AP® STATISTICS PREP

2021 Edition

The Staff of The Princeton Review

PrincetonReview.com

Penguin
Random
House

The Princeton Review
110 East 42nd Street, 7th Floor
New York, NY 10017
Email: editorialsupport@review.com

Terms of Service: The Princeton Review Online Companion Tools ("Student Tools") for retail books are available for only the two most recent editions of that book. Student Tools may be activated only once per eligible book purchased for a total of 24 months of access. Activation of Student Tools more than once per book is in direct violation of these Terms of Service and may result in discontinuation of access to Student Tools Services.

ISBN: 978-0-525-56965-7
ISSN: 2690-7011

AP is a trademark registered and owned by the College Board, which is not affiliated with, and does not endorse, this product.

The Princeton Review is not affiliated with Princeton University.

The material in this book is up-to-date at the time of publication. However, changes may have been instituted by the testing body in the test after this book was published.

If there are any important late-breaking developments, changes, or corrections to the materials in this book, we will post that information online in the Student Tools. Register your book and check your Student Tools to see whether there are any updates posted there.

Editor: Chris Chimera
Production Editors: Emily Epstein White and Jim Melloan
Production Artist: Jason Ullmeyer
Content Contributor: Lakshmi Kanikkannan and Chelsea Parlett-Pelleriti

Printed in the United States of America.

10 9 8 7 6 5 4 3 2 1

2021 Edition

Editorial

Rob Franek, Editor-in-Chief
Deborah Weber, Director of Production
Gabriel Berlin, Production Design Manager
Selena Coppock, Managing Editor
Aaron Riccio, Senior Editor
Meave Shelton, Senior Editor
Chris Chimera, Editor
Eleanor Green, Editor
Orion McBean, Editor
Brian Saladino, Editor
Patricia Murphy, Editorial Assistant

Penguin Random House Publishing Team

Tom Russell, VP, Publisher
Alison Stoltzfus, Publishing Director
Amanda Yee, Associate Managing Editor
Ellen Reed, Production Manager
Suzanne Lee, Designer

Acknowledgments

The Princeton Review would like to give special thanks to Lakshmi Kanikkannan and Chelsea Parlett-Pelleriti for their contributions to the 2020 edition of this title. We are also, as always, very appreciative of the time and attention given to each page by Jason Ullmeyer, Emily Esptein White, and Jim Melloan.

Contents

Get More (Free) Content

at **PrincetonReview.com/prep**

As easy as 1•2•3

1 Go to PrincetonReview.com/prep and enter the following ISBN for your book:

9780525569657

2 Answer a few simple questions to set up an exclusive Princeton Review account. *(If you already have one, you can just log in.)*

3 Enjoy access to your **FREE** content!

Once you've registered, you can...

- Get our take on any recent or pending updates to the AP Statistics Exam

- Take a full-length practice PSAT, SAT, and/or ACT

- Take two additional AP Statistics tests.

- Get valuable advice about the college application process, including tips for writing a great essay and where to apply for financial aid

- If you're still choosing between colleges, use our searchable rankings of *The Best 386 Colleges* to find out more information about your dream school.

- Access comprehensive study guides and a variety of printable resources, including formula sheets and tables and bubble sheets for the practice tests in this book.

- Check to see if there have been any corrections or updates to this edition

Need to report a potential **content** issue?

Contact **EditorialSupport@review.com** and include:

- full title of the book
- ISBN
- page number

Need to report a **technical** issue?

Contact **TPRStudentTech@review.com** and provide:

- your full name
- email address used to register the book
- full book title and ISBN
- Operating system (Mac/PC) and browser (Firefox, Safari, etc.)

Look For These Icons Throughout The Book

 ONLINE ARTICLES

 PROVEN TECHNIQUES

 APPLIED STRATEGIES

 STUDY BREAK

 CRITICAL CONNECTION

Part I
Using This Book to Improve Your AP Score

- Preview: Your Knowledge, Your Expectations
- Your Guide to Using This Book
- How to Begin

PREVIEW: YOUR KNOWLEDGE, YOUR EXPECTATIONS

Your route to a high score on the AP Statistics Exam depends a lot on how you plan to use this book. Respond to the following questions.

1. Rate your level of confidence about your knowledge of the content tested by the AP Statistics Exam.

   A. Very confident—I know it all
   B. I'm pretty confident, but there are topics in which I could use help
   C. Not confident—I need quite a bit of support
   D. I'm not sure

2. Circle your goal score for the AP Statistics Exam.

   5   4   3   2   1   I'm not sure yet

3. What do you expect to learn from this book? Circle all that apply to you.

   A. A general overview of the test and what to expect
   B. Strategies for how to approach the test
   C. The content tested by this exam
   D. I'm not sure yet

YOUR GUIDE TO USING THIS BOOK

This book is organized to provide as much—or as little—support as you need, so you can use this book in whatever way will be most helpful to improving your score on the AP Statistics Exam.

- The remainder of **Part I** will provide guidance on how to use this book and help you determine your strengths and weaknesses.

- **Part II** of this book contains your first practice test, answers and explanations, and a scoring guide. (Bubble sheets can be found in the very back of the book for easy tear-out.) This is where you should begin your test preparation in order to realistically determine:
  o your starting point right now
  o which question types you're ready for and which you might need to practice
  o which content topics you are familiar with and which you will want to carefully review

Once you have nailed down your strengths and weaknesses with regard to this exam, you can focus your preparation and be efficient with your time.

More AP Info Online!
We have put together even more goodies for a handful of AP Exam subjects. For short quizzes, high-level AP course and test information, expert advice, and two additional practice tests, head over to **princeton-review. com/college-advice/advanced-placement-resources**.

- **Part III** of this book will:
  - provide information about the structure, scoring, and content of the AP Statistics Exam
  - help you to make a study plan
  - point you towards additional resources

- **Part IV** of this book will explore various strategies including:
  - how to attack multiple-choice questions
  - how to write high-scoring free-response answers
  - how to manage your time to maximize the number of points available to you

- **Part V** of this book covers the content you need for your exam.

- **Part VI** of this book contains Practice Test 2, its answers and explanations, and a scoring guide. (Again, bubble sheets can be found in the very back of the book for easy tear-out.) If you skipped Practice Test 1, we recommend that you do both (with at least a day or two between them) so that you can compare your progress between the two. Additionally, this will help to identify any external issues: If you get a certain type of question wrong both times, you probably need to review it. If you only got it wrong once, you may have run out of time or been distracted by something. In either case, this will allow you to focus on the factors that caused the discrepancy in scores and to be as prepared as possible on the day of the test.

You may choose to use some parts of this book over others, or you may work through the entire book. This will depend on your needs and how much time you have. Let's now look at how to make this determination.

HOW TO BEGIN

1. **Take Practice Test 1**

   Before you can decide how to use this book, you need to take a practice test. Doing so will give you insight into your strengths and weaknesses, and the test will also help you make an effective study plan. If you're feeling test-phobic, remind yourself that a practice test is a tool for diagnosing yourself—it's not how well you do that matters but how you use information gleaned from your performance to guide your preparation.

   So, before you read further, take Practice Test 1 starting at page 11 of this book. Be sure to do so in one sitting, following the instructions that appear before the test.

2. **Check Your Answers**

   Using the answer key on page 48, count how many multiple-choice questions you got right and how many you missed. Don't worry about the explanations for now, and don't worry about why you missed questions. We'll get to that soon.

3. **Reflect on the Test**

   After you take your first test, respond to the following questions:

   - How much time did you spend on the multiple-choice questions?

   - How much time did you spend on each essay?

   - How many multiple-choice questions did you miss?

   - Do you feel you had the knowledge to address the subject matter of the essays?

   - Do you feel you wrote well-organized, thoughtful essays?

   - Circle the content areas that were most challenging for you and draw a line through each one in which you felt confident/did well.
     - Exploring Data
     - Sampling and Experimentation
     - Anticipating Patterns
     - Statistical Inference

4. **Read Part III of This Book and Complete the Self-Evaluation**

   Part III will provide information on how the test is structured and scored. It will also set out areas of content that are tested.

   As you read Part III, reevaluate your answers to the questions above. At the end of Part III, you will revisit the questions on the previous page and refine your answers to them. You will then be able to make a study plan, based on your needs and time available, that will allow you to use this book most effectively.

5. **Engage with Parts IV and V as Needed**

   Notice the word *engage*. You'll get more out of this book if you use it intentionally than if you read it passively, hoping for an improved score through osmosis.

   Strategy chapters will help you think about your approach to the question types on this exam. Part IV will open with a reminder to think about how you approach questions now and then close with a reflection section asking you to think about how/whether you will change your approach in the future.

   Content chapters are designed to provide a review of the content tested on the AP Statistics Exam, including the level of detail you need to know and how the content is tested. You will have the opportunity to assess your mastery of the content of each chapter through test-appropriate questions and a reflection section.

6. **Take Additional Practice Tests and Assess Your Performance**

Once you feel you have developed the strategies you need and gained the knowledge you lacked, you should take Practice Test 2. You should do so in one sitting, following the instructions at the beginning of the test.

When you are done, check your answers to the multiple-choice sections. See whether a teacher will read your essays and provide feedback.

Once you have taken the test, reflect on what areas you still need to work on and revisit the chapters in this book that address those deficiencies. Through this type of reflection and engagement, you will continue to improve.

Keep in mind that there are other resources available to you, including a wealth of information in your Student Tools (see "Get More (Free) Content" on page viii for more information). Find Practice Test 3 and Practice Test 4. You can continue to explore areas that can stand to be improved and engage in those areas right up to the day of the test.

Part II
Practice Test 1

Completely darken bubbles with a No. 2 pencil. If you make a mistake, be sure to erase mark completely. Erase all stray marks.

1.

YOUR NAME: _____
(Print)   Last   First   M.I.

SIGNATURE: _____   DATE: ___ / ___ / ___

HOME ADDRESS: _____
(Print)   Number and Street

_____
City   State   Zip Code

PHONE NO.: _____

IMPORTANT: Please fill in these boxes exactly as shown on the back cover of your test book.

2. TEST FORM

3. TEST CODE

4. REGISTRATION NUMBER

0	A	J	0	0	0	0	0	0	0	0
1	B	K	1	1	1	1	1	1	1	1
2	C	L	2	2	2	2	2	2	2	2
3	D	M	3	3	3	3	3	3	3	3
4	E	N	4	4	4	4	4	4	4	4
5	F	O	5	5	5	5	5	5	5	5
6	G	P	6	6	6	6	6	6	6	6
7	H	Q	7	7	7	7	7	7	7	7
8	I	R	8	8	8	8	8	8	8	8
9			9	9	9	9	9	9	9	9

5. YOUR NAME

First 4 letters of last name				FIRST INIT	MID INIT
A	A	A	A	A	A
B	B	B	B	B	B
C	C	C	C	C	C
D	D	D	D	D	D
E	E	E	E	E	E
F	F	F	F	F	F
G	G	G	G	G	G
H	H	H	H	H	H
I	I	I	I	I	I
J	J	J	J	J	J
K	K	K	K	K	K
L	L	L	L	L	L
M	M	M	M	M	M
N	N	N	N	N	N
O	O	O	O	O	O
P	P	P	P	P	P
Q	Q	Q	Q	Q	Q
R	R	R	R	R	R
S	S	S	S	S	S
T	T	T	T	T	T
U	U	U	U	U	U
V	V	V	V	V	V
W	W	W	W	W	W
X	X	X	X	X	X
Y	Y	Y	Y	Y	Y
Z	Z	Z	Z	Z	Z

6. DATE OF BIRTH

Month	Day		Year	
JAN				
FEB	0	0	0	0
MAR	1	1	1	1
APR	2	2	2	2
MAY	3	3	3	3
JUN		4	4	4
JUL		5	5	5
AUG		6	6	6
SEP		7	7	7
OCT		8	8	8
NOV		9	9	9
DEC				

7. GENDER
MALE
FEMALE

The **Princeton Review**®

1. A B C D
2. A B C D
3. A B C D
4. A B C D
5. A B C D
6. A B C D
7. A B C D
8. A B C D
9. A B C D
10. A B C D
11. A B C D
12. A B C D
13. A B C D
14. A B C D
15. A B C D
16. A B C D
17. A B C D
18. A B C D
19. A B C D
20. A B C D

21. A B C D
22. A B C D
23. A B C D
24. A B C D
25. A B C D
26. A B C D
27. A B C D
28. A B C D
29. A B C D
30. A B C D
31. A B C D
32. A B C D
33. A B C D
34. A B C D
35. A B C D
36. A B C D
37. A B C D
38. A B C D
39. A B C D
40. A B C D

Practice Test 1

AP® Statistics Exam

DO NOT OPEN THIS BOOKLET UNTIL YOU ARE TOLD TO DO SO.

At a Glance

Total Time
1 hour and 30 minutes
Number of Questions
40
Percent of Total Grade
50%
Writing Instrument
Pencil required

Instructions

Section I of this exam contains 40 multiple-choice questions. Fill in only the ovals for numbers 1 through 40 on your answer sheet.

Indicate all of your answers to the multiple-choice questions on the answer sheet. No credit will be given for anything written in this exam booklet, but you may use the booklet for notes or scratch work. After you have decided which of the suggested answers is best, completely fill in the corresponding oval on the answer sheet. Give only one answer to each question. If you change an answer, be sure that the previous mark is erased completely. Here is a sample question and answer.

Sample Question   Sample Answer

Omaha is a   Ⓐ ● Ⓒ Ⓓ Ⓔ

(A) state
(B) city
(C) country
(D) continent
(E) village

Use your time effectively, working as quickly as you can without losing accuracy. Do not spend too much time on any one question. Go on to other questions and come back to the ones you have not answered if you have time. It is not expected that everyone will know the answers to all of the multiple-choice questions.

About Guessing

Many candidates wonder whether or not to guess the answers to questions about which they are not certain. Multiple-choice scores are based on the number of questions answered correctly. Points are not deducted for incorrect answers, and no points are awarded for unanswered questions. Because points are not deducted for incorrect answers, you are encouraged to answer all multiple-choice questions. On any questions you do not know the answer to, you should eliminate as many choices as you can, and then select the best answer among the remaining choices.

GO ON TO THE NEXT PAGE.

STATISTICS
SECTION I
Time—1 hour and 30 minutes
Number of questions—40
Percent of total grade—50

Directions: Solve each of the following problems, using the available space for scratchwork. Decide which is the best of the choices given and fill in the corresponding oval on the answer sheet. No credit will be given for anything written in the test book. Do not spend too much time on any one problem.

1. In a new video game, Sea of Bandits, when you attack another character, the probability of the attack being a critical strike is 0.10. A mission requires you to attack 120 times. What is the mean and standard deviation for the number of critical strikes you would expect to get during those 120 attacks (round to the nearest hundredth)?

   (A) mean = 12 and standard deviation = 3.29

   (B) mean = 12 and standard deviation = 10.8

   (C) mean = 12 and standard deviation = 12

   (D) mean = 10 and standard deviation = 3.29

   (E) mean = 10 and standard deviation = 10.8

2. A study trained mice to push a lever and get sugar water or olive oil as a reward. On average, the sugar water mice pushed the button 5.23 times more per minute than the olive oil mice. The researchers ran a two-tailed, independent t-test and found that the difference was statistically significantly different from 0 at the $\alpha = 0.05$ level. Which of the following 95 percent confidence intervals could have come from this study?

   (A) −1.23 to 9.23

   (B) −0.02 to 10.48

   (C) −2.12 to 4.23

   (D) 1.5 to 3.45

   (E) 2.45 to 8.01

GO ON TO THE NEXT PAGE.

3. The correlation between the age (in months) when a child says her first word, and average words read to the child per week is –0.52. Given this correlation, which statement most accurately describes the relationship between the variables in the data?

(A) A higher average number of words per week is associated with a later (higher) age of first spoken word.

(B) A higher average number of words per week is associated with an earlier (lower) age of first spoken word.

(C) Average number of words per week is not associated with age of first spoken word.

(D) A lower average number of words per week is associated with an earlier (lower) age of first spoken word.

(E) Fifty percent of the variance in the age of first spoken word can be accounted for by the number of words read to a child per week.

---

4. The manager of a local taco shop surveyed 1000 randomly selected college students at a nearby community college. She asked students whether they preferred Mild, Medium, or Hot sauce and whether they were left or right-handed.

		Sauce Preference			
		Mild	Medium	Hot	Total
Handedness	Left	110	40	50	200
	Right	100	670	30	800
	Total	210	710	80	1000

Which of the following statements about a randomly selected college student is NOT true?

(A) It is more likely that the person is right-handed than left-handed.

(B) If a person prefers Medium Sauce, it is more likely that he is right-handed than left-handed.

(C) If the person is left-handed, it is more likely that he prefers Mild Sauce than that he prefers *either* Medium or Hot Sauce.

(D) It is more likely that the person likes Mild sauce than Hot sauce.

(E) It is more likely that the person is right-handed AND prefers Hot sauce than that the person is left-handed AND prefers Medium Sauce.

GO ON TO THE NEXT PAGE.

5. The probability that you will bring sunglasses with you to work given that it is sunny is 0.80. In your city, the probability that it will be sunny is 0.60. What is the probability that you will bring sunglasses AND that it is sunny?

    (A) 0.36
    (B) 0.48
    (C) 0.6
    (D) 0.8
    (E) 1.4

6. An ornithologist (a scientist who studies birds) is running an experiment to see whether African swallows weigh more or less than European swallows. He captures a random sample of 25 African swallows and weighs them. They weigh 18.27 grams with a standard deviation of 1.47 grams. He knows that European swallows weigh an average of 19 grams. He decides to run a two-tailed, one-sample t-test with an alpha level of 0.05. Using the tables provided to you, what would the critical t-value be for this experiment?

    (A) 1.96
    (B) 1.318
    (C) 1.711
    (D) 2.064
    (E) 2.060

7. A medical doctor is interested in whether a new medicine, FluBeGone treats flu symptoms better than the existing treatment. She gives a group of 100 patients FluBeGone, measures their flu symptoms and compares it to the known rate of the existing treatment. Since the existing treatment works well, she is more concerned about mistakenly deciding to switch to FluBeGone when it does not work better than the existing treatment than she is about mistakenly deciding to continue with the existing treatment when FluBeGone does work better. Which of the following is true?

    (A)   The doctor is concerned about a Type I error and has a directional hypothesis
    (B)   The doctor is concerned about a Type I error and has a non-directional hypothesis
    (C)   The doctor is concerned about a Type II error and has a directional hypothesis
    (D)   The doctor is concerned about a Type II error and has a non-directional hypothesis
    (E)   The doctor is concerned about a Type I and II error and has a non-directional hypothesis

GO ON TO THE NEXT PAGE.

8. For which of the below graphs is the mean greater than the median?

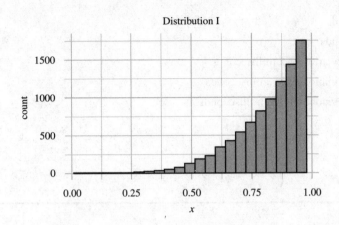

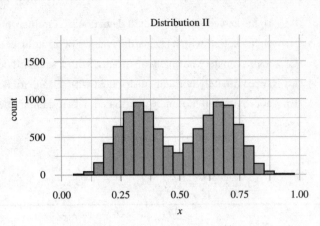

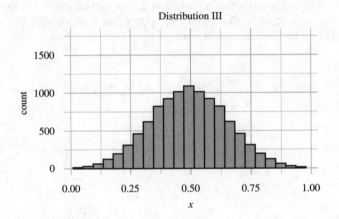

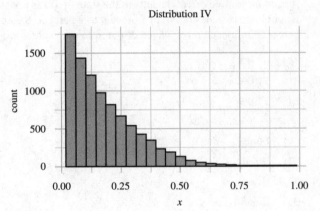

(A) I only

(B) II only

(C) III only

(D) IV only

(E) I and IV only

GO ON TO THE NEXT PAGE.

9. The distribution of reaction times for a button-pressing task is right skewed with a mean of 300 milliseconds with a standard deviation of 55 milliseconds. A random sample of 121 reaction time trials is collected. What will the shape, and standard deviation of the distribution of all possible mean reaction times be?

   (A) right skewed with a standard deviation of 5 milliseconds

   (B) right skewed with a standard deviation of 55 milliseconds

   (C) approximately normally distributed with a standard deviation of 5 milliseconds

   (D) approximately normally distributed with a standard deviation of 55 milliseconds

   (E) approximately normally distributed with a standard deviation of 300 milliseconds

---

10. A random sample of 1600 adults in the state of Texas are surveyed and asked whether they do or do not support a new law that would increase sales tax from 8 percent to 9 percent. Seventy percent of respondents said they approve the increase. At a 95 percent confidence level, which of the following values would be within the margin of error?

   I.   67.0%

   II. 71.0%

   III. 72.0%

   (A) I only

   (B) II only

   (C) III only

   (D) II and III only

   (E) I, II, and III

GO ON TO THE NEXT PAGE.

11. A new, die-based game has the following rules: a player who rolls an even number gets $10, a player who rolls an odd number gets $5, and a player who rolls a number greater than 3 gets an additional $2. How much do you expect a player to win in 10 rolls (round to the nearest cent)?

    (A) $8.50
    (B) $17.00
    (C) $56.67
    (D) $85.00
    (E) $120.00

12. A gas and electric company is interested in assessing the satisfaction of its customers. It designs a sampling procedure in which customers are randomly selected to respond to a satisfaction survey when they pay their bills online. The customer is allowed to exit out of the survey and proceed to the website. Which of the following are legitimate concerns about this sampling procedure?

    I.   Allowing customers to opt out of taking the survey could induce non-response bias.
    II. Restricting the survey to customers who pay their bills online could induce non-response bias.
    III. People who are not customers will be underrepresented in the sample.

    (A) I only
    (B) II only
    (C) III only
    (D) I and II only
    (E) I, II, and III

GO ON TO THE NEXT PAGE.

13. A new species of frog called the pvalue frog is discovered. This species has 50 percent males and 50 percent females. Twenty percent of pvalue frogs have pink dots on their skin. The rest have plain green skin. For male pvalue frogs, 25 percent have the pink dots. For female pvalue frogs, 15 percent have the pink dots. If you see a pvalue frog in the wild and it has pink dots, what is the probability that it is male?

(A) 12.5%

(B) 20%

(C) 25%

(D) 50%

(E) 62.5%

14. On average an apple weighs 100 g with a standard deviation of 20 g. On average, reusable grocery bags weight 20 g with a standard deviation of 5 g. What is the expected combined weight (and expected standard deviation) of one randomly selected bag and *three* randomly selected apples? Assume the weights of apples, and reusable bags are independent.

(A) The expected weight is 320g, and the expected standard deviation is 1,225 g.

(B) The expected weight is 320g, and the expected standard deviation is 35 g.

(C) The expected weight is 80g, and the expected standard deviation is 35 g

(D) The expected weight is 80g, and the expected standard deviation is 1,225 g

(E) The expected weight is 300g, and the expected standard deviation is 35 g

GO ON TO THE NEXT PAGE.

15. A food company has created a line of chocolate protein bites that is to be marketed to young adults around the country. They take samples of their products to the campus of Greenville College and hand the samples out to students. Students who took the samples were given a short survey and 85 percent said they would be interested in buying the product in stores. Which of the following conclusions is best supported by the data?

   (A) We expect 85 percent of college students across the country to be interested in buying chocolate protein bites.

   (B) We expect 85 percent of college students at Greenville College to be interested in buying chocolate protein bites.

   (C) We expect 85 percent of college students who accept samples at Greenville College to be interested in buying chocolate bites.

   (D) We expect that 85 percent of students at Greenville College will accept samples of chocolate protein bites.

   (E) We expect that the food company will be successful if they sell chocolate protein bites at Greenville College.

16. A school district is deciding whether to implement a new reading curriculum in their 4th grade classrooms. They currently use an older curriculum that works well, so they only care if the new reading curriculum is significantly better than the old one. If it is, they will switch curricula. The current average reading score for 4th graders in the district (R_{old}) is 49.23 points with a standard deviation of 12 points. The district plans to implement the new curriculum for a random sample of 200 4th graders and then calculate their average reading score (R_{new}). Which of the following would be an appropriate null hypothesis?

   (A) $H_0: R_{new} \geq 0$

   (B) $H_0: R_{new} \geq 0$

   (C) $H_0: R_{new} = 49.23$

   (D) $H_0: R_{new} \leq 49.23$

   (E) $H_0: R_{new} \geq 49.23$

GO ON TO THE NEXT PAGE.

17. Which of the following examples described below is *most* likely to suffer from response bias?

    (A) A study in which college students' reaction times are measured when they are tired, and when they are alert.

    (B) A study in which researchers ask local politicians how often they use illegal recreational drugs.

    (C) A study in which adults in a supermarket are asked by a neutral employee which brands of coffee they have tried.

    (D) A study in which male and female mice are trained to push a lever when a sound plays.

    (E) None of the above examples could suffer from response bias.

---

18. A company randomly selects 1000 of its employees to survey about whether or not they support the new changes in the company's vacation policy. Sixty percent of survey respondents indicated their support for the changes. The company's data scientist decides to use a one proportion z-test to test whether the proportion of employees who support the changes is different from 0 percent. What would the standard error for this test be?

    (A) 0.015

    (B) 0.05

    (C) 0.24

    (D) 0.40

    (E) 0.60

GO ON TO THE NEXT PAGE.

19. Which of the following statements about the boxplots below are true?

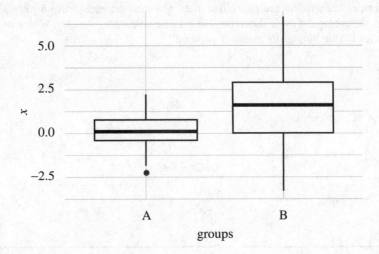

(A) About 75 percent (three quarters) of the data points in group A are greater than about 50 percent of the data points in group B.

(B) The interquartile range (IQR) for group A is larger than the IQR for group B.

(C) About 75 percent (three quarters) of the data points in group B are greater than about 50 percent of the data points in group A.

(D) The median for group A is higher than the median for group B.

(E) The smallest value in group A is smaller than any value in group B.

20. In your city, the probability of owning a dog is 0.45. The probability of owning a minivan is 0.25. The probability of owning a minivan and a dog is 0.15. Is owning a minivan independent of or dependent on dog ownership and what is the probability of owning a dog given that you own a minivan (round to the nearest hundredth)?

(A) independent and $P(\text{dog} \mid \text{minivan}) = 0.33$

(B) independent and $P(\text{dog} \mid \text{minivan}) = 0.11$

(C) dependent and $P(\text{dog} \mid \text{minivan}) = 0.33$

(D) dependent and $P(\text{dog} \mid \text{minivan}) = 0.11$

(E) dependent and $P(\text{dog} \mid \text{minivan}) = 0.60$

GO ON TO THE NEXT PAGE.

21. A biologist believes that the weight of betta fish is different when they are fed a high protein diet. To study this, she takes 200 betta fish and randomly assigns them to have either a typical or a high protein diet. She weighs the fish (in grams) before and after a two-week period where they follow their specified diets. She then subtracts the end weight from the start weight for each fish. She then takes the average of these differences to get a new variable, $weight_D$. Which of the following would be an appropriate null hypothesis for the biologist's research question?

(A) H_0: $weight_D \leq 0$ g

(B) H_0: $weight_D \geq 0$ g

(C) H_0: $weight_D = 0$ g

(D) H_0: $weight_D = 10.5$ g

(E) H_0: $weight_D \leq 10.5$ g

22. A researcher wants to look at the effect of sugar on short term memory ability. She designs a study that will look at identical twins and will randomly assign one twin to consume a sugary drink and one twin to consume an artificially sweetened (non-sugar) drink. Three hours after drink consumption, both twins will take a memory test and their scores will be recorded. Which of the following statistical tests would be *most* appropriate to answer the researcher's question?

(A) A chi-square test with sugar consumption and gender as the two variables.

(B) A matched pairs t-test looking at the difference in memory score between the sugar consuming and non-sugar consuming twin.

(C) A regression analysis with grams of sugar consumed as one variable and age as the other.

(D) An independent samples t-test looking at the difference in memory scores between the sugar consuming subjects, and the non-sugar consuming subjects.

(E) An independent samples t-test looking at the difference in sugar consumption between the sugar consuming subjects, and the non-sugar consuming subjects.

GO ON TO THE NEXT PAGE.

23. A laboratory wants to test whether cats on a new heart medication have higher blood iron levels than cats that are not on it. They plan to test 100 cats (50 with Gene X and 50 without) using a standard blood iron test. All else equal, which of the following would *increase* the statistical power?

    I.   Increasing the number of cats tested from 100 to 400 (200 with Gene X and 200 without).

    II.   Using higher doses of heart medication to increase its effect on blood iron

    III.   Switching from an alpha of 0.05 to 0.01.

    (A)   I only

    (B)   II only

    (C)   III only

    (D)   I and II only

    (E)   I, II, and III

---

24. The average apple weighs 100 grams with a standard deviation of 5 grams and is approximately normally distributed. The average grapefruit weighs 250 grams with a standard deviation of 10 grams and is approximately normally distributed. Which pair of weights for an apple and grapefruit would have the same z-score?

    (A)   apple: 100 grams, grapefruit: 100 grams

    (B)   apple: 110 grams; grapefruit: 260 grams

    (C)   apple: 107 grams; grapefruit: 264 grams

    (D)   apple: 90 grams; grapefruit: 200 grams

    (E)   apple: 250 grams; grapefruit: 100 grams

GO ON TO THE NEXT PAGE.

25. Which of the following plots is most likely to have a correlation of 0.9?

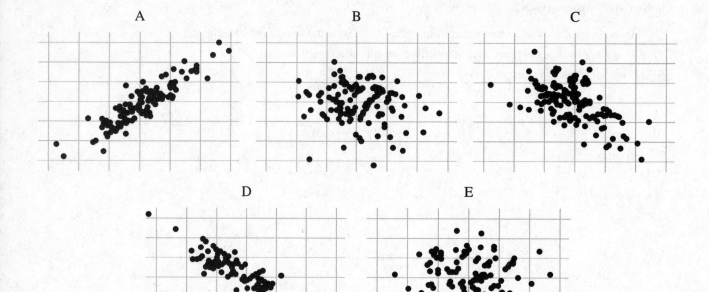

A   B   C

D   E

(A) A

(B) B

(C) C

(D) D

(E) E

26. The mean time to completion for a simple multiplication problem is 3 seconds, with a standard deviation of 0.24 seconds. What is the expected mean completion time and the corresponding standard deviation for a random sample of 16 simple multiplication problems?

(A)   mean = 3 seconds; standard deviation = 0.24 seconds

(B)   mean = 3 seconds; standard deviation = 0.06 seconds

(C)   mean = 48 seconds; standard deviation = 0.06 seconds

(D)   mean = 48 seconds; standard deviation = 0.24 seconds

(E)   mean = 48 seconds; standard deviation = 2.4 seconds

GO ON TO THE NEXT PAGE.

27. The following output is from regression analysis using an individual's income to predict the square footage of her home. Which of the following statements is consistent with the results below?

Response variable is Home Square Footage (sq. ft)

Variable	Coefficient	Std. Dev	t	p
Constant	2859.0	431.7	6.62	<0.000
Income	0.0236	0.0079	2.9	0.003

R-Sq = 8.23%

(A) Income predicts about 67.7 percent of the variability in Home Square Footage.

(B) On average, as income goes up, we expect home square footage to go down.

(C) On average, as income goes down, we expect home square footage to go down.

(D) The predicted home square footage for a person with $0 income is about 0.00237 square feet.

(E) The predicted home square footage for a person with $0 income is 0 square feet.

GO ON TO THE NEXT PAGE.

28. The graph below shows the distributions from two groups--group A and group B. Which of the following statements about the shape of the distributions is FALSE?

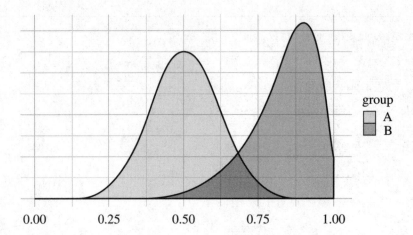

(A)   mode of A > mode of B

(B)   mean of B < median of B

(C)   group A is symmetric

(D)   group B is left skewed

(E)   mean of A ≈ median of A ≈ mode of A

---

29. An experiment is conducted to test whether college students will drink more water when the water is cold or when it is at room temperature. 100 college students were asked to come in on two separate days. Half the students were randomly selected to receive cold water on the first day and room temperature water on the second day, the other half got the waters in the reverse order. The mean difference between the amount of cold and room temperature water consumed was 1.25 ounces. The 95 percent confidence interval for the difference is 1.13 ounces to 1.37 ounces. Which of the following statements is accurate based on the provided information?

(A)   The mean difference between the amount of cold water consumed and room temperature water consumed in this experiment was not statistically significantly different from 0 at the $\alpha = 0.05$ level.

(B)   The mean amount of water consumed by students per day was 1.25 ounces.

(C)   There is a 95 percent probability that the true difference between cold and room temperature water consumption in college students is between 1.13 and 1.37 ounces.

(D)   Ninety-five percent of similarly constructed confidence intervals would contain the true mean difference between cold and room temperature water consumption in college students.

(E)   There is a 95 percent chance that the true mean difference is 1.25 ounces.

GO ON TO THE NEXT PAGE.

30. Greenville Community College (GCC) gives a survey about grades to a simple random sample of their students. They ask how many hours a week students study on average and their current GPA. They find a correlation of 0.6 between hours studied and GPA. Which of the following statements is an accurate conclusion that can be made from the study?

    (A) Studying more hours per week causes higher GPA in college students.

    (B) Studying more hours per week causes higher GPA in college students at GCC.

    (C) Studying more hours per week is associated with higher GPA in college students.

    (D) Studying more hours per week is associated with higher GPA in college students at GCC.

    (E) No conclusions can be made from this study because it was not experimental.

---

31. The mean number of hours spent per day on social media is 2.25 hours (standard deviation 0.5 hours) for college-aged students and is approximately normally distributed. How many hours would a student at the 95th percentile use social media per day (round to the nearest thousandth)?

    (A) about 2.250 hours

    (B) about 3.073 hours

    (C) about 3.225 hours

    (D) about 3.250 hours

    (E) about 3.413 hours

GO ON TO THE NEXT PAGE.

32. Which of these data sets has the highest variance?

    (A) 0, 0, 0, 0, 0, 10, 10, 10, 10, 10
    (B) 1, 2, 3, 4, 5, 6, 7, 8, 9, 10
    (C) 5, 5, 5, 5, 5, 5, 5, 5, 5, 5
    (D) 10, 10, 10, 10, 10, 90, 90, 90, 90, 90
    (E) 85, 85, 85, 85, 85, 95, 95, 95, 95, 95

33. A widget factory has its machines set to produce widgets that weigh 10 grams on average. Each week, the managers take a random sample of 100 widgets and calculate the mean widget weight in grams. They are interested in detecting whether their machines have malfunctioned and have a mean weight that is different from 10 grams. If the machines are always running correctly (i.e. the widgets have a mean weight of 10 grams), which of the following results would be expected?

    I.   The result of their statistical tests will never have p-values < 0.05.
    II. The 99 percent confidence intervals calculated from these samples will not include 10 grams 1 percent of the time.
    III. There will be no Type II errors made.

    (A) I only
    (B) II only
    (C) III only
    (D) I and III only
    (E) II and III only

GO ON TO THE NEXT PAGE.

34. The mean weight of Wheat Bits cereal boxes is 450 grams with a standard deviation of 5 grams. Assuming the weights of Wheat Bits cereal boxes are normally distributed, approximately what percentage of boxes do we expect to have a weight of more than 460 grams?

   (A) about 0.5 percent

   (B) about 1 percent

   (C) about 2.5 percent

   (D) about 5 percent

   (E) about 10 percent

---

35. A simple random sample of 500 potato chip bags were selected and weighed. The weight of each bag in grams (g) was recorded. Which of the following represents the interquartile range and the median of the weights?

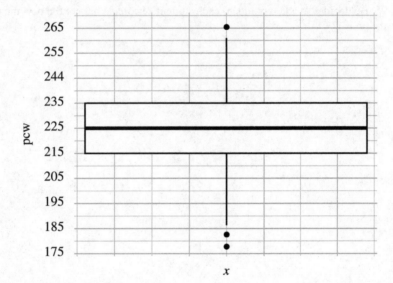

   (A) interquartile range = 20; median = 225

   (B) interquartile range = 75; median = 225

   (C) interquartile range = 20; median = 215

   (D) interquartile range = 75; median = 215

   (E) interquartile range = 86; median = 225

GO ON TO THE NEXT PAGE.

36. The product managers at Education Computing Company (ECC) are interested in testing whether their new Stats game, Linear Obsession, improves students' scores on a statistics test. They want students to come into the lab and play Linear Obsession on a Tablet for 25 minutes per day for 2 weeks. They will test all participants before and after the two weeks. Which of the following would be the best placebo group for this study?

(A) A group of students who come into the lab and spend 25 minutes a day meditating for 2 weeks.

(B) A group of students who do not do anything differently during the 2 weeks.

(C) A group of non-students who come into the lab and play Linear Obsession for 25 minutes a day for 2 weeks.

(D) A group of students who come into the lab and play Linear Obsession for an hour per day for 2 weeks.

(E) A group of students who come into the lab and play a non-statistics related but similarly structured game on a tablet for 25 minutes a day for 2 weeks.

37. Dan is an English teacher. He gives his students a test and calculates that the mean score is 74.7, the median is 74 and the standard deviation is 6.95. He decides to add 4 points to each student's score. What are the new mean, median, and standard deviation after he adds the points?

(A) 78.7, 74, 6.95

(B) 78.7, 78, 8.95

(C) 78.7, 74, 6.95

(D) 74.7, 74, 4.95

(E) 78.7, 78, 6.95

GO ON TO THE NEXT PAGE.

38. Which of the following residual plots indicates that a linear relationship between X and Y is appropriate?

Plot I

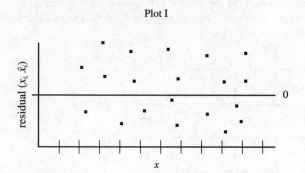

Plot II

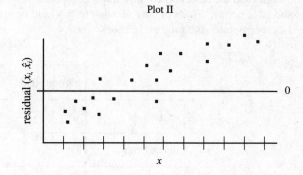

Plot III

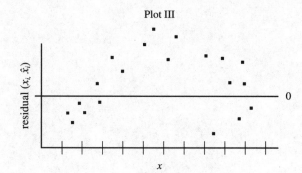

Plot IV

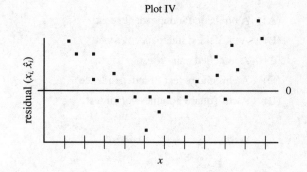

Plot V

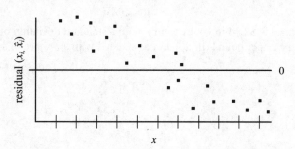

(A) Plot I

(B) Plot II

(C) Plot III

(D) Plot IV

(E) Plot V

GO ON TO THE NEXT PAGE.

39. An experimental psychologist wants to know whether rats on opiate medications and normal rats have different food preferences. He takes a group of 128 rats and randomly assigns them to be given a dose of opiates or a dose of saline. He then sets each rat in a separate cage and offers them 3 types of food: high protein, high fat, and high carbohydrate food and records which food the rats choose (chosen food is operationalized as which food they eat the most of). The results are presented in the table below. Which of the following tests would be appropriate to test the psychologist's hypothesis about the relationship between opiates and food preferences?

	high-protein	high-fat	high-carbohydrate
opiate rats	10	12	42
normal rats	14	22	28

(A) A one-sided independent *t*-test.

(B) A two-sided independent *t*-test.

(C) A matched pairs *t*-test.

(D) A chi-square test of independence.

(E) A chi-square goodness-of-fit test.

40. The mean price per pound of oatmeal is $2.34 in your country, with a standard deviation of $0.50. Assume that the price is normally distributed. What is the price per pound (in dollars) associated with a *z*-score of 1.5 (round to the nearest cent)?

(A) $1.59

(B) $2.34

(C) $3.09

(D) $3.34

(E) $3.84

END OF SECTION I

STATISTICS
SECTION II

Time—1 hour and 30 minutes
Number of questions—6
Percent of total grade—50

Part A
Questions 1–5
Spend about 65 minutes on this part of the exam.
Percent of Section II grade—75

Directions: Show all your work. Indicate clearly the methods you use, because you will be scored on the correctness of your methods as well as on the accuracy and completeness of your results and explanations.

1. A simple combat game called MoonDrop Valley has three types of attack: range attack, melee attack, and area of effect (AOE) attack. The table below gives the probability that an attack will be each of the three types of attack.

Attack Probabilities

Attack	Range	Melee	AOE
Probability	0.3	0.45	0.25

(a) The table below shows how much damage each attack does. Based on the probabilities in the first table, what is the expected amount of damage done by one attack?

Attack Damage

Attack	Range	Melee	AOE
Damage	16	12	45

GO ON TO THE NEXT PAGE.

(b) Let X be the amount of damage done after 2 subsequent attacks. Given that the three types of attacks each do a consistent amount of damage, what are the possible total damage amounts done by combinations of 2 attacks *and* the probability of those combinations (assume that attacks are independent)?

Combination	X (damage done by two attacks)	P(X)
Range, Melee		
Range, AOE		
Range, Range		
Melee, AOE		
Melee, Melee		
AOE, AOE		

(c) A professional MoonDrop Valley competition is observed and the number of attacks was recorded for all three types. Is there statistical evidence that the attack rates in the professional competition different from the rates listed in part (a)? Provide statistical justification for your answer.

Attack	Range	Melee	AOE
Probability	55	108	37

GO ON TO THE NEXT PAGE.

2. The scatterplot below shows the relationship between the average star rating (out of 5 stars) and price for 10 different pairs of shoes on a popular online store.

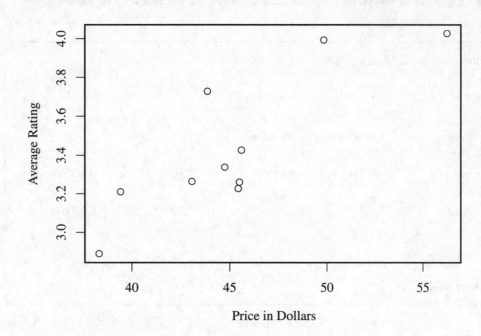

(a) Describe the relationship between price and average rating for online shoe listings. Does a linear relationship appear appropriate?

GO ON TO THE NEXT PAGE.

(b) The following results are from a regression analysis performed on shoe price and average star rating from a larger data set of 25 shoe listings. Based on the results, what would the predicted Average Rating be for a pair of shoes that cost $43.50 (round your answer to the nearest two decimal places)? Provide justification for your answer.

Response variable is Average Rating

Variable	Coefficient	Std. Dev	t	p
Constant	0.09581	0.91615	0.105	0.91762
Price	0.07547	0.02035	3.708	0.00116

R-Sq = 8.23%

(c) Describe and provide an interpretation of the slope of price in the context of this problem.

GO ON TO THE NEXT PAGE.

(d) Describe and provide an interpretation of the intercept (Constant) in the context of this problem.

GO ON TO THE NEXT PAGE.

3. A cardiologist is interested in comparing the effect of a new blood pressure medication vs a control group on the blood pressure of patients with high blood pressure. The cardiologist believes that biological sex may influence the effects of the medication. 100 participants with high blood pressure have been recruited for the study, 50 females, and 50 males.

(a) Describe an experimental design that will help the cardiologist examine his hypothesis. Your answer should include a method for random assignment.

(b) What kind of control group does your experiment have? What is the benefit of using this type of control group?

GO ON TO THE NEXT PAGE.

4. A researcher hypothesizes that mice with connective tissue disorders have slower reaction times than mice without connective tissue disorders. She plans to take 64 mice (32 with connective tissue disorders and 32 without) that have learned how to press a lever in response to an audio cue. The response time is measured as the time between the audio cue and a mouse's lever press. Reaction times will be measured in milliseconds.

The mice with connective tissue disorders have a mean reaction time of 577.89 ms with a standard deviation of 98.79 ms. The mice without connective tissue disorders have a mean reaction time of 646.21 ms with a standard deviation of 88.93 ms. Do the data provide convincing statistical evidence, at the level of $\alpha = 0.01$, that the researcher's hypothesis is correct? Explain.

GO ON TO THE NEXT PAGE.

5. An online video game has five servers. For each server, the probability of it working on a given day is 0.9. The game developers decided that if two or *fewer* servers are working, the game will shut down, otherwise, it will continue. It is reasonable to assume that the servers are independent of each other.

(a) On a given day, what is the probability that all 5 servers are working?

(b) What is the probability that the game will have to shut down?

GO ON TO THE NEXT PAGE.

(c) Given that the game is *not* shut down, what is the probability that all 5 servers are working?

(d) On average, how many days per year do we expect the game to be shut down? (Assume non-leap-year)

END OF PART A

GO ON TO THE NEXT PAGE.

STATISTICS
SECTION II
Part B
Question 6
Spend about 25 minutes on this part of the exam.
Percent of Section II grade—25

Directions: Show all your work. Indicate clearly the methods you use, because you will be scored on the correctness of your methods as well as on the accuracy and completeness of your results and explanations.

6. A clothing company sends out frequent emails to its customers. The emails include a link with a discount code. The company records how many customers click on the link for each email.

   Historically the average click-rate (the proportion of people who click on the link) over the past few years has been 0.155. Last month, people on the marketing team at the clothing company decided to explore changing the design of their emails, and they want to know whether the click-rate for the new design is higher than the existing click-rate.

   (a) The marketing people want to do an experiment to help decide design to use for their email. Design an experiment they could use to answer this question.

   (b) Describe the statistical test that the marketers should use on the experimental data they collect. Include a statement about the null hypothesis, alpha level, and what the critical test-statistic would be.

GO ON TO THE NEXT PAGE.

(c) The marketing manager now tells the team that switching to the new design will be very costly, so he wants to make sure that the switch would be worth it. A very small increase in the click-rate (like a 0.001 increase from 0.155 to 0.156 for example) might not be worth their time, and they want to be careful about deciding. They only want to switch if the click-rate for the new design is at least 0.01 higher than the click-rate of the old design. Describe at least one way that you could alter your experiment AND/OR statistical test to address these new concerns.

The company also collects a few pieces of demographic data about its customers. This includes the customer's self-identified preferred clothing category. The table below shows the frequencies of each size category for a randomly selected email from two months ago.

	Petite	Typical	Plus Size	Maternity
Clicked	302	750	323	125
Did Not Click	1756	4032	1885	827

(d) For this email, what is the probability of clicking the link given that your self-identified category is Maternity?

The marketers also look at the location of customers. Since the company operates only in the United Kingdom and the United States, they looked at the difference in click-rates between the two regions. The graph below shows the histogram of click-rates for the last 5,000 emails sent out in each region.

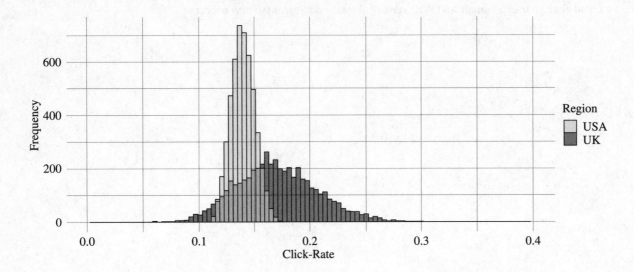

(e) Describe the shape, center, and spread for the two regions. Based on these graphs, do you think the marketers have a reason to suspect that one region has a higher click-rate than the other? Justify your response.

STOP

END OF EXAM

Practice Test 1:
Answers and
Explanations

PRACTICE TEST 1 ANSWER KEY

1.	A		21.	C
2.	E		22.	B
3.	B		23.	D
4.	E		24.	C
5.	B		25.	A
6.	D		26.	B
7.	A		27.	C
8.	D		28.	A
9.	C		29.	D
10.	D		30.	D
11.	D		31.	B
12.	D		32.	D
13.	E		33.	E
14.	B		34.	C
15.	C		35.	A
16.	D		36.	E
17.	B		37.	E
18.	A		38.	A
19.	C		39.	D
20.	E		40.	C

PRACTICE TEST 1 EXPLANATIONS

Section I—Multiple-Choice

1. **A** The critical strike probability can be described by the binomial probability distribution with $p = 0.10$. When n (the number of attacks) is 120, we expect the number of critical strikes to be $+np = (120)(0.10) = 12$. Eliminate (D) and (E). The standard deviation for a binomial distribution with $n = 120$ and $p = 0.1$ is $\sqrt{np(1-p)} = \sqrt{(120)(0.1)(1-0.1)} = \sqrt{10.8} \approx 3.29$. The answer is (A).

2. **E** This question is a great opportunity to use the process of elimination. First, use the fact that a confidence interval must include the sample estimate of 5.23. Choices (C) and (D) do not include 5.23, eliminate them. Since the two-tailed, independent t-test was statistically significant ($p < 0.05$), the confidence interval cannot contain the null value 0. This eliminates (A) and (B), which both include 0. Choice (E) is the only choice that is both centered on the sample estimate of 5.23 and does not include 0. The answer is (E).

3. **B** To answer this question, eliminate answers that you are sure are false. First of all, eliminate (E) because the coefficient of determination (the percent variance in one variable that can be accounted for by the other) is the square of the correlation coefficient. Since $(-0.52)^2 \approx 0.27$ rather than 0.50, (E) is incorrect. Choice (C) can be eliminated; it can only be said that there is no association if the correlation is close to 0. Note that (A) and (D) say the same thing (that average number of words read per week and age in months of first spoken word move in the same direction. As one goes up, the other also goes up, and likewise as one goes down the other also goes down). Since two answers cannot be correct, they can both be eliminated. Indeed, with a negative correlation, we expect the two variables to move in opposite directions, so the answer is (B).

4. **E** Use the table to check whether each choice is true. If a choice is true, put a T next to that choice. If a choice is false, put an F next to it. Choice (A) is true, because it is more likely that a randomly selected student is right-handed $\left(\dfrac{800}{1,000}\right)$ than left-handed $\left(\dfrac{200}{1,000}\right)$. Choice (B) is also true: if a student who likes Medium sauce is selected at random, he is more likely to be right-handed $\left(\dfrac{670}{710}\right)$ than left-handed $\left(\dfrac{40}{710}\right)$. Similarly, (C) is also true. If a randomly selected student is left-handed, he is more likely to like Mild Sauce $\left(\dfrac{110}{200}\right)$ than either Medium or Hot sauce $\left(\dfrac{40+50}{200} = \dfrac{90}{200}\right)$. Choice (D) is also true since it's more likely a randomly selected student likes Mild sauce $\left(\dfrac{210}{1,000}\right)$ than Hot Sauce $\left(\dfrac{80}{1,000}\right)$. Choice (E) is false; it is more likely that a randomly selected student is left-handed and prefers Medium sauce $\left(\dfrac{40}{1,000}\right)$ than that he is right-handed and prefers Hot sauce $\left(\dfrac{30}{1,000}\right)$. This question asks which of the choices is NOT true, so choose the one that's false. The answer is (E).

5. **B**   Before doing any calculations, eliminate (E) since any probability has to be between 0 and 1. Since the question provides P(sunny) and P(sunglasses | sunny) we can use these two probabilities to calculate P(sunny and sunglasses). Use the formula $P(A \cap B) = P(A) \cdot P(B|A)$. In this case, we get $P(sunny \cap sunglasses) = P(sunny) \cdot P(sunglasses | sunny) = 0.6 \cdot 0.8 = 0.48$. The answer is (B).

6. **D**   To find the critical *t*-value, look at the t distribution critical values table and go to the row where degrees of freedom equals 24 ($df = 25 - 1$). Since this is a two-sided test, look at the tail probability of 0.025 (which is the given alpha level, 0.05, divided by two) so that the critical value will have a 2.5% rejection region in each tail (for a total of 5%). There we will find that the critical value is 2.064. The answer is (D).

7. **A**   The second part of each choice is about whether the doctor had a directional or non-directional hypothesis. The doctor only cared about whether FluBeGone was better than the existing treatment (not whether it was different), so her hypothesis was directional. Eliminate (B), (D), and (E). The first part of each choice is about whether she is more concerned with a Type I or a Type II error. The question states that she would rather make the mistake of deciding to stick with the existing treatment even though FluBeGone is better. In this experiment, rejecting the null would indicate that we will act as if FluBeGone is more effective than the existing treatment. Failing to reject the null would indicate that we act as if FluBegone is the same as or worse than the existing treatment. A False Negative (Type II error) in this case would be deciding to remain with the existing treatment when FluBeGone is better, and a False Positive (Type I error) would be deciding to switch to FluBeGone when in reality it is as good as or worse than the existing treatment. The doctor is therefore more concerned with a Type I error, since the question states she is worried about mistakenly switching to FluBeGone. Eliminate (C). The answer is (A).

8. **D**   The mean is more affected by skew and outliers than the median. Graphs II and III are both symmetric, so the mean and median would be expected to be the same. Eliminate (B) and (C). It would also be expected that extreme values to the right of the graph (larger values) would have a mean that is greater than the median since the extreme tail values on the right will tend to pull the mean to the right. Only IV has a right-skewed shape consistent with data where the mean is greater than the median. We would expect that for graph I, the median is greater than the mean since the data is left-skewed. Eliminate (A) and (E). The answer is (D).

9. **C**   The Central Limit Theorem (CLT) says that as sample size increases, the distribution of sample means will become approximately normal, even if the shape of the original distribution is not normal. Though the original distribution of reaction times is right-skewed, with a sample size of 121, the distribution of sample means will be approximately normal. Eliminate (A) and (B). The standard deviation of a distribution of sample means is equal to the standard deviation of the population values (the reaction times) divided by the square root of the sample size.

$$\sigma_{\bar{x}} = \frac{\sigma}{\sqrt{n}} = \frac{55}{\sqrt{121}} = 5$$

Since the standard deviation of the distribution of the sample means (a.k.a. the standard error) is 5 milliseconds, the answer is (C).

10. **D** The margin of error is calculated by multiplying the critical z-score by the standard error. At 95% confidence, the critical z-score (z can be used since the sample size is large, and $np > 10$ and $n(1 - p) > 10$) is about 1.96.

For a sample proportion, the standard error is found using this formula:

$$s_{\hat{p}} = \sqrt{\frac{\hat{p}(1-\hat{p})}{n}}$$

$$s_{\hat{p}} = \sqrt{\frac{0.7(1-0.7)}{1600}} \approx 0.01145$$

Multiply the critical z-score by the standard error to get a margin of error of
$$1.96 \times 0.01145 \approx 0.0224 \approx 2.2\%$$

Therefore, any values within the margin of error must be *less* than 2.2% away from 70%. Statements II and III are both within 2.2% of 70%, whereas 67% is not, leaving (D) as the correct answer.

11. **D** A player would win $5 for rolling a 1, $10 for rolling a 2, $5 for rolling a 3, $12 for rolling a 4, $7 for rolling a 5, and $12 for rolling a 6. Since (on a fair die) each number 1-6 is equally likely, the expected amount of money won during one roll is the arithmetic mean of each possible value: $\frac{\$5+\$10+\$5+\$12+\$7+\$12}{6} = \$8.50$. If the player rolls 10 times, the expected winnings would be $10 \times \$8.50 = \$85.00$. The answer is (D).

12. **D** Since the company is only interested in its customers, statement III is not a concern, eliminating (C) and (E). Statement I is a concern since people with strong opinions (either negative or positive) might be more likely to respond, resulting in biased results, so eliminate (B). Statement II is also a concern, since the company wants to know about all of its customers, and it's possible that customers who pay off-line are systematically different than those who pay online (for example, age and income could be factors). Thus, the answer is (D).

13. **E** This question asks for the conditional probability of a pvalue frog being male, given that it has pink dots, $P(\text{male} \mid \text{pink dots})$. Since the question provides $P(\text{male})$ and $P(\text{pink dots} \mid \text{male})$, use Bayes' Rule to calculate the answer. Bayes' Rule says that $P(male \mid pink\ dots) = \dfrac{P(pink\ dots \mid male)\ P(male)}{P(pink\ dots)}$, so the answer is $P(male \mid pink\ dots) = \dfrac{0.25\ 0.5}{0.2} = 0.625$. Given that the frog has pink dots, there is a 62.5% chance that it is a male. The answer is (E).

14. **B** The expected value of the sum of independent random variables is the sum of their individual expectations. For three apples and one reusable bag, the expected combined weight is 100 g + 100 g + 100 g + 20 g = 320 g. Eliminate (C), (D), and (E). The standard deviation of the sum of the sum of independent random variables is the square root of the sum of their *variances* (don't forget to square the standard deviations to get the variance before adding them together). The expected standard deviation of the combined weight is $\sqrt{20^2 + 20^2 + 20^2 + 5^2} = 35$ grams. The answer is (B).

15. **C** Choices (A), (B), and (C) have similar wording but apply the conclusion *85% of … will be interested in buying chocolate protein bites* to different populations. Choice (A) applies the results to all college students, (B) to Greenville College students, and (C) to Greenville College students who took a sample. An experiment's results should be generalized to the population from which the sample was obtained. In this case, only students at Greenville who accepted a sample were surveyed. Therefore (C) is the better supported than (A) and (B). Eliminate (A) and (B). Choice (D) states that 85% of students at Greenville College will accept samples, however information about sample acceptance rates was not collected, so eliminate (D). Similarly, (E) makes a statement about the success of the food company, which we cannot assume based on the data collected. Eliminate (E). The answer is (C).

16. **D** The question provides two important pieces of information that can be used to eliminate incorrect answer choices. First, the question provides the value to compare new Reading scores to: 49.23. Choices (A) and (B) compare the new Reading scores to a Reading score of 0 and not 49.23, so eliminate (A) and (B). The district wants to reject the null if our new average reading score (R_{new}) is higher than the old one, so the null should include all cases where R_{new} is less than or equal to 49.23, which is (D).

17. **B** Response bias occurs when participants feel pressure to respond in a particular way that is untruthful or misleading (for example, they might feel that some answers are more socially or ethically acceptable). This most often happens in situations where people are being asked questions that are potentially embarrassing, incriminating, or may otherwise have outside consequences. It can also happen when people feel that the people administering the question(s) want a certain response. Choice (D) describes a study done in mice, so it can be eliminated. Choice (A) describes a study that has a relatively objective outcome (reaction time), so it can be eliminated as well. Choices (B) and (C) both describe survey-type designs that are susceptible to response bias. Choice (B) is the better answer, because the question is about a sensitive topic (drug use) and there are potentially high social consequences based on the response. Such consequence are not likely to result from a question about coffee brands, so eliminate (C). The answer is (B).

18. **A** The standard error for a one proportion z-test is $\sqrt{\dfrac{p(1-p)}{n}} = \sqrt{\dfrac{(0.6)(0.4)}{1,000}} \approx 0.015$, so the answer is (A).

19. **C** In a boxplot, the box represents the middle 50% of the data (with the horizontal line in the middle representing the median). The lower 25% ranges from the bottom-most point of the lower whisker (including any outliers) to the lower limit of the box, and similarly, the top 25% ranges from the top-most point of the top whisker (including any outliers) to the top limit of the box. Choice (A) is incorrect because less than 25% (the top whisker) of the data in group A is greater than the median for group B. Choice (B) is also incorrect because the IQR for group A is smaller than for group B (as indicated by the height of the boxes for each group). Choice (D) is incorrect since the median for group B is greater than the median for group A. Choice (E) is incorrect because the smallest value in group A (indicated by the data point just outside the bottom whisker) is inside the range of the whisker for group B. This implies that group B has values that are lower than the lowest value in group A. Choice (C) can be confirmed by checking that the 1st quartile of group B (the bottom limit of the box, above which are 75% of the data points in group B) is at or above the median of group A (the median has 50% of data points above and 50% of data points below it). The answer is (C).

20. **E** By definition, two events, A and B, are independent if $P(A \text{ and } B) = P(A) \times P(B)$. In this case, the $P(\text{dog and minivan}) = 0.15$ and $P(\text{dog}) \times P(\text{minivan}) = 0.45 \times 0.25 = 0.1125$. Since 0.1125 is not equal to 0.15, these two events are dependent, so eliminate (A) and (B). Using intersection (or the multiplication rule): $P(A \text{ and } B) = P(A) \times P(B|A) = P(B) \times P(A|B)$. Since the question provides P(dog and minivan) and P(minivan), use this formula to calculate $P(\text{dog} \mid \text{minivan})$.

$$P(\text{dog and minivan}) = P(\text{minivan}) \times P(\text{dog} \mid \text{minivan})$$
$$0.15 = 0.25x$$
$$x = \frac{0.15}{0.25} = 0.6$$

Eliminate (C) and (D). The answer is (E).

21. **C** When creating a null hypothesis, think about two main things: is the comparison one-sided or two-sided and what value is being compared to the sample statistic? In this problem, the biologist does not have a directional hypothesis. She simply asks whether their weights would be different. Therefore, there should not be a directional hypothesis, eliminating (A), (B), and (E). Since the test is on a difference score, if the betta fish in the two diets weigh the same, the difference score would be 0 rather than 10.5g, so the answer is (C).

22. **B** In this question, we need to look for two things: the correct variables (sugar consumption and memory score) and the correct test. Only answer (B) and (D) look at the correct variables, so eliminate (A), (C), and (E). Choice (B) is a matched-pairs t-test whereas (D) is an independent samples t-test. In this study, since twins are used and one of each pair is assigned to each condition, this hypothesis is best tested using a matched pairs t-test. The answer is (B).

23. **D** Statement I talks about an increase in sample size, which increases statistical power, so eliminate (B) and (C), since they do not include statement I. Statement II talks about increasing the effect size,

which also increases statistical power, eliminating (A). Statement III talks about changing the alpha level from 0.05 to 0.01 which would make it more difficult to reject the null and therefore (all else equal) *reduce* the statistical power, so eliminate (E). Thus, the answer is (D).

24. **C** Before doing any calculations, eliminate both (A) and (E). Choice (A) can be eliminated because the apple is equal to the mean apple weight and the grapefruit is not. Similarly, (E) cannot be the correct answer because the apple weighs much more than the mean apple weight, and the grapefruit weights much less than the mean grapefruit weight. Therefore, the apple would have a positive *z*-score, and the grapefruit would have a negative *z*-score. This leaves answer choices (B), (C), and (D) which all have apple and grapefruit weights that are either both over or both under their respective means (indicating that their *z*-scores would have the same sign). A *z*-score is calculated by taking a value, subtracting the mean, and dividing by the standard deviation.

$$z = \frac{(x - \mu)}{\sigma}$$

Find the *z*-scores for each of the remaining choices. For (C), the *z*-score for apple is $\frac{(107 - 100)}{5} = 1.4$, and the *z*-score for the grapefruit is $\frac{(264 - 250)}{10} = 1.4$. The answer is (C).

25. **A** A correlation coefficient communicates two main things: the direction of a relationship and its strength. A positive correlation indicates that two variables move in the same direction; as one goes up so does the other. A negative correlation indicates that the two variables move in opposite directions; as one goes up the other goes down. This question asks for a positive correlation, (A) is the only one that contains points with a positive relationship (note the points form a line that slopes upwards), meaning that (A) must be the correct answer.

26. **B** The question is providing the mean and standard deviation for one item and is asking for the mean and standard deviation of a group of samples. In other words, it is asking for the mean and standard deviation of the distribution of sample means. The mean of a distribution of sample mean is equal to the population mean (here 3 seconds), so eliminate (C), (D), and (E). The standard deviation of the distribution of sample means (also known as the standard error) is equal to the population standard deviation divided by the square root of the sample size. Here the standard deviation is 0.24 seconds, and the sample size is 16, so the standard deviation is $\frac{0.24}{\sqrt{16}} = 0.06$. This leaves (B) as the correct answer choice.

27. **C**   Choice (A) talks about one variable predicting the variability of another, which is related to R-Squared shown at the bottom of the table. However, the table shows that R-Squared is 8.23% rather than 67.7%, so eliminate (A). Choices (B) and (C) both talk about the direction of the relationship between Income and Home Square Footage. Choice (B) states that they move in opposite directions, while (C) states that they move in the same direction. The coefficient for income is positive, which means that as income goes up, so does Home Square Footage. Eliminate (B), and keep (C). Choices (D) and (E) both talk about the predicted home square footage for a person with $0 income. That value is equal to the Constant coefficient. The table shows that the Constant coefficient is 2859.0, so eliminate (D) and (E). The answer is (C).

28. **A**   Go through the statements one by one and mark each one with either T if it is True, or F if it is False. The odd one out is the correct answer. In this case, (A) is false. The mode of a distribution is the value that is at its peak. The peak of group A is around 0.5 whereas the peak of group B is around 0.9. Mark (A) as *False*. Choice (B) is true. Group B is skewed with the tail to the left, meaning that the mean will likely be closer to the tail than the median. Mark (B) as *True*. Mark (C) as *True* since it looks relatively symmetric. As noted above, group B has a skewed distribution with a tail on the left-hand side, so it is left skewed. Mark (D) as *True*. As noted above, group A is symmetric, so it follows that the mean, median, and mode are approximately the same. Mark (E) as *True* as well. This leaves answer (A) as the only *False*, and the correct answer.

29. **D**   A 95% confidence interval is a procedure that guarantees that in the long run, 95% of confidence intervals calculated in the same way (same sample size, sampled from the same population...etc) will contain the true population value. However, it does not guarantee that our specific confidence interval contains the true population value. Choice (A) makes a statement about the statistical significance of the difference. While a statistical test was not run, a 95% confidence interval that does not contain the null value (here, 0) corresponds to a significant hypothesis test with $\alpha = 1 - 0.95$. Since the confidence interval does not contain 0, (A) is false. Choice (B) asserts that the mean amount of water consumed by students is 1.25 ounces, which is false. The mean *difference* between the cold and room temperature amounts is 1.25 ounces. Choice (C) might sound correct at first glance, but recall that confidence intervals do not guarantee that there is a 95% *probability* that the true value is in this confidence interval, so this answer is also incorrect. Choice (D) gives the correct interpretation from a confidence interval. Choice (E) states that there is a 95% chance that the true mean difference is exactly 1.25 ounces. While our observed value is 1.25 ounces, the confidence interval works with ranges, not exact estimates, so (E) is also incorrect. The answer is (D).

30. **D**   To crack this question, first take a look at (E) since it is the most dissimilar to the other answer choices. Choice (E) claims that no conclusions can be made from the data since the study was not experimental. Eliminate (E), because it is possible to make some inferences from observational survey data based on the strong correlation. Now, two things are varying between the remaining four answer choices: *causes* vs. *is associated with* and *college students* vs. *college students at GCC*. Since the data is observational, we cannot make inferences about whether studying *causes* higher GPA, so (A) and (B) can be eliminated. Since the random sample was taken from just GCC students, we do not know whether the observed data generalize to all college students, so eliminate (C). The answer is (D).

31. **B**   Using the normal distribution table, we can look up a z-score associated with the 95th percentile (recall, the 95th percentile indicates a score at which 95% of scores are at or below that value). Look at Table A for the z-score that is close to a probability of 0.95. According to the table, a probability of 0.95 corresponds to a z-score between 1.64 and 1.65. Estimate that the z-score is 1.645. Using a little algebra, we can change our formula to find a z-score into a formula to take a z-score and find the raw value.

$$z = \frac{(x - \mu)}{\sigma}$$
$$1.645 = \frac{(x - 2.25)}{0.5}$$
$$0.8225 = x - 2.25$$
$$x = 3.0725$$

Rounded to the nearest thousand, someone who is at the 95th percentile for college-aged social media users spends about 3.073 hours on social media per day. The answer is (B).

32. **D**   Variance is a measure of how far numbers are from the mean (on average). If you wanted to calculate this by hand, you can use the variance formula $\frac{1}{n-1} \Sigma(x_i - \bar{x})^2$. However, we can answer this question without taking the time to calculate each list's variance. Choice (C) is automatically out. Since the numbers are all the same, the variance is 0, so it can be eliminated. Next, let's calculate the means of (A), (B), (D), and (E) to get 5, 5.5, 50, and 90 respectively. In (A) and (E), all the numbers are 5 units away from mean. For (B) all the numbers are at *most* 4.5 units away from the mean (10 − 5.5 = 4.5, 5.5 − 1 = 4.5. For (D), all the numbers are 40 units away from the mean, which is further than all the other lists. Therefore, the answer is (D).

33. **E**   In the experiments described, the null hypothesis is true, since it says *the machines are always running correctly*. Statement I says that the statistical tests will *never* have p-values < 0.05. In general, test-takers should be skeptical of answers that have absolutes like "always" or "never." In this case, statement I is incorrect since *p*-values are designed to be significant with a probability of alpha (here, alpha is 0.05). Since statement I is not true, eliminate (A) and (D). Statement II indicates that 1% of 99% confidence intervals will not contain the true value of 10 grams. By definition, 99% confidence intervals will contain the true value 99% of the time, so it is accurate that we expect them to *not* contain the true value (100 − 99)% of the time. Since II is true, eliminate (C). Statement III is also true. Type II errors are False Negatives (i.e. failing to reject the null when the null is *false*). Since we know that the null is true, it is impossible to make a Type II error. Eliminate (B). The answer is (E).

34. **C** The normal distribution has about 95% of its density within 2 standard deviations of the mean. In other words, in the long run we expect about 95% of samples drawn from this distribution to be within 2 standard deviations of the mean. In this problem, the mean is 450 grams and the standard deviation is 5 grams. Therefore, any box of cereal weighing more than 460 grams would be 2 or more standard deviations above the mean. The normal distribution is symmetric, so since we know that about 5% of cereal boxes will be 2 or more standard deviations away from the mean, we can conclude that half of that will be at least 2 standard deviations above the mean, and half will be at least 2 standard deviations below the mean. Therefore, the correct answer is (C), about 2.5%.

35. **A** Take this one item at a time. Start with the interquartile range (IQR). Looking at the graph, we can see that the box part of the boxplot, which covers the numbers counted in the IQR, goes from approximately 235 to 215. Therefore, the IQR is 235 − 215 = 20, so eliminate (B), (D) and (E). The median of a boxplot is represented by the line in the middle of the box portion of the boxplot. In this graph, it is around 225, so the answer is (A).

36. **E** The goal of placebo groups is to have a treatment that looks and feels similar to the target treatment (Linear Obsessions) but is not expected to have an effect on the outcome (scores on a statistics test). Since (C) does not use the same population that the researchers at ECC are interested in, eliminate (C). The scenario in (D) has subjects playing the same game but for longer which would be expected to have an effect on the outcome, so (D) can be eliminated. Among (A), (B) and (E), (E) has a treatment that is most similar to the experimental condition. Therefore, the answer is (E).

37. **E** Adding 4 points to each score shifts the scores up. This change affects the mean and median, but not the standard deviation. Eliminate (B) and (D), since the standard deviation is not 6.95. Both the mean and the median will be shifted up by 4 points, so the mean is 78.7, and the median is 78. Eliminate (A) and (C). The answer is (E).

38. **A** Residual plots of data where linear models are appropriate will have an even, cloud-like shape. Residuals measure how far away our predictions are from the actual y-values. There should be no discernible pattern in the residual plot. If x and y have a nonlinear relationship, using a line to predict y from x will result in residuals that are systematically different for different values of x. If there is a clear pattern, then a linear model may not be appropriate. Since (A) has no clear pattern, the answer is (A).

39. **D** In this study we have two categorical variables: rat opiate status and food type. A t-test requires one continuous variable and one categorical variable, so eliminate (A), (B), and (C). A chi-square goodness of fit test assesses whether a certain group's observed frequencies match established frequencies. In this case, there instead are two groups, and the goal is to determine whether group membership is independent of food preference, so the answer is (D).

40.   **C**   A *z*-score represents the number of standard deviations above (for positive *z*-scores) or below (for negative *z*-scores) the mean that a value is. A value that is equal to the mean ($2.34) would have a *z*-score of 0, so eliminate (B). Also, a value less than the mean has a negative *z*-score, so eliminate (A). A value with a *z*-score of 1.5 is 1.5 standard deviations above the mean, so the correct answer is equal to 1.5 × $0.50 = $0.75 above the mean. Therefore, the answer is $2.34 + $0.75 = $3.09, which is (C).

Section II—Free-Response

1.   **(a)**   The average attack damage is calculated by multiplying the probability of each attack by the amount of damage that it does and adding all of them together.

$$(0.3 \times 16) + (0.45 \times 12) + (0.25 \times 45) = 21.45 \text{ damage}$$

(b)

Combination	x (damage done by two attacks)	P(X = x)
Range, Melee	16 + 12 = 28	2 × (0.3 × 0.45) = 0.27
Range, AOE	16 + 45 = 61	2 × (0.3 × 0.25) = 0.15
Melee, AOE	12 + 45 = 57	2 × (0.45 × 0.25) = 0.225
Range, Range	16 + 16 = 32	0.3 × 0.3 = 0.09
Melee, Melee	12 + 12 = 24	0.45 × 0.45 = 0.2025
AOE, AOE	45 + 45 = 90	0.25 × 0.25 = 0.0625

(c)   For this question, use a chi-square for goodness of fit test. Our null hypothesis (H_0) is that the three attacks have proportions equal to 0.3, 0.45, and 0.25 respectively. To calculate the chi-square statistic, we first need the expected values. The total number of attacks is 200. Using the probabilities from the first part of the problem, we can calculate our expected values.

Attack	Range	Melee	AOE
Probability	200 * 0.3 = 60	200 * 0.45 = 90	200 * 0.25 = 50

Then, we can use the expected values to calculate the chi-square statistic using the formula: .

$$\chi^2 = \Sigma \frac{\left(\text{Observed} - \text{Expected}\right)^2}{\text{Expected}}$$

Attack	Range	Melee	AOE
Probability	$\frac{(55-60)^2}{60} = 0.417$	$\frac{(108-90)^2}{90} = 3.6$	$\frac{(37-50)^2}{60} = 3.38$

The sum is 0.417 + 3.6 + 3.38 = 7.397. Using the chi-square table, look at the row with ($k − 1 = 2$) degrees of freedom. Since the problem did not specify an α-level choose the one that seems reasonable. Let's use 0.01. Locate the column that says 0.01 and find the critical value which is 9.21. The value of 7.397 is less than the critical value, so don't reject at the $\alpha = 0.01$ level. There is not enough evidence that the rates of attacks are different in professional competitions.

2. (a) The relationship between average star rating and price is positive/direct. On average, as average star rating goes up, so does the price. A linear relationship does appear to be appropriate here as there are no extreme patterns or outliers.

   (b) Based on the model, the formula to predict the average star rating for any priced shoe is $0.09581 + 0.07547 \times price$, so the predicted rating for a pair of shoes that cost $43.50 is about $0.09581 + 0.07547 \times price \approx 3.38$.

   (c) The slope for price is 0.07547, which means that for every dollar increase in the price, we expect an increase of 0.07547 in the average star rating.

   (d) The constant/intercept is 0.09581. In this context, this means that if a pair of shoes cost close to $0, we would expect it to have an average star rating of close to 0.09581.

3. (a) Since the cardiologist believes that biological sex may play a role in the effect of the medication, we can use a randomized block design. Males and females will each be randomly assigned to be in either the medication or the control group. A bag with 25 black marbles and 25 white marbles (note: you could also use a fair coin, or a random number table...etc) will be used to randomly assign the males and then females into their conditions. The control group will be a placebo group and will be given a sugar pill that is similar in shape and color to the new medication. The blood pressure of the participants will be measured before and after a 6-week period during which they take their respective treatments. The change between pre- and post-measures of blood pressure will be recorded for each subject. Then we can perform an independent samples t-test on the average change blood pressure change.

   (b) This experiment has a placebo (or active) control group. This type of control group is beneficial because both groups of participants feel like they are being treated in a similar way. This can help account for the placebo effect.

4. To answer this question we can use an independent samples t-test. The two groups are mice with and without connective tissue disorders.

   $H_0 : \mu_c \geq \mu_t$ (where μ_c is the mean reaction time of mice with connective tissue disorders and μ_t is the mean reaction time of mice without)

   $H_A : \mu_c < \mu_t$

Our one-sided critical *t*-value with ($n_c + n_t - 2 = 62$) degrees of freedom and $\alpha = 0.01$ is 2.39 according to our table. The test is one-sided since we have a directional hypothesis (mice with connective tissue disorders have a *slower* reaction time).

To calculate the *t*-value, use the formulas from the formula sheets:

$$s_{\bar{x}_1 - \bar{x}_2} = \sqrt{\frac{98.79^2}{32} + \frac{88.93^2}{32}} \approx 23.50$$

$$\mu_{\bar{x}_1 - \bar{x}_2} = 646.21 - 577.89 = 68.32$$

$$t = \frac{68.32 - 0}{23.50} = 2.91$$

Since the *t*-value is greater than the critical value of 2.39, reject the null hypothesis that the reaction times are the same between the two groups of mice. This provides statistical evidence supporting the researcher's hypothesis that mice with connective tissue disorders have slower reaction times.

5. (a) Since the servers' functionality is independent of one another, the probability of all 5 servers working is $0.9^5 = 0.59049$, or about 59%.

   (b) The game will shut down if 0, 1 or 2 of the servers are working (it will remain up if 3, 4 or 5 are working). Using the binomial formula, we can figure out each of these probabilities.

   0: $0.1^5 = 0.00001$
   1: $_5C_1(0.1)^4(0.9) = 0.00045$
   2: $_5C_2(0.1)^3(0.9)^2 = 0.0081$

   $0.00001 + 0.00045 + 0.0081 = 0.00856$ or 0.856%

   (c) To do this, calculate the probability of 3, 4 and 5 servers working.

   3: $_5C_3(0.1)^2(0.9)^3 = 0.0729$
   4: $_5C_4(0.1)(0.9)^4 = 0.32805$
   5: $0.9^5 = 0.59049$

   The probability that all 5 servers are working given that the game is not shut down is $\frac{1}{n-1}\Sigma\left(x_i - \bar{x}\right)^2$.

   (d) The probability of the game being shut down is 0.00856 as calculated in part (b). Using the formula for the mean of a binomial variable, calculate that in 365 days, the game can be expected to be down $365 \times 0.00856 = 3.1244$ days per year.

6. (a) The clothing company could randomly sample 1000 of its customers using a random number generator and send them an email with the new design. Since historically the click-rate has been 0.155, the click-rate from the new design can be compared to 0.155.

(b) For this experiment, use a one proportion z-test since the observed click-rate is being compared to 0.155. The null hypothesis (H_0) could be that the click-rate for the new design is less than or equal to 0.155 since the question specifies that the marketers want to know whether the new email design has a higher click-rate than the old design (H_0: $P_{new} \leq 0.155$). Use $\alpha = 0.05$. The critical z-value would be 1.645 (remember when looking up the critical value that the test is one-tailed).

(c) The marketing manager's statement suggests that he is looking for evidence that the click-rate for the new design is at least 0.165 or higher. We can change our test by changing the null hypothesis to H_0: $P_{new} \leq 0.165$. The null value does not *always* have to be the existing value (0.155 in this case), it just has to be a number we are interested in testing against.

(d) To calculate the probability of clicking given the category Maternity, look only at the people whose self-selected category is Maternity. The total number of people in the Maternity category is the sum of those who clicked and those who did not click. Therefore, the probability is $\dfrac{125}{125+827} = 0.1313 = 13.13\%$.

(e) The UK distribution has a smaller spread than the USA distribution, but the center of the USA distribution seems higher than center of the UK distribution. Both appear unimodal, and symmetric. Based on this graph, the center of the USA's distribution is higher, however we regularly observe very low (<0.1) click rates whereas the UK's distribution almost never has values lower than 0.1. Since there is a lot more variability in the USA's distribution, more information is needed, however, because the mean/median/mode values for the USA are higher than the UK's, there is reason to suspect the USA has a higher click-rate.

HOW TO SCORE PRACTICE TEST 1

Section I: Multiple Choice

_____ × 1.8750 = _____
Number Correct   Weighted
(out of 40)   Section I Score
                                  (Do not round)

Section II: Free Response

(See if you can find a teacher or classmate to score your
Free-Response questions.)

Exact scoring can vary
from administration to
administration. Therefore,
this scoring should only
be used as an estimate.

Question 1:   _____   × 2.8125 =   _____
              (out of 4)   (Do not round)

Question 2:   _____   × 2.8125 =   _____
              (out of 4)   (Do not round)

Question 3:   _____   × 2.8125 =   _____
              (out of 4)   (Do not round)

Question 4:   _____   × 2.8125 =   _____
              (out of 4)   (Do not round)

Question 5:   _____   × 2.8125 =   _____
              (out of 4)   (Do not round)

Question 6:   _____   × 4.6875 =   _____
              (out of 4)   (Do not round)

AP Score Conversion Chart Statistics	
Composite Score Range	AP Score
112–150	5
98–111	4
80–97	3
55–79	2
0–54	1

Sum =   _____
         Weighted
         Section II Score
         (Do not round)

Composite Score _____ + _____ = _____
                    Weighted   Weighted   Composite Score
                    Section I Score   Section II Score   (Round to nearest
                                                               whole number)

Part III
About the
AP Statistics
Exam

- Structure of the AP Statistics Exam
- Overview of Content Topics
- How AP Exams Are Used
- Other Resources
- Designing Your Study Plan
- On the Day of the Test

STRUCTURE OF THE AP STATISTICS EXAM

The AP Statistics Exam is made up of two parts: a multiple-choice section and a free-response section. The entire test lasts three hours. Here's how the time is allotted:

Another Course? Of Course!

If you can't get enough AP Statistics and want to review this material with an expert, we also offer an online Cram Course that you can sign up for here: **https://www.princeton-review.com/college/ap-test-prep.**

- **Part I: Multiple Choice.** This part consists of 40 multiple-choice questions, each with five possible answers. Exactly 1 hour and 30 minutes is allotted for this part of the exam.

- **Part II: Free Response.** This part consists of six free-response questions, requiring not only that you perform the *right* computations but also that you communicate your reasoning and *justify* your answers clearly. Exactly 1 hour and 30 minutes is allotted for this part of the exam. This free-response section is further divided into two parts, Part A and Part B:
  o **Part A:** Five free-response questions, on which you are instructed to spend about 65 minutes, or about 13 minutes each.
  o **Part B:** The investigative-task question, on which you are told to spend about 25 minutes. This question typically consists of several parts linking different areas of the curriculum. As the name suggests, the investigative task question invites you to investigate a situation and arrive at a solution. It might also require you to expand your knowledge of statistics a bit beyond the course curriculum.

Using a Calculator

Regarding calculators on the AP Statistics Exam, the College Board states: "Each student will be expected to bring a graphing calculator with statistical capabilities to the exam."

For a thorough rundown of the College Board's calculator policy for this exam, go to **https://apstudent.collegeboard.org/takingtheexam/exam-policies/calculator-policy.**

Note the word *expected*. Although the Test Development Committee makes some effort to develop tests that can be passed without using a graphing calculator, the truth is that you will be at a disadvantage if you don't have one. Good graphing calculators, such as the TI-83, TI-84, and TI-89, will not only save you time and prevent you from making minor arithmetic mistakes but will also help you compute descriptive statistics such as standard deviation, correlation coefficient, and the equation of a least-squares regression line. These calculators are also capable of making useful graphs, such as histograms, scatterplot graphs, and least-squares regression lines. It goes without saying that these capabilities are extremely useful on the AP Statistics Exam.

Make sure you are thoroughly familiar with the functioning capabilities of your calculator. Don't bring an unfamiliar calculator to the AP Statistics Exam. During the months before your exam, practice using your calculator until you feel confident with it.

However, you should always remember that a graphing calculator is only a computational aid. It cannot answer problems for you. Use it carefully. Interpreting numerical answers given by the calculator is still your responsibility. The calculator cannot do it for you. Nonetheless, the calculator will definitely make your computations easier, so use it.

Certain types of calculators may be prohibited from use on exams, such as calculators with QWERTY keyboards. This policy is updated as new and modified calculators enter the market. Refer to the College Board's policy on the use of calculators on exams (it's on the website) before purchasing one.

You can find a list of acceptable calculators on the AP Calculator Policy page on AP Students.

Using Computer Outputs

Due to time constraints during the exam, students are not expected to do extensive computations. For some questions, computer outputs are provided. Students are expected to make use of these outputs and interpret them correctly. Generally, only very standard, non-program specific outputs are provided. During the weeks before the exam, become familiar with the outputs of statistical programs. Learn to read them, interpret them, and use them, so you won't be caught by surprise on the exam. When you encounter a question on the exam that comes with a computer output, be sure to read the entire question carefully before answering it, and be sure to use the given output. Do not start computing everything again. This will only waste precious time.

OVERVIEW OF CONTENT TOPICS

The curriculum for AP Statistics consists of four basic themes.

- **Exploring Data:** describing patterns and departures from patterns

- **Sampling and Experimentation:** planning and conducting a study

- **Anticipating Patterns:** exploring random phenomena using probability and simulation

- **Statistical Inference:** estimating population parameters and testing hypotheses

The following is an outline of the major topics covered by the AP Statistics Exam. The topics may be taught in a different order. Keep in mind that less emphasis is placed on actual *arithmetic computation*, and more emphasis is placed on *conceptual understanding and interpretation*.

I. Exploring Data: observing patterns and departures from patterns (20–30%)

A. Constructing and interpreting graphical displays of distributions of univariate data (dotplot, stemplot, histogram, cumulative frequency plot)

1. Center and spread
2. Clusters and gaps
3. Outliers and other unusual features
4. Shape

For more information about the course and AP Statistics Exam topics, visit AP Students online: **https://apstudent. collegeboard.org/ apcourse/ap- statistics**

B. Summarizing distributions of univariate data

1. Measuring center: median, mean
2. Measuring spread: range, interquartile range, standard deviation
3. Measuring position: quartiles, percentiles, standardized scores (z-scores)
4. Using boxplots
5. The effect of changing units on summary statistics

C. Comparing distributions of univariate data (dotplots, back-to-back stemplots, parallel boxplots)

1. Comparing center and spread: within group, between group variation
2. Comparing clusters and gaps
3. Comparing outliers and other unusual features
4. Comparing shapes

D. Exploring bivariate data

1. Analyzing patterns in scatterplots
2. Correlation and linearity
3. Least-squares regression line
4. Residual plots, outliers, and influential points
5. Transformations to achieve linearity: logarithmic and power transformations

E. Exploring categorical data

1. Frequency tables and bar charts
2. Marginal and joint frequencies for two-way tables
3. Conditional relative frequencies and association

II. Sampling and Experimentation: planning and conducting a study (10–15%)

A. Overview of methods of data collection

1. Census
2. Sample survey
3. Experiment
4. Observational study

B. Planning and conducting surveys

1. Characteristics of a well-designed and well-conducted survey
2. Populations, samples, and random selection
3. Sources of bias in sampling and surveys
4. Simple random sampling, stratified random sampling, and cluster sampling

More AP Info Online!
We have put together even more goodies for a handful of AP Exam subjects. For short quizzes, high-level AP course and test information, and expert advice, head over to **princeton-review. com/college-advice/ advanced-placement-resources.**

C. Planning and conducting experiments

 1. Characteristics of a well-designed and well-conducted experiment
 2. Treatments, control groups, experimental units, random assignments, and replication
 3. Sources of bias and confounding, including placebo effect and blinding
 4. Completely randomized design
 5. Randomized block design, including matched pairs design

D. Generalizability of results and types of conclusions that can be drawn from observational studies, experiments, and surveys

III. Anticipating Patterns: producing models using probability theory and simulation (20–30%)

A. Probability as relative frequency

 1. Interpreting probability, including long-run relative frequency interpretation
 2. "Law of Large Numbers" concept
 3. Addition rule, multiplication rule, conditional probability, and independence
 4. Discrete random variables and their probability distributions including binomial and geometric
 5. Simulation of random behavior and probability distributions
 6. Mean (expected value) and standard deviation of a random variable and linear transformation of a random variable

B. Combining independent random variables

 1. Notion of independence versus dependence
 2. Mean and standard deviation for sums and differences of independent random variables

C. The normal distribution

 1. Properties of the normal distribution
 2. Using tables of the normal distribution
 3. The normal distribution as a model for measurements

D. Sampling distributions

 1. Sampling distribution of a sample proportion
 2. Sampling distribution of a sample mean
 3. Central Limit Theorem
 4. Sampling distribution of a difference between two independent sample proportions

5. Sampling distribution of a difference between two independent sample means
6. Simulation of sampling distributions
7. *t*-distribution
8. Chi-square distribution

IV. Statistical Inference: estimating population parameters and testing hypotheses (30–40%)

A. Estimation: point estimators and confidence intervals

1. Estimating population parameters and margins of error
2. Properties of point estimators including unbiasedness and variability
3. Logic of confidence intervals, meaning of confidence level and confidence intervals, and properties of confidence intervals
4. Large sample confidence interval for a proportion
5. Confidence interval for a mean
6. Large sample confidence interval for a difference between two proportions
7. Confidence interval for a difference between two means (unpaired and paired)
8. Confidence interval for the slope of a least-squares regression line

B. Tests of significance

1. Logic of significance testing, null and alternative hypotheses; *p*-values; one- and two-sided tests; concepts of Type I and Type II errors; concept of power
2. Large sample test for a proportion
3. Test for a mean
4. Large sample test for a difference between two proportions
5. Test for a difference between two means (unpaired and paired)
6. Chi-square test for goodness of fit, homogeneity of proportions, and independence (one- and two-way tables)
7. Test for the slope of a least-squares regression line

HOW AP EXAMS ARE USED

Different colleges use AP Exam scores in different ways, so it is important that you go to a particular college's website to determine how it uses AP Exam scores. The three items below represent the main ways in which AP Exam scores can be used:

- **College Credit.** Some colleges will give you college credit if you score well on an AP Exam. These credits count towards your graduation requirements, meaning that you can take fewer courses while in college. Given the cost of college, this could be quite a benefit, indeed.

- **Satisfy Requirements.** Some colleges will allow you to "place out" of certain requirements if you do well on an AP Exam, even if they do not give you actual college credits. For example, you might not need to take an introductory-level course, or perhaps you might not need to take a class in a certain discipline at all.

- **Admissions Plus.** Even if your AP Exam will not result in college credit or even allow you to place out of certain courses, most colleges will respect your decision to push yourself by taking an AP Course or even an AP Exam outside of a course. A high score on an AP Exam shows mastery of more difficult content than is taught in many high school courses, and colleges may take that into account during the admissions process.

OTHER RESOURCES

There are many resources available to help you improve your score on the AP Statistics Exam, not the least of which are your **teachers**. If you are taking an AP class, you may be able to get extra attention from your teacher, such as obtaining feedback on your essays. If you are not in an AP course, reach out to a teacher who teaches AP Statistics, and ask whether the teacher will review your essays or otherwise help you with content.

Don't forget to check out the AP Students page as you prepare for the AP Statistics Exam. Go to **apstudent. collegeboard.org** for a course description, sample questions, and more.

Another wonderful resource is **AP Students**, the official site of the AP Exams. The scope of the information at this site is quite broad and includes:

- Course Description, which includes details on what content is covered and sample questions

- Sample questions from past exams

- Free-response question prompts and multiple-choice questions from previous years

The AP Students home page address is **https://apstudent.collegeboard.org**.

For up-to-date information about any potential changes to the AP Statistics Exam, please visit **https://apstudent.collegeboard.org/apcourse/ap-statistics**.

Finally, The Princeton Review offers tutoring and small group instruction. Our expert instructors can help you refine your strategic approach and add to your content knowledge. For more information, call 1-800-2REVIEW.

DESIGNING YOUR STUDY PLAN

You can find step-by-step study guides in your Student Tools when you register your book. Follow the instructions on the Get More (Free) Content page at the beginning of this book to access online materials to help boost your test prep.

As part of the Introduction, you identified some areas of potential improvement. Let's now delve further into your performance on Test 1, with the goal of developing a study plan appropriate to your needs and time commitment.

Read the answers and explanations associated with the multiple-choice questions (starting at page 49). After you have done so, respond to the following questions:

- Review the bulleted outline of content topics on pages 65–68. Next to each topic, indicate your rank of the topic as follows: "1" means "I need a lot of work on this," "2" means "I need to beef up my knowledge," and "3" means "I know this topic well."

- How many days/weeks/months away is your exam?

- What time of day is your best, most focused study time?

- How much time per day/week/month will you devote to preparing for your exam?

- When will you do this preparation? (Be as specific as possible: Mondays and Wednesdays from 3:00 to 4:00 P.M., for example.)

- Based on the answers above, will you focus on strategy (Part IV) or content (Part V) or both?

- What are your overall goals in using this book?

ON THE DAY OF THE TEST

- Eat a reasonable breakfast. Do not overeat, which may make you drowsy, but definitely do not skip breakfast either. Hunger pangs can prevent you from thinking straight.

- Use the bathroom before you enter the testing room. Avoid drinking beverages that will send you to the bathroom during the exam, such as coffee, tea, or other caffeinated beverages.

- Wear comfortable clothing. Dress in layers, so that you can remove them should the room be too warm.

What to Bring

Pack your bag the night before the exam. Don't forget the following:

- Several sharpened **number two pencils** and a separate eraser.

- A **snack.** Eating a piece of fruit or an energy bar during the break will give you a much-needed boost.

- If you're taking the exam at a different school from your own, or if you're homeschooled, bring a **photo I.D.** and your secondary **school code number.** (Homeschoolers will be given a code on the testing day.)

- Your **Social Security number.** Although it's not mandatory for you to provide your Social Security number, it is used for identification and appears on your AP Grade Report.

- A **watch without a calculator.** If your watch has an alarm, turn it off.

- A **calculator.** Each student is expected to bring a graphing calculator with statistical capabilities. Portable computers, tablets and iPads, pocket organizers, and devices with typewriter-style (QWERTY) keyboards, electronic writing pads, or pen-input devices are *not* allowed. Most graphing calculators currently on the market are acceptable, and you can check the most currently permitted models at the AP Statistics website: https://apstudent.collegeboard.org/apcourse/ap-statistics/calculator-policy.

- **Extra batteries** for your calculator.

Just as it's important to relax on test day, you should also take moments to relax while you prepare for the exam. Taking a study break here and there helps your mind to decompress and prepare for the next study session.

Finally...

Relax. Even if all you've done is read this book carefully, you're probably better prepared than a lot of the other students. Stay positive, and remember: everyone else is at least as nervous as you are.

Part IV
Test-Taking
Strategies for the
AP Statistics Exam

PREVIEW

Review your responses to the first three questions in Part I and then respond to the following questions:

- How many multiple-choice questions did you miss even though you knew the answer?

- On how many multiple-choice questions did you guess blindly?

- How many multiple-choice questions did you miss after eliminating some answers and guessing based on the remaining answers?

- Did you find any of the free-response questions easier or harder than the others—and, if so, why?

TIPS FOR BOTH SECTIONS OF THE AP STATISTICS EXAM

Here are two things to keep in mind for both parts of the exam.

You can find an updated copy of the AP Statistics formulas and tables in your Student Tools, so don't forget to register your book! See the Get More (Free) Content page at the beginning of this book for more information.

- **Statistical tables:** Statistical tables and formulas are provided for you in the exam booklets in both sections. A copy of those tables and formulas is available at the end of Chapter 7, as well as in your Student Tools. In the months before the exam, familiarize yourself with them and practice using them.

- **Calculators:** You may use a graphical calculator with statistical capabilities on both sections of the exam. From the beginning of your statistics course, use only one calculator, and practice with it as much as you can. Being familiar with the capabilities of your calculator will save you time on the exam. And remember that many calculators have distribution functions, which can save you from spending time looking through the tables provided. You should bring spare batteries and know how to change them.

Chapter 1
How to Approach
Multiple-Choice
Questions

CRACKING THE MULTIPLE-CHOICE SECTION

Section I of the AP Statistics Exam consists of 40 multiple-choice questions, which you're given 90 minutes to complete. That works out to 2.25 minutes per question. This section is worth 50% of your grade.

All the multiple-choice questions will have a similar format: each will be followed by five answer choices. At times, it may seem that there could be more than one possible correct answer. There is only one! Remember that the committee members who write these questions are statistics teachers. So, when it comes to statistics, they know how students think and what kinds of mistakes they make. Answers resulting from common mistakes are often included in the five answer choices to trap you.

Use the Answer Sheet

For the multiple-choice section, you write the answers *not* in the test booklet but on a separate answer sheet (very similar to the ones we've supplied at the very end of this book). Five oval-shaped bubbles follow the question number, one for each possible answer. Don't forget to fill in all your answers on the answer sheet. *Don't* just mark them in the test booklet. Marks in the test booklet will not be graded. Also, make sure that your filled-in answers correspond to the correct question numbers! Check your answer sheet after every five answers or so to make sure you haven't skipped any bubbles by mistake.

Believe it or not, there is a most efficient way to bubble in answers on the test. You may have noticed that it can be confusing and tedious to bubble in answers after every question. Alternatively, you may be the type of student who does not bubble in until the very end, a strategy that can lead to stress or running out of time before you finish bubbling all of your answers in. Of course, you want to do most of the work in your test booklet. This includes circling the correct answers as you go. Instead of immediately pausing to bubble in one answer and then moving on, however, finish answering all of the questions visible to you on a single page or two-page spread of the booklet. This method allows you to stay focused on answering questions for a longer period of time. Once you've answered all of the questions on one or two pages, bubble in your answers before turning the page. This way, you are double-checking your question numbers and bubble accuracy every 4–5 questions.

You won't be penalized (lose points) for choosing the wrong answer, so you should always guess. Use Process of Elimination to narrow down the answer choices and increase your chances of guessing correctly.

Should You Guess?

Use Process of Elimination (POE) to rule out answer choices you know are wrong and increase your chances of guessing the right answer. Read all the answer choices carefully. Eliminate the ones that you know are wrong. If you only have one answer choice left, *choose it*, even if you're not completely sure why it's correct. Remember, questions in the multiple-choice section are graded by a computer, so it doesn't care *how* you arrived at the correct answer.

Even if you can't eliminate answer choices, go ahead and guess, as you will not lose points for incorrect answers. You will be assessed only on the total number of correct answers, so be sure to fill in *all* bubbles even if you have no idea what the correct answers are. Don't just fill in any answer, however. When you get to a question that is time consuming or completely stumps you, use what we call your "Letter of the Day" (LOTD). Selecting the same answer choice each time you guess will increase your odds of getting a few of those skipped questions right.

Use the Two-Pass System

Remember that you have about two and a quarter minutes per question on this section of the exam. Do not waste time by lingering too long over any single question. If you're having trouble, move on to the next question. After you finish all the questions, you can come back to the ones you skipped.

The best strategy is to go through the multiple-choice section twice. The first time, do all the questions that you can answer fairly quickly—the ones on which you feel confident about the correct answer. On this first pass, skip the questions that seem to require more thinking or the ones you need to read two or three times before you understand them. Circle the questions that you've skipped in the question booklet so that you can find them easily in the second pass. You must be *very careful* with the answer sheet by making sure the filled-in answers correspond correctly to the questions.

Once you have gone through all the questions, go back to the ones that you skipped in the first pass. But don't linger too long on any one question even in the second pass. Spending too much time wrestling over a hard question can cause two things to happen: 1) You may run out of time and miss out on answering easier questions in the later part of the exam. 2) Your anxiety might start building up, and this could prevent you from thinking clearly and make answering other questions even more difficult. If you simply don't know the answer, or can't eliminate any choices, just use your LOTD and move on.

The two-pass system is a great way to pace yourself and use your time wisely in the multiple-choice section. During the first pass, do all the questions you can answer fairly quickly and feel confident about. Skip the ones you don't know, and save those for the second pass—but don't spend too much time on any one question! When in doubt, choose your Letter of the Day (LOTD).

REFLECT

• How long will you spend on multiple-choice questions?

• How will you change your approach to multiple-choice questions?

• What is your multiple-choice guessing strategy?

Summary

○ There are 40 multiple-choice questions on the AP Statistics Exam, which you'll have 90 minutes to complete. This section of the test is worth 50% of your total score.

○ Remember your LOTD: **L**etter **of** t**he** **D**ay. If you are stuck on a question, guess! You do not lose points for incorrect answers.

○ Use the Two-Pass System. On your first pass through the test, answer the questions that you can figure out fairly quickly, and skip the ones you don't know. Then, on your second pass, go back to the questions you skipped and either try them again or guess (remember your LOTD). Don't spend too much time on any one question.

○ Bubble in your answers every time you finish one to two pages' worth of test questions. This way, you are focused on solving the problems for longer periods, but you are still taking breaks to bubble in answers instead of saving them all until the end, which puts you at risk of running out of time. Double check your bubbles every five answers or so to keep yourself on track.

Chapter 2
How to Approach
Free-Response
Questions

CRACKING THE FREE-RESPONSE SECTION

Section II is worth 50% of your grade on the AP Statistics Exam. This section is composed of two parts. Part A contains five free-response questions; Part B contains one longer free-response question known as the "investigative task." You're given a total of 90 minutes for this section. It's recommended that you spend the first 65 minutes on the first five questions, and the next 25 minutes on the investigative task. The investigative task question is worth twice as much as each of the other free-response questions. Some students begin with the investigative task for this reason. Remember, it's not harder than the other questions—just longer.

Clearly Explain and Justify Your Answers

Remember that your answers to the free-response questions are graded by *readers* and not by computers. Communication is a very important part of AP Statistics. Compose your answers in precise sentences. Just getting the correct numerical answer is not enough. You should be able to *explain* your reasoning behind the technique that you selected and *communicate* your answer in the context of the problem. Even if the question does not explicitly say so, always explain and *justify* every step of your answer, including the final answer. Do not expect the graders to read between the lines. Explain everything as though somebody with no knowledge of statistics is going to read it. Be sure to present your solution in a systematic manner using solid logic and appropriate language.

Use Only the Space You Need

Do not try to fill up the space provided for each question. The space given is usually more than enough. The people who design the tests realize that some students write in big letters and some students make mistakes and need extra space for corrections. So if you have a complete solution, don't worry about the extra space. Writing more will not earn you extra credit. In fact, many students tend to go overboard and shoot themselves in the foot by making a mistake after they've already written the right answer.

Read the Whole Question!

Some questions might have several subparts. Try to answer them all, and don't give up on the question if one part is giving you trouble. For example, if the answer to part (b) depends on the answer to part (a), but you think you got the answer to part (a) wrong, you should still go ahead and do part (b) using your answer to part (a) as required. Chances are that the grader will not mark you wrong twice, unless it is obvious from your answer that you should have discovered your mistake.

Use Common Sense

Always use your common sense in answering questions. For example, on one free-response question that asked students to compute the mean weight of newborn babies from given data, some students answered 70 pounds. It should have been immediately obvious that the answer was probably off by a decimal point. A 70-pound baby would be a giant! This is an important mistake that should be easy to fix. Some mistakes may not be so obvious from the answers. However, the grader will consider simple, *easily recognizable errors* (e.g., giving negative probabilities) to be *very important*.

Concepts Versus Computations

The AP Statistics Exam, and particularly the free-response section, emphasizes the understanding and communication of *concepts*, rather than routine *computation*. If you show a clear understanding of why you have selected a particular technique and how you plan to use it, but you make some minor arithmetic mistake, then most likely the grader will not subtract points.

Suppose, for example, in doing a *t*-interval problem, you defined the parameter of interest, justified why using the *t*-interval was appropriate in this case, and checked all the assumptions correctly. Then you showed the correct formula for the margin of error and made the correct substitutions, but in doing the computation, you reversed the digits of the answer and got 1.61 instead of 1.16 as follows:

$$95\% \ ME = t_{0.025}(14) \ \frac{s}{\sqrt{n}} = 2.145 \left(\frac{2.1}{\sqrt{15}} \right) = 1.61$$

This mistake is not so obvious from the answer. So, you then went ahead and computed your interval correctly using the above margin of error to get 14.75 ± 1.61, which gives (13.14, 16.36). And finally, you explained and interpreted the answer correctly. In this case, because everything else was done perfectly, most likely your arithmetic error would be ignored and you would still get full credit for the question.

On the other hand, imagine the following scenario. While computing the probability under the normal curve, you make a mistake and get the wrong answer. Say you compute

$$P(X > 20) = P\left(Z > \frac{20 - 15}{2} \right) = P(Z > 2.5)$$

You look up the number in the normal table and find that the probability corresponding to 2.5 is 0.9938. Instead of subtracting this figure from 1, you subtract it from 0.5 and get the answer −0.4938. This mistake will *not* be ignored, because students are expected to know that a probability value is *always* between 0 and 1. If you get a negative value or a value larger than 1 for probability, you are expected to realize your mistake immediately. No matter how perfect the rest of the solution is, such an easily identifiable error will not be ignored.

You should use every resource available to you as you prepare for the exam, starting with the College Board website. For scoring rubrics, free-response questions from past exams, and sample responses, go to **https://apcentral. collegeboard.org/ courses/ap-statistics/exam.**

Your responses should be written as clearly as possible in complete sentences.

Think Like a Grader

When answering questions, try to think about what kind of answer the grader is expecting. Look at past free-response questions and scoring guidelines on the College Board website. These examples will give you some idea of how the answers should be phrased. The graders are told to keep in mind that there are two aspects to the scoring of free-response answers: showing statistical knowledge and communicating that knowledge. You don't need to show all the steps of a calculation, but you must explain how you got your answer and why you chose the technique you used. The table on the following page contains scoring guidelines that the College Board gives to free-response graders on the AP Statistics Exam (remember that each question is scored from 0 to 4).

Think Before You Write

Abraham Lincoln once said that if he had eight hours to chop down a tree, he would spend six of them sharpening his axe. In the free-response problems, Part A asks five questions and you have about 65 minutes to work—that's 13 minutes per question. In Part B, one question should take about 25 minutes. In both parts, it makes sense to spend some time thinking about what the question is, what answers are being asked for, what answers might make sense, and what your intuition is before starting to write. These questions aren't meant to trick you, so all the information you need is given. If you think you don't have the right information, you may have misunderstood the question. In some calculations, it is easy to get confused, so think about whether your answers make sense in terms of what the question is asking. If you have some idea of what the answer should look like before starting to write, then you will avoid getting sidetracked and wasting time on dead ends.

Scoring Guidelines for the Free-Response Questions

	Statistical Knowledge	Communication
	• Identify the important components of the problem • Demonstrate the statistical concepts and techniques that result in the correct solution of the problem	• Explain clearly what you did to get the solution to the problem and why you chose a particular method • Give a clear statement of your conclusions
Expect this score on a question	**If you do this...**	**and do this...**
4	• Through your answer, show that you understand the problem's different statistical components • Correctly analyze the relation among the different components of the problem • Correctly use the appropriate statistical techniques • Make sure all your answers are reasonable	• Explicitly explain your entire solution, not just the final answer • Describe your reasoning in getting that solution, using the correct terminology • Use the required numerical or graphical aids to explain your solution • State and check all appropriate assumptions for the statistical techniques used in your solution • Give a reasonable and complete conclusion
3	• With some minor exceptions, show an almost complete understanding of the problem's different components • Analyze the relations among the different components of the problem, with a few gaps • Use the appropriate statistical techniques • Give fairly reasonable answers, but with some computational errors	• Provide a clear but incomplete explanation of your choice of statistical techniques • Give a less-than-perfectly-organized explanation of the steps leading to your solution • Neglect a few conditions necessary for the techniques you use • Use graphical and numerical techniques to help justify your solution • Give a reasonable but somewhat incomplete conclusion
2	• Show some understanding of the problem's statistical components • Have trouble relating the different components • Use some statistical techniques correctly but omit or misuse others • Make some computational mistakes that result in unreasonable answers	• Give a vague explanation of your solution • Use inappropriate terminology • Give an explanation that is difficult to interpret • Use incomplete or ineffective graphical methods to support your solution • Totally neglect to use graphical methods to support your solution
1	• Show a limited understanding of the problem's components • Fail to identify some important components • Have difficulty organizing your solution • Use irrelevant information in your solution • Use statistical techniques incorrectly • Fail to use statistical techniques • Make arithmetic mistakes that result in unreasonable answers	• Give little explanation of your solution • Give an unclear explanation of your solution or methods • Give an explanation that does not match your solution • Fail to use diagrams or graphical methods • Use graphical methods incorrectly • Forget to write a conclusion • Give an incorrect conclusion
0	• Show little or no understanding of the problem's statistical components	• Provide no explanation of any legitimate solution

A FEW MORE TIPS

- **Include units of measurements in all your computations and answers.** You will probably not lose points for missing units, but you might *gain* an advantage by showing them. AP Statistics Exams are graded holistically. The grader will look at the whole question before assigning a grade, and every little bit helps.

- **Beware of presenting conflicting arguments.** Read your entire answer after finishing the question. If your explanation has any conflicting arguments, it will reveal a lack of understanding of the material, and you will most likely lose points.

- **Do not give parallel solutions.** For example, students often realize that a *t*-test is an appropriate procedure in a given situation, but they do not know which *t*-test to use. So they try to play it safe by giving *both* solutions (the matched and the independent sample cases, for example). This is not a good strategy. In the exam, both the solutions will be graded, and the one with the lower score will be counted.

- **Know your Greek letters.** Statistics often makes use of the following Greek letters: α (alpha), β (beta), μ (mu), χ (chi), and both Σ (upper-case sigma) and σ (lower-case sigma).

REFLECT

- How much time will you spend on the short free-response questions? What about the investigative task?

- What will you do before you begin writing your free-response answers?

- Will you seek further help, outside of this book (such as a teacher, tutor, or AP Students), on how to approach the questions that you will see on the AP Statistics Exam?

Summary

o Section II of the AP Statistics Exam is worth 50% of your total score and is broken up into two parts. Part A contains five free-response questions, and Part B contains a longer free-response question known as the "investigative task." You have 90 minutes to complete Section II, and it suggested you spend 65 minutes on Part A (the five free-response questions) and 25 minutes on Part B (the investigative task).

o Be sure to *justify* your answer at every step—that is, explain your answer as though someone who has no knowledge of statistics is reading it. Use solid logic and clear, straightforward language.

o The free-response section of the exam emphasizes understanding of concepts. So if you make a minor arithmetic error, but your answer demonstrates understanding of the concepts involved, your grader will most likely not deduct points.

o Here are some tips for maximizing your score on this section:
  • Be sure to include units of measurement for all of your calculations, as well as your final answer.
  • Beware of conflicting arguments in your answer; this may cause you to lose points.
  • Do not give parallel solutions.
  • Know your Greek letters.

Chapter 3
How to Use Your Calculator

USING THE CALCULATOR

Below is a brief outline of how to use the TI-83 or TI-84 calculator. You may need to refer to this section as you work through the examples later in the book. This is not a complete list of the useful functions of your calculator, but it does cover the functions used most often in an AP Statistics course. You may want to refer to your calculator's manual for more options.

The most commonly used statistical features of the TI-83 and TI-84 are the following:

STAT

When you press the STAT button, you are given three different options: EDIT, CALC, and TESTS.

1. **EDIT:** You can access these procedures using STAT → EDIT.

   - **Edit:** Use this option to access lists (similar to a spreadsheet), create a new list of data, or edit an existing list of data. There are six default columns labeled L_1, L_2, L_3, L_4, L_5, and L_6.

     To enter data in a list: Suppose the data to be entered is 3, 5, –2, 6. Enter the data in a list using the following steps. The data will be saved automatically.

- To **ENTER** data in a list, say, L_1
- Choose **STAT → EDIT**
- Press **ENTER**
- In the list titled L_1, type 3
- Press **ENTER**
- Type 5
- Press **ENTER**
- Type (–)2
- Press **ENTER**
- Type 6
- Press **ENTER**

To create a new list: Suppose you want to create a new list, named NEW, in addition to the six default lists. Use the following steps.

- Suppose you want to create a list between, say, L_1 and L_2
- Choose **STAT → EDIT**
- Press **ENTER**
- Put the cursor at the title of list L_2
- Press **2nd → INS** *A new column will be added to the left of L_2*
- Use the ALPHA (green) key and alphabet keys to label the new column
- Press **ENTER**

- **ClrList:** Use this option to clear all data in a given list. This option is *not* for deleting a partial list. To delete a partial list, use the DEL key. This action will delete all numbers in a given column, and *this deletion is not reversible*.

- Suppose data is in a list, say, L_1
- Choose **STAT → EDIT → ClrList**
- Press **ENTER**
- Enter the list name to read ClrList (L_1)
- Press **ENTER**

---

2. **CALC:** You can access these procedures using STAT → CALC.
    Use this option to get one or two variable summary statistics, the correlation coefficient, linear regression coefficients (slope and y-intercept), and regression using transformed variables. The steps for using these procedures are provided in Chapter 4.

    1:1-Var Stats: Use this option to compute summary statistics for one-variable (*univariate*) data. It gives the number of observations (n), mean $\left(\overline{X}\right)$, sum ($\Sigma X$), sum of squares ($\Sigma X^2$), sample standard deviation (S), population standard deviation (σ), median, quartiles (Q_1 and Q_3), minimum, and maximum.

    2:2-Var Stats: Use this option to compute summary statistics for *bivariate* data. It gives the number of pairs of observations (n), means ($\overline{X}$ and $\overline{Y}$), sums (ΣX and ΣY), sums of squares (ΣX^2 and ΣY^2), sample standard deviations (S_x and S_y), population standard deviations (σ_x and σ_y), min and max for each variable, and sum of products (ΣXY).

    8:LinReg(*a+bx*): Use this option to get the correlation coefficient and least-squares estimates for slope and y-intercept for linear regression.

    9:LnReg: Use this option for logarithmic transformation to linearize a regression model.

    0:ExpReg: Use this option for exponential transformation to linearize a regression model.

    A:PwrReg: Use this option for fitting a power model using logarithmic transformation to linearize a regression model.

3. **TESTS:** Access these procedures using STAT → TESTS.

    Procedures for creating confidence intervals and testing hypotheses are located under this option. The steps for using these procedures are provided in Chapter 7.

1:Z-Test: Use this for a one-sample z-test for population mean (known population variance).

2:T-Test: Use this for a one-sample t-test for a population mean (unknown population variance).

3:2-SampZTest: Use this for a z-test for the difference between two population means (independent samples).

4:2-SampTTest: Use this for a t-test for the difference between two population means (independent samples, unknown population variances—equal and unequal).

5:1-PropZTest: Use this for a large-sample z-test for a population proportion.

6:2-PropZTest: Use this for a large-sample z-test for the difference between two population proportions (independent samples).

7:Zinterval: Use this for a one-sample z-confidence interval for a population mean (known population variance).

8:Tinterval: Use this for a one-sample t-confidence interval for a population mean (unknown population variance).

9:2-SampZInt: Use this for a z-confidence interval for the difference between two population means (independent samples).

0:2-SampTInt: Use this for a t-confidence interval for the difference between two population means (independent samples, unknown population variances—equal and unequal).

A:1-PropZInt: Use this for a large-sample z-confidence interval for a population proportion.

B:2-PropZInt: Use this for a large-sample z-confidence interval for the difference between two population proportions (independent samples).

C:χ^2–Test: Use this for a chi-square test for independence of two categorical variables.

E:LinRegTTest: Use this for a t-test for the slope of a least-squares regression line.

MATH

Under MATH, there are four options, but the PRB option is the only one you'll need for AP Statistics. The steps for using these procedures are listed in Chapter 6.

PRB: Access these procedures using MATH → PRB.

3:nCr: Use this option to get combinations.

5:randInt(: Use this option to generate a set of random integers from a specified range.

randInt (*lower limit, upper limit, numbers to generate*)

6:randNorm(: Use this option to generate a set of random numbers from a specified normally distributed population.

randNorm (*mean, standard deviation, numbers to generate*)

7:randBin(: Use this option to generate a set of random numbers from a binomial population.

randBin (*n, p, numbers to generate*)

MATRX

Under MATRX, there are three options, but the NAMES and EDIT options are the ones you'll need to use. Access these procedures using 2nd → x^{-1} key.

1. **NAMES:** Access this option as MATRX → NAMES.
   Use this option to utilize an already-created matrix—for example, a matrix of expected counts created by a chi-square test of independence.

- Choose **MATRX → NAMES**
  A list of matrix names with their respective dimensions will be displayed.
- Use the up and down arrows to move up and down the list. Highlight the name of the matrix to be used.
- Press **ENTER** *The name of the selected matrix will be pasted in the window.*
- Press **ENTER** *The matrix will be listed in the window.*

---

2. **EDIT:** Use this option to create a new matrix or edit an existing one.

   Suppose you want to create the following 2 × 3 matrix:

$$A = \begin{bmatrix} 20 & 5 & 30 \\ 10 & 15 & 25 \end{bmatrix}$$

- Choose **MATRX** → **EDIT**
  A list of matrix names with their respective dimensions will be displayed.
- Use the up and down arrows to move up and down the list. Highlight the name of the matrix to be created, say, 1: [A]
- Press **ENTER**
- Create the appropriate dimensions for the matrix: 2 × 3
- Press **ENTER**
- Enter 20
- Press **ENTER**
- Enter 5
- Press **ENTER**
- Enter 30
- Press **ENTER**
- Enter 10
- Press **ENTER**
- Enter 15
- Press **ENTER**
- Enter 25
- Press **ENTER**

DISTR

Procedures for computing probabilities and cumulative probabilities for different distributions are listed under this option. The steps for using these procedures are provided in Chapter 6. Access these procedures in the DISTR menu, using 2nd → VARS.

2:normalcdf(: Use this option to find the area under any normal curve in a given range specified by a lower limit and an upper limit. The lower and upper limits must be x values.

normalcdf (*lower limit, upper limit, mean, standard deviation*)

If you know the lower and upper scores, you may use normalcdf (*lower z-score, upper z-score*) to find the area.

3:invNorm(: Use this option to find a z-score corresponding to the specified area (p) less than that of the z-score.

invNorm (*p, mean, standard deviation*)

5:tcdf(: Use this option to find the area under the t-distribution in a given range specified by the lower limit and the upper limit—for example, if you need to find a p-value for a t-test.

tcdf (*lower limit, upper limit, degrees of freedom*)

7:χ^2cdf(: Use this option to find the area under the chi-square distribution—for example, when you need to find a p-value for a chi-square test.

$$\chi^2 \text{ cdf } (\textit{lower limit, upper limit, degrees of freedom})$$

0:binompdf(: Use this option to find the binomial probability of a specific outcome. $P(x) = \binom{n}{x} p^x (1-p)^{n-x}$

$$\text{binompdf } (n, p, x)$$

A:binomcdf(: Use this option to find the cumulative binomial probability of a specified outcome. $P(x \le x_0) = \sum_{x=0}^{x_0} \binom{n}{x} p^x (1-p)^{n-x}$

$$\text{binomcdf } (n, p, x_0)$$

D:geometpdf(: Use this option to find the geometric probability of a specific outcome. $P(x) = p(1-p)^{x-1}$

$$\text{geometpdf } (p, x)$$

E:geometcdf(: Use this option to find the cumulative binomial probability of specified outcomes. $P(x \le x_0) = \sum_{x=1}^{x_0} \binom{n}{x} p(1-p)^{x-1}$

$$\text{geometcdf } (p, x_0)$$

DIAGNOSTICS

Use this option to get the calculator to display values for the correlation coefficient and coefficient of determination when executing regression models. You need to turn diagnostics on only once; it will stay on until you turn the diagnostics off.

- Choose 2nd → Catalog → DiagnosticOn
- On newer models of the TI-83 and TI-84 calculators, statistic diagnostics can be turned on under the MODE key as well.

STAT PLOT

Use this option to make a scatterplot, boxplot, histogram, regression line plot, and residual plot. The steps for making these graphs are given in Chapter 4.

Tips on Using the Calculator Well

The calculator is a valuable tool, but many students lose points by using it improperly or relying on it too heavily. Note that although the TI-83, TI-84, and TI-89 are popular calculators, there are many others on the market. You do not know whether the readers grading your exam will be familiar with your particular calculator.

Also, remember that readers come from both high schools and colleges. Although most high school statistics classes use calculators, many colleges do not require specific calculators in their courses. It's quite possible that your answers will be graded by people unfamiliar with statistical calculators. So, *do not use calculator talk*. Explain your answer in plain English, using the appropriate statistical terminology. For example, suppose you're faced with this question:

1. Suppose the time 8-to-12-year-olds spend playing video games per week is normally distributed with a mean of 15 hours and a standard deviation of two hours. What percent of children spend more than 20 hours per week playing video games?
    *   If your answer to this question is just the number "0.0062," you will probably not get credit. First, you did not describe your reasoning for getting this number. Second, you failed to communicate your answer appropriately. Third, the question asks for a *percentage*.
*   If your answer to this question is just "0.62%," with no further explanation or description of the steps you used to get this number, you might or might not get any credit for the answer. It depends on whether the passage above constitutes the entire question or just a sub-question of the question and how the answer to this sub-question is related to other sub-questions.
*   If your answer to this question is "normalcdf (20, 2000, 15, 2) = 0.0062," again, you should not expect to get credit. Those who are familiar with the functions of a TI-83 calculator will understand your answer, but non-users will not. Other calculators, such as Casio or HP, have different formats. This is what statistics teachers refer to as "calculator talk." Statistics teachers and, more importantly, statistics readers do not like calculator talk.
*   Instead, you should explain your answer as follows:

Let X = the time spent by 8-to-12-year-olds per week on playing video games.

Then, $P(X > 20) = P\left(Z > \dfrac{20-15}{2}\right) = P(Z > 2.5) = 0.0062$.

Therefore, about 0.62% of 8-to-12-year-olds spend more than 20 hours per week playing video games.

This will constitute a complete and well-communicated answer, without calculator talk.

> Stay away from using "calculator talk" when writing your responses. Always explain your answers in plain English, as your test may be scored by graders who are unfamiliar with statistical calculators.

Your Work Versus the Calculator's Work

Do not reproduce calculator output just as is. Do not describe how you entered numbers in the calculator or your sequence of keystrokes. This will not give you any advantage. When using confidence intervals or hypotheses-testing procedures, do not copy input or output from the calculator screen. For example, take the following problem:

Graders on free-response questions are looking for you to justify and explain answers. Don't just copy down numbers! Explain what you are calculating and, more importantly, why you are doing so.

1. A random sample of fifteen 8-to-12-year-olds was selected. All selected children were monitored for six months and the number of hours they spent playing video games was recorded. The mean number of hours they spent playing video games was 14.75 hours per week, with a standard deviation of 2.1 hours per week. Estimate the true mean time that 8-to-12-year-olds spend playing video games per week using a 95% confidence level.

    •   You might be tempted to copy the following from your calculator:

Tinterval	Tinterval
Inpt: Stats	(13.587, 15.913)
$\overline{X}$: 14.75	$\overline{X}$: 14.75
Sx: 2.1	Sx: 2.1
n: 15	n: 15
C-Level: 95	
Calculate	

Do not give in to temptation. This is calculator talk. It is not a complete answer to the question. It will not receive any credit beyond the credit allowed for arithmetic computations.

    •   Suppose you give the following answer:

$$95\% \; ME = t_{0.025}(14)\frac{s}{\sqrt{n}} = 2.145\left(\frac{2.1}{\sqrt{15}}\right) = 1.16$$

$$14.75 \pm 1.16 \text{ gives } (13.59, 15.91)$$

This is better than calculator talk, but it is still an incomplete answer. It provides the correct mechanics, but it fails to provide the proper communication. What is the parameter of interest here? Why was the *t*-interval used? Why is the *t*-interval appropriate in this situation? Are the conditions required for using the *t*-interval satisfied? What does the answer tell us in the context of the situation described? All those questions need to be answered. The above answer might get you credit for correct mechanics but nothing else. It might be worth one point out of four.

Showing Graphs

If you make plots on your calculator for, say, checking the conditions for a certain procedure used to answer a question, be sure to do more than just say that the graph shows that the required conditions were met. The grader has no way of knowing what graph you made, what your graph looked like, why you think the conditions were met, or whether you even looked at a graph. Instead, copy the graph from your calculator screen onto your answer sheet so that the grader can see what it is that you looked at when arriving at your answer. Discuss how you used the graph to make a decision. Even if your answer is wrong, you might get partial credit for using the correct reasoning. For example, you would probably lose points for using the wrong graph, but you might get some credit for drawing the correct conclusion from the wrong graph.

Summary

o   Use the STAT → EDIT function to create and clear lists of data.

o   Use STAT → CALC → 1:1-Var Stats to get summary statistics of the data, including mean, median, standard deviation, and range.

o   Common statistic tests, such as the z-test, z-interval, t-test, t-interval, and others can be found under STAT → TESTS.

o   Probability calculations for combinations and permutations are found under MATH.

o   The DISTR key can be used to calculate normal distributions and probability distributions.

o   To turn on Statistic Diagnostics on the TI-83, go to 2nd → CATALOG → DiagnosticOn and hit ENTER. For the TI-84, use the same process. On newer models, this option can be found under MODE.

o   Avoid using "calculator talk" in your responses—that is, filling your answers with references to specific calculator buttons, or answering questions with only numbers. Write your answers in plain, everyday English and provide context to the numbers, including units.

Part V
Content Review for the AP Statistics Exam

HOW TO USE THE CHAPTERS IN THIS PART

For the following content chapters, you may need to come back to them more than once. Your goal is to obtain mastery of the content you are missing, and a single read of a chapter may not be sufficient. At the end of each chapter, you will have an opportunity to test how well you understood the chapter content, as well as review the chapter's most important concepts.

These chapters are long, so don't be afraid to take breaks, even in the middle of a chapter. You might choose to read a chapter over the course of a day or two and the next day review the Key Terms, Summary, and Drill—which is a great way to test your retention of information!

Chapter 4
Exploring Data

By the end of the chapter you will be able to master:

- visualizing quantitative and qualitative data
- describing the shape, spread, and center of data from various graphs
- graphing bivariate data and describing the relationship between two variables using correlation coefficients (r) to describe direction and strength, and regression to generate a line of best fit
- determining the appropriateness of a linear relationship between two variables using residual plots
- interpreting coefficients of determination (r^2)
- calculating the expected frequency of a cell in a contingency table

OBSERVING PATTERNS AND DEPARTURES FROM PATTERNS

Statistics is a science of data. We all use data to estimate unknown quantities, to make decisions, and to develop and implement policies. To draw any sensible conclusions from collected data, we need to summarize the data or examine the patterns that it forms.

COLLECTING DATA

Who collects data and what do they do with collected data?

> This chapter will discuss graphical and numerical techniques used to study data. In the multiple-choice section, this topic appears in eight to 12 out of 40 questions. In the free-response section, this topic appears in one to two out of six questions.

*   Businesses collect data on their products and on consumers. For example, some stores collect data on when certain products—such as berries—will sell. One store found out that berries sell better in low wind weather conditions; who knew!
*   Scientists collect data on experiments they design. They might use the collected data to see whether two groups of people have different IQ scores or two types of cells grow at different rates.
*   Doctors collect diagnostic data on their patients. They might use collected data to identify the appropriate treatment for a patient.
*   Police collect data on criminal behavior and the frequency of certain crimes. They might use the collected data to determine where to increase police patrols.

Data is rarely collected in a form that is immediately useful for decision-making. For example, imagine that a polling group was conducting a telephone survey to estimate the percent of state residents in favor of the governor's new proposal. Five interviewers called a total of 1,800 residents over a period of five days and recorded the result for each resident as "supports" or "does not support." So at the completion of the survey, the polling group had a list of 1,800 responses listed as "supports" or "does not support." What could we say just by looking at a spreadsheet of this data? Unfortunately, nothing—until somebody takes the time to organize it.

To use collected data, it needs to be organized and summarized. The different methods for doing this are known as **descriptive methods**. Different descriptive methods might result in different outcomes, leading to different conclusions. Descriptive methods are useful for data presentation, data reduction, and summarization. The best method depends on the type of data being collected.

Types of Variables

There are two types of variables: **categorical** and **quantitative**. A variable is categorical if it places the individuals being studied into one of several groups or categories. Researchers generally determine the count or percent of individuals in each category. Some examples of categorical data are sex (male or female) and eye color.

A variable is quantitative if its outcomes are numerical and can be analyzed using arithmetic operations (such as taking the average). Examples of quantitative variables include age, height, weight, and IQ. Quantitative variables can be either discrete or continuous, a distinction that will be discussed in more detail later in this book. Different methods of analysis must be used for categorical and quantitative variables.

If we take only one measurement on each object, we get **univariate data**. With two measurements on each object, we get **bivariate data**. For example, measuring the heights of a group of children will result in a *univariate* data set of the heights of the children. On the other hand, if we measure the height and the weight of each child, then we will get a *bivariate* data set consisting of the heights and weights of the children.

Both types are discussed in detail later in this chapter.

Types of Descriptive Methods

We use different descriptive methods depending on the type of data collected. Descriptive methods are divided into three basic categories:

- Tabular methods
- Graphical methods
- Numerical methods

Different descriptive methods answer different questions about data. Naturally, different questions have different answers. In general, we cannot look at data from all possible angles using only one method. So it's best to use more than one method when we're summarizing a data set, even if the different methods produce some overlap of information. Let's look at each of these three categories in more detail.

TABULAR METHODS

Collected data generally need to be rearranged before analysis. One tabular method is the frequency distribution table. This table facilitates the analysis of patterns of variation among observed data.

- The letter n is used to denote the number of observations in a data set.

- The **frequency** of a value is the number of times that observation occurs. Frequency is usually denoted using the letter f.

- The **relative frequency** of a value is the ratio of the frequency (f) to the total number of observations (n). It is usually denoted by rf, and $rf = \dfrac{f}{n}$.

- The **cumulative frequency** gives the number of observations less than or equal to a specified value. It is usually denoted by cf.

- A **frequency distribution table** is a table giving all possible values of a variable and their frequencies.

Example 1: The Student Government Association (SGA) at a university was interested in how much students spend per month on housing. Because students who live in dorms pay a fixed housing fee per semester, it was decided not to include those students in the study. The SGA selected a sample of students living off campus and collected data on their housing type and on the amount they spent per month on housing. The collected information is listed in the table below. The columns titled "Exp" (for "Expenditure") give the amount each student spent per month on housing (in dollars). The columns titled "Type" give the type of housing for each student, classified as:

A = Apartment   C = Condominium   H = House   T = Townhouse

Exp	Type	Exp	Type	Exp	Type	Exp	Type	Exp	Type	Exp	Type	Exp	Type	Exp	Type
304	C	323	H	529	T	482	A	406	H	628	T	259	C	330	A
342	A	350	A	358	A	423	A	440	H	333	A	424	H	595	C
437	A	349	A	278	A	530	A	384	H	327	A	529	H	383	C
446	A	384	H	482	H	404	H	391	T	581	A	466	H	437	C
362	C	394	A	270	A	393	A	501	T	398	T	834	T	416	C
552	H	296	C	462	H	450	C	550	T	516	T	558	A	351	T
411	C	435	A	503	A	364	T	306	T	478	T	332	C	385	T
330	C	334	A	367	A	264	A	450	H	358	H	317	H	376	T
673	H	525	T	353	H	276	A	309	C	439	H	430	A	408	C
309	H	391	A	760	A	297	T	255	T	377	A	282	T	385	A

Table 1: Housing expenditure (in $) and type of housing data

These numbers are useless unless we rearrange and summarize them in a meaningful fashion. Note that data were collected for two variables: type of housing and housing expenditure per month. Type of housing is a *qualitative,* or *categorical,* variable and housing expenditure is a *quantitative,* or *continuous,* variable.

One possible grouped frequency distribution table for housing expenditure is as follows.

Housing Expenditure ($)	Frequency f	Relative Frequency rf = f/n	Percentage 100rf	Cumulative Frequency cf	Relative Cumulative Frequency rcf	Cumulative percentage 100rcf
250–299	9	0.11	11	9	0.11	11
300–349	14	0.18	18	23	0.29	29
350–399	20	0.25	25	43	0.54	54
400–449	14	0.18	18	57	0.72	72
450–499	7	0.09	9	64	0.81	81
500–549	7	0.09	9	71	0.90	90
550–599	5	0.06	6	76	0.96	96
600–649	1	0.01	1	77	0.97	97
650–699	1	0.01	1	78	0.98	98
700–749	0	0.00	0	78	0.98	98
750–799	1	0.01	1	79	0.99	99
800–849	1	0.01	1	80	1.00	100

Table 2: Frequency distribution for housing expenditure

Note the following:

- The numbers in the frequency column add up to the total number of observations, $n = 80$.
- Housing expenditures are grouped into different classes. For the class 400–449, the number 400 defines the lower limit, and the number 449 defines the upper limit.
- All classes are of length equal to 50.
- The class mark is the halfway point for each class. For class 400–449, the class mark is 424.5.
- The numbers in the relative frequency column add up to 1. In some charts, due to rounding-off errors, the total may not add to exactly 1, though it should be close.
- The numbers in the percentage column add up to 100. As with the proportions, the total should be very close to 100.
- The last entry in the cumulative frequency column is equal to the total number of observations, $n = 80$.

What do the numbers in this table mean? Below are some examples.

- The frequency for group 300–349 is 14. This means that 14 students of those interviewed spend $300 to $349 per month on housing.
- The relative frequency for group 300–349 is 0.18 and the percentage is 18. This means that 18% of students interviewed spend $300 to $349 per month on housing.
- The cumulative frequency for group 300–349 is 23. This means that 23 of the students interviewed spend less than or equal to $349 per month.

The frequency distribution table for housing type is as follows:

Relative frequency and percentage are very closely related: Percentage is just 100 × relative frequency! Often we think of percents both in their percentage form (0–100) and their decimal form (0–1).

Type of Housing	Frequency f	Relative Frequency $rf = f/n$	Percentage $100rf$
Apartment	29	0.36	36
Condominium	14	0.18	18
House	19	0.24	24
Townhouse	18	0.23	23

Table 3: Frequency distribution for housing type

Again, note the following:

- The figures in the frequency column add up to the total number of observations, $n = 80$.
- The figures in the relative frequency column add up to 1.01. This is an example of a rounding-off. Although the total is not exactly 1, it is very close.
- The figures in the percentage column add up to 101.
- For this categorical variable, there is no sensible ordering of values. So, cumulative frequency is meaningless.

We can interpret the numbers in this table as follows:

- The frequency for apartments is 29. This means that 29 of the students interviewed live in apartments.
- The relative frequency for apartments is 0.36 (36% of students interviewed live in apartments; 29/80).
- Apartments are clearly the most popular type of housing (36%), but the other housing types seem to be pretty similar in popularity among the students.
- Cumulative frequency is most useful when categories have a meaningful **order** (called ordinal data: more specific definitions later in the book). Cumulative frequency is not as useful for categories that don't have an order, like favorite pizza topping.

GRAPHICAL METHODS FOR QUALITATIVE DATA

Presenting data in tables is not always useful and will rarely give a full picture of the data. Almost every statistical problem will benefit from good charts and graphs. With today's technology, it has become much easier to generate useful charts and graphs. To summarize and describe qualitative data, bar charts are particularly useful. Pie charts are frequently used but are not recommended.

Graphical Methods for Categorical Data: Bar Charts and Pie Charts

Bar Charts

Bar charts are very common. Economists use them to display financial data. The business section of any newspaper usually has at least one bar chart. A bar chart can have either horizontal or vertical bars. Bar charts are used to display categorical data and will usually have space between each bar. They can appear similar to histograms, which are used for numerical data. (You will see an example of a histogram later in this chapter.)

This is how to make a bar chart:

- Draw horizontal (x) and vertical (y) axes.
- On the horizontal axis, mark the categories of the variable at equal intervals.
- Scale the vertical axis in order to plot frequencies, relative frequencies, or percentages.
- Note that the above three steps would result in a vertical bar chart. For a horizontal bar chart, transpose the x-axis and y-axis.
- For each category, draw a bar whose height (or whose length, for horizontal bars) is equal to the data plotted, frequency, relative frequency, percentage, etc.

Example 2: Create a bar chart summarizing the data on housing type in Table 3.

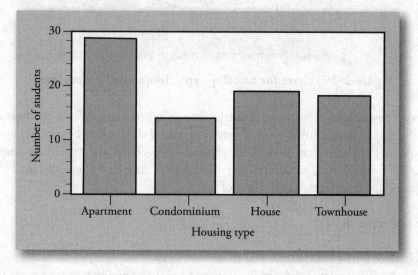

Figure 1: Bar chart for type of housing data

The bar chart above clearly shows that an apartment is the most popular type of accommodation among these students. There's not much difference in popularity between houses and townhouses, with houses leading townhouses by a narrow margin. The fewest students live in condominiums.

How do we read a bar chart?

- Each bar indicates a different category.
- The height of a frequency bar chart indicates how often that category occurred in the data set. For example, the first bar in the bar chart shown above corresponds to "Apartment." The height of this graph can be read off the vertical axis as 29; 29 students out of the 80 interviewed live in apartments.

Pie Charts

Pie charts can be difficult to make as well as to read. Choose to display your data in some other graphical method on the free-response section.

A pie chart can also display amounts and frequencies in a set of data. It is commonly used to describe the different spending categories of a budget, for example. Businesses use pie charts to display the various components of their entire production output. For example, a paper company producing copying paper, notebook paper, trifolds, etc., could use a pie chart to describe what proportion of its entire production is made up by each of these products. While popular, they are rarely, if ever, the best method of displaying data and have been shown to be misleading and hard to read accurately.

Example 3: Read the pie chart summarizing the housing type data in Table 3.

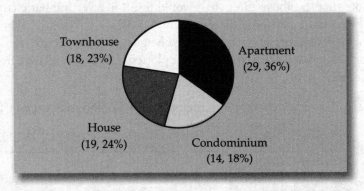

Figure 2: Pie chart for housing type (frequency, percentage)

This pie chart shows clearly that most students live in apartments. While the fewest number of students live in condominiums, there is very little visual distinction between the other three types of housing. Pie charts can be difficult to read—especially when there are many categories—because it is hard for us to determine which slice of the pie has greater area. If you have many categories, consider using other types of graphs.

How do we read a pie chart?

- Each piece of the pie corresponds to one category.
- The category corresponding to the largest piece is the one that occurs most often.

GRAPHICAL METHODS FOR QUANTITATIVE DATA

To summarize and describe quantitative data, dotplots and stemplots are used for small sets of data. For larger sets, histograms, cumulative frequency charts, and boxplots are often employed.

Examining Graphs

We can describe the overall pattern of the distribution of a quantitative variable set using the following three terms:

- The **center** of a distribution describes the "typical" or central data point. There are a few ways to measure central tendency, including **mean**, **median**, and **mode**. Each measure has different pros and cons depending on the type and shape of the data.

- The **spread** of a distribution describes how far the data points are from the center. Spread can be quantified through the range, standard deviation, or variance of a distribution.

- The **shape** of a distribution can tell us where most of the data is. For example:

  - **Symmetric distribution:** If the left half of the distribution is approximately a mirror image of the right half, then the distribution is described as symmetric. This means that the data is spread out in the same way on both sides and that there is the same amount of data on each side of the center.
  - **Skewed distribution:** If there are extreme values in only one direction that cause one side to have a longer tail, we call that distribution skewed. It's right-skewed if the longer tail is on the right, and left-skewed if the longer tail is on the left. For example, income distributions tend to be right-skewed because most people make between $17,000 and $70,000, but then you have people like Bill Gates and Oprah Winfrey who make a lot of money and pull the tail of our distribution out to the right.

The following three graphs show three basic shapes of distributions.

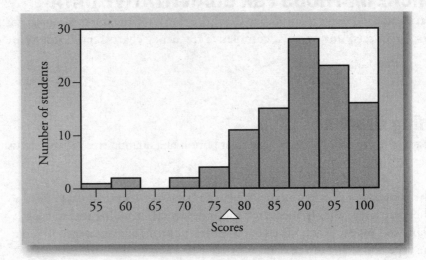

Figure 3: Left-skewed distribution

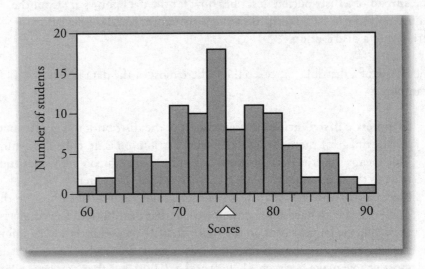

Figure 4: Symmetric distribution

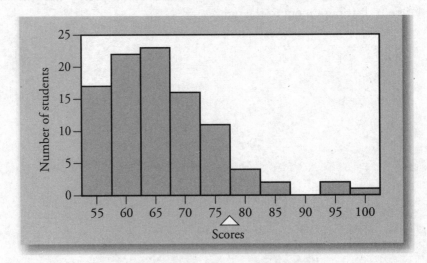

Figure 5: Right-skewed distribution

Patterns and Deviations from Patterns

When examining data, we should look for the patterns and for striking deviations from those patterns. The following terms are important for pattern recognition:

- **Clusters and gaps:** It's important to describe clusters and gaps. Are observations grouped together tightly? Are there any large gaps in the values? For example, if you plot the heights of a group of college students, the plot is likely to peak at two separate points, with a dip in between. The reason for this is that women in general tend to be a bit shorter than men. The first peak corresponds to the women's most common height, whereas the second peak corresponds to the men's most common height. Look at the following figure:

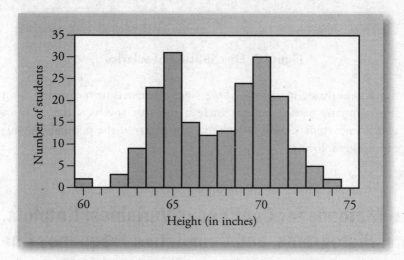

Figure 6: Distribution of student heights

- **Outliers:** An outlier is an observation that is surprisingly different from the rest of the data. Imagine you go to a high school track practice and record 100-meter dash times. Without your knowledge (you weren't paying much attention), Usain Bolt showed up and you recorded his time. When you look at your data a few days later, you notice that you have one time (Bolt's) that is surprisingly low. This is an outlier, because it doesn't belong to the group you were interested in recording: high school track team members. In the real world, we often don't know whether surprisingly extreme scores are a result of something weird like Usain Bolt showing up to a high school, or a typo made when entering the data. Because there's no easy way to tell, we often treat all extreme values as outliers. Consider the following distribution that shows the salaries of employees at one company.

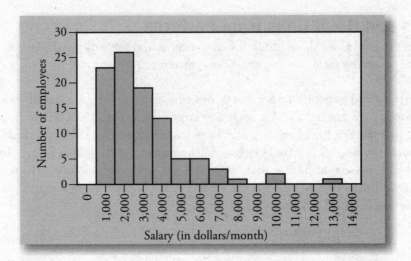

Figure 7: Distribution of salaries

The distribution is slightly right skewed. If we were interested in measuring what the typical employee at this company made, the extremely high value (perhaps the CEO's salary) is an outlier because it is so extreme that it is probably not a part of the population you're interested in measuring: typical employees.

Graphical Methods for Continuous Variables: Dotplots, Stemplots, Histograms, and Cumulative Frequency Charts

Dotplots

A dotplot is one of the easiest plots to make. It's most effective for smaller data sets. If the data set is too large, then the dotplot will be very cluttered. For large data sets, it's best to create a boxplot (described later in this chapter). Dotplots are very similar to histograms or bar plots (especially if you squint when you look at them).

This is how to make a dotplot:

- Draw a horizontal line (the *x*-axis) to indicate the data range.
- Scale the line to accommodate the entire range of data.
- Mark a dot for each observation in the appropriate place above the scaled line.
- If more than one observation has the same value, then add dots one above the other.

Example 4: Create a dotplot for the housing expenditure data in Table 1.

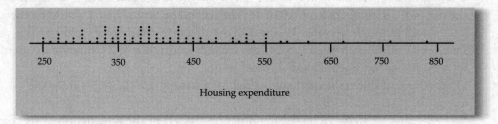

Figure 8: Dotplot for the housing expenditure data

This dotplot shows that the distribution of housing expenditure is right-skewed and that there are at least two outliers on the higher end (i.e., students paying a lot more for housing than what most of the others spend). The expenditures range from about $250 a month to almost $850 a month, with most of the amounts in the range of $250 to $550. The distribution is centered around $414 a month.

How do we read a dotplot?

- Each dot on the plot indicates the location of the value of a data point.
- For any data point, we can look directly down at the scale to determine the value of the point.

We can use the dotplot to determine:

- how the data points are spread
- what kind of shape the points make collectively
- where the approximate center of the distribution is—in other words, where this picture of dots is likely to balance if it were held on an outstretched finger

Stemplots

Stemplots, also known as stem-and-leaf plots, are also commonly used. When turned on its side, a stemplot resembles a dotplot, but with digits instead of dots. One advantage of using a stemplot is that it shows every value, but stemplots are inconvenient for very large data sets.

This is how to make a stemplot:

- Separate each observation into two parts. The left-most part of each observation is called the **stem,** and the remaining part is called the **leaf**. There is no definite rule for determining where to make the division. Use a scheme that gives a reasonable number of stems. Too few stems can distort the picture by hiding patterns, whereas too many stems can distort the picture by diluting patterns. For example, if you have a sample of 80 numbers between 1 and 99, you may want to divide the data into groups of 10. So for stems, you might choose the first digit of each number in the sample (0, 1, 2, 3, 4, 5, 6, 7, 8, 9). If the sample was of 80 numbers between 1 and 49, you might want to make 10 stems by writing in the first digit of

> **Connecting Outliers and Center**
> If we think of the data as being on a see-saw, outliers are on the very end of the see-saw. How do you think that would affect where the balancing point of the seesaw would be? Points that are far away from the bulk of the data tend to have more of an effect on the mean (or balancing point).

every number twice (0, 0, 1, 1, 2, 2, 3, 3, 4, 4). The first occurrence of 1 would be the stem for all numbers from 10 to 14; the second occurrence of 1 would be the stem for all numbers between 15 and 19. The first occurrence of 2 would be the stem for all numbers from 20 to 24; the second occurrence of 2 would be the stem for all numbers between 25 and 29; and so on.

- Draw a vertical line on the left side of the page to separate the stems from the leaves.
- Write all possible stems in increasing order on the left of the line, making sure that the entire range of the data is covered.
- For each observation, write in the leaf to the right of the corresponding stem on the right side of the vertical line in increasing order.

Example 5: Create a stemplot for the housing expenditure data in Table 1.

Stemplot of Housing Expenditure Data
N = 80

Stem	Leaf
2	55 59 64 70 76 78 82 96 97
3	04 06 09 09 17 23 27 30 30 32 33 34 42 49
3	50 51 53 58 62 64 67 76 77 83 84 84 85 85 91 91 93 94 98
4	04 06 08 11 16 23 24 30 35 37 37 39 40 46
4	50 50 62 66 78 82 82
5	01 03 16 25 29 29 30
5	50 52 58 81 95
6	28
6	73
7	
7	60
8	34

Figure 9: Stemplot for the housing expenditure data

This stemplot shows that the distribution of housing expenditure is right-skewed, with at least two outliers at the high end. Expenditures ranged from about $250 a month to almost $850 a month, with most of the amounts (all but nine) in the range of $250 to $549 per month. The distribution is centered around approximately $414 a month.

How do we read a stemplot?

- The numbers on the left of the vertical line are stems. The value of a data point is the stem plus the leaf. For the last data point, the value is 834 (stem + leaf).
- Each stem has a different number of leaves, indicating the frequency of that class. For example, stem 2 has nine leaves, which means nine observations belong to this stem. In other words, nine students pay $250–$299 per month for housing.
- Each leaf indicates a single observation. Four leaves beginning with 0 on stem 3 indicate that four students spend $300–$309 per month on housing.
- The lower stem 7 has no leaves, which means that no interviewed student pays between $700 and $749 per month for housing.

> Note: There is only one 2 because no value was under $250, and also only one 8 because no value was above $850.

We can use the stemplot to determine:

- How the data is shaped and spread. To do this, we might turn the graph on its side with the stems at the bottom.
- Where the center of this data is—just as with dotplots, where this picture of stems and leaves would balance if it were turned on its side with the stems at the bottom and held on an outstretched finger.

Histograms

A histogram is probably the most popular form of displaying data. It vaguely resembles a stemplot on its side. Histograms are especially useful for displaying patterns in large data sets. Dots or stems can get overwhelming, and provide little useful information in larger data sets. However in smaller data sets, dot plots or stem plots might be more appropriate than histograms.

When plotting the test scores of an AP stats class, you can see on all three types of graphs that 18 students got A's (90–100%). But, in a histogram, you lose the ability to see how the scores are spread out. The scores could be clustered near 100%, or 90%, or evenly spread. This can be partially improved using error bars, but for small data sets, a stemplot will allow you to see exactly what your data values are.

A histogram can be drawn using frequencies, relative frequencies, or percentages.

This is how to make a histogram:

- Create groups from continuous data (this process is called "binning").
- Draw the x-axis and the y-axis and scale to accommodate all the data groups and frequencies (or relative frequencies or percentages).
- Draw bars of heights equal to the corresponding frequencies (or relative frequencies or percentages) and add a label for each group. Draw the bars next to each other without any gaps.
- There are no gaps between histogram bars because the data values are continuous: the values in one bar flow right into the next one.

Example 6: Create a histogram to describe the housing expenditure data in Table 2.

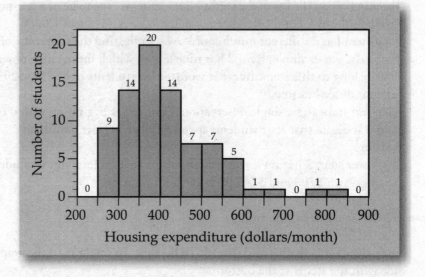

Figure 10: Frequency histogram of housing expenditure data

Notice that the shape of the distribution in both these graphs is exactly the same. The only thing that has changed is the scale of the y-axis.

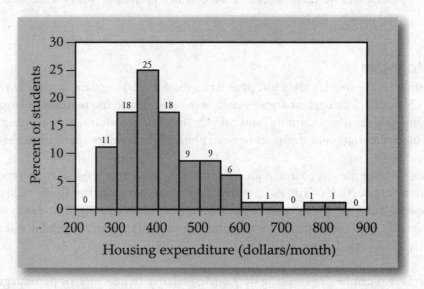

Figure 11: Percent histogram of housing expenditure data

Both these graphs show that the distribution of housing expenditure is right-skewed. In other words, more students spend lower amounts for housing, and fewer students pay higher amounts for housing. The expenditures ranged from about $250 per month to $850 per month. The expenditures seem to be centered around approximately $414 per month.

How do we read a histogram?

- Each bar represents a single group or class. There is only one bar for each class.
- The classes are placed on the x-axis in numerically increasing order, just as on a number line.
- The height of a bar in a frequency histogram corresponds to the frequency of that class. For example, the height of the first bar of Figure 10 is equal to 9. This indicates that nine students spend at least $250 but less than $300 per month on housing.
- Note that on both of the graphs on the previous page, there's one gap with no bar. This means that no student interviewed spends at least $700 but less than $750 on housing.
- The total of heights of the bars beyond 700 in Figure 10 is 0 + 1 + 1 = 2. This means that two students spend at least $700 per month on housing.
- The total of the heights of the second and third bars in Figure 10 is 14 + 20 = 34. This means that 34 students spend at least $300 but less than $400 per month on housing.
- **Percentage frequency** or **relative frequency** histograms can be read similarly. In a relative frequency histogram, the height of the bar reflects the relative frequency corresponding to the class. In a percent frequency histogram, the height of the bar reflects the percent frequency that corresponds to the class.

You can also use your calculator to draw a histogram. Here's how to do it on the TI-83 or TI-84:

TI-83 or TI-84:

Making a histogram using the entire data set:
- Choose **STAT → EDIT**
- Enter the housing expenditure data in L_1
- Choose **2nd → STAT PLOT → 1:PLOT1**
- Turn the plot1 ON by highlighting **ON** (selecting it) and pressing **ENTER**
- Out of six available choices, select "histogram" by highlighting the figure that looks like a histogram and then pressing **ENTER**
- Enter Xlist: **2nd L_1**
- Enter Freq: 1
    (a) To let calculator determine classes:
    - Choose **ZOOM → 9:ZOOMSTAT → TRACE**
    (b) To use classes of your choice:
    - Choose **WINDOW**
- Enter the required numbers in the window
    WINDOW
    Xmin = 250
    Xmax = 850
    Xscl = 50 (group width)
    Ymin = −1
    Ymax = 20 (highest frequency)
    Yscl = 1 (depends on frequency)
    Xres = 1
- Choose **GRAPH → TRACE**

Making a histogram from a frequency distribution table:
- Enter class midpoints into L1
- Enter frequencies into L2
- Choose **2nd → STAT PLOT → 1:PLOT1**
- Turn the plot1 ON by highlighting **ON** and pressing **ENTER**
- Out of six available choices, select "histogram" by highlighting it and pressing **ENTER**
- Enter Xlist: **2nd L_1**
- Enter Freq: **2nd L_2**
- Choose **WINDOW**
- Enter the required numbers in the window
    WINDOW
    Xmin = *enter minimum value*
    Xmax = *enter maximum value*
    Xscl = *enter group width*
    Ymin = −1
    Ymax = *enter highest frequency*
    Yscl = 0 (for no occurrences)
    Xres = 1
- Choose **GRAPH → TRACE**

Cumulative Frequency Charts

The cumulative frequency for any group is the frequency for that group plus the frequencies of all groups of smaller observations. Many cumulative frequency charts are S-shaped.

The cumulative frequency chart is also known as the **ogive chart**.

Here's how to draw cumulative frequency charts:

- Draw the x-axis and the y-axis.
- Scale the x-axis to accommodate the range of all groups. Mark the upper boundary of each group.
- Scale the y-axis from 0 to n for a cumulative frequency chart (from 0 to 1 for a relative cumulative frequency chart or from 0 to 100 for a percentage cumulative frequency chart).
- Place a dot at the height equal to the cumulative frequency for that group above the upper boundary for each group. Connect all the dots with straight lines. (You can also make cumulative frequency histograms which use bars instead of dots and lines).

Example 7: Create a cumulative frequency chart to describe the housing expenditure data in Table 2.

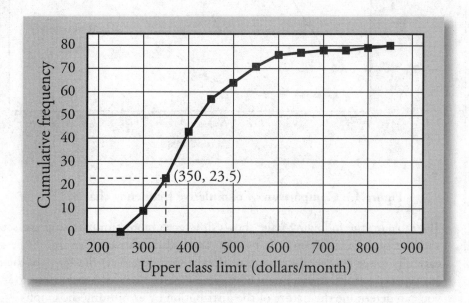

Figure 12: Cumulative frequency chart for the housing data

The line's steep climb in the beginning combined with its tapering off at the higher end of the graph indicates that the distribution is right-skewed (see Figure 13).

How do we read a cumulative frequency chart?

- From any point on the graph, we can draw a vertical line to read the *x*-value from the *x*-axis and a horizontal line to read the *y*-value from the *y*-axis. For example, take the third point from the bottom. Draw a vertical line to read *x*. It's about 350. Then draw a horizontal line to read *y*. It's about 23 or 24. This tells us that about 23 (or 24) students spend less than or equal to $350 per month on housing.

- Because a total of 80 students were interviewed, we can also say that about 80 − 23 = 57 (or 80 − 24 = 56) students spend at least $350 per month on housing.

- The steepness of the line is an indicator of the shape of the distribution. Refer to the following graph, which shows cumulative frequency lines for left-skewed, symmetric, and right-skewed distributions.

> Note that for right-skewed distributions, the curve increases quickly in the beginning but then steadies in the later part. For left-skewed distributions, the curve increases slowly in the beginning, but then steeply later on. The cumulative frequency chart for a symmetric distribution is often described as "S-shaped," because it begins with a slow increase on the left, rises rapidly in the middle, and then tapers off to a slow increase again at the right.

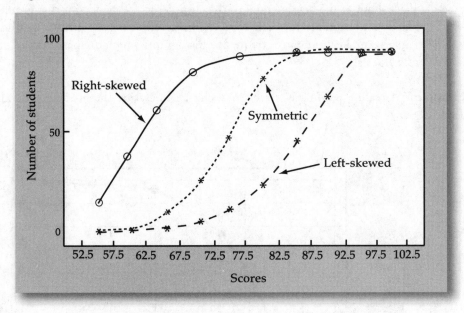

Figure 13: Comparison of cumulative frequency charts

The table on the following page shows different graphs summarizing the scores of students on an easy exam, a fair exam, and a difficult exam. Examine the graphs carefully to see how the symmetry or the skewedness affects the shape of the different types of graphs. If you know how symmetric or skewed distributions look, then you can determine the nature of the distribution by examining the graphs.

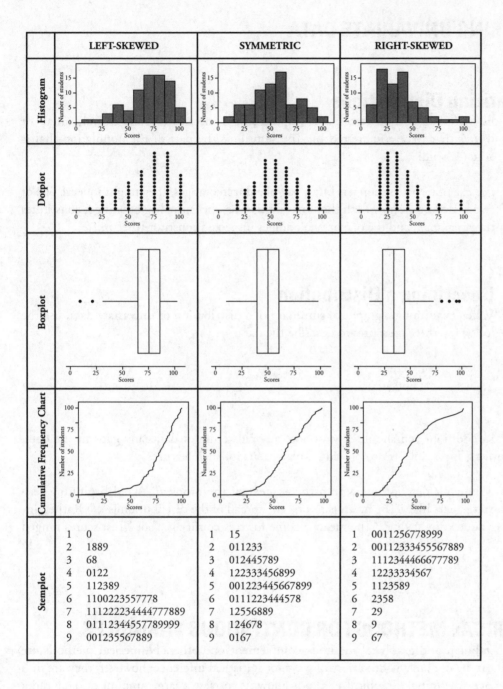

	LEFT-SKEWED	SYMMETRIC	RIGHT-SKEWED
Stemplot	1 0 2 1889 3 68 4 0122 5 112389 6 1100223557778 7 1112222344444777889 8 01112344557789999 9 001235567889	1 15 2 011233 3 012445789 4 122333456899 5 001223445667899 6 0111223444578 7 12556889 8 124678 9 0167	1 0011256778999 2 00112333455567889 3 1112344466677789 4 12233334567 5 1123589 6 2358 7 29 8 9 9 67

Note that boxplots, which are included in the table, are discussed later in this chapter, following the discussion of Graphical Summaries.

Table 4: Comparison of shapes of different graphs

Visualizations are the very first step you should take when analyzing data. The types of summary statistics, inferential tests, and analyses that can be calculated are dependent upon the shape of the distribution. While there is a lot to discuss about this topic, the key point to remember is that there are different calculations for symmetric and skewed data. Knowing the shapes of distributions will allow you to work through the test, especially the free-response section, much more efficiently.

EXPLORING UNIVARIATE DATA

Summarizing Distributions

First, two important terms: The **population** is the entire group of individuals or things that we are interested in. The **sample** is the part of the population that is actually studied.

For example, when shoppers buy a bag of a dozen oranges, they might squeeze one or two to determine how fresh they are. In this case, the entire bag of oranges constitutes the *population*, and the one or two oranges inspected constitute the *sample*.

> You can also think of the population as a Data Generating Function, or the process by which new data is created. If you look at the distribution of the height of all people, our population values technically change every time someone dies, is born, or grows. You can think of "population" values as the true values for mean, spread, etc. of the Data Generating Function that determines people's heights.

Describing a Distribution

When examining a graphical summary of a distribution of univariate data, use the following three measures to describe the data:

- Center
- Spread
- Shape

In addition, you should always note any clustering of data, any gaps in the data, and any outliers. If possible, try to provide explanations for such features.

Be sure to write your descriptions within the context of the problem. Avoid beginning sentences with statements like: "The mean is..." or "The spread of the distribution is...." Rather, include proper context by saying, "The mean income for this county is..." or "Test scores ranged from...."

NUMERICAL METHODS FOR CONTINUOUS VARIABLES

Numerical, tabular, and graphical methods complement one other. Numerical methods are precise and can be used in a wide variety of ways for statistical inference; however, they are dull and can be overwhelming. Graphical methods allow us to view a large amount of data and a large number of relationships at once, but they are not precise and are often abused. Tabular methods allow us to find precise values but are not as good for grasping relationships among variables.

There are three types of numerical measures:

- Measures of central tendency
- Measures of variation (spread)
- Measures of position

Each type is discussed in detail in the following sections, but first, let's review the notation we'll be using.

Review of Summation Notation

A Greek capital letter Σ (read as "sigma") is used to indicate the sum of a set of measurements. For example, if we denote the first through the fifth measurements of something by X_1, X_2, X_3, X_4, X_5, then

$$\sum_{i=1}^{5} X_i = X_1 + X_2 + X_3 + X_4 + X_5 = \text{the sum of first five measurements}$$

Example 8: The following list shows one student's scores on 10 quizzes:

$$8, 9, 0, 10, 10, 8, 7, 9, 10, 5$$

What is this student's total score on the quizzes?

Solution: Let X_i = the score on the ith quiz. So $X_1 = 8$, $X_2 = 9$, … $X_{10} = 5$. Then, the total score is

$$\sum_{i=1}^{10} X_i = X_1 + X_2 + \cdots + X_{10} = 8 + 9 + 0 + 10 + 10 + 8 + 7 + 9 + 10 + 5 = 76$$

Measures of Central Tendency

Measures of central tendency determine the central point of a data set or the point around which all the measurements are scattered. The two main measures of central tendency are the mean and the median.

Mean: The arithmetic mean (often called the **average**) is the most commonly used measure of the center of a set of data. The mean can be described as a data set's center of gravity, the point at which the whole group of data balances. Unlike the median, the mean is affected by extreme or outlier measurements. One very large or very small measurement can pull the mean up or down. We say that the mean is not resistant; it is not resistant to changes caused by outliers.

> Think of a seesaw—the mean is the point on the seesaw that would make it balanced. Far outliers will effect this balancing point a lot more than values that are near the balancing point.

- The **population mean** is denoted by Greek letter μ (spelled out as "mu" but pronounced "myoo"). It is computed as $\mu = \dfrac{\sum_{i=1}^{N} X_i}{N}$. That is, simply add up all of the values in the entire population and divide by the number of values.

- The **sample mean** is generally denoted by an English letter with a bar on top, such as $\overline{X}$ (read as "Xbar") or $\overline{Y}$ (read as "Ybar"). It is computed in the same way: $\overline{X} = \dfrac{\sum\limits_{i=1}^{n} X_i}{n}$, where n = the number of measurements in the sample.

Median: The median is another commonly used measure of central tendency. The median is the point that divides the measurements in half. That is, half of the values are at or below the median, and half are at or above the median. The median is *not* affected by outliers. Therefore, for skewed data sets or data sets containing outliers, it's better to use the median rather than the mean to measure the center of the data. The median is resistant; it resists changes caused by outliers.

Let's denote the median by M. Use the following steps to determine the median:

- Suppose there are n measurements in a data set.

- Arrange the measurements in increasing order (i.e., from smallest to largest).

- Compute $l = \dfrac{n+1}{2}$

- Then the median M = the value of the lth measurement.

Symmetric data? Use the mean. Skewed data? Use the median.

Note that if the data set contains an odd number of measurements, then the median belongs to the data set. But if the data set contains an even number of measurements, then the median may not belong to the data set. It is instead the mean of the middle two measurements. For example, if a data set contains five measurements, then the median is the third smallest (or third largest) measurement. But if the data set contains six measurements, then the median is the mean of the third smallest and the fourth smallest measurements (see Example 11 on page 129).

A real estate agent collects a large sample of data on the price of homes in her city and creates a histogram. It looks like this:

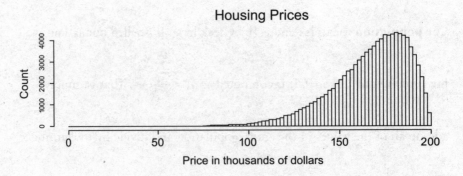

Which of the following statements about the central tendency of this data best fits with the histogram shown above (> means greater than)?

(A) mean > median > mode
(B) median > mean > mode
(C) mean > mode > median
(D) mode > mean > median
(E) mode > median > mean

Here's How to Crack It

The data in the histogram is left skewed, which means that the mean will be smaller than the median, since the mean is more affected by extreme values than the median. This eliminates (A), (C), and (D) since all three list the mean as being larger than the median.

We can visually examine the histogram to see that the mode is very far to the right and is much larger than the median (and therefore also the mean) leaving (E) as the correct answer.

Measures of Variation

Measures of variation (or "measures of spread") summarize the spread of a data set. They describe how measurements differ from each other and/or from their mean. The three most commonly used measures of variation are range, interquartile range, and standard deviation.

Range: The range is the difference between the largest and the smallest measurement in a data set.

$$R = \text{range} = \text{largest measurement} - \text{smallest measurement}$$

Range is the simplest of the measures of spread. It is very easy to compute and understand, but it is not a reliable measure because it depends only on the two extreme measurements and does not take into account the values of the remaining measurements.

Interquartile range: The interquartile range (IQR) is the range of the middle 50% of the data, the difference between the third quartile (Q_3) and the first quartile (Q_1).

$$IQR = Q_3 - Q_1$$

> Quartiles are defined in the next section under Measures of Position.

Interquartile range is not affected by outliers. If you choose to measure the center using the median, you should use the IQR to measure the spread.

Standard deviation: Standard deviation is often a more useful measure of variation than range is. Unlike range, standard deviation takes every measurement into account. However, like the range, the standard deviation is affected by outliers. When there are outliers, the IQR may be a more useful measurement. The square of the standard deviation is known as **variance**.

- A lowercase Greek letter σ (read as "sigma") is used to denote a population standard deviation. So σ^2 denotes a population variance. The population standard deviation is defined as

$$\sigma = \sqrt{\frac{\sum_{i=1}^{N}(x_i - \mu)^2}{N}}$$

That is, we square the difference between each point and the mean, add those squares, divide by the number of points, and take the square root.

- The letter *s* is used to denote a sample standard deviation. So s^2 denotes a sample variance. The sample standard deviation is defined as

$$s = \sqrt{\frac{\sum_{i=1}^{n}(x_i - \overline{x})^2}{n-1}}$$

- Note that standard deviation is measured in the same units as are data values, whereas variance is measured in squared units of the data values. For example, suppose the standard deviation of a set of housing expenditure data is 110 and the variance is 12,100. The associated units of measurement would be the following: standard deviation $s = 110$ dollars and variance $s^2 = 110^2 = 12,100$ squared dollars (or dollars^2).

- Standard deviation can be used as a unit for measuring the distance between any measurement and the mean of the data set. For example, a measurement can be described as being so many standard deviations above or below the mean. (See the discussion of *z*-scores, below.)

- A standard deviation (or variance) of 0 indicates that all of the measurements are identical. For example, if a student scores 8, 8, 8, and 8 on four quizzes, then the standard deviation of the scores is 0.

- Standard deviation is the positive square root of variance. Because variance is a squared quantity, it is *always* a positive number. So if your computation gives you a negative value for variance, go back and check your work.

- A larger standard deviation (and consequently, variance) indicates a larger spread among the measurements. The larger the standard deviation, the wider the graph. For example, two students score the following on their quizzes:

Student A: 8, 9, 4, 8, 6, 8, 7, 9, 10, 5 $s_A = 1.897$

Student B: 7, 8, 6, 7, 6, 6, 7, 5, 5, 7 $s_B = 0.917$

The dotplots and boxplots (we'll discuss boxplots in more detail later in this chapter) of scores for the two students are shown in Figures 14 and 15. Compare the spread of the scores from the plots. Both graphs show that the scores for student A are more spread out (they vary more) than the scores for student B. So it makes sense that the scores for student A have a larger standard deviation than those for student B.

Did You Know?
We divide by $n-1$ to make the standard deviation an *unbiased* estimator of the population standard deviation. When we use just *n*, the sample standard deviations are systematically larger than the population standard deviation.

Due to repeated values within a set of data, it is possible for different percentiles to have the same numeric value. For example, in the data set {1, 2, 2, 2, 2, 2, 2, 3, 4, 5, 7, 8}, the values of Q_1 (25th percentile) and the median (50th percentile) are both 2.

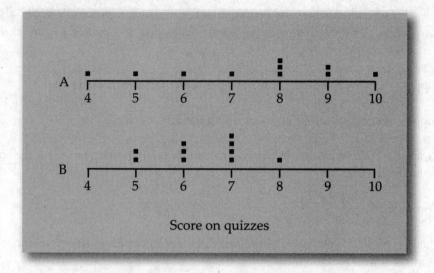

Figure 14: Dotplot of students' scores on quizzes

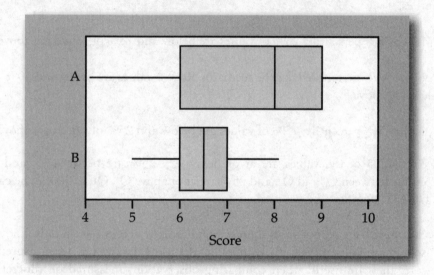

Having trouble remembering which measure of variation goes with which central tendency? Just look at the formulas! To calculate IQR, you must have the median, so those two are paired. To calculate the standard deviation you must have the mean, so those two are also paired.

Figure 15: Boxplot of students' scores on quizzes

Measures of Position

These measures are used to describe the position of a value with respect to the rest of the values of the data set. Quartiles, percentiles, and standardized scores (z-scores) are the most commonly used measures of position. To compute quartiles and percentiles, but not to compute z-scores, the data must be sorted by value.

Percentiles: Percentiles divide a set of values into 100 equal parts.

P_k = the kth percentile, which is the number such that $k\%$ of the values fall at or below it and $(100 - k)\%$ of the values fall at or above it. For example, P_{95} is the 95th percentile, which means that 95% of the values are at or below P_{95} and 5% of the values are at or above P_{95}. Note that $P_{25} = Q_1$, $P_{50} = Q_2 = M$, and $P_{75} = Q_3$.

Statistical note: Depending upon the computer software used, a percentile could also be defined as the percent of values "below" a particular data value, as opposed to the "at or below" definition that is presented above.

- Suppose there are n measurements of a particular variable in a data set.

- Suppose we are interested in determining the kth percentile.

- Arrange all measurements of that variable in increasing order, i.e., from the smallest to the largest.

- Compute $l = \dfrac{(n+1)k}{100}$

- The percentile P_k = the value of the measurement in the lth position when counted from the lowest measurement.

Quartiles: Quartiles divide a set of values into four equal parts by using the 25th, 50th, and 75th percentiles.

- Q_1 is the 25th percentile; 25% of values are below and 75% of values are above.

- Q_2 is the 50th percentile (aka the median); 50% of values are below and 50% of values are above.

- Q_3 is the 75th percentile; 75% of values are below and 25% of values are above.

In other words, 25% of the values are at or below Q_1, 25% are between Q_1 and Q_2 (the median), 25% are between Q_2 and Q_3, and 25% are at or above Q_3. Quartiles can be calculated using STAT/CALC/Var Stats on your calculator.

We need standard deviation because it gives context to the means we observe. If a scientists reported a 1-lb difference in the mean weight of a sample of people with brown eyes vs. green eyes, that would be more surprising if it was in newborn infants than grown adults. This is because the weight of newborn infants has a smaller standard deviation than that of adults.

Standardized scores or **z-scores:** Standardized scores, commonly known as z-scores, are independent of the units in which the data values are measured. Therefore, they are useful when comparing observations measured on different scales. They are computed as:

$$z\text{-score} = \frac{\text{measurement} - \text{mean}}{\text{standard deviation}}$$

A z-score gives the distance between the measurement and the mean in terms of the number of standard deviations. A negative z-score indicates that the measurement is *smaller* than the mean. A positive z-score indicates that the measurement is *larger* than the mean.

Example 9: Suppose a teacher gave her students a test. The class average was 74, and the standard deviation was 6. Suppose student A got an 88 and student B got a 70. Let's calculate the z-scores:

$$\text{Student A:} \quad z\text{-score} = \frac{\text{measurement} - \text{mean}}{\text{standard deviation}} = \frac{88 - 74}{6} = 2.33$$

Student A scored 2.33 standard deviations above the class average.

$$\text{Student B: } z\text{-score} = \frac{\text{measurement} - \text{mean}}{\text{standard deviation}} = \frac{70 - 74}{6} = -0.67$$

Student B scored 0.67 standard deviations below the class average.

Note that student B scored closer to the class average than student A.

Example 10: The mean and the standard deviation of the daily high temperatures in degrees Fahrenheit for two cities are given below:

City	Mean	Standard deviation
North Bend	80	12
South Bend	84	4

Yesterday, both cities reported a high temperature of 95 degrees. Which city had the more unusually high temperature?

Solution: Because the mean daily high temperature at North Bend is 80 degrees—which is lower than the mean daily high temperature at South Bend (84 degrees)—we are tempted to say that 95 degrees is more unusually high at North Bend. But that would be incorrect, because it does not take into account the spread of the temperatures at these two cities.

Compute z-scores for both cities:

$$\text{North Bend: } z\text{-score} = \frac{\text{measurement} - \text{mean}}{\text{standard deviation}} = \frac{95 - 80}{12} = 1.25$$

$$\text{South Bend: } z\text{-score} = \frac{\text{measurement} - \text{mean}}{\text{standard deviation}} = \frac{95 - 84}{4} = 2.75$$

Ninety-five degrees Fahrenheit is 1.25 standard deviations above the average in North Bend, whereas it is 2.75 standard deviations above the average in South Bend. This means that 95 degrees Fahrenheit was more unusually high in South Bend.

Example 11: A small used car dealer wanted to get an idea of how many cars her dealership sells per day. Listed below is the number of cars sold per day over a two-week period:

14	9	23	7	11	23	17
11	3	24	21	2	20	20

Compute:

(a) the mean number of cars sold per day

(b) the range of cars sold per day

(c) the standard deviation of the number of cars sold per day

(d) the median number of cars sold per day

(e) the first and third quartiles of the number of cars sold per day

(f) the interquartile range of the number of cars sold per day

(g) the 90th percentile of the number of cars sold per day

Solution:

(a) Let X_i = the number of cars sold on the ith day. $\sum_{i=1}^{14} X_i = 14 + 9 + \cdots$

+ 20 = 205, and the number of observations = n = 14. The sample mean is

$$\overline{X} = \frac{\Sigma X}{n} \approx \frac{205}{14} = 14.64 \text{ cars.}$$

On the average, she sells 14.64 cars per day. See the calculator instructions on page 131.

(b) The smallest number is 2, and the largest number is 24. On the best day, her dealership sold 24 cars, and on the worst day it sold only two cars. *Range* = largest measurement − smallest measurement = 24 − 2 = 22.

Therefore, the range of the number of cars sold is 22.

(c) To compute the standard deviation, use your calculator. The sample's standard deviation is s_x = 7.5611 cars. Note: the TI-83 and TI-84 denote standard deviation with the symbol σx.

(d) To find the median, first arrange the data in increasing order:

2, 3, 7, 9, 11, 11, 14, 17, 20, 20, 21, 23, 23, 24

Compute:

$$l = \frac{n+1}{2} = \frac{14+1}{2} = 7.5$$

So the median is the value of the 7.5th observation, i.e., the average of the seventh and the eighth observations. When counted from the smallest observation, the seventh observation = 14, the eighth observation = 17, and M = median = (14 + 17)/2 = 15.5. In other words, there is an even number of values in the list, so we need to take the average of the middle two values.

On half of the days, fewer than 15.5 cars were sold, and on the other half of the days, more than 15.5 cars were sold. Because you can't sell a fraction of a car, another way to say this is that, on half of the days, 15 or fewer cars were sold, and, on the other half, 16 or more were sold.

(e) The first quartile (Q_1) is the median of the lower half of the observations. The median number of cars sold on the seven days that 15 or fewer cars were sold is 9, so $Q_1 = 9$.

The third quartile (Q_3) is the median of the upper half of the observations. The median number of cars sold on the seven days that 16 or more cars were sold is 21, so $Q_3 = 21$.

(f) Interquartile range = $IQR = Q_3 - Q_1 = 21 - 9 = 12$.

(g) To find the 90th percentile (P_{90}), compute:

$$l = \frac{(n+1)k}{100} = \frac{(14+1)90}{100} = 13.5$$

So the 90th percentile is the value of the 13.5th observation, and when counted from the smallest observation, the 13th observation = 23 and the 14th observation = 24.

Interpolating between the 13th and 14th observation for the 13.5th observation, we get:

$$P_{90} = \text{90th percentile} = 23.5$$

Therefore, on 90% of the days, 23.5 (equivalently, 23) or fewer cars were sold per day, and on the remaining 10% of the days, 24 or more cars were sold per day.

TI-83 or TI-84:
- Enter data in L1
- Choose **STAT** → **CALC** → **1:1-Var Stats**
- Press **ENTER**
- Choose **2nd** → 1 (to get L1) This will result in 1-Var Stats L1
- Press **ENTER**

Note: This option gives output that contains the following:
$\overline{X}$, ΣX, ΣX^2, sx, σx, n, $Minx$, Q_1, Med, Q_3, $Maxx$
Scroll down using the down arrow to read the entire output.

GRAPHING UNIVARIATE DATA

Graphical Summaries

Graphical summary measures are a good way of conveying information, but they are also subject to misinterpretation and can be distorted very easily. Two researchers can take the same data and convey completely different messages just by manipulating the layout of a graph. So, you have to be careful when reading graphs.

The following two graphs display revenue for a business in the last calendar year.

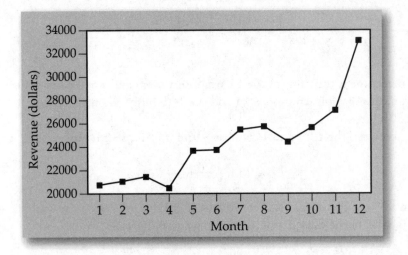

Figure 16: Revenue generated over one calendar year

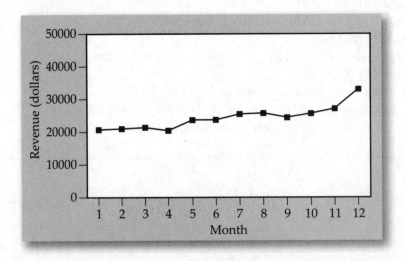

Figure 17: Revenue generated over one calendar year

- The first graph gives the impression that the revenue increased dramatically over the last calendar year.
- The second graph gives the impression that the revenue increased steadily but only slightly.

A closer inspection of the scale on the *y*-axis tells a different story. Both the graphs are displaying *exactly the same revenue data*. The only difference is that one has a more extended scale than the other. But the impressions they leave with the viewer are totally distinct.

Boxplots

A boxplot, also known as a box-and-whiskers plot, is a graphical data summary based on measures of position. It is useful for identifying outliers and the general shape of the distribution.

Here's how to make one:

- Draw a vertical number line (or alternatively a horizontal number line).
- Scale the number line to cover the range of observations.
- Draw a rectangular box to the left of (or above) the line from the first quartile to the third quartile (Q_1 to Q_3).
- Draw a line at the median, dividing the box into two compartments.
- Compute "whisker" length = $1.5IQR$.
- Compute $L = Q_1 - 1.5IQR$.
- Compute $U = Q_3 + 1.5IQR$.
- Make a lower whisker by drawing a line from the lower (left) wall of the box at Q_1 to the farthest observation greater than or equal to L.
- Make an upper whisker by drawing a line from the upper (right) wall of the box at Q_3 to the farthest observation less than or equal to U.
- Plot any points with values smaller than L or larger than U in their respective places above the number line beyond the whiskers.

How do we read a boxplot?

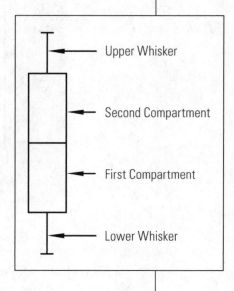

- Any points below the lower (left) whisker are identified as outliers on the lower end.
- Any points above the higher (right) whisker are identified as outliers on the higher end.
- The length of the box indicates the IQR, i.e., the range of the middle 50% of data, when the data is arranged in increasing order of value.
- The length of the lower whisker (with any outliers) shows the spread of the smallest 25% of data, when the data is arranged in increasing order of value.
- The length of the first compartment of the box shows the spread of the next smallest 25% of data.

- The length of the second compartment of the box shows the spread of the third smallest 25% of data.
- The length of the upper whisker (with any outliers) shows the spread of the largest 25% of data.
- Compare the lengths of the four parts to compare the respective spread of the data. Use the information about spread to determine the shape of the distribution.

Example 12: Make a boxplot for the car sales data given in the previous example.

Solution: As shown earlier, for the car sales data,

$$Q_1 = 9, M = 15.5, \text{ and } Q_3 = 21$$

$$IQR = Q_3 - Q_1 = 21 - 9 = 12$$

Compute $L = Q_1 - 1.5IQR = 9 - 1.5(12) = -9$

Compute $U = Q_3 + 1.5IQR = 21 + 1.5(12) = 39$

- Draw a box from 9 to 21.
- Draw a divider in the box at 15.5.
- Draw a whisker from 9 to 2 (lowest observation within the range of L).
- Draw a whisker from 21 to 24 (highest observation within the range of U).
- There are no observations beyond L and U.

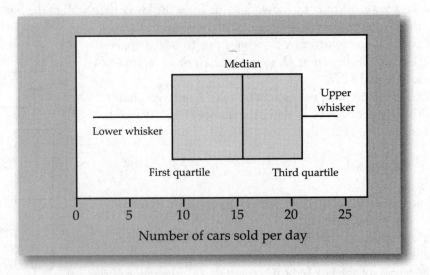

Figure 18: Boxplot of the number of cars sold per day

The longer lower whisker and the longer lower box indicate that the distribution of the number of cars sold per day has a slightly longer left tail, i.e., the distribution is slightly left-skewed. There are no outliers.

Example 13: Make a boxplot of the housing expenditure data given in the first example of this chapter (Table 1, page 104).

Solution: Compute summary measures as follows:

$$M = \$392 \text{ per month}$$

$$Q_1 = \$333.5 \text{ per month and } Q_3 = \$464 \text{ per month}$$

$$IQR = 464 - 333.5 = 130.5$$

$$L = Q_1 - 1.5IQR = 333.5 - 1.5(130.5) = 137.75$$

$$U = Q_3 + 1.5IQR = 464 + 1.5(130.5) = 659.75$$

Note that the lowest housing expenditure ($255) is higher than L, so there are no outliers on the lower side. Also note that the highest housing expenditure ($834) is larger than U. So there is at least one outlier on the higher side. The boxplot below identifies three outliers on the higher side. This means that there are three students with exceptionally high housing expenditures compared to the rest of the students. The distribution is right-skewed partly because of these outliers, though the longer right whisker indicates that the distribution would be right-skewed even without the outliers or if outliers fell within the range (Q_3, U).

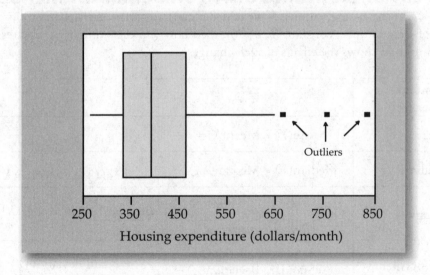

Figure 19: Boxplot of housing expenditure data

TI-83 or TI-84:

To make a boxplot

- Enter the data values into L_1
- Choose **2nd → Y** = to access STAT PLOT
- Select **1:Plot1**
- Turn on the plot by highlighting **On**
- Choose boxplot by highlighting the picture of a boxplot under Type
- Enter Xlist: L_1 (This is the default and may already be set)
- Enter Freq: 1 (This is the default.)
- Select type of marking for outliers
- Choose **ZOOM → 9:ZoomStat**
- Use the TRACE option to see the min, max, Q1, Q3, and median values

Note: The TI-83 and TI-84 do not calculate the whisker length like you should on this test.

THE EFFECT OF CHANGING UNITS ON SUMMARY MEASURES

Let X_1, X_2, ... , X_n be n observations. If we added a constant (a) to each observation or multiplied each observation by a constant (b, $b \neq 0$), then how will the summary measures change? The following chart shows the effects of such changes:

Summary Measure	$Y_i = X_i + a$	$Y_i = bX_i$
Mean	Mean(Y) = Mean(X) + a	Mean (Y) = b Mean(X)
Median	Median(Y) = Median(X) + a	Median(Y) = b Median(X)
Range	Range (Y) = Range(X) *Range is unaffected.*	Range(Y) = $\lvert b \rvert$ Range(X)
Standard Deviation	Standard deviation(Y) = Standard deviation(X) *Standard deviation is unaffected.*	Standard deviation(Y) = $\lvert b \rvert$ Standard deviation(X)
Quartiles	Quartiles(Y) = Quartiles(X) + a	Quartiles(Y) = b Quartiles(X)
Interquartile Range	IQR(Y) = IQR(X) *IQR is unaffected.*	IQR(Y) = $\lvert b \rvert$ IQR(X)

Note that all measures of spread are unaffected by adding a constant a to each observation.

Example 14: A college professor gave a test to his students. The test had five questions, each worth 20 points. The summary statistics for the students' scores on the test are as follows:

Summary Statistics for Scores	
Mean	62
Median	60
Range	45
Standard deviation	8
First quartile	48
Third quartile	71
Interquartile range	23

After grading the test, the professor realized that, because he had made a typographical error in question number 2, no student was able to answer the question. So he decided to adjust the students' scores by adding 20 points to each one. What will be the summary statistics for the new, adjusted scores?

Solution: Note that each student's score will increase by 20 points:

Summary Statistics for Adjusted Scores	
Mean	62 + 20 = 82
Median	60 + 20 = 80
Range	45 (unaffected)
Standard deviation	8 (unaffected)
First quartile	48 + 20 = 68
Third quartile	71 + 20 = 91
Interquartile range	23 (unaffected)

Example 15: The summary statistics for the property tax per property collected by one county are as follows:

Summary Statistics for Property Tax	
Mean	12,000
Median	8,000
Range	30,000
Standard deviation	5,000
First quartile	5,000
Third quartile	14,000
Interquartile range	9,000

This year, county residents voted to increase property taxes by 2% to support the local school system. What will be the summary statistics for the new, increased property taxes?

Solution: Note that each property owner will pay 2% more in taxes. So the new taxes will be:

$$\text{new tax} = 1.02(\text{old tax})$$

Summary Statistics for Increased Property Tax	
Mean	1.02(12,000) = 12,240
Median	1.02(8,000) = 8,160
Range	1.02(30,000) = 30,600
Standard deviation	1.02(5,000) = 5,100
First quartile	1.02(5,000) = 5,100
Third quartile	1.02(14,000) = 14,280
Interquartile range	1.02(9,000) = 9,180

COMPARING DISTRIBUTIONS OF TWO OR MORE GROUPS

When comparing distributions of two or more groups, use the following criteria:

- Compare the centers of the distributions.
- Compare the spreads of the distributions. Consider the differences in the spread of data within each group as well as the differences between groups.
- Compare clusters of measurements and gaps in measurements.
- Compare outliers and any other unusual features.
- Compare the shapes of the distributions.
- Compare in the context of the question.

Example 16: A department store wants to compare the optical scanners it's currently using with some new scanners. Both models occasionally have trouble reading the bar codes on labels. The store manager decides to compare the number of reading errors made by the old scanners to the number of reading errors made by the new scanners. She selects a group of 50 items and runs them through each of the scanners 20 times and then records the number of errors made. The data is shown in the following table.

Scanner	Number of Reading Errors per Group of 50 Items
New	2, 3, 3, 1, 2, 1, 2, 3, 1, 2, 2, 2, 4, 0, 1, 3, 2, 0, 2, 2
Old	6, 3, 4, 4, 6, 3, 5, 3, 1, 5, 3, 2, 5, 5, 4, 8, 4, 7, 3, 3

Display these data graphically so that the number of reading errors by the old and new scanners can be easily compared. Based on the examination of your graphical display, write a few sentences comparing the number of errors by the old and new scanners.

Solution: At least five graphs could be used here. The best is probably the boxplot because it

> **Have No Fear, Be Clear**
> To achieve the highest possible AP score for a question, avoid merely listing measures of center, spread, and shape for each distribution. You must make a clear, comparative statement. For instance, it is not sufficient to say that Group A had a mean of 82 and a standard deviation of 7, whereas Group B had a mean of 85 and a standard deviation of 5. Instead, point out that "On average Group B had higher test scores, but the distribution of test scores for Group A showed more variability."

shows the locations of the medians and quartiles most clearly.

1. **Parallel dotplots,** showing the errors made by both scanners. Parallel dotplots can be used to compare two or more data sets. Using the same scale, draw a dotplot for each data set. Label each line appropriately (see Figure 20).

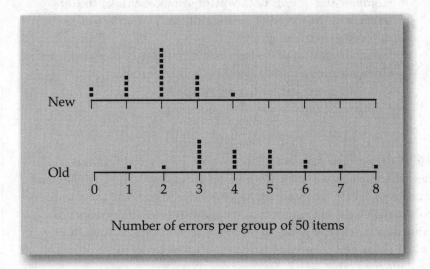

Figure 20: Parallel dotplots showing the number of errors by old and new scanners

2. **Parallel boxplots,** showing the errors made by both scanners. Parallel boxplots can also be used to compare two or more data sets. Using the same scale, draw a boxplot for each data set. Label each boxplot appropriately (see Figure 21).

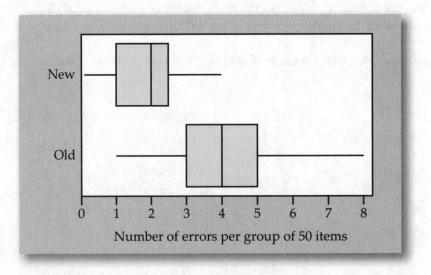

Figure 21: Parallel boxplots showing the number of errors by old and new scanners

3. **Back-to-back stemplots,** showing the errors made by both scanners, using the

same stems. Back-to-back stemplots can *only* be used to compare two data sets. Put the common stems in the middle. On one side of the stems, make a stemplot for one data set. On the other side of the stems, make a stemplot for the other data set (see Figure 22).

Old Scanner		New Scanner
Leaves	Stems	Leaves
	0	00
0	1	0000
0	2	000000000
000000	3	0000
0000	4	0
0000	5	
00	6	
0	7	
0	8	

Figure 22: Back-to-back stemplots

4. **Two histograms,** showing the errors made by both scanners. Although not incorrect, this is not a great option. Be sure to use the same scale for both histograms; otherwise the comparison will not be valid. The problem with using two histograms is that we cannot lay one histogram over the other, because the bars of one graph may be partially or totally hidden behind the bars of the other. Therefore, we have to display the histograms vertically stacked (see Figure 23).

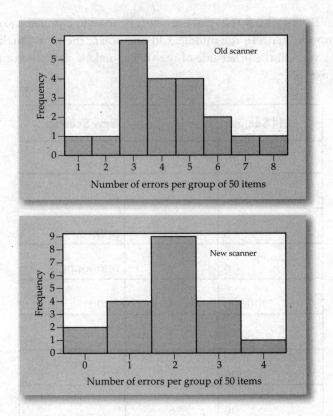

Figure 23: Stacked histograms showing the number of errors made by the old scanner and the new scanner

5. **Multiple frequency polygrams**. A **frequency polygram** is a graph showing the frequency of different values of a random variable. It is also known as a **line graph**. Basically, it can be drawn by connecting the midpoints of the tops of each bar of a histogram. Multiple frequency polygrams can be used to compare two or more data sets. Using the same scale, draw a line graph for each data set. Use different symbols and different types of lines to indicate different groups. Include the appropriate legend for correct identification (see Figure 24).

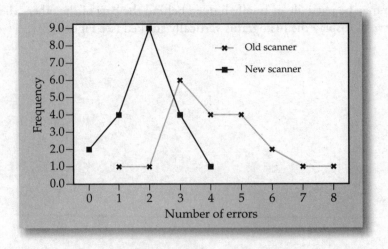

Figure 24: Line graph showing the number of errors by the old and new scanners

Examining any of these plots gives us the following information about the data:

- The distribution of the number of reading errors made by the old scanner is right-skewed, indicating that sometimes the old scanner makes a large number of errors. The distribution of the number of errors made by the new scanner is almost symmetric.

- The median number of errors made by the old scanner is four, whereas the median of those made by the new scanner is two. So with the new scanner, 50% of the time at most two errors were made; whereas with the old scanner, 50% of the time more than four errors were made.

- The number of errors made by the old scanner ranged from one to eight, whereas the number of errors made by the new scanner ranged only from zero to four. The old scanner made at least one error in each run, whereas at times the new scanner read flawlessly. The old scanner shows a larger variation in the number of errors than the new scanner shows.

Examination of the parallel boxplots gives us the following additional information about the data:

- Although the *IQR* for both scanners is close, the longer whiskers on the boxplot for the old scanner, compared to the whiskers on the boxplot for the new scanner, indicate a larger variation in the number of errors made by the old scanner as compared to the variation in errors made by the new one.

- Although the distribution of errors made by the old scanner is right-skewed, there were no outliers detected in either boxplot.

EXPLORING BIVARIATE DATA

Bivariate data is data on two different variables collected from each item in a study.

We often want to investigate the relationship between two quantitative variables. If two different quantitative variables have a linear relation, then we can measure the strength of that relationship with **linear regression**, a popular and relatively simple method discussed below. For example, we might want to know the relation between:

- high school students' scores on the midterm and their scores on the final exam
- college students' SAT or ACT scores and their GPAs when they graduate
- the price of crude oil and the price of gasoline each month
- the daily temperature and the atmospheric pressure at a given location
- advertising expenditure and either the number of items sold or amount of sales generated
- the weight of a car and its fuel efficiency

On the AP Exam, there are two commonly used measures to summarize the relation between two variables. A **scatterplot** is a *graphical* summary measure. The **correlation coefficient** is a *numerical* summary measure.

GRAPHING CATEGORICAL BIVARIATE DATA

Scatterplot

A **scatterplot** is used to describe the nature, degree, and direction of the relation between two variables x and y, where (x, y) gives a pair of measurements. Here's how to make one:

- Draw an x-axis and a y-axis.
- Scale the x- and y-axes to accommodate the ranges of data for the first and second variable.
- For each pair of measurements, mark the point on the graph where the (unmarked) lines of the x- and y-values cross.

Here's what a scatterplot can tell us about the two variables:

- **Shape:** A scatterplot tells us whether the nature of the relation between the two variables is linear or nonlinear. A linear relation is one that can be described well using a straight line (compare Figures 26 and 27 or 28).

- **Direction:** The scatterplot will show whether the y-value increases or decreases as the x increases, or that it changes direction. Specifically:
  o If a scatterplot shows an increasing or upward trend, then it indicates a **positive (or direct) relation** between the two variables. For example, the relation between the heights of fathers and the heights of their sons is a positive relation: taller fathers tend to have taller sons (see Figures 29 and 30).
  o If a scatterplot shows a decreasing or downward trend, then it indicates a **negative (or inverse) relation** between the two variables. For example, the relation between the weight of a car and its gas mileage is a negative relation: heavier cars tend to get lower gas mileage (see Figures 31 and 32).

- **Strength of relationship:** If the trend of the data can be described with a line or a curve, then the spread of the data values around the line or curve describes the degree (or strength) of the relation between the two:

  o If the data points are close to the line, then it indicates a **strong relationship** between the two variables (see Figures 29 and 31).
  o If a scatterplot has points that are more loosely scattered, then it indicates a **weaker relationship** between the two variables (see Figures 30 and 32).
  o If a scatterplot shows points scattered without any apparent pattern, then it indicates **no relationship** between the two variables (see Figure 25). The following scatterplots show various degrees of relation between the two variables.

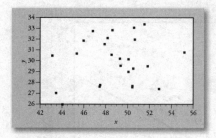

Figure 25: No relation between x and y

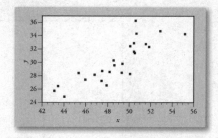

Figure 26: Linear relation between x and y

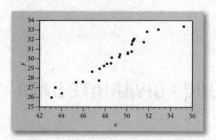

Figure 27: Nonlinear relation between x and y

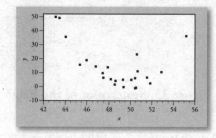

Figure 28: Nonlinear relation between x and y

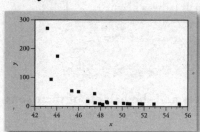

Figure 29: Strong positive linear relation between x and y

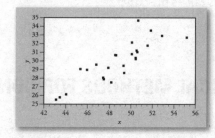

Figure 30: Weaker positive linear relation between x and y

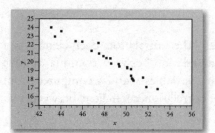

Figure 31: Strong negative linear relation between x and y

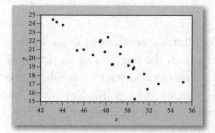

Figure 32: Weaker negative linear relation between x and y

Example 17: At the graduation ceremony of a large university, a random sample of 50 father–son pairs was selected, and the heights (in inches) of the fathers and sons were measured. Figure 33 is a scatterplot of the data collected.

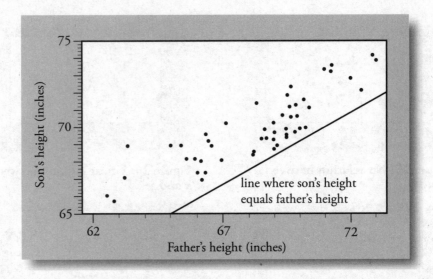

Figure 33: Scatterplot of the heights of fathers and the heights of their sons

Notice from the plot that there is a positive relationship between the father's height and the son's height. The relation is fairly strong and linear. In general, taller fathers have taller sons; also, sons are taller than fathers. In this sample, every son is at least as tall as his father.

NUMERICAL METHODS FOR CONTINUOUS BIVARIATE DATA

Correlation Coefficient

Correlation coefficients are *numerical* measures used to judge the relation between two variables.

Pearson's correlation coefficient (also known simply as "the correlation coefficient") is a numeric measure of the degree and direction of the **linear** relation between two quantitative variables. The Pearson's correlation coefficient between two variables x and y computed from a population is denoted by ρ (read as "rho"), whereas the correlation coefficient between two variables computed from a sample is denoted by r.

$$-1 \leq r \leq +1$$

Here's what the correlation coefficient tells us:

- **Direction:** The positive or negative sign of the correlation coefficient describes the direction of the linear relation between the two variables.
  - A **positive** value of the correlation coefficient indicates a **positive** relation between x and y. This means that as x increases, y also increases linearly. For example, the relation between the heights of fathers and the heights of their sons is a positive relation. Taller fathers tend to have taller sons. A scatterplot of such data will show an increasing or upward linear trend.
  - A **negative** value of the correlation coefficient indicates a **negative** relation between x and y. This means that as x increases, y decreases linearly. For example, the relation between the weight of a car and its gas mileage is a negative relation. Heavier cars tend to get lower gas mileage. A scatterplot of such data will show a decreasing or downward linear trend.
- **Strength:** The numeric value of the correlation coefficient describes the strength (or degree) of the linear relation between the two variables:
  - If the value of the correlation coefficient is equal to +1 or −1, then it indicates a **perfect correlation** between two variables. In this case, all the points in a scatterplot would fall perfectly on the line (the slope of the line is determined by direction).
  - The farther away the correlation coefficient gets from 0 (in the positive or negative direction), the stronger the relationship between the two variables, and the closer the correlation coefficient is to 0, the weaker the relationship between the two variables. For example, if the correlation coefficient between x and y is −0.86, whereas the correlation coefficient between x and z is 0.75, then x and y have a stronger relation than x and z. Note again that, unlike scatterplots, correlation coefficients do not show the shape of the relationship.

> Comparing strength? Just take the absolute value of the correlation coefficients. Now which is bigger? That coefficient represents the stronger linear relationship.

Correlation coefficients are usually computed using a calculator (see page 149) or by reading computer output from popular statistics programs. Formulas to find r are included on the AP Exam formula sheet, but they are time-consuming.

Since the further an r-value is from zero, the stronger the correlation, it can be challenging to interpret a specific number as weak, strong, or very strong. Statisticians often rely on arbitrary cutoff numbers to distinguish these values. The following diagram shows one possible set of cutoff values that you can use when interpreting your data. However, this is just one example. Ultimately, remember the axiom that the further from zero, the stronger the correlation.

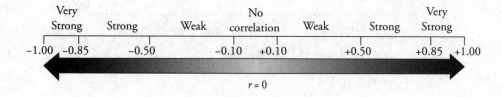

Example 18: A sample of 12 father–son pairs were selected at random. The heights (in inches) of the selected father–son pairs are listed below:

Height (in Inches) of Father (x)	Height (in Inches) of Son (y)
66	66
66	65
66	67
67	68
67	65
67	67
68	70
68	67
69	70
70	70
71	72
73	74

Compute the correlation coefficient between the heights of the fathers and the heights of their sons. Interpret the computed value.

Solution: First, let's make a scatterplot to determine the nature of the relation between the two variables. Because a correlation coefficient only applies to linear relationships, we must make sure the scatterplot is linear. See Figure 34.

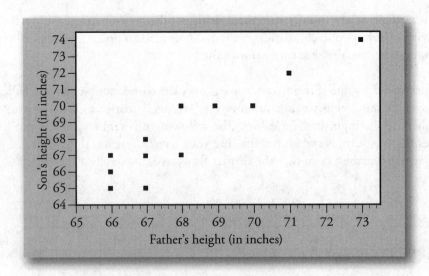

Figure 34: Scatterplot showing the heights of fathers and the heights of their sons

TI-83 or TI-84:

To make a scatterplot
- Enter X-values into L_1
- Enter corresponding Y-values into L_2
- Choose **2nd → STAT PLOT → 1:Plot1**
- Turn the plot on by highlighting **On**
- Choose scatterplot by highlighting the picture of a scatterplot under Type
- Enter Xlist: L_1
- Enter Ylist: L_2
- Select type of marking from 3 available marks
- Choose **ZOOM → 9:ZoomStat**
- Use TRACE option to trace points in the scatterplot

The scatterplot shows a positive linear relation between the heights of the fathers and the heights of their sons. Now, let's compute the correlation coefficient.

There are $n = 12$ pairs of measurements.

TI-83 or TI-84:

To compute the correlation coefficient
- Enter X-values into L_1
- Enter corresponding Y-values into L_2
- Choose **2nd → CATALOG → DiagnosticOn**

Note: This step is needed only the very first time. Once the diagnostics are turned on, omit this step. Newer models of the TI-83 and TI-84 have this option under the MODE button as well.
- Choose **STAT → CALC → 8:LinReg(a+bx)**
- On TI-83
    - o LinReg(a+bx) wil appear on your home screen
    - o Type L1,L2
- On TI-84
    - o Enter L1 for the X-list and L2 for the Y-list
    - o Scroll down and click **Calculate**
- Press **ENTER**

This option will show a, b, r^2, and r for the regression line $y = a + bx$ at r.

This gives $r \approx 0.9249$, so there is a very **strong positive linear relationship** between the heights of the fathers and the heights of their sons because r is very close to 1.

TI-83 or TI-84:

To get summary statistics for bivariate data
- Enter X-values into L_1
- Enter corresponding Y-values into L_2
- Choose **STAT → CALC → 2:2-Var Stats**
- Enter L_1, L_2. This will result in 2-Var Stats L_1, L_2.
- Press **ENTER**

  This option will provide

  $\overline{X}$, ΣX, ΣX^2, S_X, σ_X, n

  $\overline{Y}$, ΣY, ΣY^2, S_Y, σ_Y

  ΣXY, min X, max X, min Y, max Y

  Use the up arrow and down arrow to scroll up and down the list.

In a scatterplot, when these bivariate data are plotted, it shows a sort of elliptical cloud of points. Lengthwise, the cloud is centered at $\overline{X}$ and spread approximately in the range of $(\overline{X} - 3s_x, \overline{X} + 3s_x)$. Widthwise (or heightwise), the cloud is centered at $\overline{Y}$ and spread approximately in the range of $(\overline{Y} - 3s_y, \overline{Y} + 3s_y)$. The inclination of the cloud is determined by the correlation coefficient (or, equivalently, by the slope of the line, as discussed on the next page). The relation between slope of the line (b) and the correlation coefficient (r) is given by $b = r\left(\dfrac{S_y}{S_x}\right)$.

Least-Squares Regression Line

Once we have established that the two variables are related to each other, we are often interested in estimating or quantifying the relation between the two variables. When one variable explains or causes the other or when one is dependent on the other, estimating a linear regression model can be useful. Such an estimate can be useful for predicting the corresponding values of one variable for known values of the other variable.

A **linear regression model** or **linear regression equation** is an equation that gives a straight-line relationship between two variables.

The linear relation between two variables is given by the following equation for the regression line:

$$Y = \alpha + \beta X$$

where

- Y is the **dependent variable** or **response variable**.

- X is the **independent variable** or **explanatory variable**.

- α is the **y-intercept**. It is the value of Y for $X = 0$.

- β is the **slope** of the line. It gives the amount of change in Y for every unit change in X.

- ε is the random error. This general term accounts for everything besides what is accounted for by the predicted model, $Y = \alpha + \beta X$. In the case of one point, the error or residual is represented by e, and it is the difference between the observed and predicted value. For example, suppose that, using some weather models, the weather station predicted that today's highest temperature would be 75 degrees Fahrenheit. At the end of the day, the highest temperature recorded was 78 degrees. Here, the predicted temperature is 75 degrees, whereas the observed temperature is 78 degrees. The difference 78 − 75 = 3 is the residual, e. In this case, the day's high temperature was underpredicted. The goal of the linear regression is to pick the line that reduces error for all of the e's to make the model predict the observed values as closely as possible.

> Note: error, ε, is a measure of how wrong our guesses were. Low error means that our model is good at predicting real values.

The **predicted value** of Y for a given value of X is denoted by $\hat{y}$ (read as "y-hat"). It is computed using the estimated regression line

$$\hat{y} = a + bx$$

Error or residual = $e = (y - \hat{y})$ = observed value of Y for a given value of X − predicted value of Y for a given value of X.

The **least-squares regression line** is a line that minimizes the sum of the squares of the residuals. It is also known as the line of best fit. The line of best fit will always pass through the point $(\overline{X}, \overline{Y})$ and will always have the slope $\beta_1 = r \dfrac{S_y}{S_x}$.

The **coefficient of determination** measures the percent of variation in Y-values explained by the linear relation between X- and Y-values. In other words, it measures the percent of variation in Y-values attributable to the variation in X-values. It is denoted by R^2 (R-squared). It can be shown that, for a linear regression, R^2 is equal to the square of the Pearson's correlation coefficient (i.e. $R^2 = r^2$). Note that $0 \le R^2 \le 1$ always.

Example 19: A random sample of 10 office assistants hired within the last six months was selected from a large company. Each assistant's experience (in months) at the time of hire and annual starting salary (in thousands of dollars) were recorded. The data is given in the table on the following page:

Experience (in months)	Starting Salary (in 1,000 dollars)
5	28
12	34
2	24
0	19
2	24
10	32
5	25
1	20
10	29
5	26

(a) Compute the slope for the line of best fit. Interpret it.
(b) Compute the y-intercept of the line of best fit. Interpret it.
(c) Find the equation of the least-squares regression line to estimate starting salary using experience.
(d) Plot the line of best fit in a scatterplot.
(e) Predict the starting salary for an office assistant with six months of prior experience.
(f) What is the residual for the worker hired with 12 months experience?
(g) Compute the coefficient of determination. Interpret it.

Solution: In this example, note that the starting salary (in thousands of dollars) depends on the worker's experience (in months). It would make little sense to say that experience depended on starting salary! Therefore, starting salary is the **dependent,** or **response**, variable, and experience is the **independent**, or **explanatory**, variable. There are 10 pairs of measurements. The scatterplot of the data is shown in Figure 35.

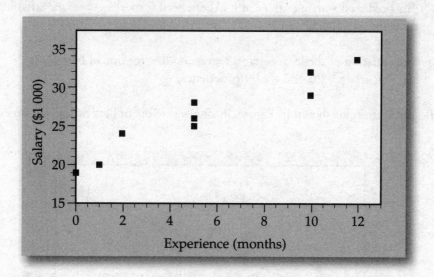

Figure 35: Scatterplot showing starting salary and experience of office assistants

The scatterplot shows that there is a *strong positive linear relationship* between the starting salary of office assistants and their prior experience.

From the data, compute: $n = 10$

TI-83 or TI-84:

To compute least-squares estimates of the slope (b), y-intercept (a), and coefficient of determination (r^2) for the line $y = a + bx$:
- Enter X-values into L_1
- Enter corresponding Y-values into L_2
- Choose **STAT → CALC → 8:LinReg(a+bx)**
- Enter L_1, L_2. This will display LinReg(a+bx) L_1,L_2
- Press **ENTER**

  This option will show a, b, r^2, r.

Do This for Due Credit
When interpreting the slope in context, you will not get full credit on the AP Exam if you forget to use the words "on average" or something equivalent, such as saying that the predicted salary increases by $1,090. The slope, b, is merely an estimate of the relationship between two variables, and your interpretation should reflect this fact.

(a) Compute the estimated slope:

$$\widehat{\beta} = b = r \frac{S_y}{S_x} = (.9514)\left(\frac{4.795}{4.185}\right) = 1.09 \text{ is the estimated slope of the line of best}$$
fit.

For every month's additional experience at the time of hiring, the starting salary increases on average by $1,090.

(b) Compute the estimated y-intercept:

$$\widehat{\alpha} = a = \overline{Y} - b\overline{X} = 26.1 - 1.09(5.2) = 20.432 \text{ is the estimated } y\text{-intercept of the}$$
line of best fit.

The predicted starting salary of inexperienced (experience = 0 months) office assistants is $20,432.

(c) The equation of the least-squares regression line (or line of best fit) is starting salary = 20.432 + 1.09(experience).

(d) The scatterplot shown in Figure 36 shows the line of best fit superimposed on it.

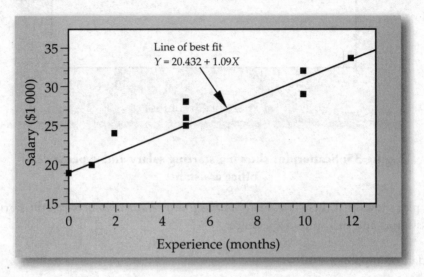

Figure 36: Line of best fit

The notation SS refers to the "sum of squares," and there are calculator functions for these: ΣX^2 and ΣY^2. The actual formula looks something like this (for SS_{xx}, the Sums of Squares for the variable X):

$$\sum_{i=1}^{n}(x_i - \bar{x})^2.$$

For SS_{xy}, the formula looks something like this:

$$\sum_{i=1}^{n}(x_i - \bar{x})(y_i - \bar{y})$$

(e) The office assistant has six months of prior experience. For X = six months: starting salary = 20.432 + 1.09(experience) = 20.432 + 1.09(6) = 26.972. The estimated starting salary for an office assistant with six months of prior experience is $26,972.

(f) The data show that an office assistant with 12 months of experience received $34,000 as a starting salary. The predicted salary is 20.432 + 1.09(12) = 33.512, i.e., $33,512. So, the residual = observed − predicted = 34,000 − 33,512 = 488. It means this office assistant received $488 more than the expected starting salary.

(g) You can find the following values on your calculator, but we've demonstrated how you could also plug into the formula. The correlation coefficient is $r = \dfrac{SS_{xy}}{\sqrt{(SS_{xx})(SS_{yy})}} = \dfrac{171.8}{\sqrt{(157.6)(206.9)}} = 0.9514$.

So, the coefficient of determination = R^2 = $(0.9514)^2$ = 0.9052, i.e., 90.52%.

This means that 90.52% of the variation among starting salaries is attributable to prior experience. So there is still about 9.5% of variation among salaries that remains unexplained. It may be due to some other factors such as education, gender, the person the assistant is working for, etc.

Figure 37 shows the observed *Y*-value, the line of best fit, and the residual for one pair of values.

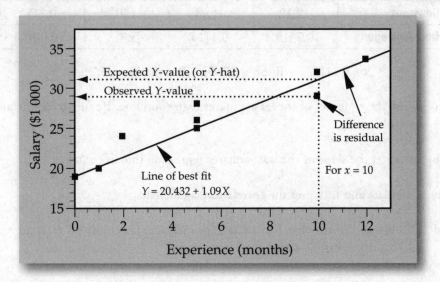

Figure 37: Plot showing observed and expected *Y*-values and the residual

---

TI-83 or TI-84:

To get a regression line superimposed on a scatterplot

- Enter *X*-values into L_1
- Enter corresponding *Y*-values into L_2
- Choose **STAT → CALC → 8:LinReg(a+bx)**
- Enter L_1, L_2, Y_1. This will display: LinReg(a+bx) L_1,L_2,Y_1

To get Y_1, *use the following sequence of commands.*

- Choose **VARS → Y-VARS → 1:Function → 1:Y₁**
- Press **ENTER**
- Press **GRAPH**

Sometimes on the AP Exam, you will be provided with a generic output from a statistical computer program and asked questions about the relationship between two variables. Usually it is not necessary to use all of the numbers presented in the output. For instance, in the example below, the columns for SE Coef, T, and P are used in inference procedures that will be discussed later in the book. For right now, you need to know the R-squared value (R-Sq, not R-Sq(adj)), the variables, and both values in the Coef (coefficient) column. For a regression equation, the Coef given for the *x*-variable is the slope and the Coef for Constant is the *y*-intercept.

Example 20: For each student, can his or her average quiz score for the semester be used to predict his or her final exam score? To answer this question, quiz averages and final exam scores were recorded for a sample of 100 students who took Statistics 101 at a nearby university. The results of a regression analysis are displayed on the next page.

Predictor	Coef	SE Coef	T	P
Constant	12.12	11.94	1.01	0.315
Quiz Average	0.7513	0.1414	5.31	0.000

$$S = 9.71152 \quad R–Sq = 37.0\% \quad R–Sq(adj) = 35.7\%$$

(a) Write the equation of the least-squares regression line. Be sure to define all variables used.

(b) Interpret the slope of the least-squares regression line in context.

(c) Calculate and interpret the correlation coefficient.

(d) One student in the class had an average quiz score of 92. If his residual was –3.753, what was his actual final exam score?

Solution:

(a) $\hat{y} = 12.12 + 0.7513x \quad x \rightarrow$ quiz average $\quad y \rightarrow$ final exam score

(b) For every one point increase in quiz average, the final exam score increases by, on average, 0.7513 points.

(c) Correlation coefficient $= r = \sqrt{R^2} = \sqrt{0.37} \approx 0.608$
Quiz average and final exam score have a moderate positive linear relationship. (Note: r is positive because the slope is positive. Beware of negative relationships.)

(d) $\hat{y} = 12.12 + 0.7513(92) = 81.2396$
Residual $= y - \hat{y}$, thus $-3.753 = y - 81.2396$
The student's actual final exam score, y, is 77.4866.

Outliers and Influential Points

As discussed earlier, an **outlier** is an observation that is surprisingly different from the rest of the data—in other words, an observation that does not conform to the general trend. An **influential observation** is an observation that strongly affects a statistic. Some outliers are influential, while others are not. If there is a considerable difference between the correlation coefficients computed with and without a specific observation, then that observation is influential. The same can be said about the line of best fit. If the estimates of the line of best fit change considerably when including or excluding a point, then that point is an influential observation.

To better understand the potential influence of any possible outlier points, look at Figures 38, 39, and 40.

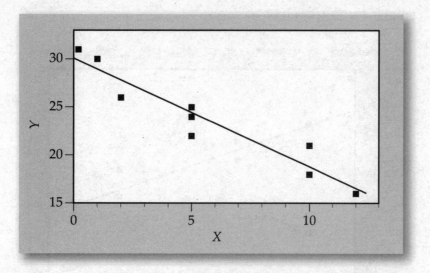

Figure 38: Scatterplot showing no outliers

This scatterplot shows no outliers. It demonstrates a strong negative linear relation between X and Y.

$$r = -0.951$$
$$R^2 = 0.904 \text{ or } 90.4\%$$

The line of best fit is $Y = 29.57 - 1.09X$.

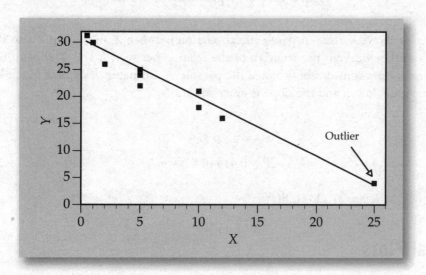

Figure 39: Scatterplot with an outlier

This scatterplot shows a very strong negative linear relation between X and Y. It also shows one outlier, which confirms the trend shown by the other observations. This outlier strengthens the relation between X and Y, but it is not an influential point because it does not change the parameter estimates.

$$r = -0.982$$
$$R^2 = 0.964 \text{ or } 96.4\%$$

The line of best fit is $Y = 29.31 - 1.03X$.

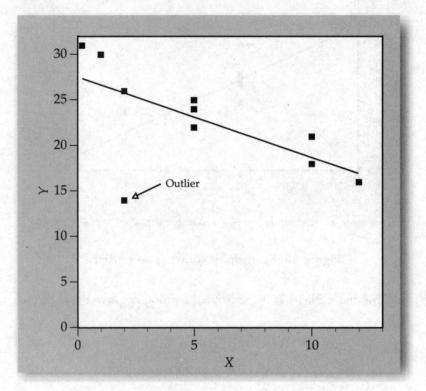

Figure 40: Scatterplot with an outlier

This scatterplot shows a strong negative linear relation between X and Y, but it also shows one outlier. This outlier weakens the strength of the relation between X and Y. It is an influential point because it does considerably change the parameter estimates. R^2 is now much lower, the intercept is slightly lower, and the slope is much lower.

$$r = -0.643$$
$$R^2 = 0.414 \text{ or } 41.4\%$$

The line of best fit is $Y = 27.21 - 0.86X$.

Residual Plots

A **residual plot** is a plot of residuals versus the predicted values of Y. This type of plot is used to assess the fit of the model. A residual plot should look random. If the residual plot shows any patterns or trends, it is an indication that the linear model is not appropriate.

Example 21: Refer to the earlier example of the office assistants. Compute the predicted value and the residual for each observed X-value.

Experience (in Months)	Starting Salary (in 1,000 Dollars)	Predicted Salary	Residual
X	Y	$\hat{Y} = 20.432 + 1.09X$	$e = Y - \hat{Y}$
5	28	25.882	2.118
12	34	33.512	0.488
2	24	22.612	1.388
0	19	20.432	−1.432
2	24	22.612	1.388
10	32	31.332	0.668
5	25	25.882	−0.882
1	20	21.522	−1.522
10	29	31.332	−2.332
5	26	25.882	0.118

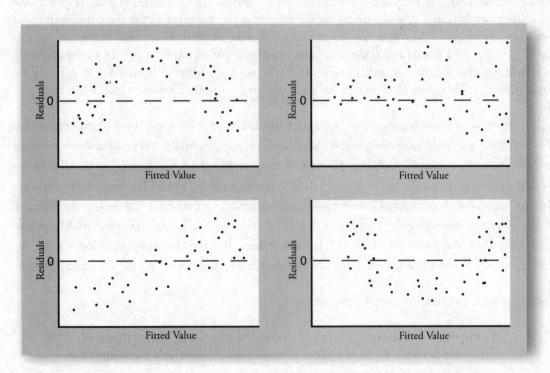

Figure 41: Examples of residual plots that suggest poor model fit

---

TI-83 or TI-84:

To get a residual plot

- Enter x-values into L_1
- Enter corresponding y-values into L_2
- Choose **STAT → CALC → 8:LinReg(a+bx)**. *Note: Failure to do this step will lead to a DIM Mismatch Error later on in this process.*
- Choose **2nd → Y =** (for STAT PLOT) → **1:Plot1**
- Turn Plot 1 On by highlighting **On** and pressing **ENTER**
- Choose scatterplot by highlighting the picture of a scatterplot under Type and pressing **ENTER**
- Enter XList: L_1
- Enter YList: **2nd → STAT** (for LIST) → **1:RESID**
- Select type of marking from the three available
- Choose **ZOOM → 9:ZoomStat**
- Use **TRACE** to trace points in the scatterplot if needed

Transformations to Achieve Linearity

Always draw a scatterplot of the data to examine the nature of the relation between two variables. You should also examine the fit of the linear model using a residual plot. If either one of these plots indicates that the linear model might not be appropriate for the data, then there are two options available: You can either use **nonlinear models,** which are not tested on the AP Exam, or use a **transformation** to achieve linearity. For example, if the data seems to have a relation of the nature $Y = aX^b$, then we can take the logarithm of both sides to get $\ln(Y) = \ln(a) + b\ln(X)$. This gives the equation of a straight line—in other words, a linear relation.

After the variables have been appropriately transformed, we can then use them to make a model. For example, we could take the natural log of all Y-values ($Z = \ln(Y)$) or the square root (square root is the most commonly applied power transformation) of all Y-values ($Z = \sqrt{Y}$). Then we would fit the model for Z as a function of X. When using a fitted model for predictions, remember to transform the predicted values back to the original scale using a reverse transformation. For example, when using the transformation $Z = \ln(Y)$ to get $\hat{Z} = a + bX$, you would need to use the reverse transformation of $\hat{Y} = e^{\hat{z}}$ for predictions. If using the transformation $Z = \sqrt{Y}$ to get $\hat{Z} = a + bX$, you would need to use the reverse transformation of $\hat{Y} = (\hat{Z})^2$ for predictions.

Here are some examples of transformations:

- The **log transformation** ($Z = \ln(Y)$) is used to linearize the regression model when the relationship between Y and X suggests a model with a consistently increasing slope.

- The **square root transformation** ($Z = \sqrt{Y} = Y^{\frac{1}{2}}$) is used when the spread of observations increases with the mean.

- The **reciprocal transformation** ($Z = \dfrac{1}{Y^1}$) is used to minimize the effect of large values of X.

- The **square transformation** ($Z = Y^2$) is used when the slope of the relation consistently decreases as the independent variable increases.

- The **power transformation** ($\ln(Y)$ and $\ln(X)$) is used if the relation between dependent and independent variables is modeled by $Y = aX^b$.

TI-83 or TI-84:

To use power transformation

This procedure will fit the model equation $Y = aX^b$ to the data using transformed values of $\ln(X)$ and $\ln(Y)$. In other words, the line $\ln(Y) = \ln(a) + b\ln(X)$ will be fitted to the data.

- Enter X-values into L_1
- Enter corresponding Y-values into L_2
- Choose **STAT → CALC → A:PwrReg**
- Enter L_1, L_2. This will display PwrReg L_1,L_2
- Press **ENTER**

TI-83 or TI-84:

To use logarithmic transformation

This procedure will fit the model equation $Y = a + b\ln(X)$ to the data using transformed values of $\ln(X)$ and Y. In other words, line $Y = a + b\ln(X)$ will be fitted to the data.

- Enter X-values into L_1
- Enter corresponding Y-values into L_2
- Choose **STAT → CALC → 9:LnReg**
- Enter L_1, L_2. This will display LnReg L_1,L_2
- Press **ENTER**

TI-83 or TI-84:

To use exponential transformation

This procedure will fit the model equation $Y = ab^X$ to the data using the X-values and the transformed values of $\ln(Y)$. In other words, the line $\ln(Y) = \ln(a) + X\ln(b)$ will be fitted to the data.

- Enter X-values into L_1
- Enter corresponding Y-values into L_2
- Choose **STAT → CALC → 0:ExpReg**
- Enter L_1, L_2. This will display ExpReg L_1,L_2
- Press **ENTER**

All of the following residual plots suggest a non-linear relationship between X and Y EXCEPT:

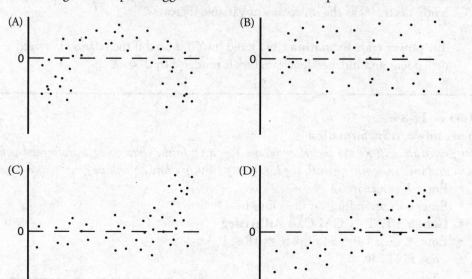

Here's How to Crack It

A residual plot shows the relationship between predicted values and errors between the actual values and predicted values (aka residuals). If there is a linear relationship between X and Y, then there should be no correlation between the residuals and the predicted values. Look for any noticeable pattern in the plots. If there is one, that's evidence a linear relationship might not be appropriate. Choice (B) is the only residual graph that shows no clear pattern (indicating that a linear model is appropriate); therefore (B) is the correct answer.

Example 22: A mathematics teacher is studying the relationship between the time children spend on computational drills and their scores on a particular standardized test. She divides students into 10 different groups. Each group spends a particular amount of time on computational drills. All students take the same standardized test after the computational drills. Their average scores on the standardized test and the time they spent on computational drills are recorded in the following table.

Time (in minutes)	Mean Score
25	45
30	56
50	68
60	87
75	89
80	96
100	105
110	112
125	118
130	126

Table 5: Average time and mean score

In this example, the scores on the standardized tests depend on the time spent on the computational drills. So time is the *independent* variable, and the score on the test is the *dependent* variable. A scatterplot and line of best fit of the data and the residual plot for a linear fit are shown in Figures 42 and 43.

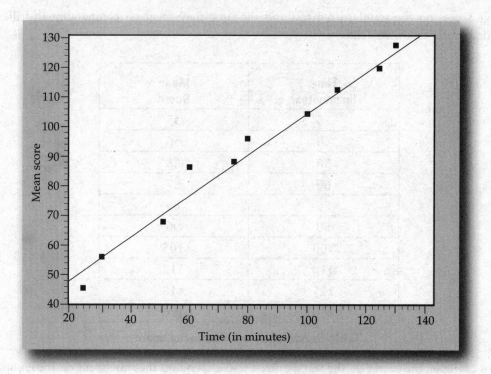

Figure 42: Scatterplot for time versus score

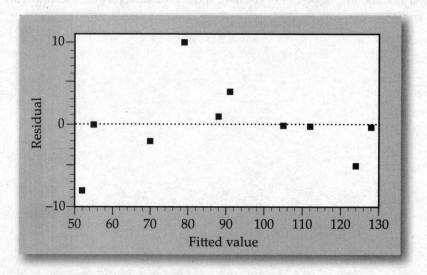

Figure 43: Residual plot for time versus score

Note that the scatterplot shows a slight curvature. Also, note that the residual plot shows a nonrandom pattern. The low and high fitted values have negative residuals, while moderate *y*-values have positive residuals, indicating that the line model is not a good fit for this data. Let's try a square root transformation. First, take the square root of the time. See Table 6.

Time (in minutes)	$\sqrt{\text{Time}}$	Mean Score
25	5.0000	45
30	5.4772	56
50	7.0711	68
60	7.7460	87
75	8.6603	89
80	8.9443	96
100	10.0000	105
110	10.4881	112
125	11.1803	118
130	11.4018	126

Table 6: Transformed data

Now, let's make a scatterplot of score versus square root of time (see Figure 44). Also fit a line using square root of time as an independent variable and score as a dependent variable. Make a residual plot for the fit (see Figure 45).

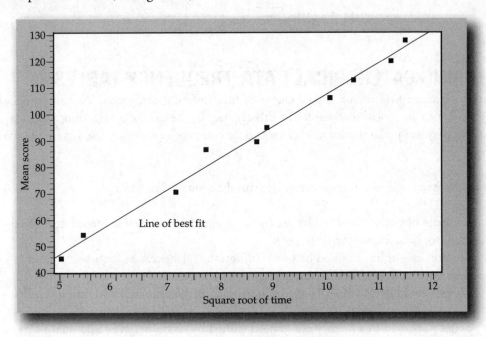

Figure 44: Scatterplot of transformed data

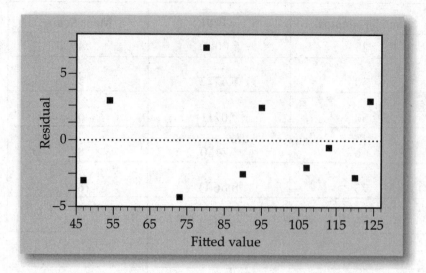

Figure 45: Residual plot for line fitted to transformed data

Now the scatterplot shows a very strong linear pattern. The residual plot shows no pattern, just randomly scattered residuals, which indicates that the line fit is good. The estimated line of best fit is

$$\text{score} = -11.2 + 11.8\sqrt{\text{time}}$$

with

$$R^2 = 0.984 \text{ or } 98.4\%$$

Suppose we are interested in predicting the mean score of students who do computational drills for 60 minutes. Then we would calculate:

$$\text{score} = -11.2 + 11.8\sqrt{\text{time}} = -11.2 + 11.8\sqrt{60} = 80.2$$

EXPLORING CATEGORICAL DATA: FREQUENCY TABLES

Remember that categorical data is data classified into different categories. We computed a frequency table for categorical data earlier in this chapter in the example regarding students' different types of housing. In that case, there was only one type of category used: namely, type of housing.

Data can also be classified into two categories simultaneously. For example:

- Students might be classified by sex (male or female) and their student status (freshman, sophomore, junior, or senior).
- Senators might be classified by party affiliation (Democrat or Republican) and their vote on a specific bill (yea or nay).
- Movies could be classified by genre (horror, comedy, drama...) and rating (G, PG, R...)
- Sodas packaged in a factory could be classified by container type and quality status (defective or nondefective).
- Cars can be classified by brand and color.

VIZUALIZING BIVARIATE CATEGORICAL DATA

Marginal and Joint Frequencies of Two-Way Tables

Suppose data is classified by two different criteria. If the classification criterion 1 has r categories and the classification criterion 2 has c categories, then the classification of data results in a table with r rows and c columns.

A table of data classified by r categories of classification criterion 1 and c categories of classification criterion 2 is known as an $r \times c$ **contingency table**.

Suppose 200 students were classified by sex and academic major. The data resulted in a 2×4 contingency table, shown in Table 7.

		Academic Major			
		Arts	**Sciences**	**Engineering**	**Education**
Sex	**Female**	35	15	5	25
	Male	10	40	50	20

Table 7: 2 × 4 contingency table

The table shows that:

- 35 female students are majoring in arts.
- 10 male students are majoring in arts.
- 15 female students are majoring in sciences.

The figures above are joint frequencies of respective categories. The **joint frequency** of two categories is the frequency with which two categories, one from each of the two classification criteria, occur together.

Let's compute row totals and column totals. See Table 8:

		Academic Major				Row Totals
		Arts	Sciences	Engineering	Education	
Sex	Female	35	15	5	25	80
	Male	10	40	50	20	120
Column Totals		45	55	55	45	200

Table 8: 2 × 4 contingency table with row and column totals

This table shows that:

- There are 80 female students in this study.
- There are 120 male students in this study.
- Out of the 200 students in this study, 45 are majoring in arts subjects.
- Out of the 200 students in this study, 55 are majoring in science subjects.
- Out of the 200 students in this study, 55 are majoring in engineering subjects.
- Out of the 200 students in this study, 45 are majoring in education subjects.

These row and column totals give the marginal frequencies for these two categories. The **marginal frequency** is the frequency with which each category occurs.

NUMERICAL METHODS FOR CATEGORICAL BIVARIATE DATA

Conditional Relative Frequencies and Association

From the above contingency table we can see that:

- Among female students, $\frac{35}{80}$ or 43.75% are majoring in arts subjects. In other words, the conditional percentage of arts majors among female students is 43.75%.
- Among male students, $\frac{50}{120}$ or 41.67% are majoring in engineering subjects. In other words, the conditional percentage of engineering majors among male students is 41.67%.

- Among science majors, $\frac{15}{55}$ or 27.27% are females. In other words, the conditional percentage of female students among the science majors is 27.2%.

- Among education majors, $\frac{20}{45}$ or 44.44% are males. In other words, the conditional percentage of male students among the education majors is 44.44%.

The **conditional relative frequency** is the relative frequency of one category given that the other category has occurred. This frequency is used to determine whether there is an association between the two classification criteria. To measure the degree of relation between two quantitative variables, we use the concept of correlation, which we discussed earlier. On the other hand, to measure the degree of relation between two *categorical* variables, we use the concept of **association**.

If the data above shows a tendency for students of one particular sex to prefer a particular academic major, then we can say that there is *an association* between sex and academic major. If there is *no association* between the two classification criteria, then the expected number of measurements in a given cell of the contingency table is equal to:

$$\frac{\text{(row total)(column total)}}{\text{total number of measurements}}$$

For example, if there is not an association between sex and the academic major of students, then the expected number of female students majoring in sciences would be $\frac{(80)(55)}{200} = 22$. We can compare the expected frequency with the observed frequency to determine whether there is an association between the two categories:

- For female students majoring in sciences:

  expected cell count = 22 > observed cell count = 15

  So we can say that there is a *negative association* between being female and majoring in science. In other words, fewer females tend to choose an academic major in the sciences than would be expected if there were no association between sex and academic major.

- For male students majoring in engineering:

  expected cell count = $\frac{(120)(55)}{200} = 33$ < observed cell count = 50

  So we can say that there is a *positive association* between being male and majoring in engineering. In other words, more males tend to choose an academic major in engineering than we would expect if there were no association between sex and academic major.

TEST YOUR UNDERSTANDING

Describe a situation in which it is better to use the median as a measure of central tendency over the mean. When data is highly skewed, the values in the tail affect the mean more than they affect the median. Since the median is more stable, it is often a better measure of central tendency when data are skewed.

Which of the three main measures of central tendency can be used with categorical (qualitative) data? The mode can be used with both categorical (qualitative) and continuous (quantitative) data. Since categories are not numeric, we cannot calculate a mean, and if the categories are not ordinal, we cannot put them in order to calculate a median.

Describe the strength and direction of the relationship between two variables with a correlation of –0.5. Since the correlation coefficient is negative, it means that there is an inverse relationship between X and Y. As X goes up, Y will go down. –0.5 indicates a moderately strong relationship, since values close to 0 indicate little relation between two variables, and values close to –1 or 1 indicate nearly perfect relationships.

If there is a clear pattern in a residual plot, is a linear relationship appropriate? Why or why not? No, if a linear relationship is appropriate, we expect to see a residual plot with near to zero correlation between residuals and predicted values. Patterns indicate that the relationship between X and Y is not linear.

Which measure of spread is least affected when there are extreme outliers in your data set? The Interquartile Range (IQR) does not include the lowest or highest 25% of data and is therefore less affected by extreme values. Both variance/standard deviation and range do include these extreme values.

Summary

o The two major categories of variables are **quantitative** and **categorical**.

o Data can be described using tables, graphs, or numbers.

o **Bar graphs** and **pie charts** are useful methods for depicting categorical data.

o There are many graphical methods for describing quantitative data. Small data sets can be depicted using **stemplots** or **dotplots**. Larger data sets can be shown as **boxplots**, **frequency charts**, and **histograms**.

o Use a **scatterplot** to organize and display bivariate quantitative data.

o Use a **two-way contingency** table to summarize bivariate categorical data.

o Ideally, data should always be visualized first, as **symmetric** data and **skewed** data are summarized using different numerical summaries.

o The table below shows different numerical summaries for quantitative data.

Type of Measure	Symmetrical	Skewed
Measure of Center	Mean	Median
Measure of Spread	Standard deviation	Interquartile range (IQR)
Visualization(s)	Relatively balanced appearance with tails of roughly equal length. Mean and median are roughly equal.	Tend to have a much longer tail on either the left or right side of the data. Median and mean are fairly different.

o The r-value, or **correlation coefficient**, is always between −1 and 1: $-1 \leq r \leq 1$.

o The r-statistic describes the strength of the correlation, with numbers closer to ±1 being stronger and values closer to 0 being weaker. The r^2 value describes how much variation in the y-values data can be attributed to changes in the x-values.

o There are two major formulas needed to calculate the **least-squares regression line**. To find the estimated slope, you need the r-statistic, the standard deviation of the x-values, and the standard deviation of the y-values. Use the formula: $b = r\dfrac{s_y}{s_x}$. To calculate the y-intercept, use the formula: $a = \bar{y} - b\bar{x}$.

o A **residual plot** shows whether a linear model is a good fit. If the points on a residual plot are randomly scattered, then a linear model is appropriate. If the points are not random, then a linear model should not be used.

Chapter 4 Review Questions

Multiple-Choice Questions

Answers can be found at the end of this section.

1. Which of the following is/are categorical variable(s)?

    I.   The mean income of teachers in Pennsylvania
    II. The types of desserts available at a restaurant
    III. The colors of cars in a parking lot

   (A) I
   (B) II
   (C) III
   (D) I & II
   (E) II & III

2. Given the following frequency distribution of the colors of cars in a parking lot, what is the relative frequency of blue cars?

Color of Cars	Number of Cars with that Color
Red	36
White	27
Blue	45
Green	12
Black	30

   (A) 0.08
   (B) 0.18
   (C) 0.20
   (D) 0.24
   (E) 0.30

3. A researcher takes a sample of 3000 flowers and measures their heights. Which is the best way to represent the data?

   (A) Bar chart
   (B) Stemplot
   (C) Histogram
   (D) Pie chart
   (E) Dotplot

4. Which of the following data sets has the largest standard deviation?

   (A) {1,4,7,10,13}
   (B) {1,1,3,5,5}
   (C) {1,3,5,7,9}
   (D) {1,2,3,4,5}
   (E) {1,1,1,1,1}

5. Which measure of center is best for skewed data?

   (A) Mean
   (B) Median
   (C) Standard deviation
   (D) Interquartile range
   (E) Mode

6. Calculate the IQR for the following data.

1	3	13	7	6	11	5	2	11	3
16	2	4	8	9	11	11	1	6	3

   (A) 3
   (B) 4
   (C) 8
   (D) 13
   (E) 15

7. A teacher grades her students' recent tests and computes the mean and median: 84 and 86, respectively. While going over the test, she realized her key had an error. To correct for it, she added 4 points to everyone's score. What are the new mean and median of the class?

   (A) Mean: 84; Median: 86
   (B) Mean: 88; Median: 86
   (C) Mean: 88; Median: 90
   (D) Mean: 84; Median: 90
   (E) Mean: 86; Median: 88

8. Which of the following does NOT show a positive correlation?

(A)

X	Y
0	4
1	8
2	12

(B)

X	Y
0	0
1	10
2	20

(C)

X	Y
0	0
1	1
2	2

(D)

X	Y
0	3
1	4
2	2

(E)

X	Y
0	0
1	2
2	6

9. Which of the following is NOT an example of a quantitative variable?

(A) Height in inches
(B) High school GPA
(C) Six-digit school ID number
(D) IQ score
(E) Age

Free-Response Questions

10. A random sample of 10 students studying for the AP Statistics Exam was taken from a large school. Each student's time studying for the class final (in hours) before the AP Exam was recorded along with their scores (out of 100) on the exam. The data is presented in the table below:

Time Studied (hours)	2	10	6	8	5	4	8	7	4	2
Score	60	95	78	88	72	73	82	86	75	63

  (a) Find the equation of the least-squares regression line to estimate scores using hours studied and interpret it.
  (b) Predict the score of a student who studied 3 hours.
  (c) Compute the coefficient of determination. Interpret it.

11. The summary statistics for the number of inches of snow in Coldland for 116 years is shown below.

N	Mean	Median	St. Dev.	Min.	Max.	Q1	Q3
116	10.443	10.364	1.541	6.213	14.578	8.746	12.379

  (a) Describe a procedure that uses this information to determine whether there are outliers.
  (b) Are there outliers? Justify using the procedure described in part (a).

CHAPTER 4 ANSWERS AND EXPLANATIONS

1. **E** A categorical variable is defined by the set of groups or categories (qualitative values) that individuals are placed into; it is not a numerical value. The mean income of teachers in Pennsylvania is a numerical value ($24,000, $12,500, $22,564.34, etc.), so it is quantitative. The types of desserts available at a restaurant will be a list of the kinds of desserts (ice cream, cake, pie, etc.) and cannot be described by numbers. The colors of cars in a parking lot will also be a list of the colors seen (red, blue, green, etc.) and cannot be described by numbers.

2. **E** The relative frequency is equal to the frequency of one case/total sample size. Therefore, Relative Frequency of Blue Cars $= \dfrac{45}{36+27+45+12+30} = \dfrac{45}{150} = 0.30$.

3. **C** The sample size is fairly large. For large sample sizes, histograms are a good representation of the data because you can see the patterns in the data, outliers, approximate center, and spread. There is too much data to be easily displayed on a stemplot or dotplot, and the data is continuous, not categorical. So neither a bar chart nor a pie chart would be appropriate.

4. **A** Standard deviation is a measure of the variation or the spread of the data, so you can quickly determine which data set has the largest standard deviation by examining which data set is the most spread out by comparing the ranges and how close the individual data points are to each other. This is only a shortcut for comparison and *not* an exact approach. Therefore, to know for sure you can use the formula for standard deviation of a population, $\sigma = \sqrt{\dfrac{\sum_{i=1}^{N}(X_i - \mu)^2}{N}}$, or the formula for standard deviation of a sample, $s = \sqrt{\dfrac{\sum_{i=1}^{N}(X_i - \bar{X})^2}{n-1}}$.

5. **B** Skewed data means that there is a shift in the data favoring one end, so the distribution has a "tail." The mean is influenced by "tails." In other words, one small or one large value can shift the mean toward that value. Median is located at the 50th percentile, so it divides the data in half. It is not affected by the actual values in each half, just that the data is split in half, so it is good for skewed data. The standard deviation and interquartile range are not measures of center; they are both measures of variation. The mode is simply the most frequently seen value, which is not as helpful as the median for skewed data.

6. **C** To determine the interquartile range (IQR), you must find the difference between the first and the third quartiles. First, arrange the data in order from smallest to largest: 1, 1, 2, 2, 3, 3, 3, 4, 5, 6, 6, 7, 8, 9, 11, 11, 11, 11, 13, 16. Next, determine the position of the value at the first and the third quartiles. The first quartile is at P_{25} and its position is at $l = \dfrac{(20+1)25}{100} = 5.25$. Similarly,

the third quartile is at P_{75} and its position is at $l = \dfrac{(20+1)75}{100} = 15.75$. Therefore, you must determine the value at the 5.25th position beginning with the least value and the value at the 15.75th position beginning with the least value. At the 5th and 6th positions, the values are both 3, so at the 5.25th position, the value is 3. At the 15th and 16th positions, the values are both 11, so at the 15.75th position, the value is 11. Finally, the IQR is determined to be the difference between these two values. Thus, the IQR is $11 - 3 = 8$.

7. **C** If you add a positive constant to every data point in a sample or population, then the measures of center (mean and median) will increase by the value of that constant, respectively. In this problem, every student's score increased by 4 points, so the mean and median each increased by four points too.

8. **D** A positive correlation between two variables is present when two variables increase together or decrease together. Because we only have three data points of each set, we must assume that none are outliers and take each into consideration. Table (A) shows that each value of Y increases with each value of X. This is also true in tables (B), (C), and (E). Table (D) has an initial increase in Y with X, but then Y decreases, so the correlation is not positive.

9. **C** Quantitative variables have two key features. First, they must be numeric. In other words, they have to be numbers. The second feature is that they have to be able to be analyzed using arithmetic operations. For example, it is possible and meaningful to find the average height, GPA, IQ score, and age of a group of students. These are all quantitative variables. While it is possible to calculate an average student ID number, this would not have any real-world meaning. The correct answer is (C).

10. **(a)** Use your calculator to calculate the equation. By hand, use the equations: $\hat{y} = a + bx$,

$b = \dfrac{\Sigma(x_i - \bar{x})(y - \bar{y})}{\Sigma(x_i - \bar{x})^2}$, and $a = \bar{y} - b\bar{x}$. Use the data to calculate a and b and then plug those

values into $\hat{y} = a + bx$. Either way, $b = 3.957$ and $a = 55.043$. Thus, the equation for the least-

squares regression line is: score = 55.043 + 3.957(time studied). This can be interpreted as:

for every hour spent studying, a student's score will increase by 3.957 points above a score of

55.043 points (the score of someone who didn't study).

(b) Use the least-squares regression line from part (a), and evaluate the equation when time studied = 3. So, score = 55.043 + 3.957(3) = 66.914. A student who studies three hours will score 66.914 points on the final exam.

(c) The coefficient of determination is the square of the correlation coefficient. Therefore, you can use your calculator data or calculate r from the data: $r = \dfrac{1}{n-1}\sum\left(\dfrac{x_i-\bar{x}}{s_x}\right)\left(\dfrac{y_i-\bar{y}}{s_y}\right) \approx 0.9654$.

Thus, $r^2 \approx 0.9321$. The statement to explain this could be: 93.21% of the variance among test scores is explained by the hours studied.

11.   (a) Using the Q_1 and Q_3 values, the bounds outside which a data point is an outlier can be calculated. Outliers are values that are less than L, where $L = Q_1 - 1.5IQR$, or greater than U, where $U = Q_3 + 1.5IQR$.

(b) $L = 8.746 - 1.5(12.379 - 8.746) = 3.2965$

$U = 12.379 + 1.5(12.379 - 8.746) = 17.8285$

Because the minimum and maximum values are not less than L or greater than U, there are no outliers in this data set.

Chapter 5
Sampling and Experimentation

By the end of the chapter you will be able to master:

- random sampling techniques
- potential sources of bias in data collection
- experimental design concepts such as blinded studies and control/placebo groups

PLANNING A STUDY

If you want to draw valid conclusions from a study, you must collect the data according to a well-developed plan. This plan must include the question or questions to be answered as well as an appropriate method of data collection and analysis. This chapter discusses various techniques for planning a study. In the multiple-choice section, this topic appears in four to six out of 40 questions. In the free-response section, this topic usually appears in one out of six questions.

OVERVIEW OF METHODS OF DATA COLLECTION

Terms and Concepts

- A **population** is the entire group of individuals or items that we are interested in.

- A **frame** (or sampling frame) is a list of all the members from which the sample is to be taken. This is usually, but not always, the same as the population—for example, a list of all account holders in a bank, a list of participants in the Boston Marathon in the year 2010, etc.

- A **sample** is the part of the population that is actually being examined.

- A **sample survey** is the process of collecting information from a sample. Information obtained from the sample is usually used to make inferences about population parameters.

- A **census** is the process of collecting information from all the units in a population. It is feasible to do a census if the population is small and the process of getting information does not destroy or modify units of the population. For example, if a school principal wants to know the educational background of the parents of all the children in her school, she can gather this information from every one of the school children. It is possible to do a census of a large population, as with the United States Census, but it requires a huge amount of work, time, and money.

As the following examples show, there are many situations in which a census is impossible or impractical:

- An advisor to a candidate for governor wants to determine how much support his candidate has in the state. Suppose the state has 4 million eligible voters. It would clearly be too time-consuming to contact each and every voter in this state, and even if it were accomplished, by the time the census was finished, the level of support for the candidate might have changed.

- Suppose an environmentalist is interested in determining the amount of toxins in a lake. Using a census would mean emptying the lake and testing all the water in the lake—obviously not a good way to gather information!

- A manufacturer of light bulbs is interested in determining the mean lifetime of 60-watt bulbs produced by his factory. Using a census would mean burning all the light bulbs produced in the factory and measuring their lifetimes. Again, a census would not be practical here.

Clearly, a census is often too costly or too time-consuming, and sometimes damaging to the population being studied. We usually have to take samples instead. How to get those samples is the subject of this chapter.

Experiments and Observational Studies

An **experiment** is a planned activity that results in measurements (data or observations). In an experiment, the experimenter *creates* differences in the variables involved in the study and then observes the effects of such differences on the resulting measurements. For example, suppose a team of engineers at an automotive factory runs cars at different predetermined and controlled speeds and then crashes the cars at a specific site. Then, the engineers measure the damage to the cars' bumpers. In this example, the team of engineers *creates* the differences in the environment by running the cars at different speeds. To sum up, in an experiment, the experimenter assigns a treatment to each subject rather than allowing subjects to make their own choices.

An **observational study** is an activity in which the experimenter *observes* the relationships among variables rather than creating them. For example, suppose an engineering student collects information from car accident reports filed by the local police department. The reports tell the student how fast the cars were traveling when the crashes occurred and how much damage was done to the cars' bumpers. In this example, the experimenter (the student) has no control over the speeds of the cars. The student observes the differences in speeds as recorded in the reports and the results of the crashes as measured by the amount of damage to the bumpers.

Experiments have some advantages, described below, but unfortunately, in some situations it is impossible, impractical, or unethical to conduct an experiment. Sometimes we must instead use an observational study. For example:

- To study the effect of smoking on people's lungs, an experiment would require that the experimenter assign one group of people to smoke and another group not to smoke. But it is clearly unethical to ask some people to smoke so that the damage to their lungs can be measured, and it may not be possible to force a smoker to quit.

- Extreme weather events like earthquakes and hurricanes can affect a city's economy, but we cannot cause extreme weather events to occur in random cities. It would be impossible to do an experimental study in this situation.

One of the problems with observational studies is that their results often cannot be generalized to a population because many observational studies use samples (such as volunteers or hospitalized patients) that aren't representative of the population of interest. These samples might simply be easiest to obtain. This problem can be solved by observing hospitalized as well as nonhospitalized patients. Another problem is that of **confounding factors**. Confounding occurs when the two variables of interest are related to a third variable instead of just to each other. For instance, in a study of elementary school children, taller students know more words. The confounding factor here is age: taller students tend to be older, and older students tend to know more words.

PLANNING AND CONDUCTING SURVEYS

Getting Samples

There are many methods of getting a sample from the population. Some sampling methods are better than others. **Biased sampling** methods result in values that are systematically different from the population values or systematically favor certain outcomes. **Judgmental sampling, samples of convenience,** and **volunteer samples** are some of the methods that generally result in biased outcomes. Sampling methods that are based on a probabilistic selection of samples, such as **simple random sampling**, generally result in unbiased outcomes.

Biased Samples

Judgmental sampling makes use of a nonrandom approach to determine which item of the population is to be selected in the sample. The approach is entirely based on the judgment of the person selecting the sample. For example, jury selection from an available pool of jurors is not a random process. Lawyers from both parties use their judgment to decide who shall be selected. The result may be a biased jury, i.e., a selection of jurors with specific opinions.

Using a **sample of convenience** is another method that can result in biased outcomes. Samples of convenience are easy to obtain. For example, suppose a real estate agent wants to estimate the mean selling price of houses in a Chicago suburb. To save time, he looks up the selling prices of houses sold in the last three months in the subdivision where he lives. Using his own subdivision may have saved him time, but the sample is not representative of all the houses in that suburb.

Volunteer samples, in which the subjects choose to be part of the sample, may also result in biased outcomes. For example, imagine that a local television station decides to do a survey about a possible tax increase to support the local school system. A telephone number is provided and respondents are asked to call and register their opinions by pressing 1 if they support the tax increase and 2 if they oppose it. The television station then counts the number of 1s and 2s to determine the degree of support for the tax increase. But the station may well have inadvertently introduced bias into the results. Only those who feel very strongly about the tax increase (either for or against) are likely to call the number and register their opinions, so the sample may not reflect the true feelings of the whole population.

Simple Random Sampling

Simple random sampling is a process of obtaining a sample from a population in which each member has an equal chance of being selected. In this type of sample, there is no bias or preference for one individual over another. Simple random samples, also known as random samples, are obtained in two different ways:

1. **Sampling with replacement from a finite population.** An example is the process of selecting cards from a deck, provided that you return each card before the next is drawn. With this scheme, the chance of selection remains the same for all cards drawn—one out of 52. If you didn't replace the first card before drawing the second, then the chance of selecting a particular second card would be higher (one out of 51) than the chance of selecting the first one (one out of 52). When two cards are drawn with replacement, the probability of selecting two particular cards is $(1/52)(1/52) = 0.0003698$ and is the same regardless of the cards selected.

2. **Sampling without replacement from an infinite population** (or a population that is simply very large compared to the sample size)—for example, selecting two voters from a list of 200,000 registered voters in a city. Here the population size (200,000) is quite large compared to the sample size (two). Note that when you're sampling without replacement, the available population size decreases as you continue sampling, but because the population size is so large compared to the sample size, the change in the chance of a particular person getting selected is negligible for practical purposes. The chance of selecting the first voter is one out of 200,000 (that is, 0.000005). Because the sample is being selected without replacement, the chance of selecting the second voter increases slightly, to one out of 199,999 (that is 0.000005000025). But this isn't much of a difference. The chance of selecting two particular voters out of 200,000 *without* replacement is $(0.000005)(0.000005000025) = 2.500125 \times 10^{-11}$; whereas the chance of selecting the same two out of 200,000 *with* replacement is $(0.000005)(0.000005) = 2.5 \times 10^{-11}$. So for all practical purposes, the chance of selection is the same.

How to Select a Simple Random Sample

To select a simple random sample from a population, we need to use some kind of chance mechanism. Here are some examples:

- Prizes offered at a baseball game. A portion of each ticket collected at the stadium entrance is put in a large box. About halfway through the game, all the ticket stubs in the box are mixed thoroughly. Then a prespecified number of ticket stubs are picked from the box. The persons sitting in the selected seats (as identified by the ticket stubs) receive prizes.

- A teacher asks each student in a class of 40 to write his or her name on a separate (but identical) piece of paper and drop it in a box. The teacher then mixes thoroughly all the pieces in the box and selects one piece at random, without looking at the name. The student whose name appears on the selected piece of paper is designated as the class representative.

- A teacher wants to select about half of the students in the class for a project, so she asks each student to toss a coin. Those who toss "heads" are selected for the project.

- A kindergarten teacher wants to select five children to perform a song at the holiday party. The teacher puts two kinds of lollipops in a jar, five of them red and the rest green. He then asks each child to take one lollipop from the jar without looking at it. The five children that pick a red lollipop are selected to sing.

The same random result can be achieved by using random number tables. A portion of a random number table is given below:

96410	96335	55249	16141	61826	57992	21382	33971	12082	91970
26284	92797	33575	94150	40006	54881	13224	03812	70400	45585
75797	18618	90593	54825	64520	78493	92474	32268	07392	73286
48600	65342	08640	78370	10781	58660	77819	79678	67621	74961
82468	15036	79934	76903	48376	09162	51320	84504	39332	26922

To demonstrate the use of random number tables, let us again consider the example of the kindergarten teacher. He could number the children using two digit numbers: 01, 02, 03, ..., 50. He would then start anywhere in the random number table and read each pair of numbers sequentially (it doesn't matter whether he reads vertically or horizontally). But the teacher is selecting from only 50 children. So he should ignore 00 and the numbers from 51 to 99. Suppose he began at the fourth line. Then he would get 48, 60, 06, 53, 42, 08, 64, 07, and so on. The child numbered 48 would be selected. The number 60 in the sequence would be ignored. The next selected child would be number 06. Number 53 in the sequence would be ignored, and so on. As a result, children numbered 48, 06, 42, 08, and 07 would be selected to participate in the program.

Computer programs and calculators can generate random numbers.

TI-83 or TI-84:

To generate random integers

- Choose **MATH → PRB → 5:randInt(**

    Enter the range of numbers from which to select and the total number of random numbers to generate. Separate the three numbers by commas.

    This will result in: randInt(1,50,5)

    Note: The first and second numbers indicate the range of numbers from which to select, and the third number indicates the number of random numbers to generate. In this case, the calculator will generate five numbers between 1 and 50.

Other Methods of Random Sampling

Besides simple random sampling, there are other sampling procedures that make use of a random phenomenon to get a sample from a population:

- In **systematic sampling** procedure, the first item is selected at random from the first k items in the frame, and then every k^{th} item is included in the sample. This method is popular among biologists, foresters, environmentalists, and marine scientists.

- In **stratified random sampling**, the population is divided into groups called *strata* (the singular is "stratum"), and a simple random sample is selected from each stratum. Strata are homogeneous groups of population units—that is, units in a given stratum are similar in some characteristics, whereas those in different strata differ in those characteristics. For example, students in a university can be grouped into strata by their majors. If a population is divided into homogeneous strata, then stratified sampling can be useful in reducing variation; that is, it can help make groups more similar and result in a more powerful test.

- In **proportional sampling**, the population is divided into groups called strata, and a simple random sample of size proportional to the stratum size is selected from each stratum. Proportional sampling is the preferred method of stratified sampling. The United States selects the number of congressional seats for each state using stratified sampling. The selection of members of Congress in the U.S. House of Representatives is a good example of proportional sampling; the U.S. Senate, on the other hand, is an example of stratified sampling in which the strata are not represented proportionally.

- In **cluster sampling**, a population is divided into existing, non-homogeneous groups called clusters. A random sample of clusters is obtained, and all individuals within the selected clusters are included in the sample. In order to safely use cluster sampling, each cluster should be representative of the population as a whole. Cluster sampling is often used to reduce the cost of obtaining a sample, especially when the population is large. For example, suppose you were doing a survey of the opinions of high school teachers. A simple random sample would not be feasible because 1) you would need a list of all high school teachers, and 2) after you selected the sample, you would have to travel to numerous schools just to administer the survey to one person at each location. A better method is to use high schools as existing clusters of teachers. Then randomly select some of the schools and survey all teachers in those schools.

A retail company has 50 locations across the world. They want to collect data about how a new type of in-person employee training performs compared to traditional methods. Which of the following sampling techniques would be most appropriate for this situation?

(A) Cluster Sampling
(B) Systematic Random Sampling
(C) Simple Random Sample
(D) Stratified Random Sampling
(E) Proportional Sampling

Here's How to Crack It

Let's look at the potential problems with this experiment. With 50 locations across the world, traveling to each one would be costly. If we used (B) or (C), we'd likely need to visit all 50 locations. The question also does not mention any notable groups in the employee population that we need to account for, so both (D) and (E) would largely be unnecessary. That leaves (A), cluster sampling, as the correct answer. Cluster sampling allows us to limit the number of stores we need to go to by treating each store as a heterogeneous cluster and randomly selecting which clusters/stores to give the new training to. Therefore, (A) is the correct answer.

BIAS IN SURVEYS

For a survey to produce reliable results, it must be properly designed and conducted. Samples should be selected using a proper randomization technique. A nonrandom selection will limit the generalizability of the results. Furthermore, interviewers should be trained in proper interviewing techniques. The attitude and behavior of the interviewer should not lead to any specific answers, because this would result in a biased outcome. Questions should be carefully worded, as the wording of a question can affect the response, and leading questions should be avoided.

Sampling error is a variation inherent in any survey. Even if a survey is repeated using the same sample size and the same questionnaires, the outcome will be different, if only slightly.

Sources of Bias in Surveys

A survey is biased if it systematically favors certain outcomes. The following are some sources of bias:

- **Response bias** occurs when a respondent provides an answer that is either factually wrong or does not accurately reflect his/her true belief/opinion. It may be caused by the behavior of the interviewer or respondent. For example, if high school children are asked in the presence of their parents whether they've ever smoked a cigarette, then they are likely to deny smoking even if they have smoked. It is possible to reduce response bias by carefully training interviewers and supervising the interview process.

- **Nonresponse bias** may occur if the person selected for an interview cannot be contacted or refuses to answer. If such individuals are different, as a group, from those who are eventually interviewed, then the results may not accurately reflect the whole population. For example, if an internet poll is conducted on the website of a news outlet, only those people who visit that outlet's website will be included. People who get their news from other outlets may have different opinions on the issue being researched than do those who participate in the poll.

- **Undercoverage bias** may occur if part of the population is left out of the selection process. For example, if you conduct a telephone survey, individuals without a telephone are left out of the selection process. In a country in which 80% of households have a telephone, only a small percent of the population would be left out of a telephone survey. But in some countries, less than 4% of households have telephones, and those that do are often affluent. A telephone survey there would give biased results. For example, in every U.S. census, a certain percent of the population is missed due to undercoverage. This undercoverage tends to be higher in poorer sections of large cities.

- **Wording effect bias** may occur if confusing or leading questions are asked. For example, imagine an interviewer who says, "The American Dental Association recommends brushing your teeth three times a day. How often do you brush your teeth on a typical day?" The respondents may feel compelled to give an answer of three or more, even if they don't brush their teeth that often. So the responses are likely to be higher than the true average of the population. In this situation, the wording effect bias could be reduced or avoided by simply asking, "How often do you brush your teeth on a typical day?"

PLANNING AND CONDUCTING EXPERIMENTS

Terms and Concepts
- A **dependent** or a **response variable** is the variable to be measured in the experiment. An **independent** or **explanatory variable** is a variable that may explain the differences in responses. We are interested in studying the effects of independent variables on dependent variables. For example, a dentist is interested in studying the duration of the effects of different amounts of anesthesia. In this case, the "amount of anesthesia" is the *explanatory* variable and the "duration of the effect" is the *response* variable.

- An **experimental unit** is the smallest unit of the population to which a treatment is applied. In the above example, each patient receiving a dose of anesthesia is an experimental unit.

- A **confounding variable** is a variable whose effect on the response cannot be separated from the effect of the explanatory variable. In properly constructed experiments, an experimenter tries to control confounding variables. Confounding can be an even more serious problem in observational studies because the experimenter has no control over the confounding variables. For example, if a new pain medication is tested on women with migraines and men with backaches, any measured differences in pain relief could be due to differences in sex or in the source of the pain. Sex and pain source are confounded.

- A **factor** is a variable whose effect on the response is of interest in the experiment. Factors are of two types: 1) **qualitative**—where the data is in non-numerical groups (red, blue, or green cars); 2) **quantitative**—where the data can be measured numerically. For example, to study the effect of income level on spending power, we can categorize annual incomes by grouping them into less than $10,000, $10,000–$24,999, $25,000–$49,999, $50,000–$99,999, and $100,000 and above.

- **Levels** are the values of a factor used in the experiment. An experiment can have one or more factors. The number of levels used in the experiment may differ from factor to factor. **Treatments** are the factor-level combinations used in the experiment. If the experiment has only one factor, then all the levels of that factor are considered treatments of the experiment.

For example, suppose that there is only one medicine on the market for controlling anxiety, but then two pharmaceutical companies come up with new medicines. A doctor is interested in comparing the effectiveness of the current medicine with those of the two new medicines. Here, "anxiety-controlling medicine" is the only *factor* of interest. There are three *levels* of this medicine, which become three *treatments*, namely, current medicine, new medicine A, and new medicine B.

Now suppose the doctor also wants to determine the effect of two types of breathing exercises along with the medicines. Let us call the exercises Exercise 1 and Exercise 2. Now this experiment has two factors, one at three levels and one at two levels, as shown in the following table.

Type of exercise	Type of medicine		
	Current medicine	New medicine 1	New medicine 2
Exercise 1	X	X	X
Exercise 2	X	X	X

Then, as defined earlier, all the factor-level combinations become treatments. To calculate the number of treatments, you will have one multiple for every factor. In the table above, there are two factors, so there will be two numbers multiplied together. Factor 1 has two levels (Exercise 1 and Exercise 2), and Factor 2 has three levels (Current medicine, New medicine 1, and New medicine 2). So there are $3 \times 2 = 6$ treatments of interest to the doctor. They are the following:

1. Current medicine and Exercise 1

2. New medicine A and Exercise 1

3. New medicine B and Exercise 1

4. Current medicine and Exercise 2

5. New medicine A and Exercise 2

6. New medicine B and Exercise 2

- A **control group** is a group of experimental units similar to all the other experimental units except that it is not given any treatment. A control group is used to establish the baseline response expected from experimental units if no treatment is given. For example, the doctor from the example above might want to know what will happen to the anxiety level of patients if no treatment at all (medicine or breathing exercises) is prescribed. Researchers then compare the baseline response from the control group to the response from the treatment group to determine whether the treatment had an effect.

- A **placebo group** is a control group that receives a treatment that looks and feels similar to an experimental treatment but is expected to have no effect. A placebo is a medicine that looks exactly like the real medicine but does not contain any active ingredients. The patients will not be able to tell the placebo and the real medicine apart by looking at them. Placebos allow researchers to observe the effect on people's expectations for improving and effects of time apart from the actual effectiveness of the treatment.

Single-Blind and Double-Blind Experiments

Similarly, it is possible that measurements or subject interaction will be biased if the person taking the measurements knows whether a patient received a placebo or not. **Blinding technique** is used in medical experiments to prevent such a bias. The blinding technique can be used in two different fashions: double blinding and single blinding. In a **single-blind experiment**, either the patient does not know which treatment he or she is receiving or the person measuring the patient's reaction does not know which treatment was given. In a **double-blind experiment**, both the patient and the person measuring the patient's reaction do not know which treatment the patient was given.

Double-blind experiments are preferred, but in certain situations they simply can't be conducted. For example, in an experiment designed to compare the drop in cholesterol level produced by a certain medication to that produced by going on a particular diet, the patients always know which treatment they are given. You can't hide from them the fact that they have been subjected to just a medication or to a new low-cholesterol diet! So a double-blind experiment would not be possible. But a single-blind experiment would be possible, because the lab technician measuring the patients' cholesterol level does not need to know which treatment the patients have been getting.

> **She Blinded Me With Science**
> Note that if test subjects are objects, such as bottles of water being tested for their volume, then double-blind experiments are not possible. The objects could not "see" the experiment, so they cannot be blinded to it!

Randomization

The technique of randomization is used to average the effects of extraneous factors on responses. In other words, it balances the effects of factors you cannot see.

- If each experimental unit is supposed to receive only one treatment, then which experimental unit receives which treatment should be determined randomly. For example, in the experiment above that compares three anxiety-controlling medicines, the doctor should use some kind of randomization mechanism (such as one of the methods described earlier) to decide which participating patient should get each one of the three medicines.

- If each experimental unit is supposed to receive all treatments, then the order of treatments should be determined randomly for each experimental unit. Suppose the doctor is interested in comparing the effects of all three medicines on each patient. Then for each patient, the doctor should use some kind of randomization mechanism to decide the order in which the three medicines will be given. All participating patients will be given all three medicines with some washout period (in order for the patient to return to baseline) in between the administration of each medicine. But the order in which the three medicines are given will differ with each patient. Some will get current medicine first, then new medicine A, and then new medicine B. Others will get new medicine B first, then current medicine, and then new medicine A, and so on.

Blocking

The technique of **blocking** is used to control the effects of known factors—factors that you *can* see. A **block** is a group of homogeneous experimental units. Experimental units in a block are similar in certain characteristics, whereas those in different blocks differ in those characteristics. For example, a doctor might suspect that the effect of a certain medicine is different on women than on men. The doctor could then control this potentially confounding factor by separating patients into two groups by gender. There would then be two blocks, male and female, and the experiment would be conducted separately within each block. Blocking may reduce unwanted variation in responses, thus allowing the experimenter to see more clearly those differences in responses due to treatments. Blocking is very similar to stratification in that the goal for both is to reduce variation. Blocking is performed prior to assigning the individuals within the sample to treatment groups, whereas stratification is done prior to choosing the sample.

Quick Tip
Make sure you understand the difference between **stratified sampling, cluster sampling,** and **blocking**.

Replication

Replication refers to the process of giving a certain treatment numerous times in an experiment, or even repeating an experiment multiple times. Replication reduces chance variation among results. It also allows us to estimate chance variation among results. In the example of comparing three medicines to control anxiety, suppose the doctor prescribes each of three medicines to only one patient each. If the responses of the three patients were different, then we would not know whether the differences were true effects of the medicines or due just to chance. Could differences among the patients have led to differences in their responses? Yes, but we don't know. What if the doctor were to prescribe each medicine to more than one patient? Each patient could receive one of three treatments selected at random. Then, on the average, the three groups of patients would likely be similar. As the differences among patients are averaged out, the effect of treatment differences will stand out.

Would all patients receiving the same treatment have the same responses? Probably not. This is why we look for average effects between groups. Randomization helps our groups to 1) be similar before there is any treatment, and 2) have similar reactions (on average) to the treatment. "On average" is the key phrase!

Completely Randomized Design

In a completely randomized design, treatments are assigned randomly to all experimental units, or experimental units are assigned randomly to all treatments. This design can compare any number of treatments. There are advantages in having an equal number of experimental units for each treatment, but this is not necessary.

Example 1: Suppose a doctor is interested in comparing an anxiety-controlling drug on the market now (let's call it "current medicine") with two new drugs ("new medicine A" and "new medicine B"). A group of patients from a local clinic is available for the experiment. Design an experiment to compare the effects of these three drugs.

Solution: In this experiment, there is one factor of interest with three levels.

- Factor of interest: anxiety-controlling medicines
- Number of levels: three
- Treatments: current medicine, new medicine A, and new medicine B
- Experimental unit: each patient
- Response variable: the anxiety level measured for each patient

Use the group of patients available from the local clinic and design the experiment as follows:

- Measure the anxiety level of each patient.
- Use a randomization scheme to divide the patients into three groups. For example, throw a six-sided die for each patient. If the numbers 1 or 2 show, then assign the patient to group 1; if the numbers 3 or 4 show, assign the patient to group 2; otherwise, assign to group 3. Or fill a jar with equal numbers of blue, red, and green beads, with the total number of beads equal to the total number of participating patients. Ask each patient to take out one bead without looking in the jar. If the patient selects a blue bead, assign that patient to group 1; if the patient selects a red bead, assign to group 2; if the patient selects a green bead, assign to group 3. Have the patient, then, replace the bead into the jar and allow the next patient to select.
- Prescribe current medicine to all patients in group 1.
- Prescribe new medicine A to all patients in group 2.
- Prescribe new medicine B to all patients in group 3.
- After a designated time period, measure the anxiety level of each patient.
- Compare the results.

This scheme can also be described using the diagram shown in Figure 1.

Quick Think
Why does this research design not include a placebo?

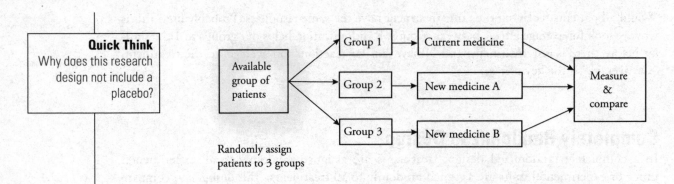

Figure 1: Schematic diagram of a completely randomized experiment

Randomized Block Design

If the treatments are the only systematic differences present in the experiment, then the completely randomized design is best for comparing the responses. But often there are other factors affecting responses. Unless they are controlled, the results will be biased. As we discussed earlier, one way to control the effects of known extraneous factors is to form groups of similar units called blocks. In a randomized block design, all experimental units are grouped by certain characteristics to form homogeneous blocks, and then a completely randomized design is applied within each block. The blocking of experimental units allows the experimenter to account for systematic differences in responses due to a known factor and leads to more precise conclusions from the experiment.

Example 2: Suppose a doctor wants to compare an anxiety-controlling drug currently on the market (current medicine) with two new drugs (new medicine A and new medicine B). A group of patients from a local clinic is available for the experiment. All three drugs are known to have different effects on men and women. Design an experiment to compare the effects of the three drugs.

Solution: In this experiment, there are two factors of interest: anxiety-controlling medicine and patient's gender. Of these two factors, anxiety-controlling medicine is a *treatment*, whereas patient's gender is a *blocking factor*. Patient responses may be different because of the treatment administered or because of the patient's gender. Separate the available group of patients by gender, so that block 1 consists only of men and block 2 only of women. Now, within each block all the patients are similar (same gender).

Measure the anxiety level of each participating patient. For each male patient, randomly assign one of the three treatments. For example, use a random number table to get one-digit random numbers. Assign numbers {1, 2, 3} to group 1, numbers {4, 5, 6} to group 2, numbers {7, 8, 9} to group 3, and ignore number 0. Then draw a random number for each patient. Separate the patients into three groups depending on the numbers they've drawn. Prescribe the current medicine to patients in group 1, new medicine A to patients in group 2, and new medicine B to patients in group 3. After a designated time, measure the anxiety level of each patient. Repeat this procedure for all female patients. When finished, compare the results. The schematic diagram shown in Figure 2 describes the design.

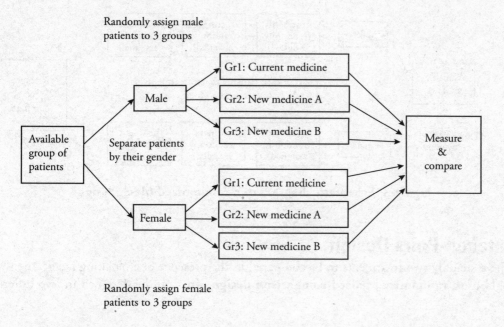

Randomly assign male
patients to 3 groups

Randomly assign female
patients to 3 groups

Figure 2: Schematic diagram of a randomized block design

Alternatively, the same experiment could be conducted as follows:

- Separate the available group of patients by gender so that block 1 consists only of men and block 2 only of women. Administer all three medicines to each patient one at a time, with a washout period in between. Determine the order in which the medicines are to be given using a randomization scheme. For example, use a random number table to get random one-digit numbers. Assign number 1 to the current medicine, number 2 to new medicine A, number 3 to new medicine B, and ignore numbers 0, 4, 5, 6, 7, 8, 9. Get two distinct random numbers for each patient to determine the order of medicines. For example, suppose the first patient draws {2, 1}. First, measure this patient's anxiety level. Next, give the patient new medicine A, and after a designated time, measure the patient's anxiety level. Then, after a washout period, measure the patient's anxiety level again, administer the current medicine, and afterward, measure the anxiety level. Again, after another washout period, measure the patient's anxiety level, administer new medicine B, and measure the anxiety level. The order of medicines given will differ for each patient, depending on the random numbers drawn. Compare the results for all three medicines, as well as for both genders.

- Here we have two sets of blocks. Gender defines one set of blocks and each patient becomes a block by itself. The schematic diagram shown in Figure 3 describes the design.

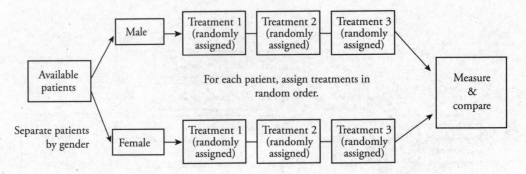

Figure 3: Schematic diagram of a randomized block design

Matched-Pairs Design

If there are only two treatments to be compared in the presence of a blocking factor, then you should use a **randomized paired comparison design**. This can be designed in two different ways:

• Form two or more blocks of two experimental units each. Experimental units within each block should be matched by some relevant characteristics. Within each block, toss a coin to assign two treatments to the two experimental units randomly. Each block will have one experimental and one control unit. Because both experimental units are similar to each other except for the treatment received, the differences in responses can be attributed to the differences in treatments. This type of experiment is called a **matched-pairs design**.

• Alternatively, each experimental unit can be used as its own block. Assign both treatments to each experimental unit, but in random order. To control the effect of the order of treatment, randomly determine the order. With each experimental unit, toss a coin to decide whether the order of treatments should be treatment 1 → treatment 2 or treatment 2 → treatment 1. Because both treatments are assigned to the same experimental unit, the individual effects of experimental units are nullified, and the differences in responses can be attributed to the differences in treatments.

Example 3: A local sickle-cell association offers programs to educate people about sickle-cell anemia. The director of the association is interested in assessing the program's effect on the participants' knowledge about the disease.

(a) Design an experiment to assess the effectiveness of this educational program.

(b) Explain why this is a matched-pairs experiment.

Solution:

(a) Prepare a test consisting of questions about sickle-cell anemia. Select a random sample of participants enrolled in the program. At the beginning of the program, administer the test to all selected participants. Let's call this the *pre-*

test. Record the results of the pre-test. Then, let all the participants complete the program. Afterward, administer the same test again. Let's call this the *post-test*. Record the results of the post-test. Finally, compare the results of the pre-test to the post-test.

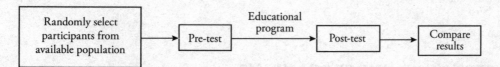

Figure 4: Schematic diagram of a matched-pairs design

Break time! Give your brain a rest with some fresh air or maybe a dance party.

(b) This is a matched-pairs design because the results of the two tests are matched by person. In this experiment, each participant's pre-test results are compared to the same participant's post-test results. A comparison of the pre-test results of one participant with the post-test results of another participant would be meaningless.

Which of these experiments is/are fully double-blind?

I. A researcher is looking at the effect of no-carb diets on depression in college students. A researcher who was not involved in assigning diets and is not aware of the participants' diets is in charge of recording depression symptoms.

II. A researcher is looking at the difference in the weight of pickle jars between two brands. A researcher who is not aware of the brand of pickle is in charge of recording weights.

III. A researcher is looking at the effect of a new drug on cold symptoms compared to similar looking placebo sugar pills. Participants are not told which pill they get. A researcher who was not involved in assigning medications and is not aware of the participants' treatment is in charge of recording cold symptoms.

    (A) I only
    (B) II only
    (C) III only
    (D) I and III
    (E) I, II, and III

Here's How to Crack It

All three of the answers make a statement about the researcher being unaware of the condition of the experimental units, so we should focus on whether the experimental units are blinded. Statement (III) explicitly states that the participants are unaware of their condition, so eliminate (A) and (B).

Statement (I) is not truly double-blind since participants are aware of the fact that they are not eating carbs, so eliminate (D) and (E), leaving (C) as the correct answer.

There is no need to continue further, as only one choice remains. However, to see why Statement (II) is also not double-blind, note that the experimental units are objects which cannot "see" (and therefore cannot be blinded to) their condition. The correct answer is (C).

TEST YOUR UNDERSTANDING

When do control groups help improve experimental design? Control groups allow us to see what would happen to experimental units over time (or without treatment). For example, in a study on a new cold medicine, a control group is necessary so that we can try to account for how symptoms normally improve over time.

Why would you use a placebo group over a control group? Placebo groups go above and beyond control groups by implementing an intervention or treatment that is similar to the target intervention/treatment. This helps us account for even more external factors. For example, in a study that gives a computerized memory training task to older adults, a placebo group might be asked to use a computer for the same amount of time as the intervention group. If our control group did nothing, it is possible that the act of being on a computer, and not the specific memory training, was the cause of any improvement. Placebo groups usually aim to be as similar as possible to the target intervention.

List 2 or more general issues that can come up when trying to sample from a particular population. What sampling technique(s) can we use to help alleviate any issues? There are many correct answers here. For example, it can be costly or impractical to travel and administer treatments to or collect surveys from many different locations like schools, corporate offices, or retail locations. Using cluster sampling allow us to treat each location as a heterogenous subpopulation and randomly sample clusters.

Often with large populations that have small minority groups, these groups are underrepresented in simple random samples. We can use proportional sampling so that we can guarantee to have a representative sample. For example, if we think handedness is important, we can divide a population into left- and right-handed people. We can then choose 10% of our sample from the left-handed group, and 90% from the right-handed group so that our sample is similar to the population.

What issues can arise when participants and/or researchers are not blind to their conditions? How do single- and double-blind studies help overcome these issues? Both subjects' and researchers' behavior can be biased if they know who gets which treatment. For example, people might feel healthier if they think they're taking a real medicine, even if it's a sugar pill. Similarly, researchers' perceptions of subjects can be unconsciously biased by what they expect to happen. Single- and double-blind experiments help alleviate these biases by preventing subjects and researchers from being aware of which treatments subjects are receiving.

Describe a scenario in which it is impossible to have a double-blind study design. If we had a study which looked at the effect of eating a vegetarian diet on cholesterol, it would be hard to blind participants to their treatment…they can tell that they're eating a vegetarian diet.

Summary

- A **census** examines every individual within a population. A **sample** examines part of a population.

- Samples can be **biased** in many ways, including judgmental bias, convenience bias, and volunteer bias.

- A **simple random sample** is the most common method used for sampling and means that every member from a population has an equal chance of being selected.

- A **survey** is a method of obtaining specific data about a sample.

- Surveys can be biased in several ways, including **response bias**, **nonresponse bias**, **undercoverage bias**, and **wording effect bias**.

- **Cluster sampling** is used when a population is very large. Statistically representative samples are taken from smaller clusters of the population, e.g., looking at high schools as clusters of groups of teachers and then sampling from a randomly selected group of high schools.

- **Stratified sampling** is used when groups share common similarities that may be relevant to the study. For example, sexes or high school grade levels can be used as strata, and a simple random sample can be taken from within each stratum.

- **Blocking** seems similar to clustering or stratified sampling, but it is used in the experimental design to create homogenous groups in order to control the effects of known factors.

- A **control group** is a group similar to the other groups in the experiment but that is not given any treatment.

- A **placebo group** is similar to the other groups but receives a treatment that appears similar to those that the other groups receive. However, this treatment is expected to have no effect on the results of the study.

- A **single-blind** study is one in which either the patient or the experimenter does not know which treatment is being given. Single-blind studies can be done on both humans and objects.

- A **double-blind** study is one in which neither the patient nor the researcher measuring results knows which treatment is being given. Double-blind studies are preferred, but they can only be done on human test subjects.

Chapter 5 Review Questions

Multiple-Choice Questions

Answers can be found at the end of this section.

1. Which of the following is an appropriate sample for a study interested in the average interest rates on home loans from a national bank?

    (A) Less than one hundred loan rates from one branch in a town

    (B) Thousands of loan rates from all branches in the Midwest

    (C) All loan rates from all branches in one town and a random sample of loan rates from other area branches

    (D) A random sample of one thousand loan rates from one hundred randomly selected branches, nationally

    (E) Loan rates from ten of your neighbors who bank at the local branch

2. Which of the following is NOT a method of random sampling?

    (A) Systematic
    (B) Stratified
    (C) Volunteer
    (D) Proportional
    (E) Cluster

3. If a study has three factors, each with three levels, how many treatments are there?

    (A) 4
    (B) 5
    (C) 6
    (D) 10
    (E) 27

4. A survey is administered to a random sample of participants. Which of the following does not describe a potential form of bias?

    (A) The survey asks about teenagers' tendency to text and drive and is administered in front of the teenagers' parents.

    (B) A small portion of the administered surveys are returned for analysis.

    (C) A study is meant to describe the behavior of high school students in general, but it is only administered to girls.

    (D) The population of a high school is divided into nonhomogeneous groups, and ten surveys are administered to a random sample from each cluster.

    (E) A question in the survey states, "Most teenagers know texting while driving is bad. How often do you text and drive?"

5. Suzy and John each claim to make the best chicken enchiladas. To test their claims, they each prepare enchiladas and serve them to a random sample of friends. Those friends are then surveyed using the same questionnaire. Results are compared. Which of the following statements about the study is true? (Note: Suzy and John do not have any friends in common.)

    (A) The results will generalize because the questionnaires were identical.

    (B) The samples were random, so the results should not be biased.

    (C) The results of this study will definitively prove whose enchiladas are better.

    (D) There is a convenience sampling bias present for both Suzy and John.

    (E) The study was a single-blind design study.

6. A student is lobbying for a new youth robotics club to be established at her high school. The school newspaper conducts a survey of students to assess interest in such a club. What is the population of interest?

   (A) All faculty, staff, and students at the school
   (B) All students at the school
   (C) All high school students in the county
   (D) All students in the district
   (E) All freshmen at the school

7. A study testing the effectiveness of a new antidepressant medication includes three groups: a group given the new antidepressant, a group given an antidepressant that has already been proven to be effective, and a group given an ineffective, non-medicated sugar pill. What is the best name for the group given the sugar pill?

   (A) Placebo
   (B) Control
   (C) Experimental
   (D) Treatment
   (E) Block

8. Why is replication a good practice in experimental designs?

   (A) It "controls" the effects of known factors.
   (B) It eliminates chance variation.
   (C) It allows for causation to potentially be determined.
   (D) It makes a study random.
   (E) It allows for chance variation to be estimated.

9. What is an example of a non-biased sampling method?

   (A) A teacher selecting only students with last names starting with the letters P through Z to take a pop quiz
   (B) A teacher selecting only students with a current A or B grade in his class to take a pop quiz
   (C) A teacher picking 10 names out of a jar containing the names of all the students in his class to take a pop quiz
   (D) A teacher selecting only students wearing long sleeves to take a pop quiz
   (E) A teacher asking the students sitting on the right side of his classroom to take a pop quiz

Free-Response Questions

10. A scientist wants to determine which catalyst, A or B, will reduce the reaction times of three reactions (1, 2, and 3) most.

    (a) Design an experiment to compare the effects of these catalysts.
    (b) What is the baseline you should compare your reaction times to?

11. A school psychologist is interested in showing whether or not stress about school can lead to poor grades in school. She interviews a random sample of 100 students from her district's schools (K–12) at the middle of the semester. She asks them how stressed they generally are on a scale from 1 to 10, 10 being the most stressed. Then, the psychologist compares the grades of these students at the end of the semester. After analyzing the data, she concludes that stress about school causes poor grades.

    (a) Is this causal conclusion appropriate based on the design of the study? Why or why not?
    (b) What are some flaws in the design? How are they flaws?
    (c) Design an experiment that corrects these flaws.

CHAPTER 5 ANSWERS AND EXPLANATIONS

1. **D** Samples from a population should use cluster sample, in which the sample is randomly selected and representative of the population as a whole. The population is the interest rates on home loans nationally, so the sample should be nationally representative. This is an example of cluster sampling. Only (D) has a sample that is representative of the population.

2. **C** Volunteer samples are a form of biased sample because the subjects self-select their participation. The results can be biased, as certain individuals can decide not to participate. The other options are all means of sampling a population randomly. For example, systematic sampling would be when a researcher selects every 5th name on a list for participation in a study. Stratified sampling would be dividing the population into strata or homogeneous groups (like boys and girls) and then randomly selecting participants from those groups. Proportional sampling would require the population to be divided into strata and samples proportional to the size of each stratum to be selected (for example, 40% of the population is girls, so 40% of the sample is from the girls stratum). Finally, cluster sampling is when the population is divided into nonhomogeneous groups and then those clusters are sampled (like when a teacher splits the classroom in half down the middle and randomly selects a sample from each half of the class—assuming the students are not seated to form strata).

3. **E** The number of values you multiply together is equal to the number of factors in a study. There are three factors, so multiply __ × __ × __. The values that go into each slot represent the number of levels for each factor. In this case, $3 \times 3 \times 3 = 27$.

4. **D** Choice (A) is an example of response bias; the teenagers may not answer honestly in front of their parents. Choice (B) is an example of nonresponse bias; a portion of the population refused to answer. Choice (C) is an example of undercoverage bias; boys are completely left out of the sample! Choice (E) is an example of wording effect bias; students may feel obliged to respond in a way to make themselves look better, because they know the behavior is not favorable. Finally, (D) is a form of random sampling; it describes a cluster sampling procedure.

5. **D** Let's walk through each choice. Choice (A): The results will not generalize because the samples who tasted the two types of enchiladas were different. Choice (B): The samples were samples of convenience, which can be biased. Choice (C): The experiment cannot definitively prove anything for the reasons in (A), (B), and (E). Choice (E): Both the subjects and administrators knew who was in each group, so there was no blinding. Choice (D) is correct for the same reason (B) is incorrect; the samples were each individual's friends only.

6. **B** The club is for the students in the high school, so all of them would be potential participants and thus the population of interest. The faculty and staff at the school will not be participants, so they are not part of the population of interest. Students anywhere else in the district or county are not important to this one high school's students' interest. Finally, freshmen are not listed as the only potential participants in the club.

7. **A** A placebo group is a special form of a control group. It helps allow researchers to determine how effective a medication actually is versus the beneficial effects produced by simply taking a pill.

8. **E** Replication within a design is beneficial because it allows researchers to determine whether the results for one participant (or group) are due to the treatment or due to characteristics of that participant (or group) or other factors. When multiple participants (or groups) are given a treatment, the variation due to chance or factors out of the researchers' control can be estimated. While replication helps control variation, it cannot eliminate it.

9. **C** A sample is considered non-biased if it is selected randomly, provides each individual with an equal chance of selection, and therefore represents the population. Choices (A), (B), and (D) can be eliminated because the teacher non-randomly selects students with particular characteristics: having a last name starting with a letter in the latter half of the alphabet, maintaining an A or B grade, or wearing long sleeves in class. Eliminate (E) because the teacher non-randomly selects the right side of the classroom to take the quiz. Therefore, the only answer that provides a scenario of random, non-biased sampling is (C), in which students' names are selected randomly from a jar.

10. **(a)** Example: Prepare 20 samples of each reaction (1, 2, and 3). Randomly assign each Catalyst A and B to 10 different samples of each reaction. For example, mix up the samples for each reaction 1, 2, and 3 and number the samples 1–20. Assign every odd-numbered reaction to Catalyst A and every even-numbered reaction to Catalyst B. Allow a lab technician to run the reactions using the catalysts and record the reaction times. This lab technician should not be involved in the assignment of catalysts to reactions. Finally, compare the results of the reaction times for each reaction under each catalyst.

    (b) You should compare your new reaction times for Reactions 1, 2, and 3 with Catalyst A and B to reaction times without any catalyst or with an established catalyst. These reaction times could be measured at the same time you do your experiment (to make sure that there's not an environmental factor influencing the reaction times, like lab temperature) or to established mean reaction times. Say that you see that Catalyst A is 0.01 seconds faster than Catalyst B in Reaction 2. If Reaction 2 takes 10 hours normally, then the improvement may not be practically useful, even if the difference is statistically significant. However, if the reaction normally takes 0.05 seconds, an improvement of 0.01 may be crucial.

11. **(a)** This causal conclusion is not appropriate because there are many factors that could have caused the poor grades in the students such as fatigue, not learning the material properly, missing class, etc. Also, this study was observational, not experimental, so causal conclusions cannot be drawn.

(b) Here are a few examples:

1. The study is observational and not experimental, so causal conclusions cannot be drawn. All other potential causal factors were not controlled.

2. The sample is only drawn from the psychologist's district. This is a sample of convenience and cannot be generalized to students outside of the district.

3. There are different types of stress, and the psychologist didn't ask about them in her survey. So students may not be experiencing stress about school alone.

4. The psychologist is comparing students at multiple ages and grades against each other. These students are at different stages of development and may experience stress at varying rates due to age and workload.

5. She measures stress at the middle of the semester and grades at the end, but stress can change over time and a final grade is cumulative. So the time periods in question between the two variables are different.

6. Stress was measured in the middle of the semester, so it is possible that prior bad grades could have caused a high stress level, not the other way around.

(c) There are potentially numerous ways of designing a more appropriate experiment to answer the psychologist's questions. The following is one example.

First, the psychologist should utilize stratified random sampling based on grade level to ensure that all ages of students are represented in the sample. Using a more representative sample will improve the generalizability of the study. Another possible improvement would be to use a block design in which students are blocked by prior academic achievement. Depending on the number of participants, block 1 could be students with a GPA from 3.5–4.0, block 2 could be students with a GPA from 3.0–3.5, and so on. The psychologist could measure stress levels at the beginning of the school year and then examine grades after a semester or marking period is completed. Grades for high-stress students will be compared to grades for low-stress students within each block. This method would ensure that the primary difference between the students would be stress level and not pre-existing differences in academic ability.

Chapter 6
Anticipating Patterns

By the end of the chapter you should be able to master:

- describing the probability of one or more events
- determining whether two events are independent
- defining and describing probability distributions using mean and variance
- using geometric and binomial distributions to answer questions about discrete events (such as coin tosses)
- describing the normal distribution and its importance in relation to sampling distributions

PROBABILITY

Words referring to probability or chance are commonly used in conversation. For example, we often come across statements like these:

- It is likely to rain today, so please take your umbrella with you.
- It was an easy test. I'll probably get an A on it.
- The Yankees have a much better chance of winning than the Mets.

Words like *probably*, *likely*, and *chance* carry similar meanings in conversation. They all convey uncertainty. By using probability, we can also make numerical statements about uncertainty. For example, bank managers can never know exactly when their depositors will make a withdrawal or exactly how much they'll withdraw. Managers also know that though most loans they've granted will be paid back, some of them will result in defaults—but they can't know exactly which ones. In other words, a variety of outcomes is possible, and therefore bank managers can never know exactly how much money the bank will have at any given moment in the future. However, the bankers can use the rules of probability and their past experience to make reasonable estimations and then use those estimations when making business decisions.

> This chapter discusses how to use probability as a tool to judge the distribution of data under a given model. In the multiple-choice section, this topic appears in eight to 12 out of 40 questions. In the free-response section, this topic appears in one or two out of six questions.

What Is Probability?

Probability is a measure of the likelihood of an event. Consider a fair coin toss. What makes this coin toss "fair?" We call it fair if the coin's chance of showing heads when flipped is the same as its chance of showing tails—in other words, if there is a 50% chance of it showing heads and a 50% chance of it showing tails. Suppose we tossed the coin twice and got two heads. Does that mean these coin tosses were not fair? What if we toss the coin three times? What do we expect to happen? Let's toss a coin 5, 10, 15, 20, 25, and more times and count the number of heads. Then we can calculate the probability of getting heads in a toss and plot that figure on a graph:

$$P(\text{Heads in a toss}) = \frac{\text{Number of heads}}{\text{Number of tosses}}$$

$$\text{Percent heads} = \frac{\text{Number of heads}}{\text{Number of tosses}} \times 100$$

Table 1 lists the results of one such experiment, and the plot in Figure 1 shows them graphically.

Number of Tosses	Number of Heads	P(Heads)	Percent of Heads	Number of Tosses	Number of Heads	P(Heads)	Percent of Heads
2	0	0	0	35	17	0.48571	48.571
3	2	0.66667	66.667	40	18	0.45	45
4	3	0.75	75	45	18	0.4	40
5	5	1	100	50	23	0.46	46
6	3	0.5	50	60	32	0.53333	53.333
7	5	0.71429	71.429	70	29	0.41429	41.429
8	5	0.625	62.5	80	34	0.425	42.5
9	7	0.77778	77.778	90	48	0.53333	53.333
10	4	0.4	40	100	49	0.49	49
15	10	0.66667	66.667	150	74	0.49333	49.333
20	9	0.45	45	200	106	0.53	53
25	12	0.48	48	500	264	0.528	52.8
30	17	0.56667	56.667	1,000	508	0.508	50.8

Table 1: Number of heads shown in different numbers of tosses

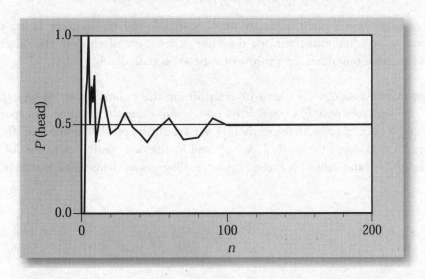

Figure 1: *P*(heads) estimated from different numbers of tosses

Notice that as the number of tosses increases, the percent of times that the coin lands on heads gets closer and closer to 50%. In other words, in the long run, the relative frequency of getting heads approaches 0.5, which is what we expected it to be. This relative frequency reflects the concept of probability. In fact, in the long run, the relative frequency of the occurrence of any specific event will always approach the expected value, also known as the probability. Random events are events that cannot be predicted in the short term, but do produce patterns (such as the 50/50 nature of a fair coin toss) in the long run.

Sample Space

Any process that results in an observation or an outcome is an experiment. An experiment may have more than one possible outcome. A set of all possible outcomes of an experiment is known as a **sample space**. It is generally denoted using the letter S.

- Tossing a coin will result in one of two possible outcomes, heads or tails. Therefore, the sample space of tossing a coin is

$$S = \{\text{Heads, Tails}\}$$

- Throwing a six-sided die will result in one of six possible outcomes. The resulting sample space is

$$S = \{1, 2, 3, 4, 5, 6\}$$

- Tossing two coins will result in one of four possible outcomes. We can indicate the outcome of each of the two tosses by using a pair of letters, the first letter of which indicates the outcome of tossing the first coin and the second letter the outcome of tossing the second coin. H is for heads and T for tails. Then the resulting sample space is

$$S = \{(H, H), (H, T), (T, H), (T, T)\}$$

The outcomes listed in a sample space are never repeated, and no outcome is left out. Two events are said to be equally likely if one does not occur more often than the other. For example, the six possible outcomes for a throw of a die are equally likely.

A **tree diagram** representation is useful in determining the sample space for an experiment, especially if there are relatively few possible outcomes. For example, imagine an experiment in which a die and a quarter are tossed together. What are all the possible outcomes? The six possible outcomes of throwing a die are 1, 2, 3, 4, 5, and 6. The two possible outcomes of tossing a quarter are heads (H) and tails (T). Figure 2 is a tree diagram of the possible outcomes:

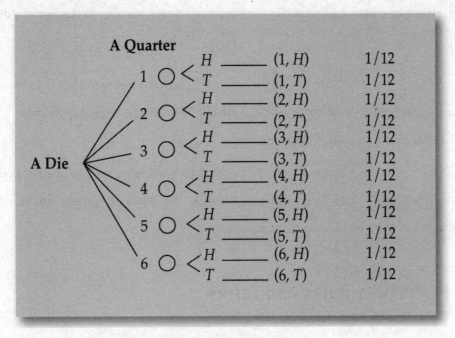

Figure 2: Tree diagram

Looking at the tree diagram, it is easy to see that the sample space is

$$S = \{(1, H), (2, H), (3, H), (4, H), (5, H), (6, H),$$

$$(1, T), (2, T), (3, T), (4, T), (5, T), (6, T)\}$$

The first number of each pair represents the outcome of throwing the die, and the second represents the outcome of tossing the coin. All 12 outcomes are equally likely. Therefore, the probability of each outcome is $\frac{1}{12}$.

An event is an outcome, or set of outcomes, of a random phenomenon. In other words, it is a subset of the sample space. It is common practice to use capital letters to indicate events. For example, one may define

A = getting an even number when a die is thrown = {2, 4, 6}
B = getting two heads when two coins are tossed simultaneously = {(H, H)}

The probability of an event is generally denoted by a capital P followed by the name of the event in parentheses: P(the event). If all the events in a sample space are equally likely, then by using the concept of relative frequency, we can compute the probability of an event as

$$P\left(\text{An event}\right) = \frac{\text{Number of outcomes in the sample space that lead to the event}}{\text{Total number of outcomes in the sample space}}$$

Applying this to the events defined earlier—A (getting an even number in the toss of a die) and B (getting two heads when two coins are tossed)—we get:

- $P(A) = \dfrac{3}{6} = \dfrac{1}{2} = 0.5$. The probability of getting an even number when a six-sided die is thrown is 0.5. In other words, there is a 50% chance of getting an even number when a six-sided die is thrown.

- $P(B) = \dfrac{1}{4} = 0.25$. The probability of getting two heads when two coins are tossed simultaneously is 0.25. In other words, there is a 25% chance of getting two heads when two coins are tossed simultaneously.

Basic Probability Rules and Terms

There are two rules that all probabilities must satisfy:

- **Rule 1:** For any event A, the probability of A is always greater than or equal to 0 and less than or equal to 1.

$$0 \leq P(A) \leq 1$$

- **Rule 2:** The sum of the probabilities for all possible outcomes in a sample space is always 1.

As a result, we can say the following:

- If an event can never occur, its probability is 0. Such an event is known as an **impossible event.**

- If an event must occur every time, its probability is 1. Such an event is known as a **sure event.**

The **odds in favor of an event** is a ratio of the probability of the occurrence of an event to the probability of the nonoccurrence of that event.

$$\text{Odds in favor of an event} = \frac{P(\text{Event } A \text{ occurs})}{P(\text{Event } A \text{ does not occur})}$$

or

$$P(\text{Event } A \text{ occurs}) : P(\text{Event } A \text{ does not occur})$$

Example 1: When tossing a die, what are the odds in favor of getting the number 2?

Solution: When tossing a die,

$$P(\text{Getting the number 2}) = \frac{1}{6} \text{ and}$$

$$P(\text{Not getting the number 2}) = P(\text{Getting the number 1, 3, 4, 5, or 6}) = \frac{5}{6}.$$

Thus, the odds in favor of getting the number 2 are $\frac{1}{6} : \frac{5}{6}$ or 1 to 5 (or 1 : 5).

More Terms

The Venn diagrams shown in Figures 3–6 illustrate some of the following terms. The rectangular box indicates the sample space. Circles indicate different events.

The **complement** of an event is the set of all possible outcomes in a sample space that do not lead to the event. The complement of an event A is denoted by A' (or A^C).

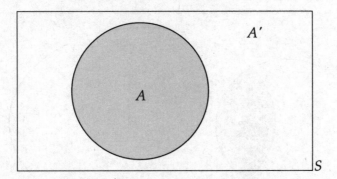

Figure 3: Event A and its complement

Disjoint or **mutually exclusive events** are events that have no outcome in common. In other words, they cannot occur together.

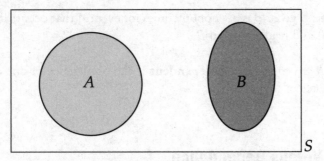

Figure 4: Disjoint events A and B

The **union** of events A and B is the set of all possible outcomes that lead to at least one of the two events A and B. The union of events A and B is denoted by $(A \cup B)$ or $(A$ or $B)$.

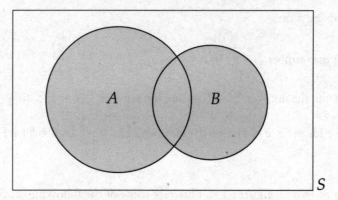

Figure 5: Union of events A and B

The **intersection** of events A and B is the set of all possible outcomes that lead to *both* events A and B. The intersection of events A and B is denoted by $(A \cap B)$ or $(A$ and $B)$.

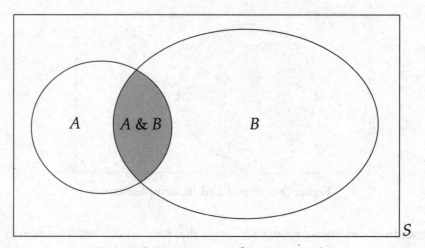

Figure 6: Intersection of events A and B

A **conditional event:** A given B is a set of outcomes for event A that occurs if B has occurred. It is indicated by $(A|B)$ and reads "A given B."

Two events A and B are considered **independent** if the occurrence of one event does not depend on the occurrence of the other.

Independence Versus Dependence

Imagine that you shuffle a standard deck of cards and then draw a card at random. The chance of your getting an ace is the same across all four suits (hearts, clubs, diamonds, and spades). In other words, the likelihood of your getting an ace does not depend on the suit of the card. So we can say that the events "getting an ace" and "getting a particular suit" are *independent*.

Now consider a doctor examining patients in an emergency room. The likelihood of a patient being diagnosed with a knee injury is higher if that patient is a football player, because football players are more likely to suffer knee injuries than non-football players. Therefore, the event "knee injury" *depends* on the event "football player" because being a football player increases the likelihood of knee injury relative to the general population.

Example 2: The sample space for throwing a die is S = {1, 2, 3, 4, 5, 6}. Suppose events A, B, and C are defined as follows:

A = Getting an even number = {2, 4, 6}
B = Getting at least 5 = {5, 6}
C = Getting at most 3 = {1, 2, 3}

Find the probability of each of these events and its complement. Then, find the union, intersection, and conditional probability of each pair of events.

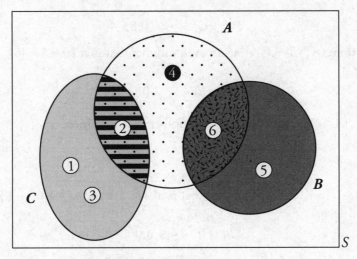

Figure 7: Venn diagram

Solution:

- **Probability:** $P(A) = \dfrac{3}{6} = 0.5$, $P(B) = \dfrac{2}{6} = 0.\overline{3}$, and $P(C) = \dfrac{3}{6} = 0.5$

- **Complement:** A' = Getting an odd number = {1, 3, 5}

$$P(A') = \frac{3}{6} = 0.5 = 1 - P(A)$$

B' = Getting a number less than 5 = {1, 2, 3, 4}

$$P(B') = \frac{4}{6} = 0.\overline{6} = 1 - P(B)$$

C' = Getting a number larger than 3 = {4, 5, 6}

$$P(C') = \frac{3}{6} = 0.5 = 1 - P(C)$$

- **Union:** $(A \cup B)$ = Getting an even number or a number greater than or equal to 5 or both

$$= \{2, 4, 5, 6\}$$

$$P(A \cup B) = \frac{4}{6} = 0.\overline{6}$$

$(A \cup C)$ = Getting an even number or a number less than or equal to 3 or both

$$= \{1, 2, 3, 4, 6\}$$

$$P(A \cup C) = \frac{5}{6} = 0.8\overline{3}$$

$(B \cup C)$ = Getting a number that is at most 3 or at least 5 or both

$$= \{1, 2, 3, 5, 6\}$$

$$P(B \cup C) = \frac{5}{6} = 0.8\overline{3}$$

- **Intersection:** $(A \cap B)$ = Getting an even number that is at least 5 = $\{6\}$

$$P(A \cap B) = \frac{1}{6} = 0.1\overline{6}$$

$(A \cap C)$ = Getting an even number that is at most 3 = $\{2\}$

$$P(A \cap C) = \frac{1}{6} = 0.1\overline{6}$$

$(B \cap C)$ = Getting a number that is at most 3 and at least 5 = $\{ \}$

$$P(B \cap C) = \frac{0}{6} = 0.000$$

In other words, B and C are disjoint or mutually exclusive events.

- **Conditional event:** $(A \mid C)$ = Getting an even number given that the number is at most 3 = $\{2\}$

$$P(A \mid C) = \frac{1}{3} = 0.\overline{3}$$

$(A \mid B)$ = Getting an even number given that the number is at least 5 = $\{6\}$

$$P(A \mid B) = \frac{1}{2} = 0.5$$

$(B \mid C)$ = Getting at least 5 given that the number is at most 3 = $\varnothing$

$$P(B \mid C) = 0$$

Note: Since the conditional probability of getting an even number given it is at most 3 is not the same as the probability of getting an even number, what does that tell us about the independence of these events? (See the next page for more on independence).

More Probability Rules

- **Complement:** The probability of the complement of an event A is given by

$$P(A') = 1 - P(A)$$

- **Union** (addition rule): The probability of the union of two events A and B is given by

$$P(A \cup B) = P(A) + P(B) - P(A \cap B)$$

If the events A and B are disjoint, then $P(A \cap B) = 0$, and

$$P(A \cup B) = P(A) + P(B)$$

> **To A or Not to A?**
> Think about it: If something is either A or not A, then everything has to be either A or not, i.e. $P(A \cup A' = 1)$.

- **Intersection** (multiplication rule): For events A and B defined in a sample space S,

$$P(A \cap B) = P(A) \cdot P(B \mid A) = P(B) \cdot P(A \mid B)$$

- **Conditional probabilities (aka Bayes' Theorem):** The probability of A given B is

$$P(A \mid B) = \frac{P(A \cap B)}{P(B)}$$

- **Independence:** Two events A and B are independent if and only if

$$P(A \mid B) = P(A) \text{ and } P(B \mid A) = P(B)$$

In other words, two events A and B are independent if and only if

$$P(A \cap B) = P(A) \cdot P(B)$$

> $P(A \mid B) = P(A)$ if and only if $P(B \mid A) = P(B)$, so it is only necessary to prove one in order to prove independence.

Example 3: Imagine that you shuffle a standard deck of 52 cards and draw a card at random.

Let

D = diamond	C = club
H = heart	S = spade
J = jack	Q = queen
K = king	1 = ace

Then $S = \{D1,..., D10, DJ, DQ, DK, C1,..., C10, CJ, CQ, CK, H1,..., H10, HJ, HQ, HK, S1,..., S10, SJ, SQ, SK\}$

Suppose we define the following events:
A = Getting an ace = $\{D1, C1, H1, S1\}$
B = Getting a diamond = $\{D1,..., D10, DJ, DQ, DK\}$
C = Getting a club = $\{C1, ...C10, CJ, CQ, CK\}$

Then

- $P(A) = \dfrac{4}{52}$, $P(B) = \dfrac{13}{52}$, $P(C) = \dfrac{13}{52}$

- A' = Getting a non-ace card

$$P(A') = 1 - P(A) = 1 - \frac{4}{52} = \frac{48}{52}$$

- B' = Getting a non-diamond card

$$P(B') = 1 - P(B) = 1 - \frac{13}{52} = \frac{39}{52}$$

- $(A \cap B)$ = Getting an ace of diamonds = {D1}

$$P(A \cap B) = \frac{1}{52}$$

Events A and B are not disjoint because an ace of diamonds ($D1$) is a common outcome for both events.

- $(B \cap C)$ = Getting a card that is a club and a diamond = { }

$$P(B \cap C) = 0$$

The events B and C are disjoint, because no outcome is common to them. Each card in a deck belongs to only one suit.

- $(A \cup B)$ = Getting an ace or a diamond or both
$\{D1,..., D10, DJ, DQ, DK, C1, H1, S1\}$

$$P(A \cup B) = \frac{16}{52}$$

Alternatively,

$$P(A \cup B) = P(A) + P(B) - P(A \cap B)$$

$$= \frac{4}{52} + \frac{13}{52} - \frac{1}{52}$$

$$= \frac{16}{52}$$

- $P(B \cup C)$ = Getting a diamond or a club or both
$= \{D1,..., D10, DJ, DQ, DK, C1,..., C10, CJ, CQ, CK\}$

$$P(B \cup C) = \frac{26}{52}$$

Alternatively, because B and C are disjoint, $P(B \cap C) = 0$. Therefore,

$$P(B \cup C) = P(B) + P(C)$$

$$= \frac{13}{52} + \frac{13}{52}$$

$$= \frac{26}{52}$$

- $(A \mid B)$ = Getting an ace given that a diamond has been drawn = $\{D1\}$

$$P(A \mid B) = \frac{1}{13}$$

Alternatively,

$$P(A \mid B) = \frac{P(A \cap B)}{P(B)} = \frac{1/52}{13/52} = \frac{1}{13}$$

Note that $P(A \mid B) = P(A)$. Therefore, events A and B are independent.

Example 4: 75% of people who purchase hair dryers are female. Of these female purchasers of hair dryers, 30% are over 50 years old. What is the probability that a randomly selected hair dryer purchaser is a female over 50 years old?

Solution: Let us define the events as follows:

W = The purchaser of a hair dryer is a female.
F = The purchaser of a hair dryer is over 50 years old.

It is known that $P(W) = 0.75$ and $P(F \mid W) = 0.30$.

Thus,

$$P(W \cap F) = P(F \mid W) \cdot P(W) = 0.30(0.75) = 0.225$$

There is a 22.5% chance that a randomly selected hair dryer purchaser is a female over 50 years old.

An alternative method for many probability questions is to make a tree diagram of the different probabilities. All branches of the tree should sum to 1. Once the numbers are filled in along the branches, multiply each number along to branch to reach the conditional probability you need. You are looking for females (0.75) who are over 50 (0.30). Thus, $0.75 \times 0.30 = 0.225$. See the following diagram.

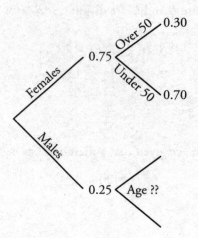

Example 5: An insurance agent knows that 70% of her customers carry adequate collision coverage. She also knows that of those who carry adequate coverage, 5% have been involved in accidents, and of those who do not carry adequate coverage, 12% have been involved in accidents. If one of her clients is involved in an auto accident, then what is the probability that the client does not have adequate collision coverage?

Solution: Let us define events as follows:

A = Client carries adequate coverage
B = Client is involved in an auto accident

We need to find $P(A' \mid B)$, which equals $\dfrac{P(A' \cap B)}{P(B)}$.

It is known that

> $P(A)$ = Probability that a client carries adequate coverage = 0.70; therefore,
> $P(A') = 1 - 0.70 = 0.30$
> $P(B \mid A)$ = Probability that a client carrying adequate coverage is involved in an auto accident = 0.05
> $P(B \mid A')$ = Probability that a client without enough coverage is involved in an auto accident = 0.12

First, let's work out the numerator. $P(A' \cap B)$, the probability that a client is not carrying enough insurance and gets involved in an auto accident.

$$P(A' \cap B) = P(B \mid A') \cdot P(A')$$

$$= 0.12(0.30)$$

$$= 0.036$$

Next, the denominator is the probability that a randomly selected client is involved in an auto accident.

$$P(B) = P(B \cap A) + P(B \cap A') = P(B \mid A) \cdot P(A) + P(B \mid A') \cdot P(A')$$

$$= 0.05(0.70) + 0.12(1 - 0.70)$$

$$= 0.071$$

Therefore,

$$P(A' \mid B) = \frac{P(A' \cap B)}{P(B)} = \frac{0.036}{0.071} \approx 0.507$$

> **Quick Tip**
> You can also sketch a tree diagram for this problem!

There is a 50.7% chance that this client does not carry adequate insurance.

An alternative method is to make a table of the possible combinations and fill in the numbers as we can. We are given that

In accident	Adequate coverage		Total
	Yes	No	
Yes	0.05 • 0.70	0.12 • ???	
No			
Total	0.70		1.00

$1.00 - 0.70 = 0.30$, so

In accident	Adequate coverage		Total
	Yes	No	
Yes	0.05 • 0.70	0.12 • 0.30	
No			
Total	0.70	0.30	

Next, do the multiplication to get

In accident	Adequate coverage		Total
	Yes	No	
Yes	0.035	0.036	
No			
Total	0.70	0.30	

Next, add across the accident–yes row, subtract in the columns, and get

	Adequate coverage		Total
In accident	Yes	No	
Yes	0.035	0.036	0.071
No	0.665	0.264	0.929
Total	0.70	0.30	1

The question asked the probability that a client does not have adequate coverage, given that he or she was in an accident. This is $0.036/0.071 = 0.507$.

○

Which of the following events are independent?

$P(A) = 0.7$
$P(B) = 0.2$
$P(C) = 0.1$
$P(B|A) = 0.5$
$P(B|C) = 0.2$
$P(A \cap C) = 0.05$

A) A and B only
B) A and C only
C) A, B and C
D) B and C only
E) None are Independent

Here's How to Crack It

For two events, E and F, to be independent, $P(E) = P(E|F)$ and $P(F) = P(F|E)$. In other words, knowing whether E occurred should not influence the probability of F occurring, and visa versa.

We're not given all the conditional probabilities, but we can calculate them using the information we have.

First, start off with the conditional probabilities we do have. $P(B|A) = 0.5$, which is not equal to $P(B)$, therefore A and B are not independent. This allows us to cross off answers (A) and (C).

Next, $P(B|C) = 0.2 = P(B)$, so B and C are independent, eliminating (B) and (E). The correct answer must be (D).

There is no need to continue, but to see why A and C are not independent, recall $P(A|C) = \dfrac{P(A \cap C)}{P(C)} = \dfrac{0.05}{0.1}$. Since $P(A|C)$ does not equal $P(A)$, A and C are not independent.

○

Example 6: The local Chamber of Commerce conducted a survey of 1,000 randomly selected shoppers at a mall. For all shoppers, the gender of the shopper and the items they were shopping for were recorded. The data collected is summarized in the following table:

Gender	Shopping For			
	Clothing	**Shoes**	**Other**	**Total**
Male	75	25	150	250
Female	350	230	170	750
Total	425	255	320	1,000

If a shopper is selected at random from this mall,

(a) What is the probability that the shopper is a female?
(b) What is the probability that the shopper is shopping for shoes?
(c) What is the probability that the shopper is a female shopping for shoes?
(d) What is the probability that the shopper is shopping for shoes given that the shopper is a female?
(e) Are the events "female" and "shopping for shoes" disjoint?
(f) Are the events "female" and "shopping for shoes" independent?

Probability =

$$\frac{\text{What we're interested in}}{\text{Possible outcomes for our population}}$$

Solution:

(a) What is the probability that the shopper is a female?

$$P = P(\text{Female}) = \frac{750}{1,000} = 0.75$$

(b) What is the probability that the shopper is shopping for shoes?

$$P = P(\text{Shopping for shoes}) = \frac{255}{1,000} = 0.255$$

(c) What is the probability that the shopper is a female shopping for shoes?

$$P = P(\text{Female} \cap \text{Shopping for shoes}) = \frac{230}{1,000} = 0.23$$

(d) What is the probability that the shopper is shopping for shoes given that the shopper is a female?

$$P = P(\text{Shopping for shoes} \mid \text{Female}) =$$

$$\frac{P(\text{Shopping for shoes} \cap \text{Female})}{P(\text{Female})} = \frac{0.23}{0.75}$$

$$\approx 0.3067$$

(e) Are the events "female" and "shopping for shoes" disjoint?
There are 230 females shopping for shoes, or
$P = P(\text{Female} \cap \text{Shopping for shoes}) = 0.23 \neq 0$. Therefore, the events
"female" and "shopping for shoes" are not disjoint.

(f) Are the events "female" and "shopping for shoes" independent?
$P = P(\text{Shopping for shoes} \mid \text{Female}) \approx 0.3067$ and $P(\text{Shopping for shoes}) = 0.255$, which means $P(\text{Shopping for shoes} \mid \text{Female}) \neq P(\text{Shopping for shoes})$.
Therefore, the events "female" and "shopping for shoes" are not independent.

RANDOM VARIABLES AND THEIR PROBABILITY DISTRIBUTIONS

A **variable** is a quantity whose value varies from subject to subject. Examples include:

*   Height (which varies from person to person)
*   The number of email messages you receive per day (which changes from day to day)
*   The number of patients examined by a doctor per day (which changes from day to day)
*   The number of home runs hit in a season by members of a baseball team (which varies from player to player)
*   The hair colors of students in a class (which varies from student to student)
*   The altitude of an airplane in flight (which varies from minute to minute)

A **probability experiment** is an experiment whose possible outcomes may be known but whose exact outcome is a random event and cannot be predicted with certainty in advance. If the outcome of a probability experiment takes a numerical value, then the outcome is a **random variable**. Random variables are usually denoted using capital letters, such as X or Y. Sometimes two or more variables are denoted using the same letter but different subscripts, such as X_1 and X_2. Let us consider random variables with numeric outcomes.

There are two types of random variables, discrete and continuous:

*   A **discrete random variable** is a quantitative variable that takes a countable number of values. The following are all discrete random variables:
    o   the number of email messages received per day
    o   the number of home runs per batter
    o   the number of red blood cells per sample of blood
    o   the number of students present in class per day
    o   the number of customers served by a bank teller per hour

> Can you have part of a unit of your variable? If not, it's discrete!
>
> For example, can you send .67 of an email?

Note that between any two possible values of a discrete random variable, there is a countable number of possible values. You may receive 10 email messages a day or 12 messages a day, but you can never receive 12.5 messages in one day, or 12.6324 messages.

- A **continuous random variable** is a quantitative variable that can take all the possible values in a given range. A person's weight is a good example. A person can weigh 150 pounds or 155 pounds or any weight between those two, including 151.5 pounds or 153.23487 pounds. Other examples of continuous random values are:
  - ○ the altitude of a plane
  - ○ the amount of rainfall in a city per day
  - ○ the amount of gasoline pumped into a car's gas tank
  - ○ the weight of a newborn baby
  - ○ the amount of water flowing through a dam per hour

THE PROBABILITY DISTRIBUTIONS OF DISCRETE RANDOM VARIABLES

A **probability distribution of a discrete random variable** or a **discrete probability distribution** is a table, list, graph, or formula giving all possible values taken by a random variable and their corresponding probabilities.

Let X be a random variable taking values x_1, x_2,..., x_n with respective probabilities $P(x_1)$, $P(x_2)$,..., $P(x_n)$. Then $\{(x_1, P(x_1)), (x_2, P(x_2)),..., (x_n, P(x_n))\}$ gives a valid probability distribution if:

- $0 \leq P(x_i) \leq 1$ for all i = 1, 2,..., n, and

- $\sum_{i=1}^{n} P(x_i) = 1$

A probability distribution is often given as a table. See the following.

Random Variable X	Probability $P(X = xi)$
x_1	$P(x_1)$
x_2	$P(x_2)$
x_3	$P(x_3)$
⋮	⋮
x_n	$P(x_n)$

Table 2: Probability distribution of a discrete random variable

Mean of a Discrete Random Variable

The mean (μ) of a discrete random variable X is also known as the **expected value**. It is denoted by $E(X)$ and is computed by multiplying each value of the random variable by its probability and then adding over the sample space.

The mean annual income for your town is $65,000 a year. You know absolutely nothing about Mr. X except that he lives in your town. What is your best guess for his annual income (i.e., what do you expect it to be)?

$$\mu_x = E(X) = \sum_{i=1}^{n} x_i P(x_i)$$

Variance of a Discrete Random Variable

The variance of a discrete random variable is defined as the sum of the product of squared deviations of the values of the variable from the mean and the corresponding probabilities:

$$\sigma^2 = \sum_{i=1}^{n} (x_i - \mu)^2 P(x_i)$$

Remember that standard deviation is simply the square root of variance.

Standard deviation is our expected value for how much any given data point will vary from the mean.

Example 7: Sophia was recently promoted to assistant manager at a small women's clothing store. One of her duties is to fill out order forms for women's shirts, which come in sizes 6, 7, 8, 9, 10, 11, and 12. She would like to determine how many shirts of each size to order. At first, she thought of ordering exactly the same number of shirts from each of the available sizes, but then she decided against doing that, because there might be a greater demand for certain sizes than for others. She looked up sales receipts from the past three months and summarized the information as follows:

Shirt Size	6	7	8	9	10	11	12
Number Sold	85	122	138	154	177	133	92

(a) Prepare a probability distribution of the number of shirts sold for each size.

(b) What is the probability that a randomly selected customer will request a shirt of size at least 11?

(c) Compute the expected shirt size of a random shopper and the standard deviation of the shirt size.

(d) If Sophia plans to order a total of 1,000 shirts, how many shirts of size 8 should she order?

Solution: (a) The total number of shirts sold is 901. Using this information, we can compute the probability of each shirt size being sold. For example, the probability of selling size 6 is 85/901 ≈ 0.09. The random variable here (X) is the shirt size, and it takes values 6, 7, 8, 9, 10, 11, and 12. Both Table 3 and the graph in Figure 8 give the probability distribution of the number of shirts sold for each size.

Shirt Size	P(x)
6	0.09
7	0.14
8	0.15
9	0.17
10	0.20
11	0.15
12	0.10

Table 3: Probability distribution of shirt size

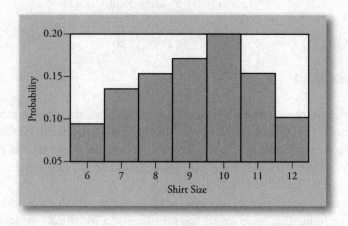

Figure 8: Probability distribution of shirt size

This probability distribution shows that 9% of the customers bought size 6 shirts, 14% bought size 7 shirts, and so on.

(b) P(A customer will request a shirt of size at least 11)

$\quad = P$(Shirt size = 11 or 12)

$\quad = P$(Shirt size = 11) + P(Shirt size = 12)

$\quad = 0.15 + 0.10$

$\quad = 0.25$

(c) The expected shirt size:

$\mu = E(x) = 6(0.09) + 7(0.14) + 8(0.15) + 9(0.17) + 10(0.20) + 11(0.15) + 12(0.10) = 9.1$

The standard deviation of shirt size:

$$\sigma = \sqrt{(6 - 9.1)^2(0.09) + (7 - 9.1)^2(0.14) + \ldots + (12 - 9.1)^2(0.10)}$$

$$= \sqrt{3.21} \approx 1.79$$

> **Defying Expectations**
> Note that the expected shirt size is a decimal, meaning it is a number you cannot "expect" to get on a single trial. That's fine. Expected value is just another term for mean, and it represents the average shirt size in the long run.

(d) From the probability distribution, $P(\text{Shirt size} = 8) = 0.15$.
Therefore, she needs to order $1{,}000(0.15) = 150$ shirts of size 8.

Combinations

A **combination** is the number of ways r items can be selected out of n items if the order of selection is *not* important. It is denoted by $\binom{n}{r}$, which reads as "n choose r," and is computed as

$$\binom{n}{r} = \frac{n!}{r!(n-r)!}$$

For any integer $n \geq 0$, $n!$ is read as "n factorial" and is computed as

$$n! = n(n-1)(n-2)(n-3)\ldots(3)(2)(1)$$

For example, $3! = (3)(2)(1) = 6$ and $5! = (5)(4)(3)(2)(1) = 120$

Note that $0! = 1$ and $1! = 1$

Example 8: A teacher wants to choose two students to represent the class in a competition. She finds that there are five students in the class who meet the eligibility criteria: Calvin, Sung, Jan, Becky, and Antoine. Because all five are eligible, she decides to select two at random. In how many different ways can this teacher select two students out of five students?

Solution: This is a combination problem because the order in which two students get selected does not matter. The following list gives all the possible ways in which two students can be selected from Calvin, Sung, Jan, Becky, and Antoine. Note that, because the order of selection is immaterial, selecting Calvin and Sung is the same as selecting Sung and Calvin.

1. Calvin and Sung
2. Calvin and Jan
3. Calvin and Becky
4. Calvin and Antoine
5. Sung and Jan
6. Sung and Becky
7. Sung and Antoine
8. Jan and Becky
9. Jan and Antoine
10. Becky and Antoine

There are 10 different ways to select two students out of five when the order of selection is not important. Using the combination function, we can find this number without having to list all the possibilities. The combination is as follows: $\binom{5}{2} = \frac{5!}{2!(5-2)!} = \frac{120}{2(6)} = 10$.

TI-83 or TI-84:
- Type the number 5 in the window
- Choose **MATH → PRB → 3:nCr**
- Type the number 2. This will result in 5 nCr 2
- Press **ENTER**

Example 9: In a dart throwing game, balloons are numbered 1 to 10 as shown:

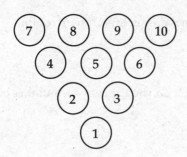

Figure 9

Suppose that following the first three dart throws, three balloons, arbitrarily located, are popped. In how many combinations can the remaining balloons be arranged after the first three are popped?

Solution: The combination is as follows:

$$\binom{10}{7} = \frac{10!}{7! \times 3!} = 120$$

Remember!

$P(x \text{ successes in } n \text{ trials}) = \binom{n}{x} p^x (1-p)^{n-x}$

Why do we use combinations? We do not care *when* in the sequence our x successes occur! We just want there to be x successes out of n trials. There are $\binom{n}{x}$ ways to get x out of n successes.

p^x is the probability of getting x successes. If the probability of getting one success is p, then the probability of getting two successes is $p \times p$, or p^2…etc.

Similarly, $(1-p)$ must be the probability of *not* getting a success. The probability of getting one failure is $(1-p)$, so the probability of getting two failures is $(1-p) \times (1-p)$ or $(1-p)^2$.

$P(A \text{ and } B) = P(A) \times P(B)$ if A and B are mutually exclusive.

So:
$P(x \text{ successes and } n - x \text{ failures}) = P(x \text{ successes}) \times P(n - x \text{ failures})$ or $p^x(1-p)^{n-x}$

Binomial Distribution

One example of a distribution of discrete random variables is the binomial distribution. A binomial distribution occurs in an experiment that possesses the following properties:

- There are n repeated trials of a number fixed in advance.
- Each trial has two possible outcomes, in general known as "success" and "failure."
- All trials are identical and independent, thus the probability for success remains the same for each trial.

The binomial variable X:

$$X = \text{the number of successes in } n \text{ trials}$$

$$= 0, 1, 2, \ldots, n$$

$$P(X = x) = \binom{n}{x} p^x (1-p)^{n-x}$$

where $p = P(\text{success in a given trial})$.

Mean of a binomial random variable (how many times do you expect to succeed?):

$$\mu = np$$

Variance of a binomial random variable (how much do you expect your number of successes to vary from sample to sample?):

$$\sigma^2 = np(1-p)$$

Some examples of binomial random variables:

- A quality control inspector takes a random sample of 20 items from a large lot, inspects each item, classifies each as defective or nondefective, and counts the number of defective items in the sample.
- A telephone survey asks 400 area residents, selected at random, whether they support the new gasoline tax increase. The answers are recorded as "yes" or "no." The number of persons answering "yes" is counted.
- A random sample of families is taken, and for each family with three children, the number of girls out of the three children is recorded.
- A certain medical procedure is performed on 15 patients who are not related to each other. The number of successful procedures is counted.
- A homeowner buys 20 azalea plants from a nursery. The number of plants that survive at the end of the year is counted.

The shape of the binomial distribution depends on the values of n and p. The distribution spreads from 0 to n. Figures 10–12 show different binomial distributions with $n = 10$.

For $n = 10$ and $p = 0.2$, the binomial distribution is right-skewed with mean $\mu = 10(0.2) = 2$. In general, as p gets closer to 0, the binomial distribution becomes more right-skewed. See Figure 10.

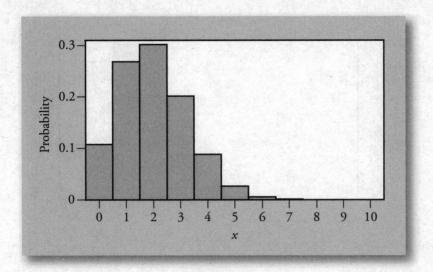

Figure 10: Binomial distribution with n = 10 and p = 0.2

For p = 0.5, the binomial distribution is symmetric with mean μ = 10(0.5) = 5. See Figure 11.

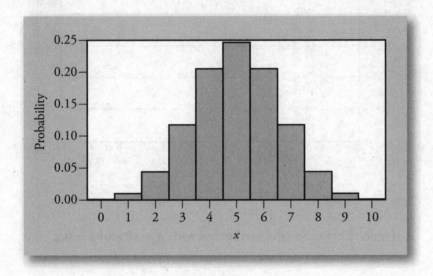

Figure 11: Binomial distribution with n = 10 and p = 0.5

For p = 0.8, the binomial distribution is left-skewed with mean μ = 10(0.8) = 8. In general, as p gets closer to 1, the binomial distribution becomes more left-skewed. See Figure 12.

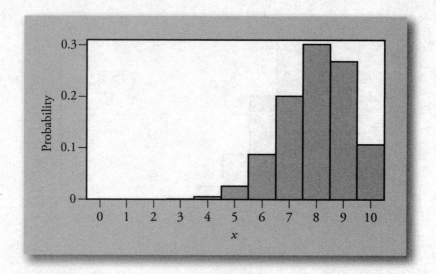

Figure 12: Binomial distribution with *n* = 10 and *p* = 0.8

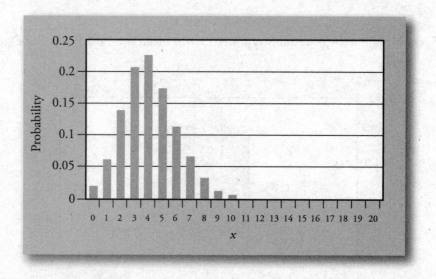

Figure 13: Binomial distribution with *n* = 20 and *p* = 0.2

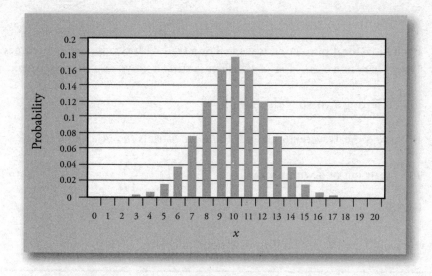

Figure 14: Binomial distribution with *n* = 20 and *p* = 0.5

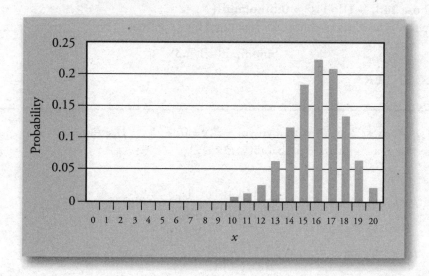

Figure 15: Binomial distribution with *n* = 20 and *p* = 0.8

Example 10: Suppose a family eats frequently at a nearby fast-food restaurant. There are three possible toys (a car, a top, or a yo-yo) given with the kids' meals. The toys are placed in the meal bags at random. Suppose this family buys a random kids' meal at this restaurant on four different days, and the chance of receiving any of the toys is the same.

(a) What is the probability that exactly three out of four meals will come with a yo-yo?

(b) What is the probability that at most two meals will come with a yo-yo?

(c) What is the probability of getting at least three yo-yos with four meals purchased?

(d) What is the expected number of yo-yos when four meals are purchased?

(e) Compute the standard deviation of the number of yo-yos when four meals are purchased.

Solution:

(a) Each kids' meal purchased is viewed as a trial with two possible outcomes, "yo-yo" or "no yo-yo." Let us consider getting a yo-yo as a success. Then:

$$p = P(\text{Getting a yo-yo with a meal}) = \frac{1}{3}$$

Because 4 meals were purchased, there are 4 trials ($n = 4$). Then:

$$P(3 \text{ meals out of 4 with a yo-yo}) = \binom{4}{3}\left(\frac{1}{3}\right)^3\left(1 - \frac{1}{3}\right)^{4-3} \approx 4(0.037)(0.667) \approx$$

0.0988.

This is how you would get the probability with your calculator:

TI-83 or TI-84:
- Choose **2nd → DISTR → 0:binompdf(**
- Enter n, p, x values in that order separated by a commas

$$\text{binompdf}(4,1/3,3)$$

- Press **ENTER**

(b) $P(\text{At most 2 meals with a yo-yo}) = P(x = 0) + P(x = 1) + P(x = 2)$
This is a cumulative probability, $P(x \leq 2)$:

$$P(\text{No yo-yo}) = P(x = 0) = \binom{4}{0}\left(\frac{1}{3}\right)^0\left(1 - \frac{1}{3}\right)^{4-0} \approx 0.1975$$

$$P(\text{One yo-yo}) = P(x = 1) = \binom{4}{1}\left(\frac{1}{3}\right)^1\left(1 - \frac{1}{3}\right)^{4-1} \approx 0.3951$$

$$P(\text{Two yo-yos}) \; P(x = 2) = \binom{4}{2}\left(\frac{1}{3}\right)^2\left(1 - \frac{1}{3}\right)^{4-2} \approx 0.2963$$

$$P(\text{At most 2 meals with a yo-yo}) = P(x = 0) + P(x = 1) + P(x = 2)$$
$$\approx 0.1975 + 0.3951 + 0.2963$$
$$= 0.8889$$

Here's how you'd get this cumulative probability with your calculator:

TI-83 or TI-84:
- Choose **2nd → DISTR → A:binomcdf(**
- Enter n, p, x values in that order, separated by commas

$$\text{binomcdf }(4,1/3,2)$$

- Press **ENTER**

(c) $P(\text{At least 3 meals with a yo-yo}) = P(x = 3) + P(x = 4)$

$$\approx 0.0988 + \binom{4}{4}\left(\frac{1}{3}\right)^4\left(1 - \frac{1}{3}\right)^{4-4}$$

$$= 0.0988 + 1\left(\frac{1}{3}\right)^4$$

$$\approx 0.0988 + 0.0123$$

$$= 0.1111$$

> **Calculator Shortcut**
> Many formulas have already been preset into your calculator. If you remember how to apply them appropriately, you can save significant time on exam day. For example, to solve this question, you could enter the following:
>
> 1 − binomcdf(4,1/3,3)

(d) $\mu_x = np = 4\left(\frac{1}{3}\right) = \frac{4}{3} = 1.33$

On the average, we expect to get 1.33 yo-yos when four meals are purchased.

(e) Standard deviation is $\sigma = \sqrt{np(1-p)} = \sqrt{4\left(\frac{1}{3}\right)\left(1 - \frac{1}{3}\right)} \approx 0.9428$

Simulating a Binomial Distribution

Let's simulate the situation in the previous example using a six-sided die. Designate the outcomes as follows:

- Getting a 1 or 2 on the die means getting a yo-yo with the meal. The probability of getting a number 1 or 2 is $\frac{2}{6} = \frac{1}{3}$.

- Getting one of the remaining numbers (3, 4, 5, or 6) means getting a different toy (not a yo-yo) with the meal. The probability of getting a 3, 4, 5, or 6 is $\frac{4}{6} = \frac{2}{3}$.

Because the family purchases four meals, roll the die four times. Each roll represents a meal purchased. Based on the outcome for each roll, determine the toy received with the meal using the above scheme. For example, imagine that the first set of four rolls resulted in the numbers

(4, 3, 2, 6). This means that only the third meal came with a yo-yo and the remaining three meals came with other toys. So from this set of four meals purchased, the family got only one yo-yo. Repeat this procedure (that of rolling the die four times and noting the number of yo-yos received out of four meals) 100 times. The results of one such simulation are listed below:

1, 1, 2, 1, 1, 1, 2, 1, 1, 1, 1, 2, 0, 0, 1, 0, 1, 1, 2, 1, 2, 0, 3, 1, 0,

0, 1, 3, 4, 1, 2, 1, 2, 2, 1, 0, 1, 1, 1, 0, 2, 2, 2, 0, 0, 1, 0, 3, 2, 2,

0, 1, 0, 1, 2, 1, 2, 1, 1, 0, 1, 1, 2, 1, 1, 2, 2, 3, 0, 2, 1, 2, 3, 2, 1,

1, 2, 0, 1, 3, 2, 1, 1, 1, 1, 1, 2, 1, 2, 2, 2, 2, 3, 1, 2, 2, 1, 1, 2, 1

This data shows that the first set of four meals resulted in getting one yo-yo, the second also resulted in one, the third resulted in two, and so on. The outcome zero means that the family got no yo-yos with the purchase of four meals; the number 4 means the family got a yo-yo with each of the four meals purchased. Now summarize the data as shown in Table 4:

Q: If we did this infinitely many times (a rather large simulation), do you think the probabilities would get closer or further away from the true probabilities that we calculated in the previous section? (Turn the page for the answer.)

Number of Meals out of 4 with a Yo-Yo	Simulated Count
0	16
1	45
2	31
3	7
4	1
Total	100

Table 4: Frequency distribution of number of meals with a yo-yo

Using these simulated results, we can estimate the probabilities and the expected value:

(a) P(Getting 3 meals with a yo-yo) = 7 out of 100 = 0.07
(b) P(Getting at most 2 meals with a yo-yo)
= P(0, 1, or 2 meals with a yo-yo)
= 92 out of 100
= 0.92
(c) P(Getting at least 3 meals with a yo-yo)
= P(3 or 4 meals with a yo-yo)
= 8 out of 100
= 0.08

(d) Expected number of yo-yos per 4 meals
= [0(16) + 1(45) + 2(31) + 3(7) + 4(1)]/100
= 132/100
= 1.32

Note that these numbers do not match the calculations in the previous section exactly, though they are close.

Geometric Distribution

Another example of a distribution of discrete random variables is the geometric distribution. The geometric distribution occurs in an experiment where repeated trials possess the following properties:

- There are n repeated trials.
- Each trial has two possible outcomes, in general known as "success" and "failure."
- Trials are repeated until a predetermined number of successes is reached.
- All trials are identical and independent; thus the probability for success remains the same for each trial.

The geometric random variable X:

X = the number of trials required to obtain the first success = 0, 1, 2, …

$P(x$ trials needed until the first success is observed$) = (1 - p)^{x-1}p$

Mean of the geometric random variable:

$$\mu = E(X) = \frac{1}{p}$$

Variance of the geometric random variable:

$$\sigma^2 = Var(X) = \frac{1-p}{p^2}$$

Some examples of the geometric random variable:

- A worker opening oysters to look for pearls counts the number of oysters she has to open until she finds the first pearl.
- A supervisor at the end of an assembly line counts the number of nondefective items produced until he finds the first defective one.
- An electrician inspecting cable one yard at a time for defects counts the number of yards she inspects before she finds a defect.

Example 11: Let's go back to the example of the fast food restaurant. Again, there are three possible toys (a car, a top, a yo-yo) given with the kids' meals, and the toys are placed in the meal bags at random. Suppose the kid in the family has his heart set on getting a yo-yo, so the family will buy him kids' meals until they get one with a yo-yo in it.

> You can think about the mean of a geometric random variable intuitively. If p gets bigger (i.e. the event is more likely), the mean number of trials until the first success goes down. If something happens often, it's very unlikely that you'll have to wait very long for it to occur.

(a) Find the probability that the family will get its first yo-yo with the third meal.

(b) Find the probability that the family will get its first yo-yo with the fifth meal.

(c) What is the expected number of meals needed to get a yo-yo?

(d) Find the probability that it will take five or fewer meals for the family to get its first yo-yo.

Solution: Each kid's meal purchased is viewed as a trial with two possible outcomes, "yo-yo" or "no yo-yo." Let us consider getting a yo-yo as a success. So,

$$p = P(\text{Getting a yo-yo with a meal}) = \frac{1}{3}$$

(a) $P(\text{Having to purchase exactly 3 meals before getting a yo-yo})$

$= P(\text{No yo-yo in first 2 meals})P(\text{Yo-yo with the 3rd meal})$

$= (1 - p)(1 - p)p$

$= (1 - p)^2 p$

$= \left(1 - \frac{1}{3}\right)^2 \left(\frac{1}{3}\right)$

≈ 0.148

TI-83 or TI-84:
- Choose **2nd → DISTR → D:geometpdf(**
- Enter p, x values in that order separated by a comma

$$\text{geometpdf } (1/3, 3)$$

- Press **ENTER**

(b) $P(\text{Having to purchase exactly 5 meals before getting a yo-yo})$

$= (1 - p)^4 p$

$= \left(1 - \frac{1}{3}\right)^4 \left(\frac{1}{3}\right)$

≈ 0.0658

A: They would get closer as we did more meal simulations. As we increase the number of simulations, any odd patterns—like getting a lot of simulations with 4/4 yo-yos—will be less likely to occur.

(c) The expected number of meals to get a yo-yo $= \mu_x = \dfrac{1}{p} = \dfrac{1}{\frac{1}{3}} = 3$

(d) $P(\text{Purchasing 5 or fewer meals to get a yo-yo})$

Without using TI-83/84 functions, this calculation will be tedious. Whereas geometpdf calculates the probability of taking x number of trials to obtain the first success, geometcdf calculates the probability of taking x or *fewer* trials.

Thus, $P(\text{Purchasing 5 or fewer meals to get a yo-yo}) = \text{geometcdf}(1/3, 5) \approx 0.86831$.

Simulating a Geometric Distribution

Consider the earlier example of purchasing kids' meals. Let's simulate the situation using a six-sided die. Designate the outcomes as follows:

- Getting a 1 and 2 on the die means getting a yo-yo with the meal. The probability of getting a number 1 or 2 is $\frac{2}{6} = \frac{1}{3}$.

- Getting one of the remaining numbers (3, 4, 5, or 6) means getting a different toy (not a yo-yo) with the meal. The probability of getting a 3, 4, 5, or 6 is $\frac{4}{6} = \frac{2}{3}$.

Because the family will purchase meals until they get a yo-yo, roll the die until the number 1 or 2 shows. Each roll represents a meal purchased. Count the number of rolls it takes to get number 1 or 2. For example, the first set of rolls resulted in faces with numbers (4, 3, 6, 5, 6, 2). This means that the sixth meal came with a yo-yo, whereas the first five meals came with different (non-yo-yo) toys. So in this set, the family had to purchase six meals to get one yo-yo. Suppose the next set of rolls resulted in (5, 5, 1). In this case, the family had to purchase only three meals to get a yo-yo. Roll 100 of these sets. From each set, note the number of meals the family had to purchase to get a yo-yo. The results of one such simulation are listed below:

6, 3, 2, 1, 8, 1, 3, 3, 2, 2, 2, 1, 3, 1, 2, 1, 7, 2, 9, 1, 1, 2, 2, 2, 7,

6, 2, 1, 1, 2, 1, 3, 2, 1, 1, 4, 5, 1, 2, 5, 1, 2, 5, 5, 2, 1, 2, 3, 2, 2,

3, 2, 2, 1, 1, 2, 1, 3, 2, 4, 3, 1, 3, 2, 1, 4, 1, 2, 2, 1, 3, 2, 2, 1, 2,

3, 3, 4, 7, 1, 1, 3, 2, 1, 3, 4, 3, 3, 4, 1, 2, 1, 2, 1, 1, 1, 1, 2, 1, 1

This shows that the first set resulted in the family's purchasing six meals to get a yo-yo; the second time, it took the family three meals to get a yo-yo; the third time, it took the family just two meals. Now summarize the results as shown in Table 5 and Figure 16:

Number of Meals Purchased Before Getting a Yo-Yo	1	2	3	4	5	6	7	8	9
Simulated Count	34	32	17	6	4	2	3	1	1

Table 5: Frequency distribution of the number of meals purchased before getting a yo-yo

You can see that the geometric distribution is very similar to the binomial distribution for getting 1 success out of *n* trials.

Binomial probability for 1 success out of *n* trials:
$$\binom{n}{p} p^1 (1-p)^{n-1}$$

Geometric probability for *n* trials needed before first success: $p^1(1-p)^{n-1}$

The only difference? Now we do care about the order our success comes in! It must be on the *n*th trial, so we do not need to multiply by $\binom{n}{p}$.

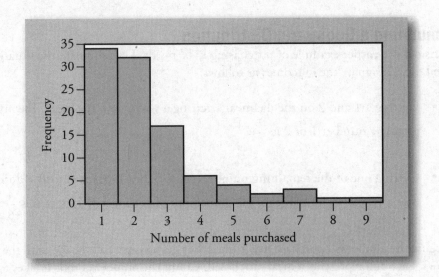

Figure 16: Frequency distribution of the number of meals purchased

Using these simulated results, we can estimate the following probabilities:

(a) P(Having to purchase 3 meals to get a yo-yo) = 17 out of 100 = 0.17.
(b) P(Having to purchase 5 meals to get a yo-yo) = 4 out of 100 = 0.04.
(c) Expected number of meals needed to get a yo-yo
= The mean number of meals needed to get a yo-yo
= [1(34) + 2(32) + 3(17) + 4(6) + 5(4) + 6(2) + 7(3) + 8(1) + 9(1)] / 100 = 2.43

On average, you would have to purchase 2.43 meals before you got a yo-yo.

Note again that these results do not match the calculations in the previous section exactly, though they are close.

Note on Binomial and Geometric Distributions

- In the binomial distribution, the number of trials (number of meals purchased) is fixed, and the number of successes (number of yo-yos received with a set of meals purchased) is a random event.
- In the geometric distribution, the number of successes (you need to get just one yo-yo) is fixed, but the number of trials required to get the success (the number of meals purchased before getting one yo-yo) is a random event.

Example 12: Suppose a large research hospital is interested in recruiting patients with a specific medical condition for an experiment. Overall, four in every 10 patients visiting this hospital suffer from this condition. The physician in charge of the project wants to determine the mean number of patients she needs to examine before she can identify two patients with this condition.

(a) Describe how you would use a table of random numbers to carry out a simulation for determining the number of patients the doctor needs to examine before she can identify two patients with the required condition. Include a description of what each digit will represent in your simulation.

(b) Use the random number table given below to show two runs of your simulation. Do this by marking up the table directly:

56085	31590	73956	27931	49899	68676	54570	95456	43655	46907
96254	15612	29355	61739	89226	18360	69722	46304	61735	10436
96880	54319	72584	10836	77289	74077	74042	27133	53459	66476
77295	82889	96136	17766	46568	31392	14120	64658	14620	90969
65508	98265	82101	29153	72906	68119	48288	16211	96864	90572

(c) Perform 100 runs of your simulation. Find the expected number of patients the doctor needs to interview before she finds two with the required condition.

Solution:

(a) With each patient, there are two possible outcomes: The patient either suffers from the condition or does not suffer from the condition. It is known that four out of every 10 patients visiting this hospital suffer from this condition. This means that the probability that a randomly selected patient will suffer from the condition is

$$\frac{4}{10} = 0.4$$

i.e., $p = 0.4$

Consider one-digit random numbers, 0 through 9. Designate numbers 1, 2, 3, 4 (any four will do) as patients with the condition and numbers 0, 5, 6, 7, 8, 9 (the remaining numbers) as patients without the condition. Start at the beginning of the first line of the random number chart. Each digit represents a patient being examined. Classify each digit as representing either "patient with condition" or "patient without condition." Stop when the second "patient with condition" is identified. Count the number of patients examined until two are found with the condition.

(b) Begin the first simulation in the first row and the second simulation in the second row.

56085 31590 73956 27931 49899 68676 54570 95456

96254 15612 29355 61739 89226 18360 69722 46304

The first run shows that a total of seven patients were examined before two with the condition were identified.

The second run shows that a total of five patients were examined before two with the specific condition were identified.

(c) The frequency distribution of a sample of 100 runs of the above-described simulation is shown in Table 6. Another simulation of 100 runs would result in slightly different counts, of course.

Number of Patients Examined to Find Two with the Condition	Simulated Count
2	39
3	27
4	15
5	7
6	6
7	3
8	1
9	2

Table 6: Frequency distribution of the number of patients examined to find two with the condition

E(Number of patients examined to identify 2 with the condition)
= [2(39) + 3(27) + 4(15) + 5(7) + 6(6) + 7(3) + 8(1) + 9(2)] / 100 = 3.37

On the average, three to four patients will be examined to find two with the required condition.

Recently you learned that that the probability of getting a critical hit on an attack in your favorite game is 15%. You've noticed that you do 20 attacks per fight. You're interested in figuring out how likely it is that you would get 5 critical hits during a fight. Which of the following distributions should you use to answer this question?

(A) a Binomial Distribution with $p = 0.15$ and $n = 20$
(B) a Binomial Distribution with $p = 0.2$ and $n = 15$
(C) a Geometric Distribution with $p = 0.15$
(D) a Geometric Distribution with $p = 0.2$
(E) a cumulative Geometric Distribution with $p = 0.15$

Here's How to Crack It
First, the question only gives you three different distributions to choose from: binomial, geometric, and cumulative geometric. If you can figure out which one to use, you can eliminate a lot of answers. Binomial Distributions tell you how likely it is to get x successes (where

x can vary from 0 to n) in n trials given that your probability of success is p. This sounds like the correct choice. You want to know how likely it is that we get $x = 5$ successes in 20 trials given that $p = 0.15$. Geometric Distributions tell us how likely it is that you'd need to wait at least k trials before you achieved your first success. This could help you answer the question "how likely is it that I'll have my first critical strike on the 5th attack," but that isn't exactly what you want to know. Cumulative Geometric Distributions are very similar to Geometric Distributions, but they help answer the question "how likely is it that I'll have to my first critical strike on or before the 5th attack," which again is similar to but not exactly what you want to know. You can now eliminate (C), (D), and (E). All you need to do is choose the correct parameters. Since p is the probability of success, and the problem tells us that the probability of a critical hit is 15%, (A) is the correct choice.

THE PROBABILITY DISTRIBUTIONS OF CONTINUOUS RANDOM VARIABLES

Recall that a continuous random variable takes all possible values in a given range. For example:

- the distance traveled by a car using one gallon of gas
- waiting time at the checkout counter of a grocery store
- the amount of water released through the Hoover Dam on a given day

Occasionally, when a discrete variable takes lots of values, it is treated as a continuous variable.

The probability distribution of a continuous random variable or **the continuous probability distribution** is a graph or a formula giving all possible values taken by a random variable and the corresponding probabilities. It is also known as the **density function (or probability density function, pdf)**.

Let X be a continuous random variable taking values in the range (a, b). Then:

- The area under the density curve is equal to the probability.
- $P(L < X < U)$ = the area under the curve between L and U, where $a \leq L \leq U \leq b$.
- The total probability under the curve = 1.
- The probability that X takes a specific value is equal to 0, i.e., $P(X = x_0) = 0$.

The reason is that the probability of getting any x exactly is 0. For example, the chance of it raining exactly 3.00233221 inches in Desert City is 0, but the chance of it raining between 3.00 and 3.01 inches is small but measurable.

The cumulative distribution function (CDF) of a random variable X is $P(X < x_0)$ for any $a < x_0 < b$. It is equal to 0 for any $x_0 < a$, and it is equal to 1 for any $x_0 > b$.

> This may seem hard to understand, but remember that there are an infinite number of points on your pdf and all of their probabilities add up to 1. Pretend you only have 10 events whose probabilities add up to 1. If they all had equal probability, then each would have a 0.1 probability. Now imagine there are 100 events (0.01 probability each). Now infinitely many events...the probability goes to 0.

Example 13: The graph in Figure 17 gives the distribution of the yearly amount of rainfall in Desert City.

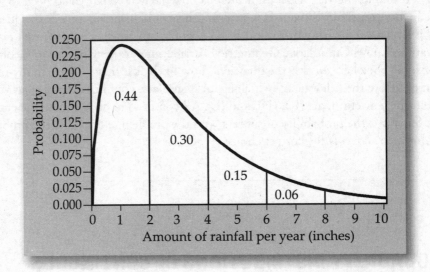

Figure 17: Probability distribution of amount of rainfall per year

In a randomly selected year,

    (a) What is the probability that Desert City got more than eight inches of rain?
    (b) What is the probability that Desert City got between two and six inches of rain?
    (c) What is the probability that Desert City got exactly two inches of rain?
    (d) What is the probability that Desert City got at most six inches of rain?

Solution: Let X = the amount of rain per year in Desert City.

    (a) P(Desert City got more than 8 inches of rain)
        $= P(X > 8) = 1 - P(X < 8) = 1 - [0.44 + 0.30 + 0.15 + 0.06] = 1 - 0.95 = 0.05$
    (b) P(Desert City got between 2 and 6 inches of rain)
        $= P(2 < X < 6) = 0.30 + 0.15 = 0.45$
    (c) P(Desert City got exactly 2 inches of rain) $= 0$
    (d) P(Desert City got at most 6 inches of rain)
        $= P(X \leq 6) = 0.44 + 0.30 + 0.15 = 0.89$

THE NORMAL DISTRIBUTION

The discovery of the normal distribution is credited to Carl Gauss. It is also known as the **bell curve** or **Gaussian distribution**. This is the most commonly used distribution in statistics because it closely approximates the distributions of many different measurements.

> Here, "~" means "is distributed as."

If a random variable X follows a normal distribution with mean μ and standard deviation σ, then it is denoted by $X \sim N(\mu, \sigma)$. The density function is shown in Figure 18.

The **standard normal** is the normal distribution with a mean of 0 and a standard deviation of 1. Any normal random variable can be transformed into the standard normal using the relation

$$Z = \frac{X - \mu}{\sigma}$$

which means $X \sim N(\mu, \sigma) \Rightarrow Z = \frac{X - \mu}{\sigma} \sim N(0, 1)$

and

$$Z \sim N(0, 1) \Rightarrow X = Z\sigma + \mu \sim N(\mu, \sigma)$$

The value of variable Z computed as $Z = \frac{X - \mu}{\sigma}$ for any specific value of X is known as the **z-score**. For example, suppose $X \sim N(10, 2)$. The z-score for $X = 12.5$ is then

$$Z = \frac{X - \mu}{\sigma} = \frac{12.5 - 10}{2} = 1.25$$

> This process is called z-scoring. It does not change the distribution at all! It simply changes the units on the x-axis, shifting it over by $-\mu$ and relabeling the axis in units of standard deviation so that 1 unit = 1 standard deviation.

Properties of the Normal Distribution

The normal distribution has the following characteristics:

- It is continuous.
- It is symmetric around its mean.
- It is bell-shaped or mound-shaped.
- Mean = median = mode.
- The curve approaches the horizontal axis on both sides of the mean without ever touching or crossing it.
- Nearly all of the distribution (99.73%) lies within three standard deviations of the mean.
- It has two inflection points: One at $\mu - \sigma$ and one at $\mu + \sigma$. (Don't worry if you don't know what this means; it is from calculus and is not a topic on the AP Exam.)
- The normal distribution is fully determined by two parameters, namely, mean and variance (or standard deviation).
- The location of the distribution on the number line depends on the mean of the distribution. See Figure 18.
- The shape of the distribution depends on the standard deviation. A normal distribution with a larger standard deviation is more spread out, while one with a smaller standard deviation is more tightly bunched. See Figure 19.

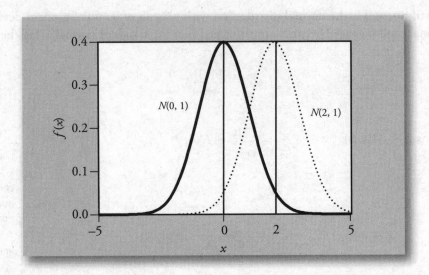

Figure 18: Normal distributions with different means 0 and 2 and standard deviations of 1

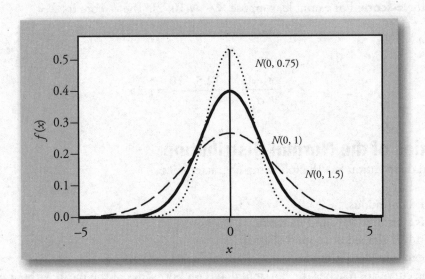

Figure 19: Normal distributions with means of 0 and standard deviations of 0.75, 1, and 1.5

Using the Normal Distribution Table

If the random variable X follows a normal distribution with mean μ and standard deviation σ, then the random variable $Z = \dfrac{X - \mu}{\sigma}$ follows a standard normal distribution, i.e., a normal distribution with mean 0 and standard deviation 1.

To find the area under the standard normal distribution—a normal distribution with mean 0 and standard deviation 1—you can simply look at the standard normal probability table, which is given to you on the AP Exam and is also reprinted on pages 383–384 (Table A). To find the area under the curve (i.e., the probability) for any normal distribution other than the standard normal, we convert it to a standard normal using the formula above.

- Approximately 68% of the area under the curve lies between $\mu - \sigma$ and $\mu + \sigma$.
- Approximately 95% of the area under the curve lies between $\mu - 2\sigma$ and $\mu + 2\sigma$.
- Approximately 99.73% (almost all) of the area under the curve lies between $\mu - 3\sigma$ and $\mu + 3\sigma$.

Example 14:

    (a) Find $P(Z < 1.27)$.
    (b) Find $P(Z < 0.82)$.
    (c) Find $P(0.82 < Z < 1.27)$.
    (d) Find $P(Z > 1.27)$.
    (e) Find the 95th percentile of the standard normal distribution.

Solution:

    (a) Refer to the normal probability table (Table A on pages 383–384).
       - Go down to the row corresponding to 1.2.
       - Go across to the column corresponding to 0.07.
       - Read the number in the cross section of the row for 1.2 and the column for 0.07.
       - It says that $P(Z < 1.27) = 0.8980$.

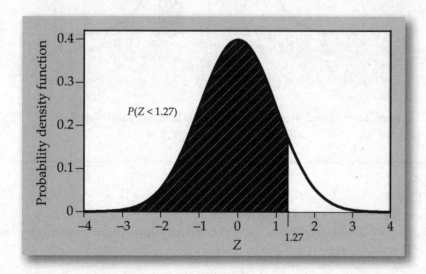

Figure 20: Shaded area under the standard normal distribution shows $P(Z < 1.27)$

TI-83 or TI-84:
- Choose **2nd → DISTR → 2:normalcdf(**
- Enter *lower bound, upper bound,* μ, and σ values in that order, separated by commas. The lower bound in this example should be negative infinity (−∞). You can simulate ∞ and −∞ by using any number beyond 5 standard deviations from the mean. This will display:

$$\text{normalcdf}(-5, 1.27, 0, 1)$$

- Press **ENTER**

(b) To find the $P(Z < 0.82)$, read the number in the cross section of row for 0.8 and column for 0.02. We see that $P(Z < 0.82) = 0.7939$.

(c) $P(0.82 < Z < 1.27) = P(Z < 1.27) - P(Z < 0.82)$
   $= 0.8980 - 0.7939$
   $= 0.1041$

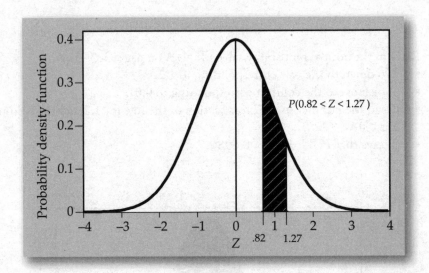

Figure 21: Shaded area under the standard normal distribution shows $P(0.82 < Z < 1.27)$

TI-83 or TI-84:
- Choose **2nd → DISTR → 2:normalcdf(**
- Enter *lower bound, upper bound,* μ, and σ values in that order separated by commas. This will display:

$$\text{normalcdf}(0.82, 1.27, 0, 1)$$

- Press **ENTER**

(d) Because the area under the entire curve equals 1, the probability that Z is *greater* than a given number is 1 − (the probability that it is *less* than that number). See Figure 22.

$P(Z > 1.27) = 1 − P(Z < 1.27)$

$= 1 − 0.8980$

$= 0.1020$

> Because the area under the curve for a single value is zero, the answer to this question would have been the same had it said, "Find $P(Z \geq 1.27)$." The same is true for parts (a)–(c).

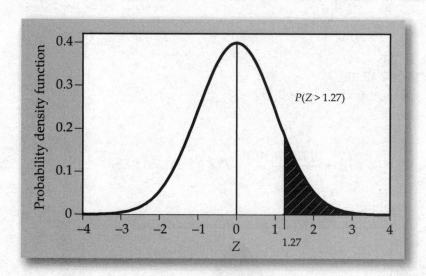

Figure 22: The darker shaded area under the standard normal distribution shows $P(Z > 1.27)$

(e) To find the 95th percentile means to find z_0 such that $P(Z < z_0) = 0.95$. To do this, we can simply use the table backward. Find the number closest to 0.95 among the probability values. Then we get $z_0 = 1.645$ (between 1.64 and 1.65).

> **Magic Numbers?**
> Statisticians use several common probability measurements. You can save time by memorizing these Z-scores and probabilities in advance!
>
> One-tailed Z-score of 95% = 1.645
> Two-tailed Z-score of 95% = 1.96
> One-tailed Z-score of 99% = 2.33
> Two-tailed Z-score of 99% = 2.58

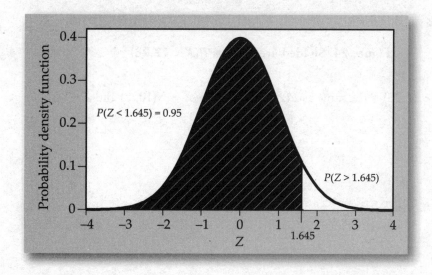

Figure 23: z-score such that $P(Z < z\text{-score}) = 0.95$

> **TI-83 or TI-84:**
> - Choose **2nd → DISTR → 3:invNorm(**
> - Enter *probability below z_0*, μ, and σ values in that order separated by commas.
> $$\text{invNorm}(0.95,0,1)$$
> - Press **ENTER**

Example 15: Suppose $X \sim N(10, 2)$. Find

(a) $P(X < 12.28)$
(b) $P(6.72 < X < 12.28)$
(c) Find x_0 such that $P(X > x_0) = 0.15$

Solution:

(a) $P(X < 12.28) = P\left(Z < \dfrac{12.28 - 10}{2}\right) = P(Z < 1.14) = 0.8729$

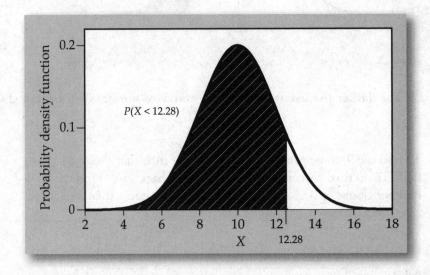

Figure 24: Shaded area shows $P(X < 12.28)$

$P(X < 12.28)$ is the same as $P(Z < 1.14)$ where $X \sim N(10, 2)$ and $Z \sim N(0, 1)$.

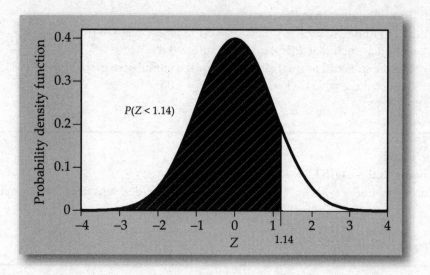

Figure 25: Shaded area shows $P(Z < 1.14)$

TI-83 or TI-84:

- Choose **2nd → DISTR → 2:normalcdf(**
- Enter *lower bound, upper bound,* μ, and σ values in that order separated by commas. Simulate $-\infty$ for the lower bound by using any number beyond 5 standard deviations below the mean. This displays:

$$\text{normalcdf}(0,12.28,10,2)$$

- Press **ENTER**

(b) $P(6.72 < X < 12.28) = P\left(\dfrac{6.72-10}{2} < Z < \dfrac{12.28-10}{2}\right)$

$$= P(-1.64 < Z < 1.14)$$

$$= P(Z < 1.14) - P(Z < -1.64)$$

$$= 0.8729 - 0.0505$$

$$= 0.8224$$

TI-83 or TI-84:

- Choose **2nd → DISTR → 2:normalcdf(**
- Enter *lower bound, upper bound,* μ, and σ values in that order separated by commas. This displays:

$$\text{normalcdf}(6.72,12.28,10,2)$$

- Press **ENTER**

(c) To find x_0 such that $P(X > x_0) = 0.15$,
i.e., to find z_0 such that $P(Z > z_0) = 0.15$, where $z_0 = \dfrac{x_0 - 10}{2}$
or find z_0 such that $P(Z < z_0) = 1 - 0.15 = 0.85$
Use the standard normal table, look for the cumulative probability of 0.85, and then read the table backward. We get $z_0 = 1.04$.

$$x_0 = 2z_0 + 10 = 2(1.04) + 10 = 12.08$$

TI-83 or TI-84:
- Choose **2nd → DISTR → 3:invNorm(**
- Enter *probability below z_0*, μ, and σ values in that order, separated by commas

$$\text{invNorm}(0.85, 10, 2)$$

- Press **ENTER**

The Normal Distribution as a Model For Measurements

The normal distribution is commonly used to describe a variety of measurements.

Example 16: At the end of the semester, a teacher determines the percent grade earned by students, taking into account all homework, test, and project scores. These student scores are normally distributed with a mean of 75 and a standard deviation of 8.

(a) If a 90-80-70-60 scheme is used to determine the letter grades of students, what percent of students earned an A?
(b) If a 90-80-70-60 scheme is used to determine the letter grades of students, what percent of students earned a B?
(c) If the teacher decides to give A's to the top 10% of the class, then what is the cutoff point for an A?
(d) If the teacher decides to give B's to the next 20% of the class, then what are the cutoff points for a B?

Solution: Remember that the grades are normally distributed with μ = 75 and σ = 8.

(a) In the 90-80-70-60 scheme, a grade of 90 or better earns an A.
Compute $P(X \geq 90)$.

$$P(X \geq 90) = P\left(Z \geq \frac{90 - 75}{8}\right) = P(Z \geq 1.875) = 1 - P(Z < 1.875) = 1 - 0.9696 = 0.0304$$

Therefore, 3.04% of the class got A's.

TI-83 or TI-84:

- Choose **2nd → DISTR → 2:normalcdf(**
- Enter *lower bound, upper bound,* μ, and σ values in that order, separated by commas. Simulate an upper bound of ∞ by using any number beyond 5 standard deviations above the mean

$$normalcdf(90,130,75,8)$$

- Press **ENTER**

(b) In the 90-80-70-60 scheme, a grade of 80 or better but less than 90 earns a B. Compute $P(80 \leq X < 90)$.

$$P(80 \leq X < 90) = P\left(\frac{80-75}{8} \leq Z < \frac{90-75}{8}\right)$$

$$= P(0.625 \leq Z < 1.875)$$
$$= P(Z < 1.875) - P(Z < 0.625)$$
$$= 0.9696 - 0.7340$$
$$= 0.2356$$

Therefore, 23.56% of the class got B's.

TI-83 or TI-84:

- Choose **2nd → DISTR → 2:normalcdf(**
- Enter *lower bound, upper bound,* μ, and σ values in that order, separated by commas

$$normalcdf(80,90,75,8)$$

- Press **ENTER**

(c) To find x_0 such that $P(X \geq x_0) = 0.10$, i.e., to find z_0 such that $P(Z \geq z_0) = 0.10$, where $z_0 = \dfrac{x_0 - 75}{8}$ or find z_0 such that $P(Z < z_0) = 1 - 0.10 = 0.90$: use the standard normal table, look for the cumulative probability of 0.90, and then read the table backward. We get $z_0 = 1.28$, so $x_0 = 8z_0 + 75 = 8(1.28) + 75 = 85.24$.

(d) Similar to part (c), you must work backwards. The next 20% will be the range from the top 10% to the top 30%. The value at the top 10% was found in part (c), so follow those steps to determine the value at the top 30% mark. $P(Z < z_0) = 1 - 0.30 = 0.70$. From the standard normal table, we get $z_0 = 0.525$, so $x_0 = 8z_0 + 75 = 8(0.525) + 75 = 79.2$. Therefore, the lower cutoff will be at 79.2 and the upper at 85.24.

COMBINING INDEPENDENT RANDOM VARIABLES

Sometimes we are interested in linear combinations of independent random variables. If we know the means and the variances of two random variables, we can determine the mean and the variance of a linear combination of these variables. Suppose X is a random variable with mean μ_X and variance σ_X^2. Suppose Y is a random variable with mean μ_Y and variance σ_Y^2. The two variables X and Y are independent.

Random Variable	Mean	Variance	
X	μ_X	σ_X^2	Independent
Y	μ_Y	σ_Y^2	

Now consider a linear combination of random variables $w = aX + bY$, where a and b are constants. Then $aX + bY$ is also a random variable, with mean $\mu_w = a\mu_X + b\mu_Y$ and variance $\sigma^2_w = a^2\sigma_X^2 + b^2\sigma_Y^2$. The following are specific cases:

Random Variable	Mean	Variance
aX	$a\mu_X$	$a^2\sigma_X^2$
$X + b$	$\mu_X + b$	σ_X^2
$aX + b$	$a\mu_X + b$	$a^2\sigma_X^2$
$X + Y$	$\mu_X + \mu_Y$	$\sigma_X^2 + \sigma_Y^2$
$X - Y$	$\mu_X - \mu_Y$	$\sigma_X^2 + \sigma_Y^2$
$aX + bY$	$a\mu_X + b\mu_Y$	$a^2\sigma_X^2 + b^2\sigma_Y^2$

If X and Y are normally distributed, then a linear combination of the two will also be normally distributed.

Example 17: A company markets 16-ounce bottles of jam. The mean amount of jam per bottle is 16 ounces, with a standard deviation of 0.1 ounces. The mean weight of the glass bottles holding the jam is five ounces, with a standard deviation of 0.5 ounces.

(a) What is the mean weight of a filled bottle?

(b) What is the standard deviation of the weight of a filled bottle?

(c) When shipped to stores, 12 random bottles are packed in each box. What is the mean and standard deviation of the weights of these random groupings of 12 bottles?

(d) The mean weight of the empty boxes is 50 ounces, with a standard deviation of four ounces. What is the mean weight and the standard deviation of the weights of the filled boxes?

(e) If the amount of jam per bottle, the weight of the bottles (with their lids), and the weight of the boxes are approximately normally distributed, what percent of boxes will weigh more than 320 ounces?

Solution: Let A = the amount of jam per bottle

B = the weight of the empty bottles (with lids)

C = the weight of a box packed with 12 filled bottles

It is known that

$$\mu_A = 16 \text{ ounces}, \sigma_A = 0.1 \text{ ounces, and}$$
$$\mu_B = 5 \text{ ounces}, \sigma_B = 0.5 \text{ ounces.}$$

(a) Let W = weight of a filled bottle = weight of bottle content + weight of a bottle (with its lid).

Therefore, the mean weight of a filled bottle is

$$\mu_W = \mu_A + \mu_B = 16 + 5 = 21 \text{ ounces}$$

(b) The standard deviation of the weight of a filled bottle is

$$\sigma_W = \sqrt{\sigma_A^2 + \sigma_B^2} = \sqrt{0.1^2 + 0.5^2} \approx 0.5099 \approx 0.51 \text{ ounces}$$

Remember that you cannot add standard deviations, only variances.

(c) Twelve random bottles are grouped together. Let G = total weight of a group of 12 filled bottles.

The mean weight of the group = $\mu_G = 12\mu_W = 12(21) = 252$ ounces.

The standard deviation of the weight of the group is

$$\sqrt{12^2 \sigma_W^2} = \sqrt{12^2 (0.51)^2} = 6.12 \text{ ounces}$$

(d) Let E = the weight of an empty box.

C = the weight of a packed box = $G + E$.

The mean weight of a packed box is $\mu_C = \mu_G + \mu_E = 252 + 50 = 302$ ounces.

The standard deviation of the weights of the packed boxes is

$$\sigma_C = \sqrt{\sigma_G^2 + \sigma_E^2} = \sqrt{6.12^2 + 4^2} \approx 7.31 \text{ ounces}$$

(e) Because all weights are approximately normally distributed, $C \sim N(302, 7.31)$. Therefore,

$$P(C > 320) = P\left(Z > \frac{320 - 302}{7.31}\right) \approx P(Z > 2.46) = 1 - P(Z < 2.46) = 0.0069$$

Thus, 0.69% of the boxes will weigh more than 320 ounces.

Example 18: Suppose that Jim's score in an 18-hole round of golf can be modeled by a normal distribution with mean of 81 and a standard deviation of 4. David's golf score can also be modeled by a normal distribution with a mean of 88 and a standard deviation of 6. Assuming that their scores are independent, what is the probability of David defeating Jim in a round of golf? (Remember that in golf, the person with the lower score wins).

Solution: Let J = Jim's score = $N(81, 4)$
Let D = David's score = $N(88, 6)$

In order to defeat Jim, David must shoot a lower score. Thus, we are looking to calculate $P(D < J)$.

If you subtract J on both sides of the inequality, you can rewrite the probability statement as $P(D - J < 0)$.

$D - J$ represents the subtraction of two random variables. You may now apply the rules for mean and variance discussed in this section. Remember that variances add even though the variables are subtracted.

$$\mu_{D-J} = \mu_D - \mu_J = 88 - 81 = 7$$

$$\sigma_{D-J} = \sqrt{\sigma_D^2 + \sigma_J^2} = \sqrt{6^2 + 4^2} \approx 7.2111$$

So the variable $D - J$ can be represented by a normal curve with mean 7 and standard deviation 7.2111. We can now use z-scores and the normal curve table to calculate $P(D - J < 0)$.

$$Z = \frac{X - \mu}{\sigma} = \frac{0 - 7}{7.2111} = -0.97$$

Using the normal curve table, $P(D - J < 0) = P(Z < -0.97) = 0.1660$.

David has a 16.6% chance of defeating Jim in a round of golf.

SAMPLING DISTRIBUTIONS

Terms and Concepts

- A **parameter** is a numerical measure of a population. For example, a student's GPA is computed using grades from all his or her courses; therefore, GPA is a parameter.

- A **statistic** is a numerical measure of a sample. An example is the percent of votes received by a presidential candidate. Generally, not every eligible voter votes in a presidential election. Therefore, the president is elected based on the support received from a sample of the eligible voters, so the percent is a statistic. (If, however, every eligible voter does vote, then the percent of votes received would be a parameter.) A good mnemonic for this is that **p**arameter and **p**opulation both start with **p**, and **s**ample and **s**tatistic both start with **s**.

- The **sample distribution** (or **distribution of sample means,** or **sampling distribution**) is the probability distribution of all possible values of a statistic. Different samples of the same size from the same population will result in different statistic values. Therefore, a statistic is a random variable. Any table, list, graph, or formula giving all possible values a statistic can take and their corresponding probabilities gives a sampling distribution of that statistic.

- The **standard error** is the standard deviation of the distribution of a statistic. Fun fact: parameters are usually represented by Greek letters, statistics by Roman letters.

Central Limit Theorem

Regardless of the shape of the distribution of the population, if the sample size is large (typically $n \geq 30$) and there is finite variance, then the distribution of the sample means will be approximately normal, with mean

$\mu_X = \mu$ and standard deviation $\sigma_{\overline{X}} = \dfrac{\sigma}{\sqrt{n}}$.

Basically, the Central Limit Theorem tells us that regardless of the shape of the population distribution, as the sample size n increases:

- The shape of the distribution of $\overline{X}$ becomes more symmetric and bell-shaped (more like a normal distribution).

- The center of the distribution of $\overline{X}$ remains at μ.

- The spread of the distribution of $\overline{X}$ decreases, and the distribution becomes more peaked.

You Down with CLT?
It might seem like it, but the Central Limit Theorem is not magic!

What is the probability of getting a mean of 6 when you roll a die (also known as getting a 6)? How about a mean of 6 when you roll two dice (getting two 6's)? In 3 rolls? Because 6 is an extreme value, it's pretty hard to get a mean of 6 when you have a lot of rolls.

Let's consider a mean of 4. If you have 3 rolls, you can get a mean of 4 with all of the following sets: {4,4,4}, {4,6,2}, {4,3,5}. What about with 4 rolls? {4,4,4,4}, {4,4,6,2}, {4,4,3,5}, {3,5,3,5}, {6,2,6,2}, {3,5,6,2}, {5,5,5,1}….Compare that with the single way to get a mean of 6 {6,6,6,6} or 1 {1,1,1,1}, and you can see why more moderate values become more likely and extreme values get less likely as your sample size gets larger, resulting in the normal distribution! As you can see, this even happens when your original distribution (probability of getting each number in a die roll) is not normally distributed.

Sampling Distribution of a Sample Proportion

Which values are most likely to occur? How do you know?

Consider a population with a proportion of successes (for example, "yes" answers to the question "Do you support the president's policies?") equal to p. Take a random sample of size n from this population and compute the sample proportion $\hat{p}$. Note that $\hat{p}$ estimates p. Different samples of size n will result in different $\hat{p}$ values. Therefore, $\hat{p}$ is a random variable. The probability of occurrence differs among the different $\hat{p}$ values. Some values of $\hat{p}$ are more likely to occur than others. All possible values of $\hat{p}$ along with their corresponding probabilities give the sampling distribution of $\hat{p}$. For a sufficiently large n, the sampling distribution of $\hat{p}$ is approximately normal, with mean $\mu_{\hat{p}} = p$ and standard deviation $\sigma_{\hat{p}} = \sqrt{\dfrac{p(1-p)}{n}}$.

Sampling Distribution of a Sample Mean

Consider a population with a mean equal to μ. Take a random sample of size n from this population and compute the sample mean $\overline{X}$. Note that $\overline{X}$ estimates μ. Different samples of size n will result in different $\overline{X}$ values. Therefore, $\overline{X}$ is a random variable. The probability of occurrence differs among the different $\overline{X}$ values. Some values of $\overline{X}$ are more likely to occur than others. All the possible values of $\overline{X}$ along with their corresponding probabilities give the sampling distribution of $\overline{X}$. For a sufficiently large n, the sampling distribution of $\overline{X}$ is approximately normal, with mean $\mu_{\overline{X}} = \mu$ and standard deviation $\sigma_{\overline{X}} = \dfrac{\sigma}{\sqrt{n}}$.

Example 19: The GPAs of graduating students at a large university are normally distributed, with a mean GPA of 2.8 and a standard deviation of 0.5. A random sample of 50 students is taken from all the graduating students.

(a)   Find the probability that the mean GPA of the sampled students is above 3.0.
(b)   Find the probability that the mean GPA of sampled students is between 2.7 and 3.0.

Solution: Because the population distribution is normally distributed, the sampling distribution will also be normal, regardless of the sample size. However, bear in mind that had the question not mentioned the shape of the population distribution, the sample size of 50 is sufficiently large for us to assume approximate normality for the sampling distribution of $\overline{X}$ with $\mu_{\overline{X}} = 2.8$ and $\sigma_{\overline{X}} = \dfrac{0.5}{\sqrt{50}} \approx 0.071$. In other words, $X \sim N(2.8, 0.071)$, approximately.

(a) $P(\text{The mean GPA of the sampled students is above } 3.0)$

$$= P(\overline{X} > 3.0)$$

$$= P\left(Z > \frac{3.0 - 2.8}{0.071}\right)$$

$$= P(Z > 2.82)$$

$$= 0.0024$$

There is less than a 1% chance (0.24%) that the mean GPA of the 50 sampled students will exceed 3.0.

(b) P(The mean GPA of sampled students is between 2.7 and 3.0)

$$= P(2.7 < \bar{X} < 3.0)$$

$$= P\left(\frac{2.7 - 2.8}{0.071} < Z < \frac{3.0 - 2.8}{0.071}\right)$$

$$= P(-1.41 < Z < 2.82)$$

$$= 0.9183$$

There is almost a 92% chance that the mean GPA of the 50 sampled students will be between 2.7 and 3.0.

Sampling Distribution of a Difference Between Two Independent Sample Proportions

Consider two populations with proportions of successes equal to p_1 and p_2, respectively. Imagine that we want to find the difference in population proportions ($p_1 - p_2$). Take independent random samples of sizes n_1 and n_2, respectively, from these populations and compute the respective sample proportions $\hat{p}_1$ and $\hat{p}_2$. Note that $(\hat{p}_1 - \hat{p}_2)$ estimates $(p_1 - p_2)$. Different samples of sizes n_1 and n_2 will result in different $(\hat{p}_1 - \hat{p}_2)$ values. Therefore, $(\hat{p}_1 - \hat{p}_2)$ is a random variable. Some values of $(\hat{p}_1 - \hat{p}_2)$ are more likely to occur than others. All the possible values of $(\hat{p}_1 - \hat{p}_2)$ along with their corresponding probabilities give the sampling distribution of $(\hat{p}_1 - \hat{p}_2)$. For sufficiently large sample sizes, the sampling distribution of $(\hat{p}_1 - \hat{p}_2)$ is approximately normal, with mean $\mu_{\hat{p}_1 - \hat{p}_2} = p_1 - p_2$ and standard deviation

$$\sigma_{\hat{p}_1 - \hat{p}_2} = \sqrt{\frac{p_1(1 - p_1)}{n_1} + \frac{p_2(1 - p_2)}{n_2}}$$

Sampling Distribution of a Difference Between Two Independent Sample Means

Consider two populations with means equal to μ_1 and μ_2, respectively. Imagine that we want to find the difference in population means ($\mu_1 - \mu_2$). Take independent random samples of sizes n_1 and n_2, respectively, from these populations, and compute the respective sample means $\bar{X}_1$ and $\bar{X}_2$. Note that $(\bar{X}_1 - \bar{X}_2)$ estimates $(\mu_1 - \mu_2)$. Different samples of size n_1 and n_2 will result in different $(\bar{X}_1 - \bar{X}_2)$ values. Therefore, $(\bar{X}_1 - \bar{X}_2)$ is a random variable. The probability of occurrence differs among the different $(\bar{X}_1 - \bar{X}_2)$ values. Some values of $(\bar{X}_1 - \bar{X}_2)$ are more likely to occur than others. All the possible values of $(\bar{X}_1 - \bar{X}_2)$, along with their corresponding probabilities, give the sampling distribution of $(\bar{X}_1 - \bar{X}_2)$. For sufficiently large n_1 and n_2, the sampling distribution of $(\bar{X}_1 - \bar{X}_2)$ is approximately normal with mean $\mu_{\bar{X}_1 - \bar{X}_2} = \mu_1 - \mu_2$ and standard deviation

$$\sigma_{\bar{X}_1 - \bar{X}_2} = \sqrt{\frac{\sigma_1^2}{n_1} + \frac{\sigma_2^2}{n_2}}$$

TEST YOUR UNDERSTANDING

Describe independent events. Two events, A and B, are independent if the outcome of one event does not affect the probability of the other. In other words, if $P(A) = P(A|B)$ and $P(B) = P(B|A)$, then A and B are independent. Knowing A would not give you any information about B. For example, a die roll and a coin flip are independent. If I flip a coin and roll a die, knowing whether I got heads or tails would not help you predict what roll I got.

What does a geometric distribution tell you? A geometric distribution tells you the probability of having your first success on the kth trial (with p = probability of success). For example, it can be used to describe the probability of a family having at least 4 boys before their first girl.

What does a binomial distribution tell you? The binomial distribution tells you the probability of having k successes in n trials (with p = probability of success). For example, it can be used to describe the probability of making 4 out of 5 free throws when your probability of making a free throw is 30%.

Explain why sampling distributions of sample means are often normally distributed. The central limit theorem (CLT) states that if you take a sample of size n from a population with finite variance (i.e. the standard deviation and variance are not ∞), and n is large enough, the distribution of sample means will be normally distributed. Even if you're sampling from a skewed distribution like height or income, the distribution of sample means will be normal!

Summary

o Probability can be conceptualized as a fraction of outcomes wanted over the total number of possible outcomes, as a tree diagram, or as a Venn diagram.

o A probability distribution is a table, list, graph, or formula that gives all the possible values taken by a random variable and their corresponding probabilities.

o The mean (μ) of a discrete random variable is calculated using the following formula:

$$\mu = E(X) = \sum_{i=1}^{n} x_i P(x_i)$$

o The variance (σ^2) of a discrete random variable is calculated using the following formula:

$$\sigma^2 = \sum_{i=1}^{n} (x_i - \mu)^2 P(x_i)$$

o A binomial distribution appears to be a symmetric distribution when $P = 0.5$. When $P < 0.5$, it is right-skewed; when $P > 0.5$, it is left-skewed.

o The only major difference between a binomial distribution and a geometric distribution is that in a geometric distribution, a success must occur on the nth trial, so there is no need to calculate the probability by the number of combinations of trials at n.

o There is zero possibility of selecting an exact value from a continuous random distribution of variables.

o   Facts to know about the normal distribution:
   •   Continuous
   •   Symmetric around the mean
   •   Bell-shaped
   •   Mean = median = mode
   •   The curve approaches, but does not cross, the horizontal axis.
   •   Nearly all data in the distribution (99.73%) lies within three standard deviations of the mean.
   •   The location of the distribution depends on the mean.
   •   The shape (width) of the distribution depends on the standard deviation.

o   Common Z-scores to know are:
   •   one-tailed score at 95% probability = 1.645
   •   two-tailed score at 95% = 1.96
   •   one-tailed score at 99% = 2.33
   •   two-tailed score at 99% = 2.58

o   When combining independent random variables, sum the means. To calculate the combined standard deviation, sum the variances (the square of the standard deviation) and then take the square root of the result.

o   The Central Limit Theorem states that as the size of a sample increases, the shape of the distribution becomes more symmetric about the mean (regardless of the shape of the original distribution), the mean of the sample equates to the population mean, and the spread of the sample data decreases.

Chapter 6 Review Questions

Multiple-Choice Questions

Answers can be found at the end of this section.

1. Sixty percent of chocolate desserts ordered at a restaurant are ordered by women. Of these women, 70 percent share their desserts. What is the probability that a randomly selected chocolate dessert was ordered by a woman who will share it?

   (A) 0.13
   (B) 0.18
   (C) 0.42
   (D) 0.45
   (E) 0.70

2. The average weight of dogs that come to a certain vet's office is 55.6 lbs, with a standard deviation of 2.2 lbs. If the weights are normally distributed, what percent of dogs weigh more than 60 lbs?

   (A) 66.8%
   (B) 47.2%
   (C) 33.4%
   (D) 15.9%
   (E) 2.28%

3. An intern goes to a coffee shop every day to buy four small coffees. Each cup contains a mean of 12 oz of coffee, with a standard deviation of 1.2 oz. The cups holding the coffee each have a mean weight of 2 oz, with a standard deviation of 0.1 oz. The intern carries the coffees in a carrier that has a mean weight of 8 oz, with a standard deviation of 0.5 oz. What is the standard deviation of the weight of the carrier holding four filled coffee cups?

   (A) 1.304 oz
   (B) 1.342 oz
   (C) 2.460 oz
   (D) 4.843 oz
   (E) 7.810 oz

4. Which of the following is FALSE about the Central Limit Theorem?

   (A) As the sample size, n, increases the center of the distribution of $\overline{X}$ remains at μ.
   (B) It is only valid if the population distribution is normal.
   (C) The distribution of $\overline{X}$ becomes more peaked as n increases.
   (D) The sample distribution will be approximately normal as n increases.
   (E) As n increases, the spread of the distribution of $\overline{X}$ decreases.

5. If you toss a fair coin seven times and get heads every time, then the eighth toss MUST be tails. Is this true?

   (A) Yes, because there have been so many heads, there must be a tails next.
   (B) Yes, otherwise the coin is not really fair.
   (C) Yes, the law of large numbers says that half the tosses must be tails, so tails is overdue.
   (D) No, the next toss cannot be predicted from the previous tosses.
   (E) No, the coin is not really fair, so it could be heads again.

6. At a certain college, 10 percent of freshmen enter without a major declared. Of those who enter with a major declared, 20 percent change it by the end of their second year. If the college admits 150 freshmen this year, how many will end their second year with the major they declared upon entry?

   (A) 12
   (B) 27
   (C) 108
   (D) 123
   (E) 147

7. At an ice cream shop, a sundae is made by selecting two flavors of ice cream and topping them with fudge, whipped cream, nuts, and a cherry. The available flavors of ice cream are chocolate, vanilla, strawberry, rocky road, chocolate chip cookie dough, and mint chip. How many different sundae combinations are possible?

(A)   2
(B)   15
(C)   24
(D) 120
(E) 720

8. The probability that Sue purchases a dress is $\frac{3}{5}$. If she does buy a dress, the probability that she buys shoes is $\frac{5}{8}$. If she does not buy a dress, the probability that she buys shoes is $\frac{1}{4}$. If you learn Sue bought shoes, what is the probability that she bought a dress?

(A) $\frac{1}{10}$

(B) $\frac{3}{8}$

(C) $\frac{19}{40}$

(D) $\frac{15}{19}$

(E) $\frac{19}{20}$

9. A math teacher and a history teacher each assign their students a textbook for class. The math textbook has an average weight of 8.00 lbs with a standard deviation of 0.4 lbs. The history textbook has an average weight of 6.00 lbs with a standard deviation of 0.2 lbs.

What is the mean weight of both the textbooks?

(A)   6.00 lbs
(B)   8.00 lbs
(C) 10.00 lbs
(D) 12.00 lbs
(E) 14.00 lbs

Free-Response Questions

10. Suppose that out of all the students in a very large school district, 17% participate in after-school sports.

    (a) If district administrators take a sample of 15 students, what is the probability that, at most, 2 of them participate in after-school sports?

    (b) In a sample of 15 students, how many should the administrators expect to play after school sports?

    (c) What is the probability that the first student who plays after-school sports will be the seventh student selected?

11. A student is selecting between two new computers for the start of the school year. Computer A costs $550 plus $100 for a lifetime warranty. Computer B costs $600 plus $50 per repair over its lifetime. The student only expects the computer he buys to last five years before he upgrades. The table shows the probability of repairs required for Computer B over five years. Based on this information, what is the difference between the mean costs of Computer A (with the warranty) and Computer B?

Number of Repairs	0	1	2	3	4
Probability	0.40	0.25	0.20	0.10	0.05

CHAPTER 6 ANSWERS AND EXPLANATIONS

1. **C** $P(W)$ = The probability that a given chocolate dessert is ordered by a woman = 0.60, and $P(S|W)$ = The probability that the chocolate dessert ordered by a woman will be shared = 0.70. You are then asked to determine the intersection of these two events: $P(W \cap S) = P(W) \cdot P(S|W) = 0.60 \cdot 0.70 = 0.42$. Thus, the probability that an ordered chocolate dessert will be ordered by a woman who then shares it is 0.42.

2. **E** In order to find the percent of dogs weighing more than 60 lbs, find the area under the normal curve that is greater than 60 lbs. Therefore, use a z-score: $P(X > 60) = (z > \frac{60 - 55.6}{2.2}) = P(z > 2) = 1 - 0.9772 = 0.0228$. (Use your calculator or the standard normal table to find the value at $z = 2$.) When you convert 0.0228 to a percentage, it is 2.28%.

3. **D** The carrier has a standard deviation of 0.5 oz. Each coffee has a standard deviation of 1.2 oz, but note that the carrier is holding four of them. There are also four cups in the carrier, each with a standard deviation of 0.1 oz. When combining standard deviations of random variables, remember you are initially combining their variances. The rules that apply here are: random variable aX has variance $a^2\sigma_x^2$, where a is a constant, and random variable $X + Y$ has variance $\sigma_x^2 + \sigma_y^2$. Therefore, the variance of four coffees is $4^2(1.2)^2 = 23.04$, and the variance of four cups is $4^2(0.1)^2 = 0.16$. Next, the random variables' variances can be combined to find the variance of four coffees, four cups, and the carrier: $4^2(1.2)^2 + 4^2(0.1)^2 + 0.5^2 = 23.04 + 0.16 + 0.25 = 23.45$. Finally, take the square root to get the standard deviation: $\sqrt{23.45} = 4.843$.

4. **B** The population can be normal or not for the Central Limit Theorem to hold; the Central Limit Theorem is not concerned with the distribution of the population. All of the other statements about the sample population are true under the Central Limit Theorem.

5. **D** Each toss is an independent event, so the seven heads that came up before do not affect the eighth toss. Further, the law of large numbers says that as the number of trials increases, the percentage of hits will approach the expected value. In this case, as we increase the number of trials (and this means to the 100s–1000s range), the percentage of heads will approach the expected value, 0.5.

6. **C** One hundred fifty freshmen enter and 90% of them declare a major, so 135 declare a major. Of those 135, 80% end their second year with that major, so 108 don't change. Or, $P(D)$ = the probability of freshmen who do not declare and $P(D')$ = the probability who declare; $P(C)$ = the probability of those who declare who change it and $P(C')$ = the probability who do not change. This problem is interested in $P(D' \cap C') = P(D') \cdot P(C'|D') = 0.90 \cdot 0.80 = 0.72$. Because there are 150 freshmen, multiply the probability by the number of freshmen, $0.72 \cdot 150 = 108$.

7. **B** Be careful about what the question says. All sundaes are made by selecting two flavors of ice cream and are topped with a standard set of toppings, so the toppings do not affect the types of possible sundaes! The only thing that affects the types of sundaes available is the combinations of flavors selected. Recall the formula for calculating the number of combinations possible: $\binom{n}{r} = \dfrac{n!}{r!\,(n-r)!}$. In this problem $n = 6$ and $r = 2$, so $\binom{6}{2} = \dfrac{6!}{2!\,(6-2)!} = 15$.

8. **D** You need to find the conditional probability that a dress was bought given that shoes were bought. Start with a tree diagram:

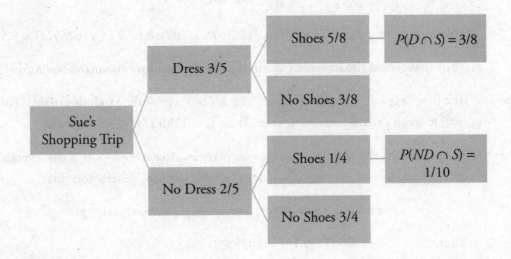

Now insert the values into the equation:

$$P(D\,|\,S) = \frac{P(D \cap S)}{P(S)} = \frac{3/8}{3/8 + 1/10} = \frac{3/8}{19/40} = \frac{15}{19}$$

9. **E** Here, the question is asking for the mean weight of both textbooks. Therefore, you need to find the sum of the average weights of the textbooks. Accordingly, 8.00 lbs + 6.00 lbs = 14.00 lbs, and (E) is correct.

10.   **(a)**   Because the problem states that the school district is very large, the selections of students to be in the sample may be considered independent; therefore, the number of students, out of 15, who play after-school sports can be considered a binomial random variable. The probability of at most 2 students is the sum of the probability of 0 students, 1 student, and 2 students. To answer the question, you can use the general formula for the probability of a binomial random variable: Thus, $\binom{n}{x} p^x (1-p)^{n-x}$.

$$P(x = 0) = (.83)^{15} \approx 0.061118$$

$$P(x = 1) = \binom{15}{1}(.17)^1(.83)^{14} \approx 0.187773$$

$$P(x = 2) = \binom{15}{2}(.17)^2(.83)^{13} \approx 0.269217$$

Finally, $P(\text{at most } 2) = P(0) + P(1) + P(2) \approx 0.061118 + 0.187773 + 0.269217 = 0.518108$.

This answer could also have been obtained using the calculator command binomcdf(15,0.17,2).

    (b)   The term "expect" refers to the *expected value* or *mean* of the random variable. For a binomial random variable, *mean* = $\mu = np$. Thus, $\mu = (15)(0.17) = 2.55$ students.

    (c)   The probability that the first student who plays an after-school sport is the seventh student is the probability of a geometric random variable with the general formula:

$$P(x \text{ trials needed until the first success is observed}) = (1-p)^{(x-1)}p.$$

Thus, $P(x = 7) = (1 - 0.17)^6(0.17) \approx 0.055580$.

11.   Computer A costs: \$650

Computer B costs: \$600 + expected cost of repairs

$\mu_{cost\ of\ repairs} = \$0(0.40) + \$50(0.25) + \$100(0.20) + \$150(0.10) + \$200(0.05) = \$57.50$

So, Computer B would be expected to cost \$657.50.

The difference between the mean costs of A and B is \$650 − \$657.50 = −\$7.50. Therefore, Computer B costs \$7.50 more than Computer A.

Chapter 7
Statistical Inference

By the end of the chapter you should be able to master:

- The difference between a null and alternative hypothesis
- How to define both types of hypothesis based on a specific experiment
- Constructing and performing a hypothesis test
- Constructing and interpreting a Confidence Interval

CONFIRMING MODELS

Important information about a population of interest is often unknown, but we can take samples from the population and gather and summarize the information from the samples. Such summary statistics can then be used to

- estimate unknown population characteristics
- make inferences about unknown population characteristics

Parameter and Statistic were also defined in the previous chapter.

PARAMETERS AND STATISTICS

In a telephone survey conducted by a local newspaper, 400 randomly selected residents of a county on the Gulf of Mexico were asked, "Are you in favor of spending tax money on measures to prevent the erosion of private beaches?" The answers were recorded as "yes," "no," or "no opinion." The newspaper found that 76% of respondents were against spending tax money to support private beaches. This percentage, known as a statistic, was calculated from the information obtained from a random sample of county residents and not the entire population of that county. Still, it provides a reasonable estimate for the unknown parameter, namely, the percentage of *all* county residents who oppose such action.

- A **parameter** is a characteristic of a population. The following are all examples of parameters, i.e., numbers describing respective populations:
  - o the mean annual household income in the state of California
  - o the percentage of voters in favor of a certain presidential candidate in the state of Florida
  - o the variance of the amount of sugar per can of a specific brand of soda

- A **statistic** is a number computed from the sample. Generally, a statistic is used to estimate an unknown parameter and make an inference about it. The following are all examples of statistics:
  - o the mean annual household income computed from 500 randomly selected households in the state of California
  - o the percentage of voters in favor of a certain presidential candidate in a sample of 385 randomly selected voters in the state of Florida
  - o the variance of the amount of sugar per can of a specific brand of soda in 12 randomly selected cans

ESTIMATION

Generally, population characteristics (parameters) are unknown. To estimate them, we take samples from the population and use information from those samples to make our best guess. This procedure of guessing an unknown parameter value using the observed values from samples is known as an **estimation process**. A specific guess or value computed from a sample is known as an **estimate**.

To estimate the mean annual income per resident of Los Angeles County, we would probably use the mean annual income per resident of a random sample of residents of Los Angeles County. The sample mean would estimate the unknown population mean. Similarly, if we were interested in estimating the proportion of voters in favor of a candidate in the state of Louisiana, then we would use the proportion of voters in favor of this candidate from any random sample of voters from Louisiana. Again, the sample proportion would estimate the population proportion.

There are two estimation methods:

- **Point estimation** gives a single value as an estimate of the unknown parameter and makes no allowance for the uncertainty of the value's accuracy.
- **Interval estimation** recognizes the uncertainty of the estimate's accuracy and compensates for it by specifying a range of values around the estimate within which the population parameter may actually lie.

For example, Paul is planning a trip to Florida during his spring break. He collects information about the trip and prepares a budget. Using the collected information, he concludes, "This trip will cost me $1,000, give or take $100." Paul is expecting the cost of his trip to be somewhere between $900 and $1,100. Because he does not know all the exact costs for the different components of this trip, his estimation procedure does not guarantee that the actual cost of the trip will be within the estimated range, but still he believes that there is a very good chance that it will be within those limits. His estimated cost of $1,000 is a point estimate of the unknown cost of the trip. The range of $100 around the point estimate of the cost is known as the **margin of error**. The estimated range of cost ($900–$1,100) is an **interval estimate** of the cost of his trip.

POINT ESTIMATION

Consider a population with an unknown parameter θ (*theta*). Let $X_1, X_2,..., X_n$ be a random sample from this population. A point estimator of θ is a statistic computed from the sample to estimate the value of the unknown parameter. That means that θ is a function of $X_1, X_2,..., X_n$. Some examples are listed below:

- If θ is the unknown population mean μ, then the point estimate is $\overline{X}$. In other words, the sample mean $\overline{X}$ is an estimator for μ. It is computed from the sampled data as

$$\overline{X} = \frac{\left(X_1 + X_2 + \cdots + X_n\right)}{n}$$

For example, the mean family income computed from a random sample of families from Miami estimates the mean family income in Miami.

- If θ is the unknown population proportion p, then the point estimate is $\hat{p}$. In other words, the sample proportion $\hat{p}$ is an estimator for p. It is computed from the sampled data as

$$\hat{p} = \frac{\text{Number of favorable occurrences}}{\text{Sample size}}$$

For example, the proportion of children receiving free lunches obtained from a random sample of 100 children in a certain county's education system estimates the proportion of children receiving free lunches in the entire education system of that county.

- If θ is the unknown population variance σ^2, then the point estimate is S^2. The sample variance S^2 is an estimator for σ^2. It is computed from the sampled data as

$$s^2 = \frac{\sum_{i=1}^{n}\left(x_i - \overline{x}\right)^2}{n-1}$$

The variance in the fat content of 2 percent milk computed from 15 randomly selected gallons of milk estimates the variance in the fat content of all the 2 percent milk bottled by that dairy.

- If θ is the unknown difference in population means $(\mu_1 - \mu_2)$, then the point estimate is $(\overline{X}_1 - \overline{X}_2)$. The difference in sample means $(\overline{X}_1 - \overline{X}_2)$ is an estimator for $(\mu_1 - \mu_2)$. It is computed from the sampled data as

$$\left(\overline{X}_1 - \overline{X}_2\right) = \left[\frac{\left(X_{11} + X_{12} + \ldots + X_{1n_1}\right)}{n_1}\right] - \left[\frac{\left(X_{21} + X_{22} + \ldots + X_{2n_2}\right)}{n_2}\right]$$

Note: Subscripts 11, 12, etc., indicate "one-one" (not eleven) and "one-two" (not twelve).

For example, if we are interested in estimating the difference in the mean life spans of two brands of tires, then we could use the difference in the mean life spans of randomly selected samples of these two brands of tires.

- If θ is the unknown difference in population proportions $(p_1 - p_2)$, then the point estimate is $(\hat{p}_1 - \hat{p}_2)$. The difference in sample proportions $(\hat{p}_1 - \hat{p}_2)$ is an estimator for $(p_1 - p_2)$.

  It is computed from the sampled data as

$$(\hat{p}_1 - \hat{p}_2) = \left[\frac{\text{Favorable occurences in sample 1}}{\text{Size of sample 1}}\right] - \left[\frac{\text{Favorable occurences in sample 2}}{\text{Size of sample 2}}\right]$$

For example, to estimate the difference in the proportions of women graduating with degrees in engineering at two major universities in Alabama, we could use the difference in those proportions computed from randomly selected samples of engineering students from each of these universities.

Sampling Distribution of a Statistic

As seen from these examples, the point estimate statistic is a function of random variables. Therefore, it is a random variable itself. Different samples will result in different estimates. How close or how far can these estimates be from the true value? We can answer this question by studying the distribution of the estimates. The **sampling distribution** of a statistic is the distribution of estimates (values taken by the statistic) from all possible samples of the same size from the same population.

Example 1: Suppose a student is interested in estimating p, the probability of getting heads when a penny is tossed. Suppose she tosses a penny 50 times and gets 24 heads. This sample of 50 tosses gives her an estimated probability ($\hat{p}$) of $\frac{24}{50}$ = 0.48. So the student decides to see what happens if she repeats the experiment. The histogram and the table on the next two pages summarize the results of 100 such experiments, each of 50 tosses:

Estimated P(Heads)	Number of Samples Giving This Estimate	Estimated P(Heads)	Number of Samples Giving This Estimate
0.32	1	0.50	14
0.34	2	0.52	10
0.36	3	0.54	16
0.38	3	0.56	5
0.40	5	0.58	5
0.42	6	0.60	2
0.44	6	0.62	3
0.46	6	0.64	2
0.48	11	0.66	0

Table 1: Distribution of P(Heads) estimated from 50 tosses

Table 1 gives a sampling distribution of a certain statistic, i.e., the probability of getting heads as estimated from 50 tosses of a penny.

Although an estimator is a random variable, we would like to get estimates close to the actual value. Three criteria used to evaluate the quality of a point estimator are

- the center of the distribution of estimates as measured by the mean
- the spread of the distribution of estimates as measured by the standard deviation
- the shape of the distribution

Let us look at a histogram of the sampling distribution given in the above example. This will help us describe the center, spread, and shape of the sampling distribution. See Figure 1.

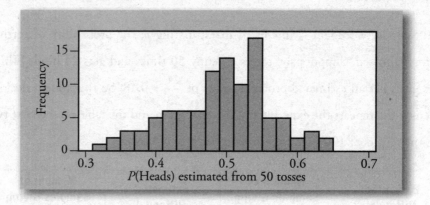

Figure 1: Sampling distribution of *P*(Heads) for a 2001 penny

- The estimates are distributed around 0.5.
- The estimates range from about 0.32 to 0.64.
- The sampling distribution is slightly left skewed.
- From the sampling distribution in Table 1, we can see that approximately 86% of the estimates are between 0.40 and 0.60.

Properties of a Statistic

The Center of a Statistic's Distribution

The property of **unbiasedness** refers to the idea that a statistic is expected to give values centered on the unknown parameter value. The **bias** of a statistic is defined as the difference between the estimated probability and the true value of the parameter being estimated. For example, in the case of the coin toss:

$$\text{Bias}(\hat{p}) = E(\hat{p}) - p$$

where $E(\hat{p})$ gives the mean of the sampling distribution of $\hat{p}$.

A statistic is unbiased if the mean of the sampling distribution of the statistic is equal to the true value of the parameter. Bias measures the average accuracy of a statistic. For an unbiased statistic, bias is equal to 0. A biased statistic has a systematic tendency to give estimates other than the actual value. In the case of the coin toss, $\text{Bias}(\hat{p}) = 0.493 - 0.48 = 0.013$, which is very close to zero, and thus indicates a relatively unbiased statistic.

The Spread of a Statistic's Distribution

The property of **variability** refers to the degree of variation in a statistic's values. Suppose more than one unbiased statistic is available to estimate an unknown parameter. The statistic with a smaller variance (or standard deviation) is considered to be more efficient. Such a statistic is more likely to give values closer to the unknown parameter value—in other words, more precise estimates.

Whenever we estimate something, we make a guess. Bias indicates that our guess is systematically wrong. **Inefficiency** (or random variability) indicates that our guess is wrong unsystematically. The dotplots shown in Figure 2 show the true weight of an item and its weight estimated from repeated weighings on four different scales.

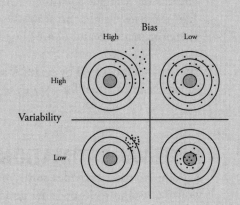

Being biased is different from just being incorrect. Bias means that you're incorrect in a similar way every time. If you've ever seen those games where you guess how many jelly beans are in a jar, think of a bias as represented by the person who always guesses too high. They're not just wrong: they're always wrong in the same direction. Someone else might just be bad at guessing: they sometimes guess too high, sometimes too low. They're also wrong, but in different ways each time.

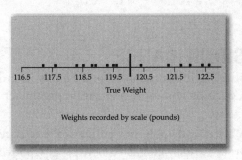

Scale A: Unbiased with large variability

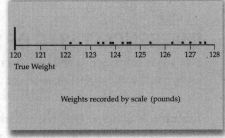

Scale B: Biased with large variability

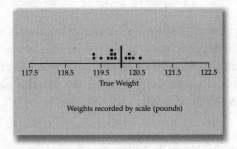

Scale C: Unbiased with small variability

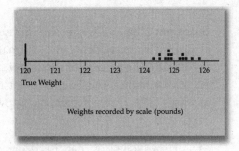

Scale D: Biased with small variability

Figure 2: Properties of a statistic

Note that the weights measured using scales A and C are scattered around the true weight, whereas the weights measured using scales B and D are scattered around some value higher than the true weight. So scales B and D have a tendency to systematically overweigh items. Therefore, scales B and D are biased, whereas scales A and C are unbiased.

The weights measured by scales A and B are spread more widely than the weights measured by scales C and D. Therefore, scales C and D are more efficient than scales A and B.

INTERVAL ESTIMATION AND THE CONFIDENCE INTERVAL

A point estimate provides some information. It is like a "best guess" of the answer. But we would also like to know how good our guess is. We have more confidence in some answers than in others. For example, you have a better idea of your own weight than of the weight of a classmate. You might guess 140 pounds for both yourself and your friend, but you would be more sure you were close to the exact number with yourself. In statistics, we talk about the goodness of an estimate using **confidence intervals** and **confidence levels**.

A confidence interval consists of two numbers between which we are reasonably certain our true parameter will fall. How certain? As certain as the confidence level we have chosen (typically 95%). More precisely, the confidence level means that in repeated sampling, a certain percentage of the intervals will contain the true parameter value.

The confidence interval can also be described in terms of margin of error (MOE). The MOE is the difference between the point estimate and the lower and upper confidence limits.

Take a Chance

In this context, chance refers to sampling variability. We analyze the situation with the understanding that, even if the true proportion is 0.65 (i.e., the sampling distribution of sample proportions had a true mean of 0.65), it is possible that a single sample proportion could be lower than 0.65. But how likely would that be? That is what inferential statistics is all about.

INFERENCE: TESTS OF SIGNIFICANCE

Statistical inference is the process of using information from a sample in order to answer a specific question or make a decision about the population parameter.

Example 2: Imagine that last month a statewide poll showed that 65% of state residents supported the governor. This week, a widely circulated newspaper reported that the governor had approved some shady financial deals. With the election approaching, the governor's advisors need to know what effect the news had on the governor's popularity. Specifically, has her support dropped from 65% as estimated by the last poll?

Solution: How can we answer this question? The best way is to take another random sample of state residents and estimate the governor's current statewide support by computing the percent of the sample still in favor of the governor. If this percentage is 65% or higher, then we have not found strong evidence that the scandal had an adverse effect. If this percentage is lower than 65%, then the question is:

- How likely is it that this decrease is due to chance?

We need to make a decision about p, the population proportion, based on $\hat{p}$, the sample proportion.

- Suppose $\hat{p} = 0.64$. How likely is such a change if $\hat{p}$ has not changed?

  What if $\hat{p} = 0.63$? What if $\hat{p} = 0.60$?

At what point do we cease considering the difference to be the result of a chance variation in the data and start believing that the governor's support has decreased? It all depends on the likelihood of our estimates. We can determine the likelihood by examining the probability that a specific sample result will occur assuming that the real statewide support for the governor has stayed at 0.65. If different samples of the same size are taken, then the estimated proportion $\hat{p}$ will change from sample to sample. Some values are more likely to occur than others. So we need to know which values are less likely to occur in a sample if the percent of support has remained unchanged. In other words, we need to know the sampling distribution of $\hat{p}$. Let's simulate it.

Assume that the proportion of voters supporting the governor is still 0.65. Then we can simulate the situation by drawing repeated samples of, say, size 500. Imagine that each sample gives a different proportion. For example, the first sample results in a $\hat{p} = 0.61$; the second sample results in a $\hat{p} = 0.63$; the third sample results in a $\hat{p} = 0.67$; and so on. A histogram of 1,000 of these estimated proportions is shown in Figure 3.

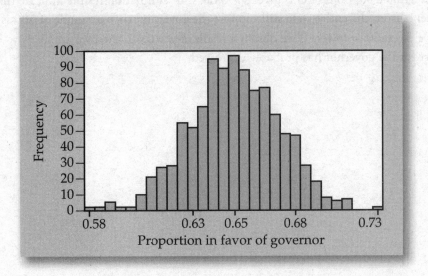

Figure 3: Frequency distribution of the estimated proportion of voters supporting the governor

This histogram shows that a sample proportion closer to 0.65 is most likely to occur, whereas values farther from 0.65 are increasingly less likely to occur. For example, from this simulated data we can estimate

- $P(\hat{p} \leq 0.63) = 0.177$. Note that to get this value, we have to add the frequency on the chart for $\hat{p} = 0.63$ to the frequencies for all $\hat{p}$ values lower than 0.63.

- $P(\hat{p} \leq 0.60) = 0.006$. Again, note that to get this value, we have to add the frequency on the chart for $\hat{p} = 0.60$ to the frequencies for all $\hat{p}$ values lower than 0.60.

You may have noticed that we said earlier that the probability of any exact result was zero, whereas here we have added the value for $\hat{p} = 0.60$ to frequencies for a lower $\hat{p}$. The reason is that here we are dealing with estimates that come from samples, not parameters that come from populations. In a sample of size n, there are a smaller number of possible proportions. With $n = 500$, there are 501 possible proportions you can get between: 0% (0 people), 0.2% (1 person), 0.4% (2 people)...and so on. Even if they have small probabilities, they're still greater than 0. In the population, there's an infinite number of possible probabilities, so each individual proportion has a probability of exactly 0.

Think about this: if you generate a random two-digit decimal, the probability of getting 0.63 or 0.46 is reasonable. If you generate a 3-digit decimal, now the probability of getting one specific number like 0.630 is smaller because there are so many options. If you generate a 100-digit decimal, then the probability of getting any exact number like 0.63478...is very very tiny. With infinite decimals, the probability of getting exactly 0.634788399...is infinitely smaller: in an infinite population, the probability of any exact value is 0.

Suppose our sample of 500 residents gives $\hat{p} = 0.60$. Our simulation results indicate that if 65% of the residents from the entire state still support the governor, then a sample of 500 is not very likely to give $\hat{p} = 0.60$ or lower. If we obtain a result of $\hat{p} = 0.60$, then we are likely to conclude that support for the governor has probably decreased.

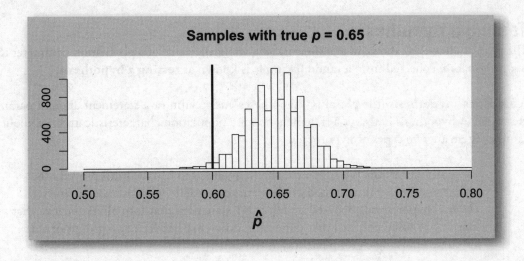

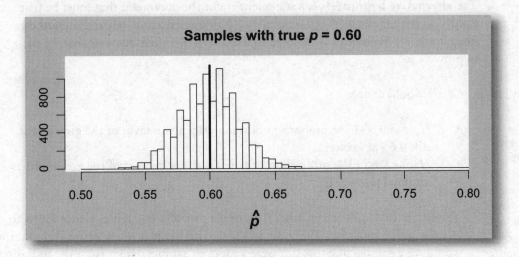

Figure 4: Frequency distribution of $\hat{p}$ based on true p.

In the top graph, we can see that if the true proportion of approval is 0.65, it's pretty unlikely that we'd get a $\hat{p}$ that is less than 0.6. We think it's more likely that the true proportion is less than 0.65, because as we see in the bottom graph (where we supposed $\hat{p}$ = 0.6), that makes the probability of getting a $\hat{p}$ of less than 0.6 much more likely.

Statistical inference is usually based on theoretical models for $\hat{p}$ or $\bar{x}$, not on simulation. On the following pages, we will use the normal model and two others to determine whether our sample result is unusual or not.

Testing a Hypothesis

The process, described above, of decision-making about the value of a population parameter using information collected from a random sample is known as **testing a hypothesis**.

A **statistical hypothesis** (the plural is "hypotheses") is a claim or a statement about a parameter value. A hypothesis is always a statement about a population characteristic and not about a sample. There are two types of hypotheses:

- The **null hypothesis** is a statement that is assumed to be true until proven otherwise. Sometimes it is described as the status quo statement about the parameter. The null hypothesis is denoted by H_0. It is a statement that formalizes the idea that "nothing is going on"; i.e., that there is no difference between two groups or that the value for a single group has stayed the same.

- The **alternative hypothesis** is a statement about the parameter that must be true if the null hypothesis is false. Sometimes it is described as the research hypothesis. The alternative hypothesis is denoted by H_1 or H_a. It is the statement that we wish to prove.

In Example 2, we would define:

> This is called a **directional** hypothesis because we are only interested in one direction (whether the proportion has decreased). We could also test whether $p = 0.65$ (null) or $p \neq 0.65$ (alternative).

- H_0: $p \geq 0.65$ (The proportion of state residents in favor of the governor is still 0.65 or greater.)
- H_a: $p < 0.65$ (The proportion of state residents in favor of the governor has dropped below 0.65.)

The goal is to determine whether the sample provides enough evidence for us to reject the null hypothesis. We want to know whether it is likely or unlikely that we would see a sample like this if it were a random sample drawn from the null distribution (where there is no difference). We're asking whether the data we saw is "typical" of the null distribution or not. From the sampled data, we compute a test statistic value and a p-value.

- The **test statistic (*TS*)** is a statistic computed from the sampled data and used in the process of testing a hypothesis. If we are using a normal model, the test statistic is the familiar z-score.

- The ***p*-value** is the probability that we would observe a test statistic value that is at least as extreme as the one computed from the sample if the null hypothesis were true. The p-value is the evidence we will use in deciding whether to reject the null hypothesis. If the p-value is large, there is a very high probability of drawing a sample like ours from the null distribution. So we do not reject the null hypothesis. However, if the p-value is small, then there is a very low probability of drawing a random sample like ours from the null distribution, and because it is very unlikely that we would get this sample from the null distribution, we assume it probably came from a different distribution (the alternative one).

- The alpha (α) level is a predetermined cutoff point for what is to be considered strong evidence against the null hypothesis. The most common alpha-level is 0.05, but 0.10, 0.01, and even 0.005 are also used.

Using the information from the sample, we make one of the following decisions:

- The sample provides enough evidence to reject the null hypothesis and accept the alternative hypothesis (p-value $< \alpha$); or

- Because of the lack of evidence, we do not reject the null hypothesis (p-value $\geq \alpha$). (Note that failing to *reject* the null hypothesis does not imply *accepting* the null hypothesis. No amount of evidence allows us to accept the null hypothesis.)

Possible Errors

Using the sampled data does not guarantee that our decision is correct. Because our decision is based on a sample and not on the entire population, it's possible for us to make the wrong decision because of random sampling variability. There are two types of errors we could make.

A **Type I error** is the error of rejecting the null hypothesis when it is true. The probability of a Type I error occurring is denoted by α.

A **Type II error** is the error of failing to reject the null hypothesis when it is false. The probability of Type II error is denoted by β.

For a given sample size, we cannot control both Type I and Type II errors. If we try to reduce one type of error, the other type of error will increase. The only exception is an increase in the sample size. Increasing the sample size reduces Type II errors while leaving Type I the same. Also, keep in mind that in certain tests, it's more important to reduce one type of error than the other. For example, when trying a defendant, the null hypothesis is that the defendant is not guilty. The legal system considers the Type I error (to reject the null hypothesis when the null hypothesis is true—in other words, to convict an innocent defendant) to be worse than the Type II error (to fail to reject the null when the alternative hypothesis is true—in other words, acquit a guilty defendant), because our judicial system believes that it's more important to protect an innocent person than to punish a guilty person.

> **What Does an Alpha of 0.05 Mean?**
> Because alpha is a cutoff point for our *p*-value, and *p*-values are probabilities of drawing a sample like ours from the null distribution, then our alpha represents how unlikely a sample needs to be under the null distribution for us to say, "eh, this sample is probably not from the null distribution." An alpha of 0.05 means that we want there to be less than a 5% chance of getting a sample like this under the null distribution.

> If someone came up to you and said, "There are no black swans in the world!" how many swans would they need to show you before you were 100% sure that they were correct?

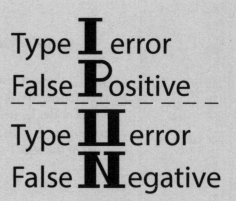

Type **I** error
False **P**ositive
Type **II** error
False **N**egative

		True Situation	
		Null hypothesis is true	Alternative hypothesis is true
Decision	Fail to reject null hypothesis	Correct decision $P(\text{Correct decision}) = 1 - \alpha$	Type II error $P(\text{Type II error}) = \beta$
	Reject null hypothesis	Type I error $P(\text{Type I error}) = \alpha$	Correct decision $P(\text{Correct decision}) = 1 - \beta$ = Power of the test

Table 2: Two types of errors

The power of the test is the probability of correctly detecting an effect (rejecting the null) when there really is an effect and is $1 - \beta$. For a specific alternative,

$$\text{Power of a test} = 1 - P(\text{Type II error})$$

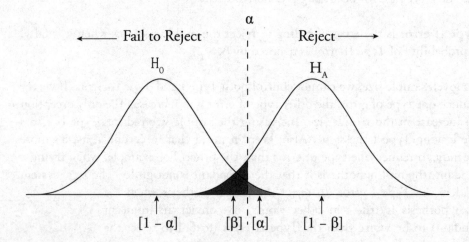

Figure 5: Visualization of the null and alternative hypothesis distributions

Figure 5 shows a visualization of the null and alternative hypothesis distributions. From this, the confidence level, the power of the test, and the four possible decisions are shown as distinct regions of the figure. The unshaded part of the H_0 is the confidence level $(1 - \alpha)$. The shaded part of the H_0 to the right of α is the region of rejection. The unshaded part of the H_A is the power of the test $(1 - \beta)$. The shaded part of the H_A to the left of α is the β region.

A good test has a high power. The following features can affect the power of a test:

- The power of a test increases as the sample size increases.
- The power of a test increases as the Type I error rate (α) increases.
- The power of a test increases as the effect size increases. The effect size is essentially the difference between the hypothesized value of a parameter and its true value.

Example 3: All else being equal, which of the following will increase statistical power? An increase in the sample size? A decrease in the population standard deviation? A decrease in the effect size? An increase in alpha level?

Solution: Sample size, population standard deviation, effect size, and alpha level all directly affect statistical power. A good rule to remember is that (all else being equal) the less the Null (H_0) and Alternative (H_A) distributions overlap, the more statistical power there will be.

Both increasing the sample size and decreasing the population standard deviation have the effect of squeezing the distributions to make them thinner by decreasing the standard error (which is $\frac{\sigma}{\sqrt{n}}$). This causes less overlap, and therefore increases statistical power.

Decreasing the effect size decreases the statistical power because it moves H_A and H_0 closer together, causing more overlap between them.

Increasing the alpha level increases statistical power but does not affect the overlap between the distributions. Instead, it simply moves the rejection region so that more of the alternative distribution is in the rejection region.

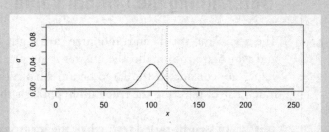

As in Figure 5, we can see the power of the test in the above graph.

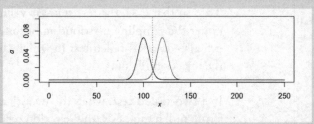

If we increase our sample size, our distributions get thinner, even though their means are the same. This is due to fact that the standard error gets smaller as *n* gets bigger. Thinner distributions mean less overlap between the distributions, which leads to greater statistical power.

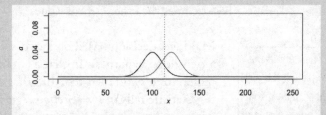

Increasing our alpha cutoff (in this image, it moved further left) means that more of the alternative distribution is to the right of the cutoff, leading to increased statistical power.

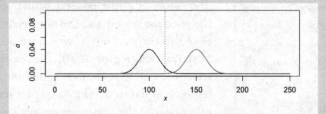

A larger effect size also creates less overlap between the null and alternative distribution by increasing the distance between the distribution means. Again, less overlap leads to greater statistical power since more of the alternative distribution is to the right of the rejection region.

Determining the Critical Value

The terms "too small" and "too large" are vague. How do we decide which values are too large and which are too small? The answer is simple: Values of the test statistic beyond the critical values are considered too large or too small. The critical value is determined based on how much risk of rejecting the true null hypothesis the investigator is willing to take. For example:

- In a **right-tailed test**, when the investigator is willing to take a 5% risk (i.e., $\alpha = 0.05$) of rejecting a true null hypothesis, the rejection region is formed by the largest values of the test statistic with a probability of occurrence totaling 0.05. In that case, the test statistic value above which 5% of the possible values are under the sampling distribution becomes the critical value. For z- and t-tests we can also do a left-tailed test in which the smallest (often negative) values make up the rejection region.

- In a **two-tailed test**, when the investigator is willing to take a 5% risk of rejecting a true null hypothesis, the rejection region is formed by the largest and smallest values of the test statistic with a probability of occurrence totaling 0.05. Therefore, the entire rejection region is divided equally into two parts, one in the left tail and the other in the right tail. The size of each part of the rejection region equals $\alpha/2$ (here, 0.025). In this case, there are two critical values. The test statistic value below which the bottom 2.5% of the sampling distribution lies becomes one critical value, and the test statistic value above which the top 2.5% of the sampling distribution lies becomes the other critical value.

Think about this: rejecting the null hypothesis means that the observed statistic is at least $t\alpha/_2 \cdot \frac{\sigma}{\sqrt{n}}$ or $z\alpha/_2 \cdot \frac{\sigma}{\sqrt{n}}$ away from the null statistic.

A confidence interval gives you the range of all values around your observed value that are less than $t\alpha/_2 \cdot \frac{\sigma}{\sqrt{n}}$ or $z\alpha/_2 \cdot \frac{\sigma}{\sqrt{n}}$ units away.

If the null value is in your CI, then it's by definition less than the required distance away to reject the null.

Making a decision based on a two-sided confidence interval is equivalent to testing a two-sided hypothesis in that a two-sided confidence interval gives a non-rejection region for a two-tailed test. In other words, rejecting the null hypothesis when the test statistic falls *in the rejection region* is equivalent to rejecting the null hypothesis when the hypothesized parameter value falls *outside the confidence interval*.

The Rejection and Non-Rejection Regions

The entire set of the possible values of a test statistic can be divided into two regions: the rejection region and the non-rejection region. The **rejection region (RR)** is the set of test statistic values for which we should reject the null hypothesis. It is also known as the **critical region (CR)**. The set of test statistic values for which we should fail to reject the null hypothesis is called the **non-rejection region**. The area of the rejection region is equal to α. The value of a test statistic that gives the boundary between the rejection and the non-rejection region is known as the **critical value (CV)**. The critical value is shown as z^* or t^* on the AP Statistics Exam.

The location of the rejection region is determined by the nature of the alternative hypothesis, such as $\mu < 10$, $\mu > 10$, or $\mu \neq 10$. We can use three different types of tests, as defined by the location of the rejection region:

- **Left-tailed test:** In a left-tailed test, "too-small" values of the statistic as compared to the hypothesized parameter value lead to the rejection of the null hypothesis. Therefore, the entire rejection region falls in the left tail of the sampling distribution of the test statistic.

  For example, a brewery markets bottles labeled "net contents 12 oz." A consumer advocacy group suspects that the average content of the bottles is lower than that printed on the labels and decides to investigate. The group is interested in testing H_0: μ = 12 oz against H_a: μ < 12 oz, where μ = the mean amount filled per bottle. This is a left-tailed test. Too-small values of the sample mean will result in the rejection of the null hypothesis and the acceptance of the alternative hypothesis. So the rejection region is located in the left tail of the sampling distribution, as shown in Figure 6.

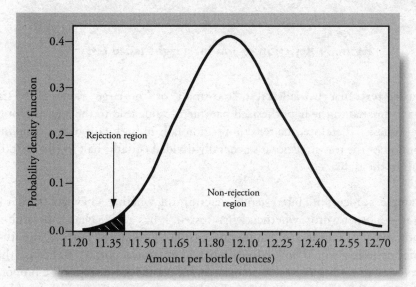

Figure 6: Rejection region for a left-tailed test

- **Right-tailed test:** In a right-tailed test, "too-large" values of the statistic as compared to the hypothesized parameter value lead to the rejection of the null hypothesis. Therefore, the entire rejection region falls in the right tail of the sampling distribution of the test statistic.

  For example, an honors program at a local high school claims that its students have a higher GPA than the general student population average of 2.8. The superintendent is interested in testing this claim H_0: $\mu \le 2.8$ H_a: $\mu > 2.8$ where μ = the average student GPA for the whole school. This is a right-tailed test. Large values of the sample mean will result in the rejection of the null hypothesis and the acceptance of the alternative hypothesis. So, the rejection region is located in the right tail of the sampling distribution as shown in Figure 7.

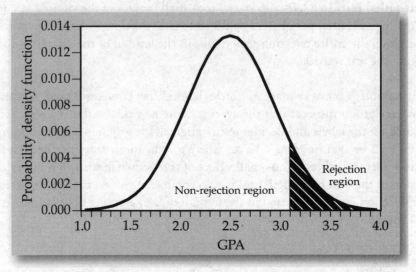

Figure 7: Rejection region for a right-tailed test

- **Two-tailed test:** In a two-tailed test, "too-small" or "too-large" values of the statistic as compared to the hypothesized parameter value lead to the rejection of the null hypothesis. Therefore, the rejection region falls in both tails of the sampling distribution of the test statistic. It's generally divided equally, half in the left tail and half in the right.

For example, students are interested in determining whether a new gold dollar is a fair coin—in other words, whether, when tossed, it has a 50% chance of landing on heads and a 50% chance of landing on tails. To evaluate its fairness, the students decide to toss a gold dollar 100 times and count the number of heads. They are interested in testing $H_0: p = 0.50$ against $H_a: p \neq 0.50$, where p = the proportion of heads. This is a two-tailed test. Too-large or too-small proportions of heads in 100 tosses will result in the rejection of the null hypothesis and the acceptance of the alternative hypothesis. So the rejection region is located in both tails of the sampling distribution, half in the left and half in the right, as shown in Figure 8.

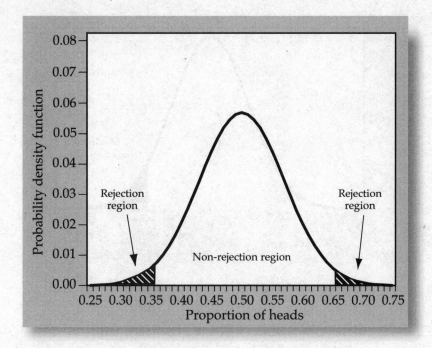

Figure 8: Rejection region for a two-tailed test

Determining Sample Size

Experimenters are often interested in determining the sample size needed to achieve certain reliable results. This helps the experimenter in planning the experiment and in budgeting its cost. The sample size needed to estimate the parameter within a specified margin of error and the required confidence level can be determined using the formula for the margin of error.

Note: When computing sample size, round up the numerical answer to attain the desired level of accuracy. For example, if the answer is 96.012, then we need at least 97 observations to attain the desired level of accuracy.

Finding Z_α

When determining sample size, you'll often need to find the value for the z-score Z_α, or z-(alpha). In most AP textbooks, the critical z-score is designated as z^*, which stands for the critical value for either a one- or two-tailed test. In this book, for increased clarity about the value of z^* for each test, we will use the designations Z_α and $Z_{\alpha/2}$. Z_α = the z-score such that the area under the standard normal distribution beyond the z-score is equal to α. As shown in Figure 9, Z_α is the number on the baseline. It is a z-score. The subscript α (of Z_α) gives the area in the right tail.

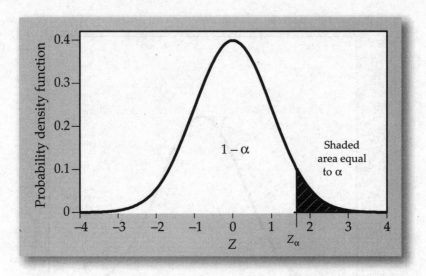

Figure 9: Graphical representation of Z_α

Example 4: Find $Z_{0.05}$ (z^* of a 5% rejection region in a one-tailed test).

Solution: As described earlier, $Z_{0.05}$ = the z-score such that the area under the standard normal distribution beyond the z-score is equal to 0.05. In other words, 95% of the area under the curve is to the left of $Z_{0.05}$. This makes $Z_{0.05}$ the 95th percentile. So, as shown in Figure 10, finding $Z_{0.05}$ is the same as finding the 95th percentile for the standard normal distribution.

Quick Tip

The Z-distribution and T-distribution tables you will use on the AP Exam are right-tailed tables. Make sure that you are using the correct alpha value to find the critical value for the test you are running! If you have a one-tailed test, then find Z_α. If you are using a two-tailed test, divide the α in half, denoted $Z_{(\alpha/2)}$.

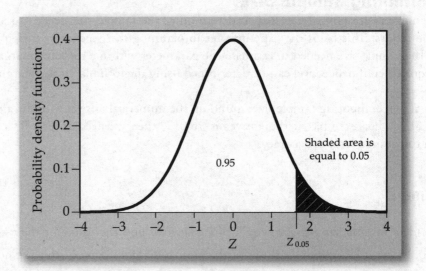

Figure 10: Graphical representation of $Z_{0.05}$

- **Finding $Z_{0.05}$ using the standard normal table:** Inside the body of the table, locate the number closest to 0.95. It is halfway between 0.9495 and 0.9505. Note that 0.9495 corresponds to the z-score 1.64, and 0.9505 corresponds to the z-score 1.65. So 0.95 corresponds to the z-score 1.645. In other words, $z^* = Z_{0.05} = 1.645$.

- **Finding $Z_{0.05}$ using the TI-83 or TI-84: 2nd → DISTR → 3:invNorm(0.95)**

This gives $z^* = Z_{0.05} \approx 1.6448$, which is approximately 1.645.

Example 5: For $\alpha = 0.05$, find $Z_{\alpha/2}$ (z^* of a 5% rejection region in a two-tailed test).

Solution: It is given that $\alpha = 0.05$, which means $\alpha/2 = 0.025$. So, as described earlier, $z^* = Z_{\alpha/2}$ $= Z_{0.025} =$ the z-score such that the area under the standard normal distribution beyond the z-score is equal to 0.025.

Therefore, we are interested in finding the 97.5th percentile for the standard normal distribution.

- **Using the standard normal table:** Inside the body of the table, locate the number closest to 0.975. In this case, it is exactly equal to 0.9750 and corresponds to the z-score 1.96. Therefore, $z^* = Z_{0.025} = 1.96$.
- **Using the TI-83 or TI-84: 2nd $\rightarrow$ DISTR $\rightarrow$ 3:invNorm(0.975)** This gives $Z_{0.025} \approx 1.95996$, which can be rounded to 1.96.

Some of the commonly used z-scores and the corresponding tail probabilities are listed in Table 3.

α Area in the Right Tail of the Standard Normal Distribution	Z_α (z^* for one-tailed test)	$Z_{\alpha/2}$ (z^* for one-tailed test)
0.20	0.84	1.28
0.10	1.28	1.645
0.05	1.645	1.96
0.02	2.05	2.33
0.01	2.33	2.576

Table 3: z-scores associated with commonly used values of α

Determining the Sample Size to Estimate Population Mean μ

- The margin of error to estimate μ is $ME = Z_{\alpha/2}\left(\dfrac{\sigma}{\sqrt{n}}\right)$. First, determine the desired level of confidence and the margin of error. Then estimate n by plugging the desired margin of error into this formula.

- We can estimate the required sample size as

$$n \geq \left(\frac{Z_{\alpha/2}\sigma}{ME}\right)^2$$

- If the population standard deviation is unknown, use the sample standard deviation in place of the population standard deviation.

When determining the desired *ME*, you can ask yourself how *precise* you would like your interval estimate to be. We can easily calculate an interval that is so wide that it's practically useless: for example, if we calculated a confidence interval for the mean annual cost of maintaining an electric vehicle and got a range between $0 and $1 million. If we can estimate the standard deviation of the sample, we can use that to approximate how wide our CI will be. As *n* gets bigger, the interval will get narrower.

Determining the Sample Size to Estimate Population Proportion *p*

- The maximum margin of error to estimate p is $Z_{\alpha/2}\sqrt{\dfrac{p(1-p)}{n}}$. First, determine the desired level of confidence and the margin of error. Then estimate n by equating the desired margin of error with this expression.

- If an estimate of p is available from past experiments, then estimate the required sample size as

$$n \geq \left(\frac{Z_{\alpha/2}}{ME}\right)^2 p(1-p)$$

- If no information about p is available, then use $p = \dfrac{1}{2}$ and estimate the required sample size as

$$n \geq \left(\frac{Z_{\alpha/2}}{2ME}\right)^2$$

  This gives a conservative estimate for the sample size in the absence of any prior information about p.

- For a 95% confidence level, $z^* \approx Z_{\alpha/2} = 1.96 \cong 2.0$. By substituting this in the above formula, we get

$$n \geq \left(1/ME\right)^2$$

Note that, to cut the margin of error in half, the sample size needs to be quadrupled.

It can be seen from the above formulas that:

- Sample size increases as the desired margin of error decreases.
- Sample size increases as the required confidence level increases.
- Sample size increases as the standard deviation increases.

Example 6: A factory cans fresh pineapple in sugar syrup. The manager in charge is interested in estimating the average amount of sugar per can to within 2 mg of the true mean. From previous experiments, he knows that the standard deviation of the sugar content is approximately 15 mg. Each test of measuring the amount of sugar in a can costs $5.00. One thousand dollars have been budgeted for this experiment. Does the manager have enough funds to estimate the average amount of sugar per can with a 95% confidence?

Solution: The manager is interested in determining the sample size needed to estimate

μ = the mean amount of sugar per can.

Confidence level = $0.95 \Rightarrow \alpha = 0.05 \Rightarrow z^* = Z_{\alpha/2} = Z_{0.025} = 1.96$

The desired ME = 2 mg, and the standard deviation is 15 mg.

So the required sample size is

$$n \geq \left(\frac{Z_{\alpha/2}\sigma}{ME} \right)^2 = \left(\frac{1.96(15)}{2} \right)^2 = 216.09$$

The manager should sample at least 217 cans. It will cost him at least 217(5) = $1,085. Because he has a budget of $1,000, he does not have enough money.

Example 7: Officials at a large university want to estimate the proportion of students in favor of changing from a quarter system to a semester system. They would like the estimate to be within 0.04 of the true proportion with a 95% confidence level.

(a) Estimate the required sample size if no prior information is available.
(b) Assume that a similar poll was conducted two years ago. It resulted in 35% of the students favoring a change from the quarter system to the semester system. Estimate the required sample size.

Solution: The officials are interested in estimating p = the proportion of students in favor of changing from a quarter system to a semester system.

Confidence level = $0.95 \Rightarrow \alpha = 0.05 \Rightarrow z^* = Z_{\alpha/2} = Z_{0.025} = 1.96$

The desired ME = 0.04

(a) Because no prior information is available, use $\hat{p} = \frac{1}{2}$ to get a conservative estimate of the required sample size.

$$n \geq \left(\frac{Z_{\alpha/2}}{2ME} \right)^2 = \left(\frac{1.96}{2(0.04)} \right)^2 = 600.25$$

The university officials need to poll at least 601 students at random.

(b) Using information from the prior poll, we get $\hat{p} = 0.35$. Then the required sample size is

$$n \geq \left(\frac{Z_{\alpha/2}}{ME} \right)^2 \hat{p}(1-\hat{p}) = \left(\frac{1.96}{0.04} \right)^2 (0.35)(1 - 0.35) \approx 546.23$$

The university officials need to poll at least 547 students at random.

ESTIMATION AND INFERENCE PROBLEMS

To do well on the AP Statistics Exam, you will need to be able to estimate and make inferences about the following parameters:

- population proportion (p)
- population mean (μ)
- the difference between two population proportions ($p_1 - p_2$)
- the difference between two population means ($\mu_1 - \mu_2$)
- the slope of the least-squares regression line (β)

In addition, you also need to know how to make inferences about categorical data. **Estimation procedures**, such as constructing confidence intervals, are used to estimate unknown population parameters; whereas **inference procedures**, such as testing hypotheses, are used for testing claims about unknown population parameters.

Below are the general steps you need in order to solve problems involving confidence intervals and the testing of hypotheses. All these steps are covered in detail later in this chapter. Before answering any estimation or inference problem, read the entire question carefully. Some problems may require you to use all the steps listed below, whereas others may require only a few.

Steps for Constructing a Confidence Interval

1. Set up the problem correctly.
   - Identify the parameter of interest—for example:
     - population proportion (p)
     - population mean (μ)
     - difference in population proportions ($p_1 - p_2$)
     - difference in population means ($\mu_1 - \mu_2$)
     - population mean of differences (μ_d)

   - Describe the parameter in the context of the problem. For example, write p = the proportion of voters in Iowa in favor of the governor's position or μ_d = the mean difference in the cholesterol level of patients before and after taking the new medicine.

2. Identify the appropriate type of confidence interval, and check its requirements.

   - Give the correct name or formula for the type of confidence interval you've selected. For example, to construct a confidence interval for p = the proportion of voters in Iowa in favor of the governor's position, you could write either

   (a) A large sample's z-interval for proportion, or

   (b) The confidence interval for p is constructed as $\hat{p} \pm Z_{\alpha/2}\sqrt{\dfrac{\hat{p}(1-\hat{p})}{n}}$

- Check the requirements for the selected confidence interval. For example, to construct a confidence interval for p, ask yourself whether $n\hat{p} > 10$ and $n(1 - \hat{p}) > 10$ (all requirements will be discussed in detail later in this chapter). Show your work. Just stating the assumptions or saying they are satisfied is not enough.

  Note: If you use the wrong type of confidence interval, then you will not get any credit for this part of the problem on the AP Statistics Exam!

3. Provide the correct mechanics to solve the problem.

- Give the correct values obtained from statistical tables or your calculator. For example, for a 95% confidence interval for p, give $z^* = Z_{\alpha/2} = Z_{0.025} = 1.96$.

- Compute the confidence interval correctly. Show you're putting the correct numbers into the formula you already gave in step 2. After you've computed the correct confidence interval, be sure to state it as (lower limit, upper limit).

4. State the correct conclusion in the context of the problem, using your confidence interval.

  For example, if your 95% interval for p is (0.62, 0.68), then write, "We are 95% confident that the proportion of voters in Iowa in favor of the governor's position is between 0.62 and 0.68."

Steps for Testing a Hypothesis

1. State a correct set of hypotheses.
   - State the null and alternative hypotheses correctly, defining any notation used.
   - State both hypotheses in the context of the problem. For example, write:
     (a) H_0: $p = 0.5$ against H_a: $p > 0.5$, where p = the proportion of voters in the state of Iowa in favor of the governor's position, or
     (b) H_0: $\mu_d = 0$ against H_a: $\mu_d > 0$, where μ_d = the mean difference in the cholesterol level of patients before and after taking the new medicine.

   Note: If you switch the null and alternative hypotheses around, you will lose all credit for this step on the AP Statistics Exam.

2. Identify the appropriate statistical test and check the appropriate requirements.

   - Give the correct name of the test, or give the correct symbol or formula for the test statistic. For example, to test for p as defined in step 1, write either:
     (a) Use a large samples z-test for proportion, or

     (b) The test statistic is $z = \dfrac{\hat{p} - p_0}{\sqrt{\dfrac{p_0(1 - p_0)}{n}}}$

   - Check the requirements for the selected test. (Use the same procedure as in step 3 of the estimation problem process above.)

Note: If you use the wrong statistical test (for example, if you use a paired *t*-test when an independent samples *t*-test is more appropriate), then you will not get any credit for this part of the problem on the AP Statistics Exam.

3. Provide the correct mechanics to solve the problem.

    *   Give the correct numerical value of the test statistic. Be sure to show that you're putting the correct numbers into the formula you gave in step 2. For example, write:

$$\text{Test statistic} = z = \frac{\hat{p} - p_0}{\sqrt{\frac{p_0(1 - p_0)}{n}}} = \frac{0.64 - 0.5}{\sqrt{\frac{0.5(1 - 0.5)}{250}}} \approx 4.43$$

    *   At this point there are two ways to do the problem: the ***p*-value approach** and the **rejection region approach** (again, both are described in detail later in this chapter). The *p*-value approach is generally the easier way to go if you're using a TI-83 or TI-84 calculator. The TEST option on the calculator will give the *p*-value. The rejection region approach is a bit more complicated, but it can be done just by using the tables supplied on the AP Statistics Exam—it does not require a calculator. Both approaches are equally acceptable to the AP graders. **Note:** Minor computational errors will not necessarily lower your score on this part of the AP Statistics Exam.

4. State the correct conclusion in the context of the problem using the results of your statistical test.

    *   Use your test results from the earlier step to arrive at the conclusion, using either the *p*-value approach or the rejection region approach. State clearly the link between the conclusion and the test result. For example, write:
        (a) Because *p*-value = 0.0000047 < α (here α = 0.01), we reject the null and accept the alternative hypothesis; or
        (b) Because the test statistic value 4.43 falls in the rejection region, we reject the null and accept the alternative hypothesis; or
        (c) Because the test statistic value 4.43 > 1.645, we reject the null and accept the alternative hypothesis.

Note: If the rejection rule is applied incorrectly, you will not get any credit for this part of the problem on the AP Statistics Exam!

    *   Write the conclusion in the context of the problem, consistent with the defined hypotheses. In other words, do not stop after saying "reject" or "do not reject" the null hypothesis. For the above example, you should write the following: "There is significant evidence to suggest that the proportion of voters in Iowa in favor of the governor's position is more than 0.5."

ESTIMATION FOR AND INFERENCE ABOUT A POPULATION PROPORTION *p*

Newspapers, television stations, and manufacturers routinely use public opinion polls to estimate the proportion of a population in favor of a certain issue, candidate, or product.

Parameter of interest: population proportion *p*

- Select a random sample of size *n*.
- Define what a "success" will be. For example, if you are interested in the proportion of pet owners in a neighborhood, define a "success" as owning a pet.
- Count the number of successes in your sample (x).

- The estimated proportion from the sample is $\hat{p} = \dfrac{x}{n}$. $\hat{p}$ is a point estimate of an unknown population proportion. Different random samples of size *n* from the same population will result in different sample proportions, giving different estimates. The distribution of the estimated proportions from all possible random samples of size *n* is the sampling distribution of $\hat{p}$.

- The mean of all possible sample proportions is *p*. Therefore, $\hat{p}$ is an unbiased estimator of *p*.

- The standard deviation of the sampling distribution of $\hat{p}$ is $\sigma_{\hat{p}} = \sqrt{\dfrac{p(1-p)}{n}}$. When we use our sample proportion $\hat{p}$ in this formula, we refer to it as the standard error. Standard error = $\sqrt{\dfrac{\hat{p}(1-\hat{p})}{n}}$.

- For a large *n*, the sampling distribution of $\hat{p}$ is approximately normally distributed. Therefore, for a large *n*, we can construct a *z*-interval or use a *z*-test. For a small *n*, we may need to use a different test, but these tests are not on the AP Exam.

> **Estimating *p* using $(1 - \alpha)100\%$ confidence interval:**
> Large sample case: Construct a *z*-interval
>
> $$\text{Margin of Error: } z^* \sigma_{\hat{p}} = Z_{\alpha/2}\sqrt{\dfrac{\hat{p}(1-\hat{p})}{n}}$$
>
> $$\text{Confidence Interval: } \hat{p} \pm Z_{\alpha/2}\sqrt{\dfrac{\hat{p}(1-\hat{p})}{n}}$$

Example 8: Suppose a pollster needs to determine the proportion of adult Americans who favor universal health care. Of the 2,000 Americans surveyed, 1,355 respond in favor of universal health care.

   (a) Find the true proportion of all adult Americans favoring universal health care according to this survey. Use a sample proportion point estimator.

   (b) Assume it is binomial: either the respondents favor universal health care or they do not. Find the standard deviation from point estimators. Assume the entire population surveyed is normally distributed.

Solution:

   (a) The sample proportion point estimator is $\hat{p} = \dfrac{1355}{2000} = 0.678$. This represents the true proportion of all adult Americans favoring universal health care.

   Those who do not favor it are represented by $1 - \hat{p} = 0.322$.

   (b) σ = standard deviation of sample proportions =
   $$\sqrt{\frac{\hat{p}(1-\hat{p})}{n}} = \sqrt{\frac{(0.678)(0.322)}{2,000}} \approx 0.010$$

Making an inference about the population proportion p:
Large sample case: Use a z-test.

H_0: $p = p_0$ (specified)
H_a: $p > p_0$ or
$\quad\;\; p < p_0$ or
$\quad\;\; p \neq p_0$

$$z = \frac{\hat{p} - p_0}{\sqrt{\dfrac{p_0(1 - p_0)}{n}}}$$

	Rejection Rule	
Alternative hypothesis:	Rejection region approach:	p-value approach:
H_a: $p > p_0$ H_a: $p < p_0$ or H_a: $p \neq p_0$	Reject H_0 if $z > Z_\alpha$ $z < -Z_\alpha$ $z > Z_{\alpha/2}$ or $z < -Z_{\alpha/2}$	Reject H_0 if p-value $< \alpha$, where p-value $= P(Z > z)$ p-value $= P(Z < z)$ p-value $= P(Z > |z|) + P(Z < -|z|)$

Conditions:

   (a) An independent random sample of size n is taken from the population.

   (b) The sample size is large enough so that the distribution of $\hat{p}$ is approximately normal (see below).

Checking the normality condition (b):

If the following conditions are satisfied, then the sample size is large enough to assume that the distribution of $\hat{p}$ is approximately normal.

- $n\hat{p}$ and $n(1 - \hat{p}) > 10$ for an estimation problem, where $\hat{p}$ = sample proportion.
- $np_0 > 10$ and $n(1 - p_0) > 10$ for an inference problem, where p_0 = claimed proportion.

Example 9: The CEO of a cable company claims that at least 80% of his more than 1 million customers are satisfied with the service his company provides. You are one of his customers and you are not happy with the service. You have also heard several of your friends complain about the cable service. Based on these complaints, you believe that the CEO's statement may be false. To test the claim, you select a simple random sample of 103 customers and find that 77 of them are satisfied with the service. Based on your sample result, do you think the CEO's claim is false? Test the CEO's claim at the 5% significance level.

Solution:

Step 1: State the hypotheses and define the parameter.

$H_0: p \geq 0.80$ (Writing $p = 0.80$ is also acceptable.)

$H_a: p < 0.80$

P represents the proportion of customers who are satisfied with the cable company's service.

Step 2: State the appropriate test by name or formula, and check the necessary conditions.

We will conduct a one-sample z-test for a population proportion.

(a) The problem states that an SRS is taken from a large population of customers (greater than 10 times the sample size); thus, the condition for having an independent random sample is met.

(b) $np_0 = 103(0.80) = 82.4$; $n(1 - p_0) = 103(0.20) = 20.6$. Both values are greater than 10, so we may assume that the sampling distribution for $\hat{p}$ is approximately normal.

Step 3: Perform the necessary calculations for the chosen test.

The point estimator sample proportion is $\hat{p} = \dfrac{77}{103} \approx 0.748$

The standard deviation for the sampling distribution is

$$\sqrt{\frac{\hat{p}(1-\hat{p})}{n}} = \sqrt{\frac{(0.748)(0.252)}{103}} \approx 0.0428$$

At 5% significance, the one-sided valued interval yields $z^* = z_\alpha = -1.645$

$$z = \frac{\hat{p} - p_o}{\sigma} = \frac{0.748 - 0.80}{0.0428} \approx -1.215$$

Step 4: Write your conclusion in context.

Because $-1.215 > -1.645$, the results are not significant. We fail to reject the H_0 claim at 95% confidence (5% significance). We do not have sufficient evidence to say that the proportion of satisfied customers is less than the CEO's claim of 0.80.

Note: A lack of significance does not mean that the CEO's claim is correct. The sample proportion *is* less than 0.80, but it's just not far enough away to conclude that the CEO was making false statements.

Example 10: A large national bank randomly selected 300 checking accounts from all its checking accounts and found that 45 were overdrawn at least once in the past two years.

- (a) Estimate the true proportion of checking accounts at this bank that were overdrawn at least once in the last two years, using a 95% confidence interval.
- (b) The bank manager reported that the bank has a significantly lower percentage of overdrawn checking accounts compared to the nation as a whole. If 20% of accounts nationally are overdrawn, can we believe the bank manager's report?

Solution:

(a) Estimation:

Step 1: The bank is interested in estimating p = the true proportion of checking accounts overdrawn at least once in the last two years.

Step 2: A random sample of $n = 300$ accounts was taken. Of the sampled accounts, $x = 45$ were overdrawn at least once in the last two years.

The sample proportion is $\hat{p} = \frac{x}{n} = \frac{45}{300} = 0.15$.

Conditions:

- (1) The accounts are independent because it is given that a random sample of accounts was taken and there are over 3,000 checking accounts at the bank.

- (2) $n\hat{p} = 300(0.15) = 45 > 10$ and $n(1 - \hat{p}) = 300(1 - 0.15) = 255 > 10$.
  Therefore, the sample size is large enough to assume that the sampling distribution of $\hat{p}$ is approximately normal.

Both conditions are satisfied, so we can construct a large sample z-interval for proportion.

Step 3: To construct a 95% confidence interval, we use $\alpha = 0.05$. Therefore, as discussed in the section "Finding Z_α," we can find $z^* = Z_{\alpha/2} = Z_{0.05/2} = Z_{0.025} = 1.96$.

The 95% $ME = Z_{\alpha/2}\sqrt{\dfrac{\hat{p}(1-\hat{p})}{n}} = 1.96\sqrt{\dfrac{0.15(1-0.15)}{300}} \approx 0.04$.

So, $\hat{p} \pm ME \Rightarrow 0.15 \pm 0.04 \Rightarrow (0.11, 0.19)$.

Therefore, a 95% confidence interval to estimate p is (0.11, 0.19).

Step 4: We are 95% confident that the true proportion of checking accounts at this bank that were overdrawn at least once in the last two years is between 0.11 and 0.19.

In other words, we are 95% confident that 11% to 19% of checking accounts at this bank were overdrawn at least once in the last two years.

TI-83 or TI-84:
- Choose **STAT → TESTS → A:1-PropZInt**
- Enter appropriate values
  1-PropZInt
  X: 45
  n: 300
  C-Level: .95
  Calculate
- Highlight **Calculate**
- Press **ENTER**

(b) Inference:

Step 1: We are interested in making an inference about p = the true proportion of checking accounts at this bank overdrawn at least once in the last two years.

Nationally, 20% of checking accounts are overdrawn. The manager reported that $p < 0.20$. We are looking for evidence to support the manager's report. Therefore, use $p_0 = 0.20$, and define the null and alternative hypotheses as H_0: $p \geq 0.20$ (the proportion of overdrawn accounts at this bank is the same as the national proportion, or higher) and H_a: $p < 0.20$ (the proportion of overdrawn accounts at this bank is lower than the national proportion).

Step 2: A random sample of $n = 300$ accounts was taken.

Of the sampled accounts, $x = 45$ were overdrawn at least once in the last two years.

The sample proportion is

$$\hat{p} = \frac{x}{n} = \frac{45}{300} = 0.15$$

Conditions:

(a) It is given that a random sample of accounts was taken.
(b) $np_0 = 300(0.20) = 60 > 10$ and $n(1 - p_0) = 300(1 - 0.20) = 240 > 10$.

Therefore, the sample size is large enough to assume that the sampling distribution of $\hat{p}$ is approximately normal.

The conditions are satisfied, so we can use a large sample z-test for proportion.

Step 3: The alternative hypothesis indicates that this is a left-tailed test. Suppose we are willing to take a 5% risk of rejecting a true null hypothesis. In this case, $\alpha = 0.05$.

Using the p-value approach: The rejection rule is "reject H_0 if p-value < 0.05."

Compute the test statistic value as

$$z = \frac{\hat{p} - p_0}{\sqrt{\dfrac{p_0(1 - p_0)}{n}}} \approx \frac{0.15 - 0.20}{\sqrt{\dfrac{0.20(1 - 0.20)}{300}}} = \frac{-0.05}{0.023} \approx -2.165$$

Compute the p-value using either the standard normal table or the TI-83 or TI-84.

- Using the standard normal table: The probability corresponding to the z-score of $-2.165 \approx -2.17$ is 0.015.
- Using the TI-83 or TI-84: **2nd → DISTR → 2:normalcdf(−5000,−2.165,0,1)**. This gives about 0.01519, which can be rounded to 0.015. Therefore, value $P(Z < -2.165) \approx 0.015$. See Figure 11.

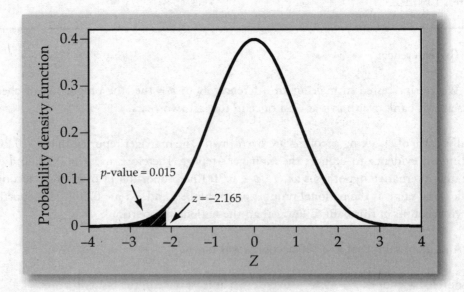

Figure 11: p-value approach

Using the rejection region approach:

The rejection rule is "reject H_0 if $z < z^* = -Z_\alpha = -Z_{0.05} = -1.645$."

The graph in Figure 12 shows the rejection region.

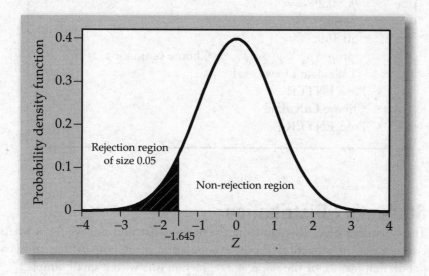

Figure 12: Rejection region and non-rejection region

Compute the test statistic value as

$$z = \frac{\hat{p} - p_0}{\sqrt{\dfrac{p_0\left(1 - p_0\right)}{n}}} = \frac{0.15 - 0.20}{\sqrt{\dfrac{0.20\left(1 - 0.20\right)}{300}}} \approx \frac{-0.05}{0.023} \approx -2.165$$

Step 4: Make a decision using either the rejection region approach or the p-value approach as follows:

The rejection region approach: Because $z = -2.165$, which is less than -1.645 (or because, from the above graph, we can see that the z falls in the rejection region), we should reject the null hypothesis and accept the alternative hypothesis.

The p-value approach: Because p-value $= 0.015$, which is less than 0.05, we should reject the null hypothesis and accept the alternative hypothesis.

Now state the conclusion in the context of the problem: at a 5% risk of error, we can conclude that the data provides sufficient evidence to support the manager's report that the bank's proportion of overdrawn accounts is lower than the national proportion.

When we do a *t*-test what we are really doing is comparing the means of two samples. Because we are comparing sample means, we are working with the sampling distribution of sample means! That is why the denominator in the *t*-statistic is the standard error $\left(\frac{s}{\sqrt{n}}\right)$ —we're looking at the difference between the two sample means and how big it is compared to the standard error.

TI-83 or TI-84:
- Choose **STAT → TESTS → 5:1-PropZTest**
- Enter appropriate values
  1-PropZTest
  p_0: 0.20
  x: 45
  n: 300
  prop $\neq p_0$ $< p_0$ $> p_0$ Choose option $< p_0$
  Calculate Draw
- Press **ENTER**
- Choose **Calculate**
- Press **ENTER**

Student's *t*-Distribution

The *t*-distribution is different from the normal distribution. We use it when making estimates of, or inferences about, a population mean, the difference between two population means, or the slope of a regression line with a small sample.

The *t*-distribution can be described as follows: Consider a sample of size *n* taken from a normally distributed population with unknown mean μ and unknown standard deviation σ. Then the unknown population standard deviation is estimated using the sample standard deviation *s*. The statistic $\frac{\bar{x} - \mu}{\text{SE}}$ (remember that $\text{SE} = \frac{s}{\sqrt{n}}$) is computed from the sample. Different samples of size *n* will result in different values for the statistic.

Cheers!
William Gosset, while working for the Guinness brewery, discovered the sampling distribution that the above statistic follows. He published his results under the pen name "Student." Since then, this sampling distribution has been known as student's *t*-distribution.

The characteristics of the *t*-distribution include the following:

- It's a continuous distribution.
- Its mean is 0.
- It's symmetric about its mean.
- It's bell shaped.
- Its shape depends on a parameter, called **degrees of freedom**, denoted by *df*. For smaller degrees of freedom, the distribution is more spread out, which means that its tails are thicker. As the degrees of freedom get larger, the *t*-distribution's tails get thinner and the *t*-distribution looks more and more like the standard normal (*z*) distribution. In other words, as the degrees of freedom increase, the standard deviation of the *t*-distribution decreases.
- It has a larger standard deviation than the standard normal distribution. In other words, it has thicker tails than the standard normal distribution. As the degrees of freedom increase, the standard deviation of the *t*-distribution approaches 1, making it the shape of the standard normal distribution.

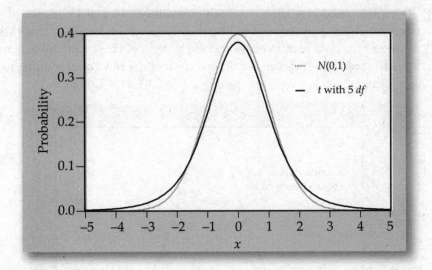

Figure 13: Comparison of standard normal and *t*-distribution

How to Read the *t* Table

The critical *t*-value (*t**) is the value of *t* required to achieve a certain upper tail probability. On the table for *t*-distribution critical values, the degrees of freedom (*df*) are listed in the leftmost column, the confidence levels (*C*) are listed across the bottom, and the corresponding upper tail probability (*p*) for each confidence level is listed across the top of the table.

- Determine the required degrees of freedom *df*. There are different formulas for degrees of freedom depending on which test or confidence interval you're using.
- Determine the area in the right tail of the distribution, namely the upper tail probability.
- In the *t* table, go down to the row that corresponds to the degrees of freedom, and then go across to the column that corresponds to the tail probability. Read the number in the cross section of the selected row and column.

Example 11: (a) Find *t** for tail probability 0.05 and 8 degrees of freedom.
(b) Find *t** for tail probability 0.01 and 15 degrees of freedom.

Solution:

(a) We are interested in finding *t** for tail probability 0.05 and 8 degrees of freedom. This means we need to find the *t* score for a *t*-distribution with 8 degrees of freedom such that the area to the right of this *t* score is equal to 0.05. Thus, read the number in the cross section of the row corresponding to *df* = 8 and the column corresponding to *p* = 0.05: *t** = 1.860.

What's a Degree of Freedom?

Say we tell you that we know the weights of 3 different people. Person A weighs 100 lbs, and Person B weighs 175 lbs. What do you know about Person C's weight? Nothing! It is a "free" variable: it could be anything! There are three pieces of independant information, because knowing Person A's and B's weight did not change your ability to predict Person C's weight.

But say we told you that the mean of their weights was 160, now do you know what Person C weighs?

Calculating the mean results in losing 1 piece of "free" information. If we know the mean, that third person's weight can no longer be any number.

(b) We are interested in finding t^* for tail probability 0.01 and 15 degrees of freedom. This means we need to find the t score for a t-distribution with 15 degrees of freedom such that the area to the right of this t score is equal to 0.01. So read the number in the cross section of the row corresponding to $df = 15$ and the column corresponding to $p = 0.01$: $t^* = 2.602$.

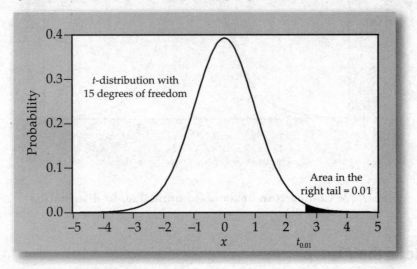

Figure 14: Finding the t score for a specified area in the right tail

ESTIMATION FOR AND INFERENCE ABOUT A POPULATION MEAN μ

Another important parameter is population mean. Here are some examples of the usefulness of a mean:

- Manufacturers are often interested in estimating the mean amount of a product per box filled by a filling machine, the mean amount of time spent by robots per assembly of a specific number of units, etc.
- The Department of Education might be interested in the mean amount of money per child spent by the state on education, the mean amount of time spent by parents on volunteer activities in their children's schools, etc.
- Local television stations might be interested in the mean amount of time viewers spend watching a particular station.

Parameter of interest: Population mean μ

- Select a random sample of size n.
- For each item or subject in the sample, measure the numerical characteristic of interest, X.

$$\text{Sample: } (x_1, x_2, x_3, ..., x_n)$$

- Compute the sample mean $\bar{x} = \dfrac{\sum x_i}{n}$ and sample standard deviation s.

This sample mean $\bar{x}$ is a point estimate of the unknown population mean. Different random samples of size n from the same population will result in different sample means, giving different estimates. The distribution of means from all possible random samples of size n is the sampling distribution of $\bar{x}$.

- The mean of all possible sample means is μ. Therefore, $\bar{x}$ is an unbiased estimator of μ.

- The standard deviation of the sampling distribution of $\bar{x}$ is $\sigma_{\bar{x}} = \dfrac{\sigma}{\sqrt{n}}$.

- Sampling distribution of $\bar{x}$:
  o If the population is normally distributed and the population standard deviation is known, then the sampling distribution of $\bar{x}$ is also a **normal distribution**.
  o If the population is normally distributed and the population standard deviation is unknown, then the sampling distribution of $\bar{x}$ is a **t-distribution** with $(n - 1)$ degrees of freedom.

To construct a confidence interval or make an inference using a normal (z) or a t-distribution, decide between a normal and a t-distribution using the following scheme:

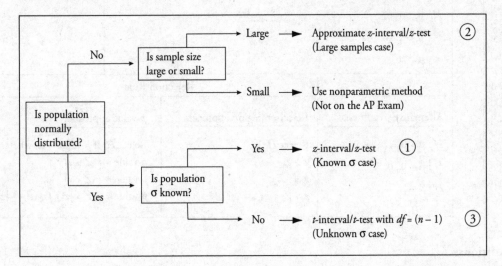

Figure 15: Scheme for selecting t- or z-interval for estimation of and inference about sample mean

In most cases on the AP Exam, if the problem is about a mean or a difference of two means, you will use ③, the t-test.

① *z*-Interval or *z*-Test: Known Standard Deviation Case

The population standard deviation σ is known, and the population is normally distributed. This case is unusual because if we are trying to estimate the population mean, we probably don't know the population standard deviation.

> **Estimating μ using $(1 - \alpha)100\%$ confidence interval:**
> Known standard deviation case:
>
> Construct a *z*-interval
>
> Confidence Interval: $\quad \bar{x} \pm z^* \dfrac{\sigma}{\sqrt{n}}$

Both the rejection region approach and the *p*-value approach operate on the same principles. Each is a measure of how extreme a value is. Each test (*z*, *t*, χ^2) will have different critical values depending both on the test and the degrees of freedom (in the *t* and χ^2 cases). *p*-values are test-independent. A *p*-value of 0.05 means the same thing whether you just did a *z*, *t*, or χ^2 test—there is a 5% chance of getting a sample this extreme from a null distribution.

Making an inference about the population mean μ:
Known standard deviation case: Use a *z*-test.

$H_0: \mu = \mu_0$	
$H_a: \mu > \mu_0$ or	$z = \dfrac{\bar{x} - \mu_0}{\sigma / \sqrt{n}}$
$\quad \mu < \mu_0$ or	
$\quad \mu \neq \mu_0$	

	Rejection Rule	
Alternative hypothesis:	Rejection region approach:	*p*-value approach:
$H_a: \mu > \mu_0$	Reject H_0 if	Reject H_0 if *p*-value $< \alpha$, where
$H_a: \mu < \mu_0$ or	$z > Z_\alpha$	*p*-value $= P(Z > z)$
$H_a: \mu \neq \mu_0$	$z < -Z_\alpha$	*p*-value $= P(Z < z)$
	$z > Z_{\alpha/2}$ or $z < -Z_{\alpha/2}$	*p*-value $= P(Z > |z|) + P(Z < -|z|)$

Conditions:

(a) The subjects are independent, which is satisfied if a random sample is taken from the population, and the sample size *n* is less than 10% of the population.
(b) The sampled population is normally distributed.

Checking the normality condition:

- Make a dotplot or a stem-and-leaf plot for the sample. Ask yourself whether the distribution is fairly symmetric and bell-shaped, without any outliers. In other words, ask yourself whether the distribution resembles the normal distribution. Alternatively, use a normal probability plot.

② Approximate *z*-Interval or *z*-Test: Large Sample Case

The population distribution σ is unknown, but the sample is large. If σ is unknown then estimate it using the sample standard deviation s.

> **Estimating μ using $(1 - \alpha)100\%$ confidence interval:**
>
> Unknown standard deviation case:
>
> Construct an approximate *z*-interval
>
> Confidence Interval: $\quad \bar{x} \pm z^* \dfrac{\sigma}{\sqrt{n}}$

Making an inference about the population mean μ:
Large sample case: Use an approximate *z*-test.

$H_0: \mu = \mu_0$ (specified)

$H_a: \mu > \mu_0$ or

$\quad \mu < \mu_0$ or $\qquad z = \dfrac{\bar{x} - \mu_0}{\sigma/\sqrt{n}}$

$\quad \mu \neq \mu_0$

	Rejection Rule	
Alternative hypothesis:	Rejection region approach:	*p*-value approach:
$H_a: \mu > \mu_0$ $H_a: \mu < \mu_0$ or $H_a: \mu \neq \mu_0$	Reject H_0 if $z > Z_\alpha$ $z < -Z_\alpha$ $z > Z_{\alpha/2}$ or $z < -Z_{\alpha/2}$	Reject H_0 if *p*-value $< \alpha$, where *p*-value $= P(Z > z)$ *p*-value $= P(Z < z)$ *p*-value $= P(Z > |z|) + P(Z < -|z|)$

Conditions:

(a) The subjects are independent, which is satisfied if a random sample is taken from the population, and the sample size n is less than 10% of the population.

(b) The sample size is large enough to apply the Central Limit Theorem and get an approximate normal distribution for the sample mean.

Checking the sample size condition:

There is no fixed value that determines whether a sample size is large or small; this depends on the shape of the sampled population. If there are no outliers and the population distribution is not extremely skewed, then $n \geq 30$ is large enough to get approximately normal sampling distribution of $\overline{X}$.

③ *t*-Interval or *t*-Test

The population distribution is normal, but the population standard deviation σ is unknown. Estimate σ using the sample standard deviation s.

Estimating μ using $(1 - \alpha)$100% confidence interval:

Construct a *t*-interval with $df = (n - 1)$ degrees of freedom

Confidence Interval: $\quad \bar{x} \pm t^* \dfrac{s}{\sqrt{n}}$

Making an inference about the population mean μ:

Unknown variance case: Use a *t*-test with $df(n - 1)$ degrees of freedom.

H_0: $\mu = \mu_0$ (specified)

H_a: $\mu > \mu_0$ or

$\quad \mu < \mu_0$ or

$\quad \mu \neq \mu_0$

$$t = \dfrac{\bar{x} - \mu_0}{s/\sqrt{n}}$$

	Rejection Rule	
Alternative hypothesis:	Rejection region approach:	*p*-value approach:
H_a: $\mu > \mu_0$ H_a: $\mu < \mu_0$ or H_a: $\mu \neq \mu_0$	Reject H_0 if $t > t_\alpha(df)$ $t < -t_\alpha(df)$ $t > t_{\alpha/2}(df)$ or $t < -t_{\alpha/2}(df)$	Reject H_0 if *p*-value $< \alpha$, where *p*-value $= P(t(df) > t)$ *p*-value $= P(t(df) < t)$ *p*-value $= P(t(df) > |t|) + P(t(df) < -|t|)$

Conditions:

(a) The subjects are independent, which is satisfied if a random sample is taken from the population, and the sample size n is less than 10% of the population.

(b) The sampled population is normally distributed.

Checking the normality condition:

- Make a dotplot or a stem-and-leaf plot for the sample. Ask yourself whether the shape of the distribution is fairly symmetric and bell-shaped, without any outliers. In other words, ask yourself whether the distribution resembles the normal distribution. Alternatively, use a normal probability plot.

Example 12: A company that manufactures bicycles receives steel rods in large shipments from a supplier. From past experience, the bicycle company manager knows that σ = 0.12 inches (approximately) and that the lengths are approximately normally distributed. The manager takes a random sample of 10 rods. The lengths of the sampled rods in inches are as follows:

11.90, 11.94, 12.05, 12.07, 11.97, 12.01, 12.08, 12.05, 12.12, 12.14

(a) The manager wants to estimate the mean length of the latest shipment of rods using a 90% confidence interval. Help this manager construct a confidence interval, and then interpret it.

(b) The company needs rods with a length of 12 inches in order to assemble the bikes properly. Because too-large and too-small rods are unsuitable, shipments not meeting the requirement are sent back to the supplier. Help this manager determine whether the shipment should be accepted or rejected.

Solution: (Remember that this is an unusual example because we usually do not know the population standard deviation.)

Step 1: (a) The manager is interested in estimating μ = true mean length of rods received in the latest shipment.

Step 2: A random sample of *n* = 10 rods was taken.

For each sampled rod, *x* = the length of the rod in inches.

It is given that the population standard deviation is σ = 0.12 inches.

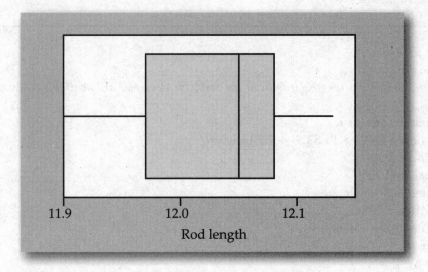

Figure 16: Distribution of rod lengths

Conditions:

(1) The rods are independent because it is given that a random sample of rods was taken from the shipment and $10 < 10\%$ of the large shipment of rods.

(2) It is also given that the lengths of the rods are approximately normally distributed. The conditions are therefore satisfied, and the population standard deviation is known. So this is a known standard deviation case, and we can use a z-interval to estimate the population mean.

Step 3: To construct a 90% confidence interval, we need $\alpha = 0.10$. Therefore,

$$z^* = Z_{\alpha/2} = Z_{0.10/2} = Z_{0.05} = 1.645$$

The sample mean is $\bar{x} = \dfrac{\sum x}{n} = \dfrac{120.33}{10} = 12.033$ inches.

The 90% $ME = z^* \dfrac{\sigma}{\sqrt{n}} = 1.645 \left(\dfrac{0.12}{\sqrt{10}} \right) \approx 0.0624$.

$$\bar{x} \pm ME \Rightarrow 12.033 \pm 0.0624 \Rightarrow (11.9706, 12.0954)$$

Therefore, the 90% confidence interval to estimate μ is (11.97, 12.10) inches.

Step 4: We are 90% confident that the true mean length of rods from this shipment is between 11.97 and 12.10 inches.

TI-83 or TI-84:
Using the data
If the actual measurements (the lengths of the rods, for example) are available, then use this option.

- Enter data in list L_1
- Choose **STAT** → **TESTS** → **7:ZInterval**
- Choose **Data**
- Press **ENTER**
- Enter appropriate values
    ZInterval
    Input: Data Stats
    σ : 0.12
    List: L_1
    Freq: 1
    C-Level: .90
    Calculate
- Highlight **Calculate**
- Press **ENTER**

Note: The ZInterval test assumes a two-tailed test. To correctly generate the interval for a one-tailed test, double the confidence level, or use the formula $1 - 2(\alpha)$.

TI-83 or TI-84:

Using summary statistics

If the actual measurements are not available, but the sample mean and the population standard deviation are available, then use this option.

- Choose **STAT → TESTS → 7:ZInterval**
- Choose **Stats**
- Press **ENTER**
- Enter appropriate values
    ZInterval
    Input: Data Stats
    σ : 0.12
    $\bar{x}$: 12.033
    n: 10
    C-Level: .90
    Calculate
- Highlight **Calculate**
- Press **ENTER**

(b) Make an inference about the mean.

Step 1: μ = the true mean length of rods received in the latest shipment.

The manager is interested in making an inference about the mean length of the rods in this shipment—in other words, she wants to test

$$H_0: \mu = 12 \text{ inches (accept the shipment)}$$

against $H_a: \mu \neq 12$ inches (reject the shipment)

Step 2: A random sample of $n = 10$ rods was taken.

For each sampled rod, x = the length of the rod measured in inches.

It is given that the population standard deviation $\sigma = 0.12$ inches.

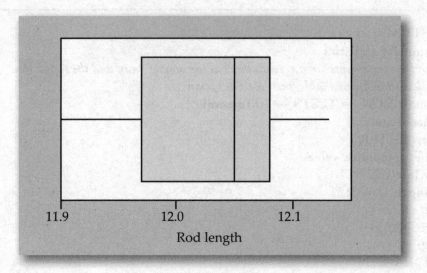

Figure 17: Distribution of rod lengths

Conditions: It is given that a random sample of rods is taken from the shipment. It is also given that the lengths are approximately normally distributed. The conditions are satisfied, and the population standard deviation is known. So this is a known standard deviation case, and we can use a z-test for mean.

Step 3: Let's use $\alpha = 0.10$. $z^* = Z_{\alpha/2} = Z_{0.10/2} = Z_{0.05} = 1.645$.

The rejection rule is:

- Reject the null hypothesis if p-value < 0.10 (using a p-value approach).

- Reject the null hypothesis if $z > 1.645$ or if $z < -1.645$ (using the rejection region approach).

The sample mean is $\bar{x} = 12.033$ inches.

$$z = \frac{\bar{x} - \mu_0}{\sigma / \sqrt{n}} = \frac{12.033 - 12}{0.12 / \sqrt{10}} \approx 0.87$$

$$p\text{-value} = P(Z > 0.87) + P(Z < -0.87) = 0.3844$$

Step 4: Because p-value = 0.3844 > 0.10 (or if using the rejection region approach, because $-1.645 < z < 1.645$), we do not reject the null hypothesis. The manager should not reject the shipment. Note that p-value = 0.3844 indicates that if the manager rejects the shipment, then there is a 38.44% chance that she is rejecting a shipment that meets specifications. Because the manager is only willing to take a 10% risk of rejecting the true null hypothesis, she must not reject the shipment.

TI-83 or TI-84:

Using the data

If the actual measurements are available, then use this option.

- Enter data in list L_1
- Choose **STAT → TESTS → 1:Z-Test**
- Choose **Data**
- Press **ENTER**
- Enter appropriate values

    Z-Test

    Input: Data Stats

    μ_0: 12

    σ: 0.12

    List: L_1

    Freq: 1

    $\mu : \neq \mu_0 < \mu_0 > \mu_0$ Choose option $\neq \mu_0$

Calculate Draw

- Press **ENTER**
- Choose **Calculate**
- Press **ENTER**

TI-83 or TI-84:

Using summary statistics

If the actual measurements are not available, but the sample mean and the population standard deviation are available, then use this option.

- Choose **STAT → TESTS → 1:Z-Test**
- Choose **Stats**
- Press **ENTER**
- Enter appropriate values

    Z-Test

    Input: Data Stats

    μ_0: 12

    σ : 0.12

    $\bar{x}$: 12.033

    n: 10

    $\mu : \neq \mu_0 < \mu_0 > \mu_0$ (Choose option $\neq \mu_0$)

Calculate Draw

- Press **ENTER**
- Choose **Calculate**
- Press **ENTER**

Example 13: Consider a vending machine that is supposed to dispense eight ounces of a soft drink. A random sample of 20 cups taken over a one-week period contained the following amounts in ounces:

| 8.1 | 7.7 | 7.9 | 8.0 | 7.7 | 7.8 | 7.9 | 8.0 | 7.6 | 7.9 |
| 8.0 | 7.9 | 7.6 | 7.5 | 8.1 | 7.8 | 7.8 | 7.9 | 8.2 | 7.5 |

(a) Estimate the true mean amount dispensed by the machine using a 95% confidence level.

(b) Is there significant evidence to conclude that the machine is dispensing less than 8 ounces?

Solution:

(a) Estimation:

Step 1: We are interested in estimating μ = the true mean amount of soft drink per cup dispensed by the machine.

Step 2: A random sample of n = 20 cups was taken.

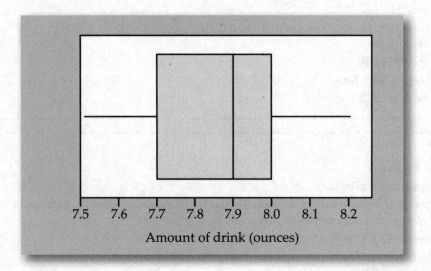

Figure 18: Boxplot of amount of drink dispensed per cup

Conditions:

(1) It is given that a random sample of cups was examined. Because the cups were filled over a period of one week, we can assume that the amounts filled are independent.

(2) Let's use a boxplot to summarize the data (see Figure 18). There are no outliers, and the distributions are fairly symmetric. Therefore, the above plot shows that it is reasonable to assume that the amounts dispensed per cup by the machine are approximately normally distributed.

The amount of soft drink dispensed per cup is approximately normally distributed, but the population standard deviation of the distribution of the amount of drink per cup is unknown. Therefore, we should construct a t-interval for the mean.

Step 3: Compute the sample mean and sample standard deviation using the formulas we already learned in Chapter 4.

$$\bar{x} = 7.845 \text{ and } s \approx 0.1986$$

With a sample of size 20, the degrees of freedom = 20 − 1 = 19.

To construct a 95% confidence interval, use $\alpha = 0.05$. Using the *t*-table for 19 degrees of freedom we get

$$t^* = t_{\alpha/2}(19) = t_{0.05/2}(19) = t_{0.025}(19) = 2.093$$

$$95\% \ ME = t_{0.025}(19)\left(\frac{s}{\sqrt{n}}\right) = 2.093\left(\frac{0.1986}{\sqrt{20}}\right) \approx 0.0929 \text{ ounces}$$

$$\bar{x} \pm ME \Rightarrow 7.845 \pm 0.0929 \Rightarrow (7.752, 7.938)$$

The 95% confidence interval to estimate μ is (7.75, 7.94).

Step 4: Interpretation.

- We are 95% confident that the true mean amount dispensed by the machine is between 7.75 ounces and 7.94 ounces.
- We are 95% confident that our best estimate of 7.845 ounces is within 0.0929 ounces of the true mean amount dispensed by the machine.

TI-83 or TI-84:
Using the data
If the actual measurements are available, then use this option.
- Enter the data into L_1
- Choose **STAT → TESTS → 8:TInterval**
- Choose **Data**
- Press **ENTER**
- Enter the appropriate values
    TInterval
    Inpt: Data Stats
    List: L_1
    Freq: 1
    C-Level: .95
    Calculate
- Highlight **Calculate**
- Press **ENTER**

Note: The TInterval test assumes a two-tailed test. To correctly generate the interval for a one-tailed test, double the confidence level, or use the formula $1 - 2(\alpha)$.

TI-83 or TI-84:
Using summary statistics
If the actual measurements are not available, but the sample mean and sample standard deviation are available, then use this option.

- Choose **STAT** → **TESTS** → **8:TInterval**
- Choose **Stats**
- Press **ENTER**
- Enter the appropriate values
  TInterval
  Inpt: Data Stats
  $\bar{x}$: 7.845
  Sx: 0.1986
  n: 20
  C-Level: .95
  Calculate
- Highlight **Calculate**
- Press **ENTER**

(b) Inference:

Step 1: We are interested in testing the hypothesis about

$\mu \geq$ the true mean amount of soft drink dispensed by the machine

H_0: μ = 8 ounces (The true mean amount of soft drink dispensed by the machine is eight ounces.)

H_a: μ < 8 ounces (The true mean amount of soft drink dispensed by the machine is less than eight ounces.)

Step 2: A random sample of n = 20 cups was taken.

Conditions:

(1) It is given that a random sample of cups filled was examined.
(2) Let's use a boxplot to summarize the data. The amount of soft drink dispensed per cup is approximately normally distributed, but the population standard deviation of the distribution of the amount of soft drink per cup is unknown. Therefore, we should use a t-test for the mean.

Step 3: Compute the sample mean and sample standard deviation using the formulas already learned in Chapter 4.

$$\bar{x} = 7.845 \text{ and } s \approx 0.1986$$

With a sample of size 20, df = 20 − 1 = 19.

Suppose we use $\alpha = 0.05$. Then, using a t-table for 19 degrees of freedom, we get $t^* = t_\alpha(19) = t_{0.05}(19) = 1.73$.

So the rejection rule is to reject the null hypothesis and accept the alternative hypothesis if:

- $t < -1.73$ (rejection region approach)
- p-value < 0.05 (p-value approach)

Compute the test statistic (and p-value if using p-value approach):

$$t = \frac{(\bar{x} - \mu_0)}{s/\sqrt{n}} = \frac{(7.845 - 8.000)}{0.1986/\sqrt{20}} \approx -3.49$$

$$p\text{-value} = P(t < -3.49) = 0.0012$$

Step 4: Write a conclusion.

- Using the **p-value approach:** Because p-value $= 0.0012 < \alpha = 0.05$, we should reject the null hypothesis and accept the alternative hypothesis.
- Using the **rejection region approach:** Because $t = -3.49 < -1.73$ (in other words, the test statistic falls in the rejection region), we should reject the null hypothesis and accept the alternative hypothesis.

Conclusion: At the 5% level of significance, there is sufficient evidence to conclude that the true mean amount dispensed by the machine is less than 8 ounces.

TI-83 or TI-84:
Using the data
If the actual measurements are available, then use this option.
- Enter the data into L_1
- Choose **STAT → TESTS → 2:T-Test**
- Choose option **Data**
- Press **ENTER**
- Enter appropriate values
    T-Test
    Input: Data Stats
    μ_0: 8.0
    List: L_1
    Freq: 1
    $\mu : \neq \mu_0$ $< \mu_0$ $> \mu_0$ (Choose option $< \mu_0$)
    Calculate Draw
- Press **ENTER**
- Choose option **Calculate**
- Press **ENTER**

TI-83 or TI-84:

Using summary statistics

If the actual measurements are not available, but the sample mean and sample standard deviation are available, then use this option.

- Choose **STAT → TESTS → 2:T-Test**
- Choose option **Stats**
- Press **ENTER**
- Enter appropriate values

    T-Test

    Input: Data Stats

    μ_0: 8.0

    $\bar{x}$: 7.845

    Sx: 0.1986

    n: 20

    μ_0: $\neq \mu_0$ $< \mu_0$ $> \mu_0$ (Choose option $< \mu_0$)

    Calculate Draw
- Press **ENTER**
- Highlight **Calculate**
- Press **ENTER**

Example 14: A spring water bottling plant fills bottles labeled 12 ounces. The floor supervisor noticed that in the past couple of days the plant had had several bottles overflow during the filling process. Suspecting that the mean filling-process amount had increased, he took 40 oversized bottles, filled them using the normal process for 12 ounce bottles, and measured the contents of each selected bottle (in ounces). The amounts are as follows:

13.19	12.87	12.20	11.97	12.05	12.68	12.41	13.30
12.89	12.23	12.39	13.13	12.74	13.17	12.40	11.97
12.39	12.67	12.07	13.37	12.74	12.26	12.47	12.16
12.24	12.86	12.11	12.60	12.03	12.19	12.92	12.35
12.53	12.30	12.64	12.52	13.22	12.84	13.09	12.20

(a) Estimate the filling-process mean using a 90% confidence interval.

(b) Is there significant evidence to support the supervisor's suspicions? Justify your answer using statistical evidence.

Solution:

(a) Estimating the filling-process mean:

Step 1: The supervisor is interested in estimating.

μ = the true mean amount of spring water filled per bottle (in ounces).

Step 2: A random sample of $n = 40$ bottles was taken.

For each sampled bottle, x = the amount of water measured in ounces.

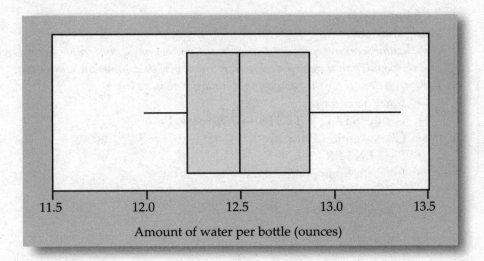

Figure 19: Boxplot of the amount of water filled per bottle

Conditions:

(1) It is given that a random sample of bottles was taken from those filled in the last eight-hour shift.

(2) A boxplot of the data (see Figure 19) shows no outliers. We do not know the distribution of the amount filled per bottle, but the sample size is large enough that we can apply the Central Limit Theorem and assume that $\bar{x}$ is approximately normally distributed. Therefore, we can use a z-interval to estimate the population mean.

Step 3: To construct a 90% confidence interval, we need $\alpha = 0.10$. Therefore,

$$z^* = Z_{\alpha/2} = Z_{0.10/2} = Z_{0.05} = 1.645$$

The sample mean $\bar{x} = \dfrac{502.36}{40} = 12.559$ oz.

The sample standard deviation is

$$s_x = \sqrt{\frac{\sum\left(x_i - \bar{x}\right)^2}{n-1}} = \sqrt{\frac{6315.52 - \left(502.36^2 / 40\right)}{40 - 1}} \approx 0.405 \text{ oz.}$$

Then

$$90\% \; ME = Z_{\alpha/2}\frac{s}{\sqrt{n}} = 1.645\left(\frac{0.405}{\sqrt{40}}\right) \approx 0.105 \text{ oz.}$$

$$\bar{x} \pm ME \Rightarrow 12.559 \pm 0.105 \Rightarrow (12.454, 12.664).$$

Therefore, the 90% confidence interval to estimate μ is (12.45, 12.66) oz.

Step 4: We are 90% confident that the true mean amount per bottle filled is between 12.45 and 12.66 oz.

Q: If your *p*-value is less than alpha, can you be sure that the null is true?

(Turn the page for the answer.)

TI-83 or TI-84:
Using the data
If the actual measurements are available, use this option. If the sample size is large and the population standard deviation is unknown, then input the sample standard deviation (s) for the population standard deviation (σ).
- Enter data in list L_1
- Choose **STAT → TESTS → 7:ZInterval**
- Choose option **Data**
- Press **ENTER**
- Enter the appropriate values
  Zinterval
  Input: Data Stats
  σ : 0.405
  List: L_1
  Freq: 1
  C-Level: .90
  Calculate
- Highlight **Calculate**
- Press **ENTER**

TI-83 or TI-84:
Using summary statistics
If the actual measurements are not available, but the mean of a large sample and the population standard deviation are available, then use this option. If the sample size is large and the population standard deviation is unknown, then input the sample standard deviation (s) for the population standard deviation (σ).
- Choose **STAT → TESTS → 7:ZInterval**
- Choose option **Stats**
- Press **ENTER**
- Enter the appropriate values
  ZInterval
  Input: Data Stats
  σ: 0.405
  $\bar{x}$: 12.559
  n: 40
  C-Level: .90
  Calculate
- Highlight **Calculate**
- Press **ENTER**

(b) The supervisor is interested in determining whether the filling-process mean has increased.

Step 1: The filling-process mean is

μ = true mean amount of spring water filled per bottle (in ounces).

To decide whether the filling-process mean has increased, the supervisor will test

H_0: μ = 12 oz. (The plant is still filling on the average 12 oz. per bottle.)

H_a: μ > 12 oz. (On the average, the plant is filling more than 12 oz. per bottle.)

Step 2: A random sample of n = 40 bottles was taken.

For each sampled bottle, x = the amount of water per bottle measured in ounces.

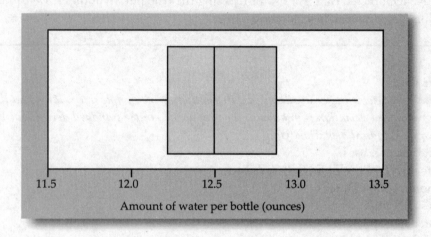

Figure 20: Boxplot of the amount of water filled per bottle

Conditions:

(1) It is given that a random sample of bottles was taken from the bottles filled in the last eight-hour shift.
(2) A boxplot of the data (Figure 19) shows no outliers. We do not know the distribution of the amount filled per bottle, but the sample size is large enough that we can apply the Central Limit Theorem and assume that $\bar{x}$ is approximately normally distributed. Therefore, we can use a z-test to make an inference about the filling-process mean.

Step 3: Suppose we use α = 0.05. Then

$$z^* = Z_\alpha = Z_{0.05} = 1.645$$

The sample mean is $\bar{x}$ = 12.559 oz and the sample standard deviation is $s \approx 0.405$ oz.

The rejection rule is "reject the null hypothesis if p-value < 0.05" (or, "reject the null hypothesis if $z > 1.645$," if using a rejection region approach).

Compute the test statistic value (and compute the p-value, if using a p-value approach).

$$z = \frac{\bar{x} - \mu_0}{s/\sqrt{n}} = \frac{12.559 - 12}{0.405/\sqrt{40}} \approx 8.73$$

$$p\text{-value} = P(Z > 8.73) = \text{almost } 0$$

Step 4: Because the p-value < 0.05 (or $z = 8.73 > 1.645$), reject the null hypothesis and accept the alternative hypothesis. At a 5% risk of rejecting the true null hypothesis, we can conclude that the filling-process mean has increased.

TI-83 or TI-84:
Using the data
If the actual measurements are available, use this option. If the sample size is large and the population standard deviation is unknown, then input the sample standard deviation (s) for the population standard deviation (σ).

- Enter data in list L_1
- Choose **STAT → TESTS → 1:Z-Test**
- Choose option **Data**
- Press **ENTER**
- Enter appropriate values
  Zinterval
  Input: Data Stats
  μ_0: 12
  σ: 0.405
  List: L_1
  Freq: 1
  $\mu: \neq \mu_0 \quad < \mu_0 \quad > \mu_0$ (Highlight option $> \mu_0$)
  Calculate Draw
- Press **ENTER**
- Choose option **Calculate**
- Press **ENTER**

A: No. By definition there's still a chance that your sample could have come from the null distribution (the p-value is the probability of that happening).

> **TI-83 or TI-84:**
> **Using summary statistics**
> *If the actual measurements are not available, but the mean of a large sample and the population standard deviation are available, then use this option. If the population standard deviation is unknown, then use the sample standard deviation to estimate the population standard deviation.*
>
> - Choose **STAT → TESTS → 1:Z-Test**
> - Choose option **Stats**
> - Press **ENTER**
> - Enter appropriate values
>   Z-Test
>   Input: Data Stats
> μ_0: 12
> σ : 0.405
> $\bar{x}$: 12.559
>   n: 40
> $\mu : \neq \mu_0 \quad < \mu_0 \quad > \mu_0$ (Highlight option $> \mu_0$)
>   Calculate Draw
> - Press **ENTER**
> - Choose option **Calculate**
> - Press **ENTER**

ESTIMATION OF AND INFERENCE ABOUT THE DIFFERENCE IN POPULATION PROPORTIONS ($p_1 - p_2$)

Large Samples Case

Often we are interested in comparing proportions from two different populations. For example:

- comparing the proportion of residents of Mobile County in favor of using tax money to rebuild private beaches to the proportion of residents of Baldwin County in favor of the same proposal
- comparing the proportion of Florida residents who support the patients' bill of rights to that of Texas residents who support the bill
- comparing the proportion of Visa cardholders assessed late-payment penalties to that of MasterCard cardholders assessed late-payment penalties

Let

p_1 = the proportion of interest in population 1

p_2 = the proportion of interest in population 2

Parameter of interest: Difference between two population proportions $(p_1 - p_2)$

- Select a random sample of size n_1 from population 1.
- Select a random sample of size n_2 from population 2.
- Be sure to select the two samples independently of each other.
- For each item or subject in the sample, note the presence or absence of the specific criteria of interest.
- Count the number of subjects meeting required criteria (x_1) from sample 1.
- Count the number of subjects meeting required criteria (x_2) from sample 2.

- The estimated proportion from sample 1 is $\hat{p}_1 = \dfrac{x_1}{n_1}$.

- The estimated proportion from sample 2 is $\hat{p}_2 = \dfrac{x_2}{n_2}$.

$\hat{p}_1$ and $\hat{p}_2$, respectively, provide point estimates of the unknown population proportions p_1 and p_2. The difference $(\hat{p}_1 - \hat{p}_2)$ gives a point estimate of $(p_1 - p_2)$. Different random samples of the same size from the same population will result in different sample proportions, giving different estimates. Therefore, the difference $(\hat{p}_1 - \hat{p}_2)$ is a random variable. The distribution of estimated differences from all possible random samples of sizes n_1 and n_2 is the sampling distribution of $(\hat{p}_1 - \hat{p}_2)$.

- The mean of the sampling distribution of $(\hat{p}_1 - \hat{p}_2)$ is $(p_1 - p_2)$.

  Therefore, $(\hat{p}_1 - \hat{p}_2)$ is an unbiased estimator of $(p_1 - p_2)$.

- The standard deviation of the sampling distribution of $(\hat{p}_1 - \hat{p}_2)$ is

$$\sigma_{\hat{p}_1 - \hat{p}_2} = \sqrt{\frac{p_1(1-p_1)}{n_1} + \frac{p_2(1-p_2)}{n_2}}$$

- For large sample sizes, the sampling distribution of $(\hat{p}_1 - \hat{p}_2)$ is approximately normally distributed.

Estimating $(p_1 - p_2)$ using $(1 - \alpha)100\%$ confidence interval:

Large samples case: Construct a z-interval

Margin of Error:

$$Z_{\alpha/2} s_{(\hat{p}_1 - \hat{p}_2)} = Z_{\alpha/2} \sqrt{\frac{\hat{p}_1(1-\hat{p}_1)}{n_1} + \frac{\hat{p}_2(1-\hat{p}_2)}{n_2}}$$

Confidence Interval:

$$(\hat{p}_1 - \hat{p}_2) \pm Z_{\alpha/2} \sqrt{\frac{\hat{p}_1(1-\hat{p}_1)}{n_1} + \frac{\hat{p}_2(1-\hat{p}_2)}{n_2}}$$

Making an inference about the difference in population proportions ($\hat{p}_1 - \hat{p}_2$): Large samples case: Use a z-test.

H_0: $p_1 - p_2 = D_0$ (D_0 is "pooled $\hat{p}$")

H_a: $p_1 - p_2 > D_0$ or
$p_1 - p_2 < D_0$ or
$p_1 - p_2 \neq D_0$

$$z = \frac{(\hat{p}_1 - \hat{p}_2) - D_0}{\sqrt{\hat{p}_c(1 - \hat{p}_c)\left(\frac{1}{n_1} + \frac{1}{n_2}\right)}} \qquad \text{where} \quad \hat{p}_c = \frac{x_1 + x_2}{n_1 + n_2}$$

Rejection Rule		
Alternative hypothesis:	Rejection region approach:	p-value approach:
H_a: $p_1 - p_2 > D_0$ H_a: $p_1 - p_2 < D_0$ H_a: $p_1 - p_2 \neq D_0$	Reject H_0 if $z > Z_\alpha$ $z < -Z_\alpha$ $z > Z_{\alpha/2}$ or $z < -Z_{\alpha/2}$	Reject H_0 if p-value $< \alpha$, where p-value $= P(Z > z)$ p-value $= P(Z < z)$ p-value $= P(Z > |z|) + P(Z < -|z|)$

Conditions:

(a) Random samples are taken from both the populations.

(b) The samples are taken independently.

(c) Both sample sizes are large enough that the distribution of ($\hat{p}_1 - \hat{p}_2$) is approximately normal.

Note that when constructing a confidence interval, the separate sample proportions are used to calculate the standard deviation and to check the normality condition. When making an inference, the pooled or common $\hat{p}$ is used to calculate the standard deviation and check the normality condition.

Checking the normality condition:

If $n_1 \hat{p}_1 > 10$, $n_1(1 - \hat{p}_1) > 10$, $n_2 \hat{p}_2 > 10$, and $n_2(1 - \hat{p}_2) > 10$, then it is reasonable to assume that the distribution of ($\hat{p}_1 - \hat{p}_2$) is approximately normal.

Example 15: A large manufacturer of jeans has two factories, one in Mexico and one in the Philippines. At the end of the assembly lines, each finished pair of jeans is inspected for quality and classified as either good or defective. The business manager wants to compare the proportion of defective jeans produced by the two factories. From one day's production, she randomly selects 500 pairs of jeans from the factory in Mexico and finds 25 defective. Similarly, she randomly selects 350 pairs of jeans from the factory in the Philippines and finds 27 defective. Estimate the difference in the proportion of defective jeans produced by the two factories, using a 98% confidence interval.

Solution:

Step 1: The business manager wants to estimate ($p_1 - p_2$), where

p_1 = The true proportion of defective jeans manufactured at the plant in Mexico.

p_2 = The true proportion of defective jeans manufactured at the plant in the Philippines.

Step 2: A random sample of $n_1 = 500$ pairs of jeans was taken from the plant in Mexico.

Of the sampled jeans, $x_1 = 25$ were defective.

The sample proportion is $\hat{p}_1 = \dfrac{x_1}{n_1} = \dfrac{25}{500} = 0.05$.

A random sample of $n_2 = 350$ pairs of jeans was taken from the plant in the Philippines.

Of the sampled jeans, $x_2 = 27$ were defective.

The sample proportion is $\hat{p}_2 = \dfrac{x_2}{n_2} = \dfrac{27}{350} \approx 0.077$.

Conditions:

(a) It is given that random samples of jeans were taken. It is reasonable to assume that both samples were taken independently.

(b) $n_1\hat{p}_1 = 500(0.05) = 25 > 10$ and $n_1(1 - \hat{p}_1) = 500(1 - 0.05) = 475 > 10$.

$n_2\hat{p}_2 = 350(0.077) \approx 27 > 10$ and $n_2(1 - \hat{p}_2) = 350(1 - 0.077) \approx 323 > 10$.

Therefore, the sample sizes are large enough that we can assume that the sampling distribution of $(\hat{p}_1 - \hat{p}_2)$ is approximately normal.

The conditions are satisfied and we can therefore use a large-samples z-interval for difference in proportions.

Step 3: To construct a 98% confidence interval, we use $\alpha = 0.02$.

$$z^* = Z_{\alpha/2} = Z_{0.02/2} = Z_{0.01} = 2.33$$

$$(\hat{p}_1 - \hat{p}_2) = 0.05 - 0.077 = -0.027$$

$$98\% \ ME = Z_{\alpha/2}\sqrt{\dfrac{\hat{p}_1(1 - \hat{p}_1)}{n_1} + \dfrac{\hat{p}_2(1 - \hat{p}_2)}{n_2}}$$

$$= 2.33\sqrt{\dfrac{0.05(1 - 0.05)}{500} + \dfrac{0.077(1 - 0.077)}{350}}$$

$$\approx 0.04$$

$$(\hat{p}_1 - \hat{p}_2) \pm ME \Rightarrow -0.027 \pm 0.04 \Rightarrow (-0.067, 0.013)$$

Therefore, a 98% confidence interval to estimate $(p_1 - p_2)$ is $(-0.067, 0.013)$.

Step 4: We are 98% confident that the difference between the proportion of defective jeans produced by the plant in Mexico and the proportion of defective jeans produced by the plant in the Philippines is between -0.067 and 0.013. Because 0 falls in this interval, we cannot conclude that $p_1 - p_2 \neq 0$. In other words, there is no significant difference between the proportion of defective jeans produced by the factory in Mexico and the proportion produced by the factory in the Philippines.

TI-83 or TI-84:
- Choose **STAT → TESTS → B:2-PropZInt**
- Enter appropriate values
  2-PropZInt
  x1: 25
  n1: 500
  x2: 27
  n2: 350
  C-Level: .98
  Calculate
- Highlight **Calculate**
- Press **ENTER**

ESTIMATION OF AND INFERENCE ABOUT THE DIFFERENCE IN POPULATION MEANS ($\mu_1 - \mu_2$)

We are often interested in comparing the means of two different populations. For example:

- Comparing the mean lifetimes of two comparable brands of tires
- Comparing the mean costs of education at two state universities
- Comparing the mean grades of students taught using two different methods
- Comparing the mean number of asthma attacks per month before and after patients are given a new medication

In each of the above examples, we want to compare the means of two populations. To make such a comparison, we need to take a random sample from each of the two populations and compare their sample means. But notice that, in some cases, the two samples are independent, whereas in others the samples are dependent. By "dependence," we mean that there is some kind of matching involved between the first sample and the second sample. Data collected from independent samples is analyzed differently from data collected from dependent samples:

- **Independent samples.** To compare the effects of two different teaching methods (traditional and new) on students' grades, take a group of students with similar educational backgrounds. Assign these students randomly to one of two different groups. Teach the students in group 1 using the traditional method and those in group 2 using the new method. At the end of the course, give the same exam to both groups and measure the students' grades. In this situation, there is no specific matching between the students in one group and the students in the other group. So the two samples are independent or unpaired.

- **Dependent samples.** To measure the effectiveness of a new diet, select a group of patients, and measure their cholesterol levels before starting on a new diet. Then measure the cholesterol levels of the same patients after they've been put on the diet for three months. In this situation, note that there is a specific match between the "before diet" cholesterol level sample and the "after diet" cholesterol level sample. Both samples are taken from the same patients. It does not make sense to compare the "before diet" cholesterol level for Bob with the "after diet" cholesterol level for Ann. Dependence does not necessarily mean taking measurements on the same item or person, however.

Case of Independent or Unpaired Samples

Two samples are considered independent if the selection of one sample has no bearing on the selection of the other sample. For example, to compare the lifetimes of Goodyear tires to the lifetimes of Firestone tires, we could select a sample of tires from Goodyear's production line and a sample from Firestone's. Which tires get selected in one sample has no connection to which tires get selected in the other sample.

Here, we will let

μ_1 = The mean of population 1, and σ_1 = the standard deviation of population 1.
μ_2 = The mean of population 2, and σ_2 = the standard deviation of population 2.

Suppose we are interested in estimating the difference between two population means. Parameter of interest: Difference between two population means ($\mu_1 - \mu_2$).

- Select a random sample of size n_1 from population 1.
- Select a random sample of size n_2 from population 2.
- Select the two samples independently of each other.
- For each selected item, measure the specific variable of interest. Let x_{11}, x_{12}, ..., x_{1n_1} be the measurements from the first sample and x_{21}, x_{22}, ..., x_{2n_2} be the measurements from the second sample.
- Compute both sample means.

- The mean of sample 1 is $\bar{x}_1 = \dfrac{\sum\limits_{i=1}^{n_1} x_{1i}}{n_1}$. The mean of sample 2 is $\bar{x}_2 = \dfrac{\sum\limits_{i=1}^{n_2} x_{2i}}{n_2}$. Note

that $\bar{x}_1$ estimates μ_1 and $\bar{x}_2$ estimates μ_2. The difference ($\bar{x}_1 - \bar{x}_2$) gives a point

estimate of the difference ($\mu_1 - \mu_2$). Different random samples of the same size

from the same population will result in different sample means, giving different

estimates. Therefore, the difference ($\bar{x}_1 - \bar{x}_2$) is a random variable. The distribution of the estimated differences in sample means from all possible random and

independent samples of sizes n_1 and n_2 is the sampling distribution of $(\bar{x}_1 - \bar{x}_2)$.

- The mean of the sampling distribution of $(\bar{x}_1 - \bar{x}_2)$ is $(\mu_1 - \mu_2)$. Therefore, $(\bar{x}_1 - \bar{x}_2)$ is an unbiased estimator of $(\mu_1 - \mu_2)$.

- Because the samples were taken independently, the standard deviation of the sampling distribution of $(\bar{x}_1 - \bar{x}_2)$ is

$$\sigma_{\bar{x}_1 - \bar{x}_2} = \sqrt{\frac{\sigma_1^2}{n_1} + \frac{\sigma_2^2}{n_2}}$$

- Note the following about the sampling distribution of $(\bar{x}_1 - \bar{x}_2)$:
  If both the populations are normally distributed and the population standard deviations are known, then the sampling distribution of $(\bar{x}_1 - \bar{x}_2)$ is also a **normal distribution**.

  If both the populations are normally distributed and the population standard deviations are unknown but equal, then the sampling distribution of $(\bar{x}_1 - \bar{x}_2)$ is a **t-distribution** with $(n_1 + n_2 - 2)$ degrees of freedom.

  If both the populations are normally distributed and the population standard deviations are unknown and unequal, then the sampling distribution of $(\bar{x}_1 - \bar{x}_2)$ is an approximate **t-distribution** with degrees of freedom equal to

$$df = \frac{\left(\dfrac{s_1^2}{n_1} + \dfrac{s_2^2}{n_2}\right)^2}{\dfrac{\left(s_1^2/n_1\right)^2}{n_1 - 1} + \dfrac{\left(s_2^2/n_2\right)^2}{n_2 - 1}}$$

In most cases, this formula gives a fractional value for the required degrees of freedom. We would therefore need computers or calculators to find the true corresponding t-values. When using tables, use the next smallest degree of freedom to the calculated df. For example, if the above formula gives degrees of freedom equal to 17.35, then use 17 degrees of freedom in the t-distribution table.

You do not need to memorize this (or any other) formula; you will be provided with all of the formulas you need. This calculation can be done on your calculator. On the TI-83 or TI-84, use the **0:2-SampTInt** function from the STATS-Tests menu.

If both the sample sizes are large, then according to the Central Limit Theorem, the sampling distribution of $(\bar{x}_1 - \bar{x}_2)$ is approximately **normal**, regardless of the population distributions.

- To construct a confidence interval using a normal or a *t*-distribution, decide between the two distributions using the scheme shown in Figure 21.

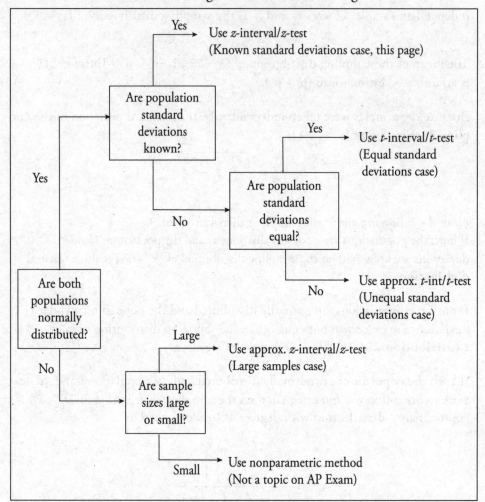

**Figure 21: Scheme for selecting a confidence interval or test
for difference of population means**

Known Standard Deviations Case

The two population standard deviations σ_1 and σ_2 are known, and both populations are normally distributed. Again, this case is unusual. If we want to estimate the difference in means, we most likely do not know the standard deviations.

Estimating $(\mu_1 - \mu_2)$ **using** $(1 - \alpha)100\%$ **confidence interval:**

Known standard deviations case: Construct a z-interval

$$\text{Margin of Error: } Z_{\alpha/2}\, \sigma_{(\bar{x}_1 - \bar{x}_2)} = Z_{\alpha/2}\sqrt{\frac{\sigma_1^2}{n_1} + \frac{\sigma_2^2}{n_2}}$$

$$\text{Confidence Interval: } \left(\bar{x}_1 - \bar{x}_2\right) \pm Z_{\alpha/2}\sqrt{\frac{\sigma_1^2}{n_1} + \frac{\sigma_2^2}{n_2}}$$

Making an inference about the difference in population means $(\mu_1 - \mu_2)$**:**
Known standard deviations case: Use a z-test.

$H_0: \mu_1 - \mu_2 = D_0$ (D_0 is specified)

$H_a: \mu_1 - \mu_2 > D_0$

$\quad \mu_1 - \mu_2 < D_0$ or

$\quad \mu_1 - \mu_2 \neq D_0$

$\quad D_0$ is specified difference

$$z = \frac{(\bar{x}_1 - \bar{x}_2) - D_0}{\sqrt{\dfrac{\sigma_1^2}{n_1} + \dfrac{\sigma_2^2}{n_2}}}$$

	Rejection Rule	
Alternative hypothesis:	Rejection region approach:	p-value approach:
$H_a: \mu_1 - \mu_2 > D_0$	Reject H_0 if	Reject H_0 if p-value $< \alpha$, where
$H_a: \mu_1 - \mu_2 < D_0$	$z > Z_\alpha$	p-value $= P(Z > z)$
$H_a: \mu_1 - \mu_2 \neq D_0$	$z < -Z_\alpha$	p-value $= P(Z < z)$
	$z > Z_{\alpha/2}$ or $z < -Z_{\alpha/2}$	p-value $= P(Z > |z|) + P(Z < -|z|)$

Conditions:

(a) Random samples are taken from both the populations.
(b) The samples are taken independently.
(c) The sampled populations are normally distributed.

Checking the normality condition:

Make a dotplot or stem-and-leaf plot for each sample. Ask yourself whether each distribution is fairly symmetric and bell-shaped, without any outliers. In other words, ask yourself whether the distribution resembles the normal distribution. Alternatively, use a normal probability plot. There are more formal tests, but they are not topics on the AP Exam.

Large Samples Case
Both samples are large.

If the population standard deviations (σ_1 and σ_2) are unknown, estimate them using the sample standard deviations (s_1 and s_2, respectively).

Estimating $(\mu_1 - \mu_2)$ **using** $(1 - \alpha)100\%$ **confidence interval:**

Large samples case: Construct a z-interval

$$\text{Margin of Error: } Z_{\alpha/2} s_{x_1 - x_2} = Z_{\alpha/2} \sqrt{\frac{s_1^2}{n_1} + \frac{s_2^2}{n_2}}$$

$$\text{Confidence Interval: } \left(x_1 - x_2\right) \pm Z_{\alpha/2} \sqrt{\frac{s_1^2}{n_1} + \frac{s_2^2}{n_2}}$$

Making an inference about the difference in population means $(\mu_1 - \mu_2)$:

Large samples case: Use a z-test.

$H_0: \mu_1 - \mu_2 = D_0$ (D_0 is specified)

$H_a: \mu_1 - \mu_2 > D_0$

$\mu_1 - \mu_2 < D_0$ or

$\mu_1 - \mu_2 \neq D_0$

(D_0 is specified difference)

$$z = \frac{(\overline{x}_1 - \overline{x}_2) - D_0}{\sqrt{\dfrac{\sigma_1^2}{n_1} + \dfrac{\sigma_2^2}{n_2}}}$$

	Rejection Rule	
Alternative hypothesis:	Rejection region approach:	p-value approach:
$H_a: \mu_1 - \mu_2 > D_0$	Reject H_0 if	Reject H_0 if p-value $< \alpha$, where
$H_a: \mu_1 - \mu_2 < D_0$	$z > Z_\alpha$	p-value $= P(Z > z)$
$H_a: \mu_1 - \mu_2 \neq D_0$	$z < -Z_\alpha$	p-value $= P(Z < z)$
	$z > Z_{\alpha/2}$ or $z < -Z_{\alpha/2}$	p-value $= P(Z > |z|) + P(Z < -|z|)$

Conditions:

(a) Random samples are taken from both populations.

(b) The samples are taken independently.

(c) The samples are large enough that the distribution for $(\overline{x}_1 - \overline{x}_2)$ is approximately normal.

Checking the normality condition:

There is no unique value that determines in general whether a sample size is large or small; this depends on the shape of the distribution of the sampled population. If there are no outliers and the population distributions are not extremely skewed, then $n_1 \geq 30$ and $n_2 \geq 30$ are large enough to get approximately normal sampling distributions for $\overline{x}_1$ and $\overline{x}_2$, and consequently for $(x_1 - x_2)$, too.

Equal Standard Deviations Case

Two population standard deviations σ_1 and σ_2 are unknown but are assumed to be equal. Let's say $\sigma_1 = \sigma_2 = \sigma$. Compute sample standard deviations from each sample. Let s_1 be the standard deviation computed from sample 1 and s_2 be the standard deviation computed from sample 2. We know that s_1 estimates σ_1 and s_2 estimates σ_2. But remember that $\sigma_1 = \sigma_2 = \sigma$. So we have two estimates (s_1 and s_2) for one unknown quantity σ. By pooling information from both samples, we can get an improved estimate of σ. The pooled estimate of σ is computed as

$$s_p = \sqrt{\frac{(n_1 - 1)s_1^2 + (n_2 - 1)s_2^2}{n_1 + n_2 - 2}}$$

Estimating $(\mu_1 - \mu_2)$ **using $(1 - \alpha)100\%$ confidence interval:**

Equal standard deviations case: Construct a t-interval with df degrees of freedom, where $df = (n_1 + n_2 - 2)$.

Margin of Error: $t_{\alpha/2}(df)s_{(\bar{x}_1 - \bar{x}_2)} = t_{\alpha/2}(df)s_p\sqrt{\dfrac{1}{n_1} + \dfrac{1}{n_2}}$

Where $s_p = \sqrt{\dfrac{(n_1 - 1)s_1^2 + (n_2 - 1)s_2^2}{n_1 + n_2 - 2}}$

Confidence Interval: $(\bar{x}_1 - \bar{x}_2) \pm t_{\alpha/2}(df)s_p\sqrt{\dfrac{1}{n_1} + \dfrac{1}{n_2}}$

Making an inference about the difference in population means $(\mu_1 - \mu_2)$:
Equal standard deviations case: Use a t-test with $df = (n_1 + n_2 - 2)$ degrees of freedom.

$H_0: \mu_1 - \mu_2 = D_0$

(specified difference)

$H_a: \mu_1 - \mu_2 > D_0$

$\quad \mu_1 - \mu_2 < D_0$ or

$\quad \mu_1 - \mu_2 \neq D_0$

$$t = \frac{(\bar{x}_1 - \bar{x}_2) - D_0}{s_p\sqrt{\dfrac{1}{n_1} + \dfrac{1}{n_2}}}$$

where $s_p = \sqrt{\dfrac{(n_1 - 1)s_1^2 + (n_2 - 1)s_2^2}{(n_1 + n_2) - 2}}$

Rejection Rule		
Alternative hypothesis:	Rejection region approach:	p-value approach:
$H_a: \mu_1 - \mu_2 > D_0$	Reject H_0 if	Reject H_0 if p-value $< \alpha$, where
$H_a: \mu_1 - \mu_2 < D_0$	$t > t_\alpha(df)$	p-value $= P(t(df) > t)$
$H_a: \mu_1 - \mu_2 \neq D_0$	$t < -t_\alpha(df)$	p-value $= P(t(df) < t)$
	$t > t_{\alpha/2}(df)$ or $t < -t_{\alpha/2}(df)$	p-value $= P(t(df) > |t|) + P(t(df) < -|t|)$

Conditions:

    (a) Random samples are taken from both the populations.
    (b) The samples are taken independently.
    (c) The sampled populations are normally distributed.
    (d) The population standard deviations are equal ($\sigma_1 = \sigma_2$).

Checking the normality condition:

Make a dotplot, histogram, or stem-and-leaf plot for each sample. Ask yourself whether each distribution is fairly symmetric and bell-shaped, without any outliers. In other words, ask yourself whether both the distributions resemble the normal distribution. Alternatively, use a normal probability plot.

Checking the condition of equal standard deviations:

Make dotplots or histograms and visually compare the spread of the measurements. If they are fairly comparable, without any outliers, then it is reasonable to assume that the standard deviations are equal. Alternatively, use a two-tailed F-test for equality of standard deviations (you may have learned how to do this in your statistics class, but it is not a topic on the AP Exam).

Unknown Standard Deviations Case

Two population standard deviations σ_1 and σ_2 are unknown. Estimate the unknown population standard deviations using the sample standard deviations s_1 and s_2, respectively.

> **Estimating** $(\mu_1 - \mu_2)$ **using** $(1 - \alpha)100\%$ **confidence interval:**
>
> Unequal standard deviations case: Construct a t-interval with
>
> $$df = \frac{\left(\dfrac{s_1^2}{n_1} + \dfrac{s_2^2}{n_2}\right)^2}{\dfrac{\left(s_1^2/n_1\right)^2}{n_1 - 1} + \dfrac{\left(s_2^2/n_2\right)^2}{n_2 - 1}} \text{ degrees of freedom}$$
>
> Margin of Error: $t_{\alpha/2}(df)\, s_{\bar{x}_1 - \bar{x}_2} = t_{\alpha/2}(df)\sqrt{\dfrac{s_1^2}{n_1} + \dfrac{s_2^2}{n_2}}$
>
> Confidence Interval: $(\bar{x}_1 - \bar{x}_2) \pm t_{\alpha/2}(df)\sqrt{\dfrac{s_1^2}{n_1} + \dfrac{s_2^2}{n_2}}$

On the TI-83 or TI-84, df can be obtained using the **0:2-SampTInt** function under the STATS-Tests menu.

Making an inference about the difference in population means ($\mu_1 - \mu_2$):

Unequal standard deviations case: Use a t-test with $df = \dfrac{\left(\dfrac{s_1^2}{n_1} + \dfrac{s_2^2}{n_2}\right)^2}{\dfrac{\left(s_1^2/n_1\right)^2}{n_1 - 1} + \dfrac{\left(s_2^2/n_2\right)^2}{n_2 - 1}}$ degrees of freedom

H_0: $\mu_1 - \mu_2 = D_0$ (specified difference)

H_a: $\mu_1 - \mu_2 > D_0$

$\qquad \mu_1 - \mu_2 < D_0$ or

$\qquad \mu_1 - \mu_2 \neq D_0$

$$t = \frac{(\bar{x}_1 - \bar{x}_2) - D_0}{\sqrt{\dfrac{s_1^2}{n_1} + \dfrac{s_2^2}{n_2}}}$$

	Rejection Rule	
Alternative hypothesis:	Rejection region approach:	p-value approach:
H_a: $\mu_1 - \mu_2 > D_0$ H_a: $\mu_1 - \mu_2 < D_0$ H_a: $\mu_1 - \mu_2 \neq D_0$	Reject H_0 if $t > t_\alpha(df)$ $t < -t_\alpha(df)$ $t > t_{\alpha/2}(df)$ or $t < -t_{\alpha/2}(df)$	Reject H_0 p-value $< \alpha$, where p-value $= P(t(df) > t)$ p-value $= P(t(df) < t)$ p-value $= P(t(df) > |t|) + P(t(df) < -|t|)$

Conditions:

(a) Random samples are taken from both the populations.

(b) The samples are taken independently.

(c) The sampled populations are normally distributed.

Checking the normality condition:

Make a dotplot or stem-and-leaf plot for each sample. Ask yourself whether the shape of each distribution is fairly symmetric and bell-shaped, without any outliers. In other words, ask yourself whether each distribution resembles the normal distribution. Alternatively, use a normal probability plot.

Checking the condition of unequal standard deviations:

In most cases, if the ratio of sample variances is larger than 4, then it is safe to assume that the standard deviations are unequal. Alternatively, use a two-tailed F-test for equality of standard deviations (you may have learned how to do this in your statistics class, but it is not a topic on the AP Exam).

Example 16: An economist wants to compare the hourly rates charged by automobile mechanics in two suburbs. She randomly selects auto repair facilities from both suburbs and records their hourly rates (in dollars). The data are as follows:

Suburb 1: 40.0 38.0 38.0 37.0 36.0 39.0 41.5 38.0 39.5 37.5 35.0 40.0

Suburb 2: 35.0 37.0 31.0 39.0 31.5 35.0 32.5 34.0 39.0 36.0

Is there sufficient evidence to indicate a difference in the mean hourly rates for these two suburbs?

Solution: The economist wants to make an inference about the hourly rates charged by auto mechanics.

Step 1: Let

μ_1 = the mean rate charged by mechanics in suburb 1

μ_2 = the mean rate charged by mechanics in suburb 2

We are interested in the difference $(\mu_1 - \mu_2)$. Because the economist wants to determine whether there is a difference in the two population means, we should use a two-tailed test.

H_0: $(\mu_1 - \mu_2) = 0$ (There is no difference in the mean rates charged in the two suburbs.)

H_a: $(\mu_1 - \mu_2) \neq 0$ (There is a difference in the mean rates charged in the two suburbs.)

Step 2: The sample sizes n_1 = 12 and n_2 = 10 are both small. Let us plot both the samples.

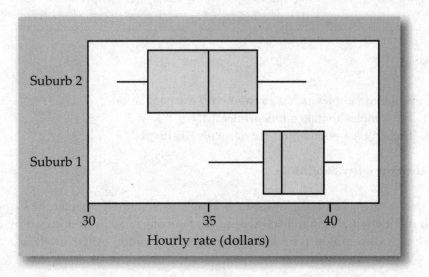

Figure 22: Boxplots of mechanics' hourly rates

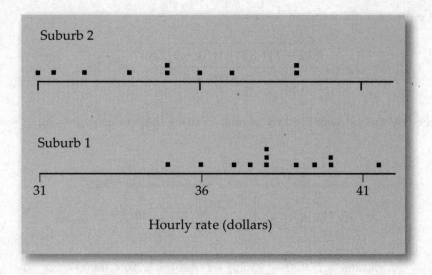

Figure 23: Parallel dotplots showing distribution of hourly rates

Conditions:

(a) It is given that random samples of auto repair facilities were obtained.

(b) There is no reason for the selection of facilities in one suburb to have any bearing on the selection of facilities in another suburb. Therefore, it is reasonable to assume that the samples were selected independently of each other.

(c) The graphs in Figures 22 and 23 show that the distributions of hourly rates are fairly symmetric, with no outliers. It is reasonable to assume that both the populations are approximately normally distributed.

All the conditions for a *t*-test are satisfied. Even though the population standard deviations are unknown, the dotplots show a similar spread for both samples, so it is reasonable to assume equal population standard deviations and to use an equal standard deviations *t*-test.

Step 3: Suppose we use a 5% level of significance. The degrees of freedom

$$df = 12 + 10 - 2 = 20 \text{ and } t^* = t_{\alpha/2}(df) = t_{0.025}(20) = 2.086$$

The rejection rule is "reject the null hypothesis if *p*-value < 0.05" (or, if using the rejection region approach, "reject the null hypothesis if $t < -2.086$ or $t > 2.086$").

Compute sample means and standard deviations, using the formulas we've learned before:

	n	Average	Standard Deviation
Suburb 1	12	38.29	1.83
Suburb 2	10	35.0	2.84

The pooled estimate of the standard deviation is

$$s_p = \sqrt{\frac{(12-1)1.83^2 + (10-1)2.84^2}{12 + 10 - 2}} \approx 2.34$$

Compute the test statistic value (and the p-value, if using the p-value approach).

$$t = \frac{(\bar{x}_1 - \bar{x}_2) - 0}{s_p\sqrt{\left(\dfrac{1}{n_1} + \dfrac{1}{n_2}\right)}} = \frac{38.29 - 35.00}{2.34\sqrt{\left(\dfrac{1}{12} + \dfrac{1}{10}\right)}} = 3.29$$

$$p\text{-value} = P(t(20) < -3.29) + P(t(20) > 3.29) = 0.0037$$

Step 4: Because p-value $= 0.0037 < 0.05$ (or, if using the rejection region approach, because the test statistic, $t = 3.29$, falls in the rejection region, or $t = 3.29 > 2.086$), we should reject the null hypothesis and accept the alternative hypothesis.

Because there is less than a 5% risk of making the wrong decision, we can conclude that there is a significant difference in the mean hourly charges in the two suburbs.

Because $\bar{x}_1 > \bar{x}_2$, we can say that the mean rates charged in suburb 1 are higher than the mean rates charged in suburb 2.

TI-83 or TI-84:

Inference using data

If the actual measurements are available, use this option.

- Enter data in 2 columns, say Suburb 1 in L_1 and Suburb 2 in L_2
- **Choose STAT → TESTS → 4:2-SampTTest**
- Press **ENTER**
- Choose option **Data**
- Press **ENTER**
- Enter appropriate values

  2-SampTTest

  Input: Data   Stats

  List1: L_1

  List2: L_2

  Freq1: 1

  Freq2: 1

  $\mu_1: \neq \mu_2$ $< \mu_2$ $> \mu_2$ (Choose option $\neq \mu_2$)
- Press **ENTER**

  Pooled: No   Yes   (Select Yes or No)
- Press **ENTER**

  Calculate   Draw
- Choose option **Calculate**
- Press **ENTER**

Note:

- For equal standard deviation case choose
  Pooled: Yes
- For unequal standard deviation case choose
  Pooled: No

TI-83 or TI-84:

Estimation using data

If the actual measurements are available, use this option.

- Enter data in 2 columns, say Suburb 1 in L_1 and Suburb 2 in L_2
- **Choose STAT → TESTS → 0:2-SampTInt**
- Press **ENTER**
- Choose option **Data**
- Press **ENTER**
- Enter appropriate values

    2-SampTInt

    Input: Data   Stats

    List1: L_1

    List2: L_2

    Freq1: 1

    Freq2: 1

    C-Level: .95

    Pooled: No   Yes   (Select No or Yes)

- Press **ENTER**

    Calculate

- Highlight **Calculate**
- Press **ENTER**

Note:

- For equal standard deviation case choose
  Pooled: Yes
- For unequal standard deviation case choose
  Pooled: No

You design a study to look at the difference in weight between two brands of potato chips. The mean difference between the two samples from Cronch Chips and Salty Seas Chips was 0.25 ounces, and your *t*-test resulted in a *p*-value of 0.001. Which of the following is/are true?

I. There is a 0.1% chance that there is no difference between Cronch and Salty Seas Chips.

II. There is a 0.1% chance that if there were no true population difference between Cronch and Salty Seas we would see a sample of chips with a difference of 0.25 oz or greater.

III. The difference between the bags of Cronch and Salty Seas chips is exactly 0.25 oz.

A) I only

B) II only

C) III only

D) I and II only

E) None of the Above

Here's How to Crack it

Most of the answers here use the value 0.1%, which comes from the p-value of 0.001. Let's tackle I and II first since they both use the same value. To figure out which one(s) could be correct, we have to think about the definition of a p-value. A p-value tells you the probability of getting a sample as or more extreme than yours if there were no difference between Cronch and Salty Seas Chip weights. Since we assume that there is no difference between the two chip weights in order to calculate the p-value, it cannot tell you the probability that there truly is no difference. So (I) is false. Eliminate (A) and (D). Statement (II) does give the correct interpretation of the p-value, so eliminate (C) and (E). The correct answer must be (B). Although there is no need to continue, to see why (III) is also incorrect note the sample difference doesn't necessarily equal the true population difference. The given sample difference of 0.25 oz is just an estimate of the population difference and is often not exactly correct.

Example 17: Students in a course at a large university felt that using a calculator would give them an advantage on an exam. Their instructor decided to check it out. Because she was teaching two of the 18 sections of this course and students were assigned randomly to different sections, she decided to allow one section to use calculators on the test and not the other. The students' scores on the test are approximately normally distributed. The average class scores and variances of the class scores are as follows:

	n	Class Average	Class Variance
Calculators	23	80.7	49.5
No Calculators	22	78.9	60.4

Is it advantageous for students to use calculators on the test? Justify using statistical evidence.

Solution: The instructor wants to compare two population means, namely, the mean test score of students using a calculator and the mean test score of students not using a calculator.

Step 1: Let

μ_1 = the mean score of students using a calculator

μ_2 = the mean score of students not using a calculator

We are interested in making an inference about $(\mu_1 - \mu_2)$.

$$H_0: \mu_1 = \mu_2 \text{ or } \mu_1 - \mu_2 = 0$$

(There's no difference between the mean scores of the two groups.)

$$H_a: \mu_1 > \mu_2 \text{ or } \mu_1 - \mu_2 > 0$$

(The mean score of the students using a calculator is higher than the mean score of students not using a calculator.)

Step 2: It is given that the students are assigned randomly to different sections. So it is reasonable to assume that the selected students are random, independent samples of all students taking this course. Also, it is given that the scores are approximately normally distributed.

The sample variances are fairly close to each other, and we can assume that the unknown population variances (and hence, their standard deviations) are equal. We can use the equal standard deviations t-test with $df = 23 + 22 - 2 = 43$ degrees of freedom. Let's use a 5% error rate.

Step 3: The rejection rule is to "reject null if p-value < 0.05" (or, if using the rejection region approach, "reject null if $t > 1.681$").

The pooled estimate of the standard deviation is

$$s_p = \sqrt{\frac{(23-1)49.5 + (22-1)60.4}{23 + 22 - 2}} \approx 7.40$$

Compute the test statistic value (and p-value if using p-value approach).

$$t = \frac{(\bar{x}_1 - \bar{x}_2) - 0}{s_p \sqrt{\left(\frac{1}{n_1} + \frac{1}{n_2}\right)}} = \frac{80.7 - 78.9}{7.40 \sqrt{\left(\frac{1}{23} + \frac{1}{22}\right)}} \approx 0.815$$

p-value = $P(t(43) > 0.815) = 0.2097$.

If it were not reasonable to assume equal population variances, then we could use the unequal variances t-test with

$$\upsilon = \frac{\left(\frac{s_1^2}{n_1} + \frac{s_2^2}{n_2}\right)^2}{\frac{\left(s_1^2/n_1\right)^2}{n_1 - 1} + \frac{\left(s_2^2/n_2\right)^2}{n_2 - 1}} = \frac{\left(\frac{49.5}{23} + \frac{60.4}{22}\right)^2}{\frac{\left(49.5/23\right)^2}{23 - 1} + \frac{\left(60.4/22\right)^2}{22 - 1}} \approx 42.12$$

where υ is the symbol for degrees of freedom.

Again, use a 5% error rate. The rejection rule is to "reject null if p-value < 0.05" (or, if using the rejection region approach, reject null if $TS > 1.682$). Compute the test statistic value (and p-value if using p-value approach).

$$t = \frac{(\bar{x}_1 - \bar{x}_2) - 0}{\sqrt{\left(\frac{s_1^2}{n_1} + \frac{s_2^2}{n_2}\right)}} = \frac{80.7 - 78.9}{\sqrt{\left(\frac{49.5}{23} + \frac{60.4}{22}\right)}} = 0.813$$

p-value $= P(t(42.12) > 0.813) = 0.2103$

Step 4: Because, in either case, the p-value > 0.05 (or the t falls in the non-rejection region), we do not reject the null hypothesis. At a 5% risk, we can conclude that there is insufficient evidence to suggest that the use of calculators improves the mean student grade.

TI-83 or TI-84:

Inference using summary statistics

If the actual measurements are not available, but the sample means and sample standard deviations are available, then use this option.

- Choose **STAT → TESTS → 4:2-SampTTest**
- Press **ENTER**
- Choose option **Stats**
- Press **ENTER**
- Enter appropriate values

    2-SampTTest

    Input: Data   Stats

    x̄1: 80.7

    Sx1: $\sqrt{49.5}$

    n1: 23

    x̄2: 78.9

    Sx2: $\sqrt{60.4}$

    n2: 22

    μ_1: $\neq \mu_2$ $<\mu_2$ $>\mu_2$ (Select option $> \mu_2$)
- Press **ENTER**

    Pooled: No   Yes   (Select Yes or No)
- Press **ENTER**

    Calculate   Draw
- Choose option **Calculate**
- Press **ENTER**

Note:

- For equal standard deviations case choose

    Pooled: Yes
- For unequal standard deviations case choose

    Pooled: No

Note: For equal standard deviations cases, choose "Pooled: Yes." For unequal standard deviations cases, choose "Pooled: No."

TI-83 or TI-84:

Estimation using summary statistic

If the actual measurements are not available, but the sample means and sample standard deviations are available, then use this option.

- Choose **STAT → TESTS → 0:2-SampTInt**
- Press **ENTER**
- Choose option **Stats**
- Press **ENTER**
- Enter appropriate values

  2-SampTInt

  Input: Data   Stats

  $\bar{x}1$: 80.7

  Sx1: $\sqrt{49.5}$

  n1: 23

  $\bar{x}2$: 78.9

  Sx2: $\sqrt{60.4}$

  n2: 22

  C-Level: .95

  Pooled: No   Yes   (Choose No)

  Calculate

- Highlight **Calculate**
- Press **ENTER**

Example 18: A student waiting tables at a restaurant near a university in Chicago felt that customers tend to tip female waiters better than they tip male waiters. To confirm his suspicion, he contacted 50 female students and 75 male students who waited tables at different restaurants near the university and asked them to keep a record of tips received for one week. At the end of the week, he compiled the data in terms of the mean amount of tips received per hour worked by each student and summarized the data as follows:

	n	Average	Standard Deviation
Females	50	15.50	4.25
Males	75	12.25	3.20

(a) Estimate the difference in the mean amount of tips received hourly by female and male waiters. Use $\alpha = 0.10$.

(b) Does this data provide evidence to justify the student's suspicions?

(c) Would you do anything differently in this experiment if you repeated it? Why?

Solution:

    (a) We are interested in the difference in the mean amount of tips received by female and male waiters.

Step 1: Let

    μ_1 = The mean amount of tips received by female waiters per hour

    μ_2 = The mean amount of tips received by male waiters per hour

We are interested in estimating

$(\mu_1 - \mu_2)$ = the difference in the mean amount of tips received by female and male waiters.

Step 2: The sample sizes are large enough that we can apply the Central Limit Theorem and use a z-interval. Let us assume that

- There are no outliers in the data. (Because there is no data available, we cannot check.)
- All male and female waiters were selected randomly and independently.

Step 3: Using $\alpha = 0.10$, we get $z^* = Z_{\alpha/2} = 1.645$. The population standard deviations are unknown, so we estimate them using the sample standard deviations.

$$\text{The 90\% } ME = Z_{\alpha/2}\sqrt{\frac{s_1^2}{n_1} + \frac{s_2^2}{n_2}} = 1.645\sqrt{\frac{4.25^2}{50} + \frac{3.20^2}{75}} \approx 1.16$$

$$(\bar{x}_1 - \bar{x}_2) \pm ME \Rightarrow (15.50 - 12.25) \pm 1.16 \Rightarrow (2.09, 4.41)$$

The 90% confidence interval to estimate $(\mu_1 - \mu_2)$ is (2.09, 4.41) dollars.

Step 4: We are 90% confident that the difference in mean amounts of tips received per hour by female and male waiters is between $2.09 and $4.41.

    (b) Refer to the confidence interval constructed in part (a). Note that the interval does not contain zero. Therefore, at a 10% risk, we can conclude that there is a significant difference in the mean amount of tips received by female and male waiters.

Also note that the entire interval for $(\mu_1 - \mu_2)$ lies above 0. So, we can conclude that $(\mu_1 - \mu_2) > 0$. In other words, the mean amount of tips received by female waiters is significantly higher than the mean amount of tips received by male waiters.

Alternatively, we could test

$$H_0: (\mu_1 - \mu_2) < 0$$

(Female waiters do not receive higher tips on average than male waiters.)

$$H_a: (\mu_1 - \mu_2) > 0$$

(Female waiters receive on the average higher tips than male waiters.)

The large-samples z-test results in $z = 4.60$, p-value $= 0.000002$ (almost 0).

For this p-value, we should reject the null for any reasonable level of significance and conclude that there is evidence to support the student's suspicions. The data suggests that, on average, female waiters tend to receive higher tips than male waiters.

(c) A better way to do the study would be to take a random sample of waiters, regardless of whether or not they're students. It is not clear whether these samples were selected at random. Because only student waiters were included in the experiment, the results will only be applicable to student waiters at this particular university, rather than all male and female waiters.

Case of Dependent or Paired Samples

Sometimes it is necessary or useful to collect samples that are not independent. For example, when checking the effectiveness of a certain weight loss program, you need to measure and compare the weights of the same participants before starting the program and after completing the program. Comparison of Bill's "before" weight with Leslie's "after" weight is meaningless. We need to compare Bill's "before" and "after" program weights and Leslie's "before" and "after" weights. This also allows us to better account for the differences between people. Even if Bill weighs 250 lbs to start and Leslie weighs 145 lbs, we are now comparing each person to him- or herself when we do paired samples. Therefore, we have to use dependent or paired measurements.

Pairing or matching does not necessarily mean taking both measurements on the same subject. For example, suppose we are interested in comparing two different brands of calculators (say, TI and HP) in terms of ease of computation. If we did some computations on TI calculators and some other computations on HP calculators, then it's possible that some of the differences in the ease of computation would be due to the differences in the types of computations performed. The responses would not be comparable. The best way to perform this experiment would be to do the same type of computations on both calculators and to do each calculation in random order, to avoid giving any specific calculator the advantage of the practice effect. This would result in the matching or pairing of samples. The samples would therefore not be independent. Is this a problem? No, in fact it can be helpful in many cases. It just means that the data would need to be analyzed differently.

Some of the ways in which pairing or matching can be achieved are the following:

- Take both measurements on the same subject, as discussed in the diet example above.
- Use naturally occurring pairs (such as twins or spouses) and assign the two subjects in each pair to two different groups, using some kind of randomization

scheme. Then take measurements on both groups and compare.

- Match subjects by some characteristics, the effects of which might otherwise obscure the difference in responses. For example, to compare the effects of two headache medicines, we could match patients by their ages, because the effect of the medicine may differ depending on the patient's age. Two patients in the same age group could each be given a different medicine, and then the medicine's effects could be compared. The age effect would then not be confounded with the medicine effect.

Let μ_X be the mean of one population and μ_Y be the mean of the other. Each of the members of the X-population is paired in some way with each of the members of the Y-population. We are interested in the differences $(X - Y)$. Parameter of interest: Population mean of differences μ_d.

Here, $\mu_d = \mu_X - \mu_Y$, but this case differs from that of the two-sample cases described earlier in that the two populations are not independent, so the responses or measurements of the subjects will not be independent either.

- Select a random sample of size n items (or n pairs of items).
- For each selected item, measure the characteristic of interest, resulting in a sample of pairs of measurements.

$$\text{Sample: } (x_1, y_1), (x_2, y_2), (x_3, y_3),..., (x_n, y_n)$$

- Compute the differences $d_i = x_i - y_i$, $i = 1, 2,..., n$. Note that the two-sample case reduces to a one-sample case.
- Compute the mean difference and the standard deviation of the differences.

$$\bar{d} = \frac{\sum d_i}{n} \text{ and } s_d = \sqrt{\frac{\sum (d_i - \bar{d})^2}{n - 1}}$$

This sample mean $\bar{d}$ is a point estimate of the unknown population mean μ_d. Different random samples of size n from the same population will result in different sample means, giving different estimates. The distribution of means from all possible random samples of n differences is the sampling distribution of $\bar{d}$.

- The mean of all possible sample means is μ_d. Therefore, $\bar{d}$ is an unbiased estimator of μ_d.

- The standard deviation of the sampling distribution of $\bar{d}$ is $\sigma_{\bar{d}} = \frac{\sigma_d}{\sqrt{n}}$, where σ_d is the standard deviation of the population of differences.

- If the population of differences is normally distributed and the population standard deviation σ_d is unknown, then the sampling distribution of $\bar{d}$ is a t-distribution with $(n - 1)$ degrees of freedom.

Estimating μ_d using $(1 - \alpha)100\%$ confidence interval:

Construct a t-interval with $df = (n - 1)$ degrees of freedom

Margin of Error: $t_{\alpha/2}\left(df\right)S_{\bar{d}} = t_{\alpha/2}\left(df\right)\dfrac{s_d}{\sqrt{n}}$

Confidence Interval: $\bar{d} \pm t_{\alpha/2}\left(df\right)\dfrac{s_d}{\sqrt{n}}$

Making an inference about the difference in population means μ_d:
Use a t-test with $df = (n - 1)$ degrees of freedom.

$H_0: \mu_d = \mu_0$ (Specified Difference)

$H_a: \mu_d > \mu_0$

    $\mu_d < \mu_0$ or

    $\mu_d \neq \mu_0$

$$t = \frac{\bar{d} - \mu_0}{s_d / \sqrt{n}}$$

	Rejection Rule	
Alternative hypothesis:	Rejection region approach:	p-value approach:
$H_a: \mu_d > \mu_0$	Reject H_0 if	Reject H_0 if p-value $< \alpha$, where
$H_a: \mu_d < \mu_0$ or	$t > t_\alpha(df)$	p-value $= P(t(df) > t)$
$H_a: \mu_d \neq \mu_0$	$t < -t_\alpha(df)$	p-value $= P(t(df) < t)$
	$t > t_{\alpha/2}(df)$ or $t < -t_{\alpha/2}(df)$	p-value $=$
		$P(t(df) > \lvert t \rvert) + P(t(df) < -\lvert t \rvert)$

Conditions:

(a) A random sample of differences is taken from the population differences.

(b) The sampled population of differences is normally distributed.

Checking the normality condition:

Make a dotplot or stem-and-leaf plot for the sample of differences $(d_1, d_2, \ldots d_n)$. Ask yourself whether the distribution is fairly symmetric and bell-shaped, without any outliers. In other words, ask yourself whether the distribution of differences resembles the normal distribution. Alternatively, use a normal probability plot. The AP Exam may or may not tell you that the distribution of differences is normal.

Example 19: Workers at a factory asked their supervisor to provide music during their shift. The supervisor wanted to know whether the music really helped improve the workers' performance. Because all the workers were assigned to different rooms at random, the supervisor randomly selected one room. For one week, she provided music in this room, and for one week, she provided none. She flipped a coin to determine which week to provide music. Afterward, she recorded the productivity of the workers, using the average number of items assembled per day:

Worker	1	2	3	4	5	6	7	8	9	10
With Music	29.38	31.53	27.45	27.76	29.31	27.69	29.07	27.48	29.83	28.96
Without Music	24.55	25.59	23.17	24.71	25.26	24.88	24.34	26.13	25.57	26.63

(a) Estimate the difference between the workers' performance in the presence of music and their performance in the absence of music using a 95% level of confidence.

(b) Does music improve the performance of workers as measured by the mean number of items assembled per day? Give statistical evidence.

Solution:

(a) Estimation.

Step 1: Let X = the performance with music

Y = the performance without music

μ_x = the mean performance with music

μ_y = the mean performance without music

We are interested in $\mu_d = \mu_x - \mu_y$ = the mean difference in performance.

Step 2: Because the performances "with music" and "without music" are measured on the same group of workers, this is a dependent samples case. The specific person's effect on the performance will be nullified when we look at the differences.

Define difference $d = X - Y$. Compute the differences in the performance of each worker.

Worker	1	2	3	4	5	6	7	8	9	10
With Music	29.38	31.53	27.45	27.76	29.31	27.69	29.07	27.48	29.83	28.96
Without Music	24.55	25.59	23.17	24.71	25.26	24.88	24.34	26.13	25.57	26.63
Difference	4.83	5.94	4.28	3.05	4.05	2.81	4.73	1.35	4.26	2.33

Plot the differences (see Figure 24). Please note that the differences were each rounded to the nearest whole number.

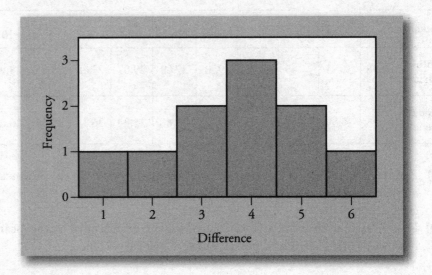

Figure 24: Histogram of the differences in performance

Conditions:

(1) It is given that a random sample of one room was taken. Because the workers are randomly assigned to different rooms, workers in the selected room where the sample was taken can be assumed to be a random sample of all workers at this factory.

(2) A histogram of the differences shows that there are no outliers, and its shape suggests it is reasonable to assume that the differences in performance are approximately normally distributed.

Because the population standard deviation of the differences is unknown, we should construct a *t*-interval for the mean.

Step 3: Now the two-sample problem has been reduced to a one-sample problem. Compute the sample mean and standard deviation of the differences.

$$\bar{d} = 3.763 \text{ items per day, and } s_d = 1.362 \text{ items per day}$$

With a sample of size 10, degrees of freedom = 10 − 1 = 9.

To construct a 95% confidence interval, use α = 0.05. Using a *t*-table for 9 degrees of freedom we get

$$t^* = t_{\alpha/2}(9) = t_{0.05/2}(9) = t_{0.025}(9) = 2.262$$

The 95% $ME = t_{0.025}(9)\left(\dfrac{s_d}{\sqrt{n}}\right) = 2.262\left(\dfrac{1.362}{\sqrt{10}}\right) \approx 0.974$ items/day.

$$\bar{d} \pm ME \Rightarrow 3.763 \pm 0.974 \Rightarrow (2.789, 4.737)$$

The 95% confidence interval to estimate μ_d is (2.79, 4.74).

Step 4: Interpretation:

We are 95% confident that the true mean difference in performance is between 2.79 and 4.74 items per day. We are 95% confident that our best estimate of the difference, 3.763 items per day, is within 0.974 items of the true mean difference in performance.

Note that the confidence interval falls entirely above zero. Therefore, we can conclude that the mean difference in performance is significant and that the mean number of items produced per day with music is higher than the mean number produced without music.

TI-83 or TI-84:

Using data

- Enter the data into two lists, "with music" in L_1, and "without music" in L_2
- Move cursor to the column labeled L_3
- Type $L_1 - L_2$
- Press **ENTER** (all the differences should appear in list L_3)
- Choose **STAT → TESTS → 8:TInterval**
- Highlight **Data**
- Press **ENTER**
- Enter appropriate values

    TInterval
    Input: Data Stats
    List: L_3
    Freq: 1
    C-Level: .95
    Calculate

- Highlight **Calculate**
- Press **ENTER**

(b) Inference.

Step 1: We are interested in testing a hypothesis about

μ_d = The true mean difference in performance of workers as measured by the number of items assembled per day = mean with music – mean without music.

H_0: $\mu_d = 0$ (There is no difference in the performance of workers with and without music.)

H_a: $\mu_d > 0$ (Music improves performance, i.e., the mean performance is better with music than without music.)

Step 2: A random sample of $n = 10$ workers was taken.

Because the performances "with music" and "without music" were measured on the same group of workers, this is a dependent-samples case. The specific person's effect on the performance will be nullified when we look at the differences.

Define difference $d = X - Y$. Compute the differences in the performance of each worker.

Worker	1	2	3	4	5	6	7	8	9	10
With Music	29.38	31.53	27.45	27.76	29.31	27.69	29.07	27.48	29.83	28.96
Without Music	24.55	25.59	23.17	24.71	25.26	24.88	24.34	26.13	25.57	26.63
Difference	4.83	5.94	4.28	3.05	4.05	2.81	4.73	1.35	4.26	2.33

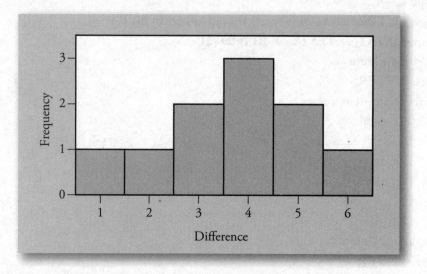

Figure 25: Histogram of difference in performance
(Note: Differences were rounded to the nearest whole number)

Conditions:

(1) It is given that a random sample of one room was taken. Because the workers are randomly assigned to different rooms, workers in the selected room can be assumed to be a random sample of all workers at this factory.

(2) A histogram of differences (see Figure 25) shows that there are no outliers, and its shape suggests it is reasonable to assume that the differences in performance are approximately normally distributed.

Because the population standard deviation of the differences is unknown, we should use a t-test for the mean.

Step 3: Now the two-sample problem has been reduced to a one-sample problem. Compute the sample mean and standard deviation of the differences.

$$\bar{d} = 3.763 \text{ items per day, and } s_d = 1.362$$

With a sample of size 10, degrees of freedom = $10 - 1 = 9$.

Suppose we use $\alpha = 0.05$. Then, using the t-table for 9 degrees of freedom, we get

$$t^* = t_\alpha(9) = t_{0.05}(9) = 1.833$$

The rejection rule is to reject the null hypothesis and accept the alternative hypothesis if

- $t < -1.833$ or $t > 1.833$ (rejection region approach)
- p-value < 0.05 (p-value approach)

Compute the test statistic (and p-value if using p-value approach)

$$t = \frac{\left(\bar{d} - \mu_0\right)}{s_d / \sqrt{n}} = \frac{(3.763 - 0)}{1.362 / \sqrt{10}} \approx 8.737$$

$$p\text{-value} = P(t > 8.737) = \text{almost } 0$$

Step 4: Write conclusion.

- Using p-value approach:
  Because the p-value is almost 0, for any reasonable α we should reject the null hypothesis and accept the alternative hypothesis.
- Using the rejection region approach:
  Because $t = 8.737 > 1.833$ (or the test statistic falls in the rejection region), we should reject the null hypothesis and accept the alternative hypothesis.

Conclusion: At a 5% level of significance, there is sufficient evidence to conclude that the performance of workers has improved in the presence of music.

TI-83 or TI-84:

Using data

- Enter the data into two lists, "with music" in L_1, and "without music" in L_2
- Move cursor to the column labeled L_3
- Type $L_1 - L_2$
- Press **ENTER** (all the differences should appear in list L_3)
- Choose **STAT → TESTS → 2:T-Test**
- Choose option **Data**
- Press **ENTER**
- Enter appropriate values
  T-Test
  Input: Data Stats
  μ_0: 0
  List: L_3
  Freq: 1
  μ: $\neq \mu_0$ $< \mu_0$ $> \mu_0$ (Choose option $> \mathbf{\mu_0}$)
- Press **ENTER**
  Calculate Draw
- Choose option **Calculate**
- Press **ENTER**

MAKING AN INFERENCE USING CATEGORICAL DATA

A categorical variable is a variable that classifies the outcomes of an experiment into different categories. These categories can be numerical or nonnumerical. For example:

- A teacher classifies students according to the student status (freshman, sophomore, junior, or senior).
- A biologist classifies crossbred varieties of flowers according to the color of petals (white, red, or pink).
- A doctor classifies patients by sex (male, female).
- A factory classifies each item produced by its status (good, minor defect, major defect).
- A postal worker classifies letters by the state of the addressee (AL, … WA).
- To issue tax rebates in 2001, the Internal Revenue Service divided taxpayers according to the last two digits of their social security numbers (00, 01, … 99). This grouping was used to determine in which week each taxpayer would receive a check.

Suppose there are k different groups into which the measurements are categorized. These groups are typically referred to as cells. The **observed frequency** is the number of measurements from one experiment falling into that particular cell. The observed counts of cells, 1 through k, are denoted by O_1, O_2,..., O_k. If n observations are taken in one experiment, then

$$O_1 + O_2 + \cdots + O_k = n$$

Often, we devise a theory about the distribution of measurements into different categories, and we wish to check out our theory by conducting an experiment. The **expected frequency** is the number of measurements expected to fall into that cell according to our theory. The expected counts for cells 1 through k are denoted by $E_1, E_2,..., E_k$ and

$$E_1 + E_2 + \cdots + E_k = n$$

For example, a biologist might suspect that when two varieties of a flowering plant are cross-bred, the result would be 20%, 30%, and 50% of the plants bearing white, red, and pink flowers, respectively. Then, to check her theory, the biologist might crossbreed and grow, say, 150 plants and classify each one by the resulting color of flowers that it produces. Suppose the experiment results in 28 plants bearing white flowers, 46 bearing red, and 76 bearing pink. In this case, 28, 46, and 76 are the observed counts. The theoretical proportions of 20, 30, and 50% lead to the expected counts in 150 plants as 30 bearing white flowers, 45 bearing red, and 75 bearing pink.

The question of interest here is whether the observed counts seem to agree with the expected counts, or how likely the observed counts would be if the truth were really described by the expected counts. The test statistic value that determines the extent of agreement between the observed and expected counts is computed as

$$\chi^2 = \sum_{\text{all cells}} \frac{\left(O_i - E_i\right)^2}{E_i}$$

> If our observed values are close to what we expect, $O - E$ will be very close to 0.

The smaller the value of the test statistic, the higher the agreement between the expected and observed counts. Larger values of the test statistic indicate more discrepancy between the observed and expected counts. This test statistic follows an approximate χ^2 (chi-square) distribution.

The Chi-Square Distribution

Another commonly used sampling distribution, besides the t-distribution and the standard normal, is the χ^2 (or "chi-square") distribution. This distribution is commonly observed when we use inferential procedures for categorical data. It has the following properties:

- It is a continuous distribution.
- It is a distribution of the sums of squared normal random variables. So the chi-square variable takes only positive values.
- It is a right-skewed distribution.
- The shape of the chi-square distribution, like that of the t-distribution, depends on its degrees of freedom (df). Figure 26 shows how the shape of the distribution changes with the degrees of freedom.
- The mean of the chi-square distribution = df. Note, in Figure 26, that the center of the distribution shifts to the right as degrees of freedom increase.
- The standard deviation of the chi-square distribution = $\sqrt{2df}$.

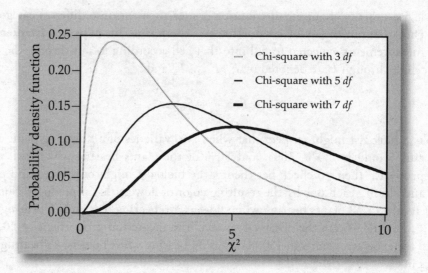

Figure 26: Chi-square distribution for different degrees of freedom

Reading a Chi-Square Table

χ_α^2: A chi-square value such that the area to the right under the distribution is equal to α.

- To find $\chi_{0.05}^2$ with 10 degrees of freedom from the table, go down to the row corresponding to 10 degrees of freedom, and then go across to the column corresponding to the right-tail area 0.05. Read the number in the cross section of the row for 10 degrees of freedom and the column for right-tail area 0.05. It gives $\chi_{0.05}^2(10) = 18.31$.

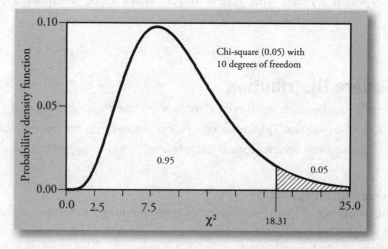

Figure 27: Chi-square (0.05) with 10 degrees of freedom

- To find $\chi_{0.01}^2(10)$, read the number in the cross section of the row corresponding to 10 degrees of freedom and the column corresponding to the right-tail area 0.01. It gives $\chi_{0.01}^2(10) = 23.21$.

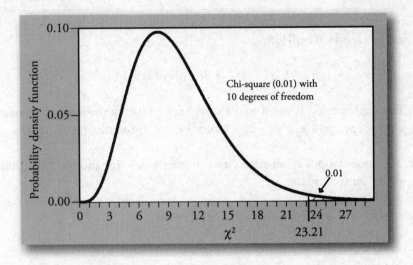

Figure 28: Chi-square (0.01) with 10 degrees of freedom

The Test of Goodness-of-Fit

This test is used to check whether the observed data counts confirm the expected distribution of counts into different categories. Read the problem carefully to determine the expected proportion for each category. For example, if there are five categories and the problem states that each category is equally likely, then the expected proportion for each is $\frac{1}{5}$ or 0.20.

- Suppose the population is divided into k different categories.
- Take a random sample of size n from the population of interest.
- Classify each selected item of the sample into one of the k categories.
- Count the number of items in each category. These are the observed counts, $O_1, O_2,..., O_k$.
- To get each expected count, multiply the sample size n by the proportion for that cell.

- Compute the test statistic $\chi^2 = \sum_{\text{all cells}} \frac{(O_i - E_i)^2}{E_i}$.

- For a sufficiently large random sample, the distribution of the test statistic is approximately a chi-square with $df = (k - 1)$ degrees of freedom.

$\mathcal{X}^2$ **Test of Goodness-of-Fit:**

Use a chi-square test with $df = (k - 1)$ degrees of freedom.

H_0: The population is divided into k categories in the following proportions: $p_1, p_2, ..., p_k$. ($p_1 + p_2 + ... + p_k = 1$ and $0 < p_i < 1$, for all $i = 1, 2, ..., k$)

H_a: The population is divided into k categories in proportions that differ from $p_1, p_2, ..., p_k$.

The rejection rule: Reject the null hypothesis if

- $TS > \mathcal{X}^2(df)$ (using the rejection region approach)

- p-value $< \alpha$, where p-value $= P(\mathcal{X}^2(df) > TS)$ (using the p-value approach)

Conditions:

(a) Data are counts, not percentages or averages.
(b) A random sample of size n is taken.
(c) The sample size n is large enough to get an approximate chi-square distribution for the test statistic.

Checking the condition of a large n:

If all expected counts are at least 5 ($E_i \geq 5$), then we have a large enough sample to use a chi-square approximation. If some cells have $E_i < 5$, then such cells should be combined with other adjoining cells in a logical manner to satisfy the requirement of expected counts. If no such combining is possible, exact tests may be used, but they are not a topic on the AP Exam.

Example 20: An accounting firm in Mississippi has clients from various states. The chief accountant knew that last year the firm had the following distribution of clients from different states:

State of Residence	Mississippi	Alabama	Louisiana	Arkansas	Florida	Tennessee
Proportion of Clients	0.60	0.15	0.15	0.04	0.03	0.03

But the accountant thought that the distribution had changed this year. So he took a random sample of 400 clients and classified them according to their state of residence. The summarized data is as follows:

State of Residence	Mississippi	Alabama	Louisiana	Arkansas	Florida	Tennessee
Number of Clients	200	87	68	27	8	10

What does the data suggest? Is the distribution of clients the same as last year or has it changed?

Solution: The clients are classified by their state of residence, which is a categorical variable.

Step 1: We are interested in testing

H_0: The proportion of clients from Mississippi, Alabama, Louisiana, Arkansas, Florida, and Tennessee is the same this year as last year.

H_a: This year, at least two proportions have changed from those of last year.

Step 2: Use a chi-square test of goodness-of-fit. Compute the expected counts as $400p_i$, where p_i is the proportion of clients from the ith state. For example, last year, 60% of clients were from Mississippi. If the proportions this year are the same, then out of 400, 60% of clients—i.e., $400(0.60) = 240$ clients—should be from Mississippi.

State of Residence	Mississippi	Alabama	Louisiana	Arkansas	Florida	Tennessee
Observed Number of Clients (O_i)	200	87	68	27	8	10
Expected Number of Clients (E_i)	240	60	60	16	12	12

A random sample of clients was selected. All the expected counts are higher than five. Therefore, it is reasonable to use the chi-square test.

Step 3: The firm's clients are from six different states. So for $k = 6$, we get $df = k - 1 = 5$ degrees of freedom. Suppose we use 0.05-level of significance. The rejection rule is to "reject the null hypothesis if p-value < 0.05" (or, if using rejection region approach, "reject the null hypothesis if $TS > \chi^2_{0.05}(5) = 11.1$").

$$\chi^2 = \sum_{i=1}^{6} \frac{(O_i - E_i)^2}{E_i}$$

$$= \frac{(200-240)^2}{240} + \frac{(87-60)^2}{60} + \frac{(68-60)^2}{60} + \frac{(27-16)^2}{16} + \frac{(8-12)^2}{12} + \frac{(10-12)^2}{12}$$

$$\approx 6.67 + 12.15 + 1.07 + 7.56 + 1.33 + 0.33$$

$$= 29.11$$

The p-value $= P(\chi^2(5) > 29.11) = .000022$, which is almost 0.

Step 4: Because p-value $= 0.000022 < 0.05$ (or $TS = 29.11 > 11.1$, if using the rejection region approach), we should reject the null hypothesis and accept the alternative hypothesis. The p-value indicates that if this year's proportion of clients had remained the same as last year's, then the probability of observing the test statistic value of 29.11 or higher is 0.000022. Therefore, we can conclude that the data suggests that the proportions have changed from those of last year.

TI-83 or TI-84:
- Clear lists L_1, L_2, and L_3
- Enter the observed counts in L_1
- Enter the expected counts in L_2
- Define list L_3 to be $(L_1 - L_2)^2/L_2$
  Bring the cursor to the list heading L_3
  Type $(L_1 - L_2)^2/L_2$
- Press **ENTER**
- Choose **2nd → LIST → MATH 5:sum(**
- Press **ENTER**
- Type (L_3) to give
  sum(L_3)
- Press **ENTER**

To compute the p-value:

Use the chi-square *CDF* from the distribution menu to compute the area between the *TS* value (given by the sum command as described above) and infinity (simulated using some large number).

- Choose **2nd → DISTR → 7:χ^2 cdf**
- Press **ENTER**
- Type 29.11,1E50,5) to give
  χ^2 cdf(29.11,1E50,5)
  (Enter *TS*, simulated ∞, and *df* separated by commas)
- Press **ENTER**

Example 21: A nursery ships plants by truck in trays of 12 plants each. At the end of one such journey, 100 randomly selected trays were inspected, and the number of plants in each tray that did not survive the journey was counted. The data was recorded as follows:

Number of Plants That Did Not Survive the Journey	0	1	2	3	4
Number of Trays	31	44	15	8	2

Is the binomial distribution an appropriate model to determine the chance of a single plant surviving?

Solution: There are 12 plants per tray, i.e., $n = 12$ trials. There are a total of $12 \times 100 = 1,200$ plants. Associated with each plant are two possible outcomes, namely, "surviving the journey" and "not surviving the journey." If we define success as "not surviving the journey," then the probability of success associated with each plant is estimated as follows:

Out of 1,200 plants inspected, $(31(0) + 44(1) + 15(2) + 8(3) + 4(2)) = 106$ did not survive the journey. So the estimated probability of not surviving the journey = $\hat{p} = 106/1,200 \approx 0.088$.

Step 1: Here we are interested in testing the following hypotheses:

H_0: A binomial distribution with $n = 12$ and $p = 0.088$ is an appropriate model to describe this data.

H_a: A binomial distribution with $n = 12$ and $p = 0.088$ is not an appropriate model to describe this data.

Step 2: We can use the chi-square goodness-of-fit test to check the appropriateness of the binomial distribution to describe the data above. Assuming that the null hypothesis is true (i.e., assuming that the data comes from a binomial population with $n = 12$, and $p = 0.088$), compute the likelihood of 0, 1, 2, 3, etc., plants not surviving the journey. For example:

$$P(X = 2 \text{ did not survive the journey}) = \binom{12}{2} 0.088^2 (1 - 0.088)^{10} \approx 0.2034$$

Number of Plants That Did Not Survive the Journey (x)	0	1	2	3	4	5 or more
$P(X = x)$	0.3311	0.3834	0.2034	0.0654	0.0142	0.0025

$$P(X \geq 5) = 1 - [P(X = 0) + P(X = 1) + \cdots + P(X = 4)]$$

Using these probabilities, compute the expected number of trays with the number of plants not surviving the journey equal to 0, 1, 2, etc., as $100 \times P(x)$. This gives the expected counts as follows:

Number of Plants That Did Not Survive the Journey (x)	0	1	2	3	4	5 or more
$P(X = x)$	0.3311	0.3834	0.2034	0.0654	0.0142	0.0025
Expected Counts	33.11	38.34	20.34	6.54	1.42	0.25

Because the expected counts for the last two categories are less than five, the chi-square test cannot be applied successfully. So let us combine the last three cells (this combination makes sense—three or more is a reasonable category) to give the expected counts as follows:

Number of Plants That Did Not Survive the Journey (x)	0	1	2	3 or more
Observed Counts (O_i)	31	44	15	10
Expected Counts (E_i)	33.11	38.34	20.34	8.21

All the expected counts are larger than five, and all trays were selected at random. So, the conditions for the chi-square test are satisfied.

Step 3: With four categories in the table, degrees of freedom = df = 3. If we are willing to take a 5% risk of rejecting the true null hypothesis, then the rejection rule is "reject the null hypothesis if p-value < 0.05" (or if using the rejection region approach, "reject the null hypothesis if the $TS > \chi^2_{0.05}(3) = 7.81$").

Compute the test statistic value (and p-value if using a p-value approach).

$$\chi^2 = \sum_{i=1}^{4} \frac{(O_i - E_i)^2}{E_i}$$

$$= \frac{(31 - 33.11)^2}{33.11} + \frac{(44 - 38.34)^2}{38.34} + \frac{(15 - 20.34)^2}{20.34} + \frac{(10 - 8.21)^2}{8.21}$$

$$\approx 2.76$$

$$\text{The } p\text{-value} = P(\chi^2(3) > 2.76) = 0.4301$$

Step 4: Because p-value $= 0.4301 > 0.05$ (or since $TS = 2.76 < \chi^2_{0.05}(3) = 7.81$), we fail to reject the null hypothesis. Thus, we can conclude that there is insufficient evidence against the null hypothesis. In other words, it is reasonable to assume that the data follows a binomial model with $n = 12$ and $p = 0.088$.

Contingency Tables

In many experiments, data is classified by two different criteria, each criterion with two or more categories. Such a classification of data results in a table with two or more rows and two or more columns, where rows represent categories of one factor and columns represent categories of the other factor. For example, students might be classified by sex and academic major, athletes by athletic specialty (track, football, gymnastics, etc.) and the type of injury sustained, or patients by sex and race.

An $r \times c$ contingency table is an arrangement of data into a table with r rows and c columns, creating a total of rc cells.

Test of Independence

Often, scientists are interested in determining whether two different categorical variables are independent or dependent. For example, television stations might want to know whether the type of program a viewer watches is associated with his or her sex, sociologists might want to know whether children's behavior patterns are associated with the marital status of parents, and marine biologists might want to know whether the behavior patterns of dolphins are associated with the time of year.

- Identify two factors of interest and their categories.
- Take a random sample of n items from the population of interest.
- Determine the category of each of two factors to which each item in the sample belongs.
- Summarize the observed data into an $r \times c$ contingency table, where $r =$ the number of rows = the number of categories of interest for factor 1, and $c =$ the number of columns = the number of categories of interest for factor 2.
- Count the number of items in each cell. These are the observed counts O_{ij}

$(i = 1, 2,..., r,$ and $j = 1, 2,..., c)$.

		Columns			Row Total R_i
		1	2	. . .	c	
Rows	1	O_{11}	O_{12}	. . .	O_{1c}	R_1
	2	O_{21}	O_{22}	. . .	O_{2c}	R_2
	.	.	.		.	.
	.	.	.		.	.
	.	.	.		.	.
	r	O_{r1}	O_{r2}	. . .	O_{rc}	R_r
Column Totals C_j		C_1	C_2	. . .	C_c	n

Table 4: $r \times c$ contingency table of observed counts

- Compute the row totals and the column totals. Note that the sum of the row totals and the sum of the column totals is n. This is a good way to check your math.
- If the two factors of interest are independent, then

P(A randomly selected item belongs to the $(i, j)^{th}$ cell) =

P(It belongs to the ith category of factor 1)
$\times P$(It belongs to the jth category of factor 2)

Therefore, out of n observations, the $(i, j)^{th}$ cell is expected to contain

$$E_{ij} = \frac{R_i C_j}{n} \text{ observations.}$$

In other words, find the expected value for each cell using $\dfrac{\text{(row total)(column total)}}{\text{grand total}}$.

Compute the expected counts for all cells and place them in parentheses next to the observed counts.

		Columns				Row Total R_i
		1	2	...	c	
Rows	1	$O_{11}(E_{11})$	$O_{12}(E_{12})$	...	$O_{1c}(E_{1c})$	R_1
	2	$O_{21}(E_{21})$	$O_{22}(E_{22})$	...	$O_{2c}(E_{2c})$	R_2
	.	.	.		.	.
	.	.	.		.	.
	.	.	.		.	.
	r	$O_{r1}(E_{r1})$	$O_{r2}(E_{r2})$	...	$O_{rc}(E_{rc})$	R_r
Column Totals C_j		C_1	C_2	...	C_c	n

Table 5: $r \times c$ contingency table of observed and (expected) counts

- Compute the test statistic value as

$$\chi^2 = \sum_{j=1}^{c} \sum_{i=1}^{r} \frac{\left(O_{ij} - E_{ij}\right)^2}{E_{ij}}$$

- For a sufficiently large n, the test statistic follows a chi-square distribution with $df = (r-1)(c-1)$ degrees of freedom.

χ^2 **Test of Independence:**

Use a chi-square test with $df = (r - 1)(c - 1)$ degrees of freedom.

H_0: The two factors of interest are independent. Or, there is no association between two factors of interest. (This should always be the null hypothesis.)

H_a: Two factors of interest are not independent. Or, there is an association between two factors of interest.

$$\chi^2 = \sum_{j=1}^{c} \sum_{i=1}^{r} \frac{\left(O_{ij} - E_{ij}\right)^2}{E_{ij}}$$

where $E_{ij} = \dfrac{R_i C_j}{n}$

The rejection rule: Reject the null hypothesis if

- $\chi^2 > \chi^2(df)$ (using the rejection region approach)

- p-value $< \alpha$, where p-value $= P(\chi^2(df) > TS)$ (using the p-value approach)

Conditions:

(a) Data are counts, not percentages or averages.
(b) A random sample of size n is taken.
(c) The sample size n is large enough to get an approximate chi-square distribution for the test statistic.

Checking the assumption of a large n:

If all expected counts are at least five, then we have a large enough sample to use the chi-square approximation. If some cells have $E_i < 5$, then the corresponding rows and/or columns should be combined with other rows and/or columns in a logical manner to satisfy the requirement of expected counts.

	Coffee	Tea	Hot Chocolate	Row Total
College	150			250
High School		75		200
Column Total	200	150	100	450

Why $(r - 1)(c - 1)$? Check out the above table. According to the formula, we have $(2 - 1)(3 - 1) = 2$ degrees of freedom. That means that if we know the row and column totals, we only need 2 pieces of information to figure out all the cell values. Try it yourself!

Example 22: The State Department of Education wanted to see whether there is any connection between the education levels of fathers and sons. A random sample of 1,000 father–son pairs was selected from the available census data for the state of Alabama, and the level of education for both father and son was recorded as "less than high school (< HS)," "high school (HS)," or "more than high school (> HS)." The resulting data is summarized in the following table:

		Father's Education Level		
		< HS	HS	> HS
Son's Education Level	< HS	120	80	25
	HS	210	170	60
	> HS	110	140	85

Does this data provide significant evidence of an association between a father's education level and his son's education level?

Solution:

Step 1:

H_0: There is no association between a father's education level and his son's education level.

H_a: There is an association between a father's education level and his son's education level.

or

H_0: A father's education level and his son's education level are independent.

H_a: A father's education level and his son's education level are not independent.

Step 2: Use a chi-square test for independence. Compute all row totals and column totals. Then compute the expected cell counts as

$$\text{Expected count for a cell} = \frac{(\text{Row total})(\text{Column total})}{\text{Grand total}}$$

Below is a table of observed and expected counts, with the expected counts in parentheses.

		Father's Education Level			
		<HS	HS	>HS	**Total**
Son's Education Level	<HS	120 (99.0)	80 (87.8)	25 (38.3)	225
	HS	210 (193.6)	170 (171.6)	60 (74.8)	440
	>HS	110 (147.4)	140 (130.7)	85 (57.0)	335
	Total	440	390	170	1000

All expected counts are greater than or equal to five, and the sample was chosen randomly. So the chi-square test of independence is appropriate.

Step 3: This is a 3 × 3 contingency table. So the degrees of freedom = (3 − 1)(3 − 1) = 4. Suppose we use α = 0.05. The rejection rule is "reject null if p-value < α" (or if using the rejection region approach, "reject null if $TS > \chi^2_{0.05}(4) = 9.49$").

Compute the test statistic (and p-value if using the p-value approach).

$$TS = \sum_{i=1}^{3}\sum_{j=1}^{3}\frac{\left(O_{ij} - E_{ij}\right)^2}{E_{ij}}$$

$$= \frac{(120 - 99)^2}{99} + \frac{(80 - 87.8)^2}{87.8} + \cdots + \frac{(85 - 57)^2}{57}$$

$$= 38.03576$$

p-value = $P(\chi^2 > 38.03576) = 0.00000011 \approx 0$

Step 4: Because the p-value is too small for any reasonable level of significance (or since $TS = 38.036 > 9.49$, if using the rejection region approach), we should reject the null hypothesis and accept the alternative hypothesis. There is significant evidence to conclude that there is an association between a father's education level and his son's education level.

```
TI-83 or TI-84:
    • Choose MATRX → EDIT
    • Select 1: [A]
    • Press ENTER
    • 3 ▷ ▷ 3
    • Press ENTER
    • Enter observed counts in a 3 × 3 matrix
    • Choose STAT → TESTS → C:χ²-Test
    • Press ENTER
            χ²-Test
            Observed: [A]
            Expected: [B]
            Calculate   Draw
    • Choose option Calculate
    • Press ENTER
To get the expected counts:
    • Choose MATRX → EDIT
    • Select 2: [B]
    • Press ENTER
```

Test for Homogeneity of Proportions

To compare two or more populations, we use the chi-square test for homogeneity of proportions, which is an extension of the large-samples z-test for the difference of two independent proportions $(p_1 - p_2)$. In the chi-square test, independent samples are taken from two or more populations of interest. When comparing only two population proportions, the two-tailed z-test gives the same results as the chi-square test. The procedure for the test of homogeneity of proportions is similar to the procedure for the test of independence, except for one criterion. In the test of homogeneity, because the samples are taken from different populations of interest, row or column totals are fixed in the resulting contingency table.

- Identify k populations of interest, for which we are interested in comparing the proportions $p_1, p_2,..., p_k$, where p_i is the proportion for ith population of interest $0 < p_i < 1$ $(i = 1, 2,..., k)$.
- We want to make an inference about the equality of $p_1, p_2,..., p_k$.
- Take a random sample from each population of interest. Take the samples independently. Let the sample sizes be equal to $n_1, n_2,...,n_k$, respectively, from k populations. The total number of observations is $n = n_1 + n_2 + \cdots + n_k$.
- Count the number of items in favor of and against the criterion of interest from each sample. These are the observed counts.
- Summarize the observed data into a $k \times 2$ contingency table, where in each row the number in the first column indicates the number in favor and the number in the second column indicates the number against the criterion of interest in that sample.

- The row totals are equal to the sample sizes; i.e.,

$$R_i = n_i, \ (i = 1, 2,..., k)$$

- Compute the column totals

$$C_j = \sum_{i=1}^{k} O_{ji}, \ j = 1, 2$$

Note that

$$\sum_{i=1}^{k} R_i = \sum_{j=1}^{2} C_j = n$$

- If all k population proportions are equal, then the expected count in each cell of the table (in favor of and against the criterion in each sample) can be computed as

$$E_{ij} = \frac{R_i C_j}{n}$$

So compute the expected counts for all cells.

- Compute the test statistic value as

$$\chi^2 = \sum_{j=1}^{2} \sum_{i=1}^{k} \frac{\left(O_{ij} - E_{ij}\right)^2}{E_{ij}} \ (i = 1, 2,..., k \text{ and } j = 1, 2)$$

- For a sufficiently large n, the test statistic follows a chi-square distribution with $df = (k - 1)$ degrees of freedom.

χ^2 Test for homogeneity of proportions:

Use a chi-square test with $df = (k - 1)$ degrees of freedom.

H_0: $p_1 = p_2 = \ldots = p_k$, i.e., all population proportions are equal (this should always be the null hypothesis).

H_a: At least two population proportions are different.

$$\chi^2 = \sum_{j=1}^{2} \sum_{i=1}^{k} \frac{\left(O_{ij} - E_{ij}\right)^2}{E_{ij}}, \text{ where } E_{ij} = \frac{R_i C_j}{n}$$

The rejection rule: Reject the null hypothesis if

- $TS > \chi^2(df)$ (using the rejection region approach)

- p-value $< \alpha$, where p-value $= P(\chi^2(df) > TS)$ (using the p-value approach)

Assumptions:

(a) Each sample is selected at random from the population.

(b) All samples are taken independently of each other.

(c) The sample size n is large enough to get an approximate chi-square distribution for the test statistic.

Checking the assumption of a large n:

If all expected counts are at least five, then we have a large enough sample to use the chi-square approximation.

Example 23: On the campus of a large boarding school, students are housed in Alpha, Beta, Gamma, and Delta dormitories according to their grade levels (9, 10, 11, and 12, respectively). The school officials had heard several complaints about the food services for the dormitories but felt that the complaints differed across the four dormitories. To get student input, a random sample of students was selected from each dormitory (100 students each from Alpha and Beta dormitories, and 75 students each from Gamma and Delta dormitories). Each selected student was asked, "Are the current food services in your dormitory satisfactory?" The answers were recorded as "satisfactory" or "not satisfactory." The results were summarized as follows:

In this case, the degrees of freedom are still $(r - 1)(c - 1)$ but we're making the assumption that $c = 2$ (see table on page 364). That leaves us with $(r - 1)(2 - 1)$ or just $(r - 1)$. Since we often refer to groups with the variable k, we write the degrees of freedom formula as $k - 1$.

	Satisfactory	Sample Size
Alpha	78	100
Beta	72	100
Gamma	49	75
Delta	44	75

Is there significant evidence to indicate whether the proportion of students satisfied with the current food services differs in different dormitories?

Solution: Here we are interested in comparing four proportions:

p_1 = The proportion of students from Alpha dormitory satisfied with the food services.

p_2 = The proportion of students from Beta dormitory satisfied with the food services.

p_3 = The proportion of students from Gamma dormitory satisfied with the food services.

p_4 = The proportion of students from Delta dormitory satisfied with the food services.

Step 1: Define the null and alternative hypotheses as follows:

H_0: $p_1 = p_2 = p_3 = p_4$, i.e., the proportion of students satisfied with the food services is the same across all four dormitories.

H_a: At least two dormitories differ in the proportion of students satisfied with the food services.

Step 2: Use a chi-square test of homogeneity of proportions.

Complete the table of observed counts (add a "Not Satisfactory" column), and then compute the column totals.

	Satisfactory	Not Satisfactory	Row Totals ($R_i = n_i$)
Alpha	78	22	100
Beta	72	28	100
Gamma	49	26	75
Delta	44	31	75
Column Total (C_j)	243	107	$n = 350$

Compute the expected counts as

$$E_{ij} = \frac{R_i C_j}{n}$$

For example:

The expected number of students satisfied with the food services from the Alpha dormitory $= \frac{(100)(243)}{350} = 69.43$.

The following table shows the observed and expected counts, with the expected counts in parentheses:

	Satisfactory	Not Satisfactory
Alpha	78 (69.429)	22 (30.571)
Beta	72 (69.429)	28 (30.571)
Gamma	49 (52.071)	26 (22.929)
Delta	44 (52.071)	31 (22.929)

All the students were selected at random. All four samples were taken independently of each other. All the cell counts are larger than five. Therefore, the conditions for the chi-square test of homogeneity are satisfied.

Step 3: Suppose we are using a 5% level of significance. With $k = 4$ population proportions to compare, the degrees of freedom = $df = 3$. The rejection rule is "reject the null hypothesis if p-value < 0.05" (or if using the rejection region approach, "reject the null hypothesis if $TS > \chi^2_{0.05}(3) = 7.81$").

Compute the test statistic (and the p-value if using the p-value approach).

$$\chi^2 = \sum_{j=1}^{c} \sum_{i=1}^{r} \frac{\left(O_{ij} - E_{ij}\right)^2}{E_{ij}}$$

$$= \frac{(78 - 69.429)^2}{69.429} + \frac{(22 - 30.571)^2}{30.571} + \cdots + \frac{(31 - 22.929)^2}{22.929}$$

$$\approx 8.45$$

$$p\text{-value} = P(\chi^2 > 8.45) = 0.037$$

Step 4: Because p-value $= 0.037 < 0.05$ (or if using the rejection region approach, because $\chi^2 = 8.45 > 7.81$), we should reject the null hypothesis and conclude that at least two dormitories differ in terms of the proportion of students satisfied with the current food services.

Inference for the Slope of a Least-Squares Line (Linear Regression)

It's common practice to estimate the relation between correlated variables and use the estimated relation to predict a response for a given value of an independent variable. Some examples of such estimates are:

- Car manufacturers estimating the mean miles per gallon given by a model of a car from the weight of the car
- Real estate agents estimating the price of a house using the age and/or the location of the house
- Colleges estimating the grade point averages of prospective students at graduation using their scores on college entrance examinations
- Crime labs using the dimensions of bones to estimate the age of a victim

A statistical relation between two variables X (the **independent** or **explanatory** variable) and Y (the **dependent** or **response** variable) is a relation described by a line. Suppose the true linear relation between X and Y is given by

$$Y = \alpha + \beta X \text{ where}$$

$$\alpha = Y\text{-intercept of the line}$$

$$\beta = \text{slope of the line}$$

Here, α and β are population parameters.

The statistical relationship between X and Y could be represented as $Y = \alpha + \beta X + \varepsilon$, where ε = random error.

The difference between a linear and statistical relationship is the error term. In a true linear relationship, we expect X to perfectly predict Y. In a statistical relationship, we expect that there is some true linear relationship, but we expect error around that relationship.

Using the **least-squares regression technique**, the slope and the Y-intercept, respectively, can be estimated from n pairs of measurements as

$$b = r \frac{s_y}{s_x} \quad \text{and} \quad a = \overline{y} - b\overline{x}$$

The sample statistics a and b estimate α and β.

The **error (residual)** is the difference between the observed response and the response predicted by the estimated regression line: i.e., $e = (y - \hat{y})$, where $\hat{y} = b_0 + b_1 x$. The standard deviation of all the error terms in the sample is denoted by s_e.

- Note that this quantity, the standard deviation of the residuals, is often designated in computer output of linear regression problems.

Then the question that arises is: is there a significant relationship between Y and X? In other words: does Y depend significantly on X? Or: does X provide a significant amount of prediction of Y?

If the slope of the line of true relation is zero—i.e., if the relation between Y and X is a horizontal line—then there is no relation between Y and X. A line of slope zero gives the same value for Y regardless of the value of X. In other words, the value of Y does not depend on the value of X. The scatterplot of such population data will show a cloud of measurements with no specific direction; however, in a sample, this may not be true. Even for a population with $\beta = 0$, the slope estimated from the sample (and not computed from the whole population) will not necessarily be equal to zero because of the sampling variation involved. If the estimated slope is non-zero, then the following questions arise:

- Is $b \neq 0$ because the slope of true relation is non-zero, i.e., $\beta \neq 0$?
  OR
- Is $b \neq 0$ just because of sampling variation, when in fact $\beta = 0$?

How much variation among b_1 values can be explained away as a chance variation? That can be determined using the sampling distribution of b. To check the likelihood of b from a population with a specified β (of zero or non-zero value), use the **t-test for slope**.

- Take a random sample of n pairs of observations from the population of interest, or take a random sample of n objects from the population, and make a pair of measurements on each selected object.

$$(x_1, y_1), (x_2, y_2), ..., (x_n, y_n)$$

It is possible for X and Y to be related non-linearly; however, that is beyond the scope of this test.

- Assume that random variables X and Y are linearly related. Make a scatterplot of the n pairs of observations. A quick review of the scatterplot will indicate whether an assumption of linear relation between X and Y is reasonable.

- If the assumption of linear relation is reasonable, then estimate the slope of the line of best fit (also known as "the least-squares regression line").

$$b = \frac{n\sum xy - (\sum x)(\sum y)}{n\sum x^2 - (\sum x)^2}$$

- Different random samples of size n will result in different estimates for b. If for any fixed value of X the responses are normally distributed with the same standard deviation σ, then the sampling distribution of b is also a normal distribution with a mean of β and a standard deviation given by σ_β.

Because the standard deviation of errors σ_ε is unknown, estimate it using S_b. Then the ratio b/S_b follows a t-distribution with $df = (n - 2)$ degrees of freedom.

Estimating β using $(1 - \alpha)100\%$ confidence interval:

Construct a t-interval with $df = (n - 2)$ degrees of freedom.

Margin of Error: $t^* s_b$

Confidence Interval: $b \pm t^* s_b$

Making an inference about the slope (β) of a regression line:
Use a t-test with $df = (n - 2)$ degrees of freedom.

H_0: $\beta = 0$ (or other specified slope)

H_a: $\beta > 0$
 $\beta < 0$ or
 $\beta \neq 0$

$$t = \frac{b - \beta}{s_b}$$

	Rejection Rule	
Alternative hypothesis:	Rejection region approach:	p-value approach:
H_a: $\beta > 0$ (or other specified slope) H_a: $\beta < 0$ H_a: $\beta \neq 0$	Reject H_0 if $t > t_\alpha(df)$ $t < -t_\alpha(df)$ $t > t_{\alpha/2}(df)$ or $t < -t_{\alpha/2}(df)$	Reject H_0 if p-value $< \alpha$, where p-value $= P(t(df) > t)$ p-value $= P(t(df) < t)$ p-value $=$ $P(t(df) > |t|) + P(t(df) < -|t|)$

Conditions:

(a) A random sample of n pairs is obtained.
(b) The residuals (errors) are normally distributed.
(c) The mean error is 0.
(d) The standard deviation of errors, σ_ε, is the same for all values of X.
(e) The residuals are independent.

Checking the conditions:

(a) From the description of the experiment, determine whether it is reasonable to assume that the sample was randomly selected from the population of interest.
(b) Make a boxplot or stem-and-leaf plot of the residuals. If the distribution is fairly symmetric and bell-shaped, then it is reasonable to assume that the errors are normally distributed. Alternatively, use a normal probability plot to make the decision.
(c) Plot the errors to get a residual plot. If all the errors are evenly scattered around 0, then it is reasonable to assume that the mean is 0.
(d) If the residual plot shows a somewhat similar spread of errors across all values of X, then it is reasonable to assume a constant standard deviation.
(e) If the residual plot shows no specific trends or patterns, it is reasonable to assume that the errors are independent.

Example 24: Some of the members of the faculty of the College of Education believe that reading performance is related to the point size of the letters in the document read. A group of randomly selected students were given a test. They were asked to read certain passages in different point sizes on a computer. The letter sizes were randomized. The average time (in minutes) required for the subjects to read the passages was determined. The data is given in the following table:

Letter Size (in Points)	7	8	9	10	11	12	13	14
Average Reading Time (in Minutes)	7.10	7.14	6.50	6.78	6.44	6.94	6.30	6.46

The regression analysis performed on the data by a computer gave the following results:

Predictor	Coef	StDev	T	P
Constant	7.6700	0.4225	18.15	0.000
Letter size	−0.09167	0.03931	−2.33	0.058

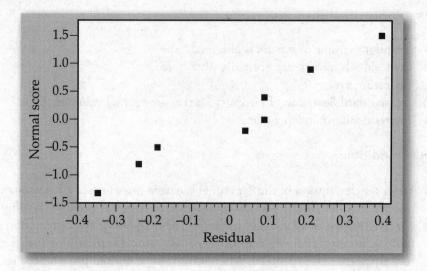

Figure 29: Normal probability plot for residuals

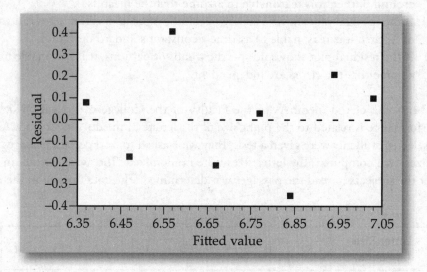

Figure 30: Residual plot

Is there a significant relation between the letter point size and the reading performance as measured by average reading time?

Solution:

Step 1: The faculty are interested in determining whether average reading time depends on the point size of the letter. So test

H_0: There is no relation between average reading time and letter size, or $\beta = 0$.

H_a: There is a relation between average reading time and letter size, or $\beta \neq 0$.

Step 2: Use the *t*-test for slope (or a *t*-test for correlation coefficient).

(a) A random sample of students was used.

(b) The normal probability plot in Figure 29 shows a fairly linear pattern. So it is reasonable to assume that the distribution of residuals is normal.

(c) The residual plot in Figure 30 shows that the residuals are scattered around 0. It is reasonable to assume that the mean is 0.

(d) The residual plot shows a somewhat similar spread of errors across all values of *X*. It is reasonable to assume a constant standard deviation.

(e) The residual plot shows no specific trends or patterns. It is reasonable to assume that the errors are independent.

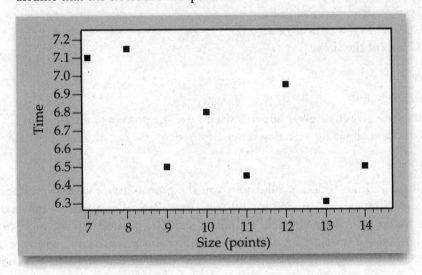

Figure 31: Scatterplot of reading time versus letter size

This scatterplot shown in Figure 31 indicates a slightly downward trend. It is reasonable to assume that a linear relation exists between the reading time and the letter point size.

Step 3: With *n* = 8 pairs of measurements, degrees of freedom = *n* − 2 = 6. Suppose we use $\alpha = 0.10$, then

$$t^* = t_{\alpha/2}(df) = t_{0.10/2}(6) = t_{0.05}(6) = 1.943$$

The rejection rule is to "reject null if *p*-value < 0.10" (or "reject null if $t > 1.943$ or $t < -1.943$," if using the rejection region approach).

From the results of the regression analysis provided we get

$$b = -0.092, \quad t = \frac{b}{S_b} = \frac{-0.092}{0.03931} = -2.33 \text{ and } p\text{-value} = 0.058$$

Step 4: Because the p-value = 0.058 < 0.10 (or, if using the rejection region approach, $t = -2.33$, which falls in the rejection region), reject the null hypothesis and accept the alternative hypothesis. At a 10% error rate, we can conclude that there is a linear relation between letter size and reading performance.

---○---

Which of the following statements is accurate? You can reject the null when:

    (A) $p < \alpha$, or $\chi^2 <$ critical value
    (B) $p < \alpha$, or $\chi^2 >$ critical value
    (C) $p > \alpha$, or $\chi^2 <$ critical value
    (D) $p > \alpha$, or $\chi^2 >$ critical value
    (E) None of the above

Here's How to Crack It

This question style gives us a great opportunity to use the process of elimination (POE). If we can make a decision about the rejection criteria for p or χ^2, we can automatically eliminate two answers.

Starting with p, we know that a p-value tells you the probability of getting a value at least as extreme as our observed statistic if the null were true. Basically, it tells us how extreme our sample data would be in a world where the null is true. We assume that the more extreme the data is, the less likely it is that the null is true. Therefore, we reject the null when we have small p-values since smaller p-values indicate more extreme data. We can eliminate (C) and (D).

In general, extreme sample data will generate test statistics that are further from 0. Since the χ^2 test statistic can only be positive, we only reject the null when χ^2 is larger than the critical value. Therefore, we can eliminate (A). Since (B) is true, eliminate (E). The correct answer is (B).

---○---

QUICK QUIZ

Fill in the blanks in the scheme for selecting *t*- or *z*-intervals for estimation and inference. This chapter contains similar flow charts, but try to complete these without help. Answers can be found on page 392.

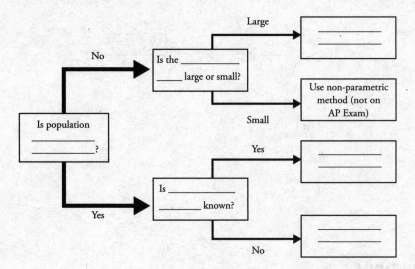

Fill in the blanks in the scheme below for selecting a confidence interval or test for difference of population means. Answers can be found on page 392.

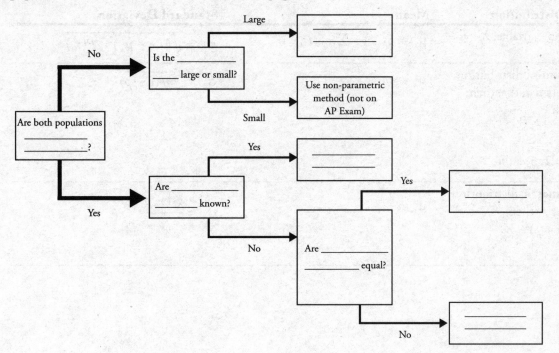

FORMULAS FOR AP STATISTICS

I.   Descriptive Statistics

$$\overline{x} = \frac{1}{n}\sum x_i = \frac{\sum x_i}{n}$$

$$s_x = \sqrt{\frac{1}{n-1}\sum(x_i - \overline{x})^2} = \sqrt{\frac{\sum(x_i - \overline{x})^2}{n-1}}$$

$$\hat{y} = a + bx$$

$$\overline{y} = a + b\overline{x}$$

$$r = \frac{1}{n-1}\sum\left(\frac{x_i - \overline{x}}{s_x}\right)\left(\frac{y_i - \overline{y}}{s_y}\right)$$

$$b = r\frac{s_y}{s_x}$$

II.   Probability and Distributions

$$P(A \cup B) = P(A) + P(B) - P(A \cap B)$$

$$P(A\,|\,B) = \frac{P(A \cap B)}{P(B)}$$

Probability Distribution	Mean	Standard Deviation
Discrete random variable, X	$\mu_x = E(X) = \sum x_i \cdot P(x_i)$	$\sigma_x = \sqrt{E(x_i - \mu_x)^2 \cdot P(x_i)}$
If X has a **binomial** distribution with parameters n and p, then: $P(X = x) = \binom{n}{x}p^x(1-p)^{n-x}$ where $x = 0, 1, 2, 3, ..., n$	$\mu_x = np$	$\sigma_x = \sqrt{np(1-p)}$
If X has a **geometric** distribution with parameter p, then: $P(X = x) = (1-p)^{n-1}p$ where $x = 1, 2, 3, ...$	$\mu_x = \dfrac{1}{p}$	$\sigma_x = \dfrac{\sqrt{1-p}}{p}$

III. Sampling Distributions and Inferential Statistics

$$\text{standardized test statistic:} \frac{\text{statistic} - \text{parameter}}{\text{standard error of the statistic}}$$

$$\text{confidence interval: statistic} \pm (\text{critical value})(\text{standard error of statistic})$$

$$\text{Chi-square statistic:} \quad \boxed{\chi^2 = \sum \frac{(\text{observed} - \text{expected})^2}{\text{expected}}}$$

Random Variable	Parameters of Sampling Distribution	Standard Error* of Sample Statistic
For one population: $\hat{p}$	$\mu_{\hat{p}} - p$ $$\sigma_{\hat{p}} = \sqrt{\frac{p(1-p)}{n}}$$	$$s_{\hat{p}} = \sqrt{\frac{\hat{p}(1-\hat{p})}{n}}$$
For two populations: $\hat{p}_1 - \hat{p}_2$	$\mu_{\hat{p}_1 - \hat{p}_2} = p_1 - p_2$ $$\sigma_{\hat{p}_1 - \hat{p}_2} = \sqrt{\frac{p_1(1-p_1)}{n_1} + \frac{p_2(1-p_2)}{n_2}}$$	$$s_{\hat{p}_1 - \hat{p}_2} = \sqrt{\frac{\hat{p}_1(1-\hat{p}_1)}{n_1} + \frac{\hat{p}_2(1-\hat{p}_2)}{n_2}}$$ when $p_1 = p_2$ is assumed: $$s_{\hat{p}_1 - \hat{p}_2} = \sqrt{\hat{p}_c(1-\hat{p}_c)\left(\frac{1}{n_1} + \frac{1}{n_2}\right)}$$ where $\hat{p}_c = \frac{X_1 + X_2}{n_1 + n_2}$

Sampling distributions for means:

Random Variable	Parameters of Sampling Distribution	Standard Error* of Sample Statistic
$\bar{X}$	$\mu_{\bar{X}} = \mu$ $\sigma_{\bar{X}} = \dfrac{\sigma}{\sqrt{n}}$	$s_{\bar{X}} = \dfrac{s}{\sqrt{n}}$
$\bar{X}_1 - \bar{X}_2$	$\mu_{\bar{X}_1 - \bar{X}_2} = \mu_1 - \mu_2$ $\sigma_{\bar{X}_1 - \bar{X}_2} = \sqrt{\dfrac{\sigma_1^2}{n_1} + \dfrac{\sigma_2^2}{n_2}}$	$s_{\bar{X}_1 - \bar{X}_2} = \sqrt{\dfrac{s_1^2}{n_1} + \dfrac{s_2^2}{n_2}}$

Sampling distributions for simple linear regression:

Random Variable	Parameters of Sampling Distribution	Standard Error* of Sample Statistic
For slope: b	$\mu_b = \beta$ $\sigma_b = \dfrac{\sigma}{\sigma_x \sqrt{n}}$	$s_b = \dfrac{s}{s_x \sqrt{n-1}}$
	where $\sigma_x = \sqrt{\dfrac{\sum(x_i - \bar{x})^2}{n}}$	where $s = \sqrt{\dfrac{\sum(y_i - \hat{y}_i)^2}{n-2}}$ and $s_x = \sqrt{\dfrac{\sum(x_i - \bar{x})^2}{n-1}}$

TABLES FOR AP STATISTICS

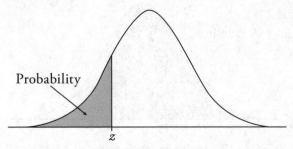

Probability

z

Table entry for z is the probability lying below z.

TABLE A

					Standard Normal Probabilities					
z	.00	.01	.02	.03	.04	.05	.06	.07	.08	.09
−3.4	.0003	.0003	.0003	.0003	.0003	.0003	.0003	.0003	.0003	.0002
−3.3	.0005	.0005	.0005	.0004	.0004	.0004	.0004	.0004	.0004	.0003
−3.2	.0007	.0007	.0006	.0006	.0006	.0006	.0006	.0005	.0005	.0005
−3.1	.0010	.0009	.0009	.0009	.0008	.0008	.0008	.0008	.0007	.0007
−3.0	.0013	.0013	.0013	.0012	.0012	.0011	.0011	.0011	.0010	.0010
−2.9	.0019	.0018	.0018	.0017	.0016	.0016	.0015	.0015	.0014	.0014
−2.8	.0026	.0025	.0024	.0023	.0023	.0022	.0021	.0021	.0020	.0019
−2.7	.0035	.0034	.0033	.0032	.0031	.0030	.0029	.0028	.0027	.0026
−2.6	.0047	.0045	.0044	.0043	.0041	.0040	.0039	.0038	.0037	.0036
−2.5	.0062	.0060	.0059	.0057	.0055	.0054	.0052	.0051	.0049	.0048
−2.4	.0082	.0080	.0078	.0075	.0073	.0071	.0069	.0068	.0066	.0064
−2.3	.0107	.0104	.0102	.0099	.0096	.0094	.0091	.0089	.0087	.0084
−2.2	.0139	.0136	.0132	.0129	.0125	.0122	.0119	.0116	.0113	.0110
−2.1	.0179	.0174	.0170	.0166	.0162	.0158	.0154	.0150	.0146	.0143
−2.0	.0228	.0222	.0217	.0212	.0207	.0202	.0197	.0192	.0188	.0183
−1.9	.0287	.0281	.0274	.0268	.0262	.0256	.0250	.0244	.0239	.0233
−1.8	.0359	.0351	.0344	.0336	.0329	.0322	.0314	.0307	.0301	.0294
−1.7	.0446	.0436	.0427	.0418	.0409	.0401	.0392	.0384	.0375	.0367
−1.6	.0548	.0537	.0526	.0516	.0505	.0495	.0485	.0475	.0465	.0455
−1.5	.0668	.0655	.0643	.0630	.0618	.0606	.0594	.0582	.0571	.0559
−1.4	.0808	.0793	.0778	.0764	.0749	.0735	.0721	.0708	.0694	.0681
−1.3	.0968	.0951	.0934	.0918	.0901	.0885	.0869	.0853	.0838	.0823
−1.2	.1151	.1131	.1112	.1093	.1075	.1056	.1038	.1020	.1003	.0985
−1.1	.1357	.1335	.1314	.1292	.1271	.1251	.1230	.1210	.1190	.1170
−1.0	.1587	.1562	.1539	.1515	.1492	.1469	.1446	.1423	.1401	.1379
−0.9	.1841	.1814	.1788	.1762	.1736	.1711	.1685	.1660	.1635	.1611
−0.8	.2119	.2090	.2061	.2033	.2005	.1977	.1949	.1922	.1894	.1867
−0.7	.2420	.2389	.2358	.2327	.2296	.2266	.2236	.2206	.2177	.2148
−0.6	.2743	.2709	.2676	.2643	.2611	.2578	.2546	.2514	.2483	.2451
−0.5	.3085	.3050	.3015	.2981	.2946	.2912	.2877	.2843	.2810	.2776
−0.4	.3446	.3409	.3372	.3336	.3300	.3264	.3228	.3192	.3156	.3121
−0.3	.3821	.3783	.3745	.3707	.3669	.3632	.3594	.3557	.3520	.3483
−0.2	.4207	.4168	.4129	.4090	.4052	.4013	.3974	.3936	.3897	.3859
−0.1	.4602	.4562	.4522	.4483	.4443	.4404	.4364	.4325	.4286	.4247
−0.0	.5000	.4960	.4920	.4880	.4840	.4801	.4761	.4721	.4681	.4641

TABLE A

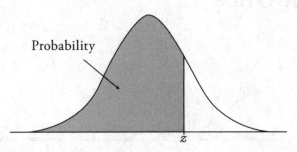

Probability

Table entry for *z* is the probability lying below *z*.

Standard Normal Probabilities—Continued									
z	.00	.01	.02	.03	.04	.05	.06	.07	.08	.09
0.0	.5000	.5040	.5080	.5120	.5160	.5199	.5239	.5279	.5319	.5359
0.1	.5398	.5438	.5478	.5517	.5557	.5596	.5636	.5675	.5714	.5753
0.2	.5793	.5832	.5871	.5910	.5948	.5987	.6026	.6064	.6103	.6141
0.3	.6179	.6217	.6255	.6293	.6331	.6368	.6406	.6443	.6480	.6517
0.4	.6554	.6591	.6628	.6664	.6700	.6736	.6772	.6808	.6844	.6879
0.5	.6915	.6950	.6985	.7019	.7054	.7088	.7123	.7157	.7190	.7224
0.6	.7257	.7291	.7324	.7357	.7389	.7422	.7454	.7486	.7517	.7549
0.7	.7580	.7611	.7642	.7673	.7704	.7734	.7764	.7794	.7823	.7852
0.8	.7881	.7910	.7939	.7967	.7995	.8023	.8051	.8078	.8106	.8133
0.9	.8159	.8186	.8212	.8238	.8264	.8289	.8315	.8340	.8365	.8389
1.0	.8413	.8438	.8461	.8485	.8508	.8531	.8554	.8577	.8599	.8621
1.1	.8643	.8665	.8686	.8708	.8729	.8749	.8770	.8790	.8810	.8830
1.2	.8849	.8869	.8888	.8907	.8925	.8944	.8962	.8980	.8997	.9015
1.3	.9032	.9049	.9066	.9082	.9099	.9115	.9131	.9147	.9162	.9177
1.4	.9192	.9207	.9222	.9236	.9251	.9265	.9279	.9292	.9306	.9319
1.5	.9332	.9345	.9357	.9370	.9382	.9394	.9406	.9418	.9429	.9441
1.6	.9452	.9463	.9474	.9484	.9495	.9505	.9515	.9525	.9535	.9545
1.7	.9554	.9564	.9573	.9582	.9591	.9599	.9608	.9616	.9625	.9633
1.8	.9641	.9649	.9656	.9664	.9671	.9678	.9686	.9693	.9699	.9706
1.9	.9713	.9719	.9726	.9732	.9738	.9744	.9750	.9756	.9761	.9767
2.0	.9772	.9778	.9783	.9788	.9793	.9798	.9803	.9808	.9812	.9817
2.1	.9821	.9826	.9830	.9834	.9838	.9842	.9846	.9850	.9854	.9857
2.2	.9861	.9864	.9868	.9871	.9875	.9878	.9881	.9884	.9887	.9890
2.3	.9893	.9896	.9898	.9901	.9904	.9906	.9909	.9911	.9913	.9916
2.4	.9918	.9920	.9922	.9925	.9927	.9929	.9931	.9932	.9934	.9936
z	.00	.01	.02	.03	.04	.05	.06	.07	.08	.09
2.5	.9938	.9940	.9941	.9943	.9945	.9946	.9948	.9949	.9951	.9952
2.6	.9953	.9955	.9956	.9957	.9959	.9960	.9961	.9962	.9963	.9964
2.7	.9965	.9966	.9967	.9968	.9969	.9970	.9971	.9972	.9973	.9974
2.8	.9974	.9975	.9976	.9977	.9977	.9978	.9979	.9979	.9980	.9981
2.9	.9981	.9982	.9982	.9983	.9984	.9984	.9985	.9985	.9986	.9986
3.0	.9987	.9987	.9987	.9988	.9988	.9989	.9989	.9989	.9990	.9990
3.1	.9990	.9991	.9991	.9991	.9992	.9992	.9992	.9992	.9993	.9993
3.2	.9993	.9993	.9994	.9994	.9994	.9994	.9994	.9995	.9995	.9995
3.3	.9995	.9995	.9995	.9996	.9996	.9996	.9996	.9996	.9996	.9997
3.4	.9997	.9997	.9997	.9997	.9997	.9997	.9997	.9997	.9997	.9998

TABLE B

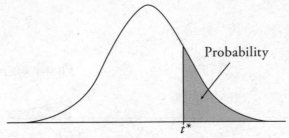

Probability

t^*

Table entry for p and C is the point t^* with probability p lying above it and probability C lying between $-t^*$ and t^*.

t Distribution Critical Values

df	.25	.20	.15	.10	.05	.025	.02	.01	.005	.0025	.001	.0005
1	1.000	1.376	1.963	3.078	6.314	12.71	15.89	31.82	63.66	127.3	318.3	636.6
2	.816	1.061	1.386	1.886	2.920	4.303	4.849	6.965	9.925	14.09	22.33	31.60
3	.765	.978	1.250	1.638	2.353	3.182	3.482	4.541	5.841	7.453	10.21	12.92
4	.741	.941	1.190	1.533	2.132	2.776	2.999	3.747	4.604	5.598	7.173	8.610
5	.727	.920	1.156	1.476	2.015	2.571	2.757	3.365	4.032	4.773	5.893	6.869
6	.718	.906	1.134	1.440	1.943	2.447	2.612	3.143	3.707	4.317	5.208	5.959
7	.711	.896	1.119	1.415	1.895	2.365	2.517	2.998	3.499	4.029	4.785	5.408
8	.706	.889	1.108	1.397	1.860	2.306	2.449	2.896	3.355	3.833	4.501	5.041
9	.703	.883	1.100	1.383	1.833	2.262	2.398	2.821	3.250	3.690	4.297	4.781
10	.700	.879	1.093	1.372	1.812	2.228	2.359	2.764	3.169	3.581	4.144	4.587
11	.697	.876	1.088	1.363	1.796	2.201	2.328	2.718	3.106	3.497	4.025	4.437
12	.695	.873	1.083	1.356	1.782	2.179	2.303	2.681	3.055	3.428	3.930	4.318
13	.694	.870	1.079	1.350	1.771	2.160	2.282	2.650	3.012	3.372	3.852	4.221
14	.692	.868	1.076	1.345	1.761	2.145	2.264	2.624	2.977	3.326	3.787	4.140
15	.691	.866	1.074	1.341	1.753	2.131	2.249	2.602	2.947	3.286	3.733	4.073
16	.690	.865	1.071	1.337	1.746	2.120	2.235	2.583	2.921	3.252	3.686	4.015
17	.689	.863	1.069	1.333	1.740	2.110	2.224	2.567	2.898	3.222	3.646	3.965
18	.688	.862	1.067	1.330	1.734	2.101	2.214	2.552	2.878	3.197	3.611	3.922
19	.688	.861	1.066	1.328	1.729	2.093	2.205	2.539	2.861	3.174	3.579	3.883
20	.687	.860	1.064	1.325	1.725	2.086	2.197	2.528	2.845	3.153	3.552	3.850
21	.686	.859	1.063	1.323	1.721	2.080	2.189	2.518	2.831	3.135	3.527	3.819
22	.686	.858	1.061	1.321	1.717	2.074	2.183	2.508	2.819	3.119	3.505	3.792
23	.685	.858	1.060	1.319	1.714	2.069	2.177	2.500	2.807	3.104	3.485	3.768
24	.685	.857	1.059	1.318	1.711	2.064	2.172	2.492	2.797	3.091	3.467	3.745
25	.684	.856	1.058	1.316	1.708	2.060	2.167	2.485	2.787	3.078	3.450	3.725
26	.684	.856	1.058	1.315	1.706	2.056	2.162	2.479	2.779	3.067	3.435	3.707
27	.684	.855	1.057	1.314	1.703	2.052	2.158	2.473	2.771	3.057	3.421	3.690
28	.683	.855	1.056	1.313	1.701	2.048	2.154	2.467	2.763	3.047	3.408	3.674
29	.683	.854	1.055	1.311	1.699	2.045	2.150	2.462	2.756	3.038	3.396	3.659
30	.683	.854	1.055	1.310	1.697	2.042	2.147	2.457	2.750	3.030	3.385	3.646
40	.681	.851	1.050	1.303	1.684	2.021	2.123	2.423	2.704	2.971	3.307	3.551
50	.679	.849	1.047	1.299	1.676	2.009	2.109	2.403	2.678	2.937	3.261	3.496
60	.679	.848	1.045	1.296	1.671	2.000	2.099	2.390	2.660	2.915	3.232	3.460
80	.678	.846	1.043	1.292	1.664	1.990	2.088	2.374	2.639	2.887	3.195	3.416
100	.677	.845	1.042	1.290	1.660	1.984	2.081	2.364	2.626	2.871	3.174	3.390
1000	.675	.842	1.037	1.282	1.646	1.962	2.056	2.330	2.581	2.813	3.098	3.300
∞	.674	.841	1.036	1.282	1.645	1.960	2.054	2.326	2.576	2.807	3.091	3.291
	50%	60%	70%	80%	90%	95%	96%	98%	99%	99.5%	99.8%	99.9%

Confidence level C

TABLE C

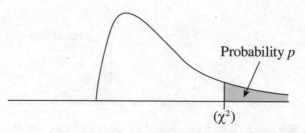

Probability p

(χ^2)

Table entry for p is the point (χ^2) with probability p lying above it

χ^2 Critical Values

						Tail Probability p						
df	.25	.20	.15	.10	.05	.025	.02	.01	.005	.0025	.001	.0005
1	1.32	1.64	2.07	2.71	3.84	5.02	5.41	6.63	7.88	9.14	10.83	12.12
2	2.77	3.22	3.79	4.61	5.99	7.38	7.82	9.21	10.60	11.98	13.82	15.20
3	4.11	4.64	5.32	6.25	7.81	9.35	9.84	11.34	12.84	14.32	16.27	17.73
4	5.39	5.99	6.74	7.78	9.49	11.14	11.67	13.28	14.86	16.42	18.47	20.00
5	6.63	7.29	8.12	9.24	11.07	12.83	13.39	15.09	16.75	18.39	20.51	22.11
6	7.84	8.56	9.45	10.64	12.59	14.45	15.03	16.81	18.55	20.25	22.46	24.10
7	9.04	9.80	10.75	12.02	14.07	16.01	16.62	18.48	20.28	22.04	24.32	26.02
8	10.22	11.03	12.03	13.36	15.51	17.53	18.17	20.09	21.95	23.77	26.12	27.87
9	11.39	12.24	13.29	14.68	16.92	19.02	19.68	21.67	23.59	25.46	27.88	29.67
10	12.55	13.44	14.53	15.99	18.31	20.48	21.16	23.21	25.19	27.11	29.59	31.42
11	13.70	14.63	15.77	17.28	19.68	21.92	22.62	24.72	26.76	28.73	31.26	33.14
12	14.85	15.81	16.99	18.55	21.03	23.34	24.05	26.22	28.30	30.32	32.91	34.82
13	15.98	16.98	18.20	19.81	22.36	24.74	25.47	27.69	29.82	31.88	34.53	36.48
14	17.12	18.15	19.41	21.06	23.68	26.12	26.87	29.14	31.32	33.43	36.12	38.11
15	18.25	19.31	20.60	22.31	25.00	27.49	28.26	30.58	32.80	34.95	37.70	39.72
16	19.37	20.47	21.79	23.54	26.30	28.85	29.63	32.00	34.27	36.46	39.25	41.31
17	20.49	21.61	22.98	24.77	27.59	30.19	31.00	33.41	35.72	37.95	40.79	42.88
18	21.60	22.76	24.16	25.99	28.87	31.53	32.35	34.81	37.16	39.42	42.31	44.43
19	22.72	23.90	25.33	27.20	30.14	32.85	33.69	36.19	38.58	40.88	43.82	45.97
20	23.83	25.04	26.50	28.41	31.41	34.17	35.02	37.57	40.00	42.34	45.31	47.50
21	24.93	26.17	27.66	29.62	32.67	35.48	36.34	38.93	41.40	43.78	46.80	49.01
22	26.04	27.30	28.82	30.81	33.92	36.78	37.66	40.29	42.80	45.20	48.27	50.51
23	27.14	28.43	29.98	32.01	35.17	38.08	38.97	41.64	44.18	46.62	49.73	52.00
24	28.24	29.55	31.13	33.20	36.42	39.36	40.27	42.98	45.56	48.03	51.18	53.48
25	29.34	30.68	32.28	34.38	37.65	40.65	41.57	44.31	46.93	49.44	52.62	54.95
26	30.43	31.79	33.43	35.56	38.89	41.92	42.86	45.64	48.29	50.83	54.05	56.41
27	31.53	32.91	34.57	36.74	40.11	43.19	44.14	43.96	49.64	52.22	55.48	57.86
28	32.62	34.03	35.71	37.92	41.34	44.46	45.42	48.28	50.99	53.59	56.89	59.30
29	33.71	35.14	36.85	39.09	42.56	45.72	46.69	49.59	52.34	54.97	58.30	60.73
30	34.80	36.25	37.99	40.26	43.77	46.98	47.96	50.89	53.67	56.33	59.70	62.16
40	45.62	47.27	49.24	51.81	55.76	59.34	60.44	63.69	66.77	69.70	73.40	76.09
50	56.33	58.16	60.35	63.17	67.50	71.42	72.61	76.15	79.49	82.66	86.66	89.56
60	66.98	68.97	71.34	74.40	79.08	83.30	84.58	88.38	91.95	95.34	99.61	102.7
80	88.13	90.41	93.11	96.58	101.9	106.6	108.1	112.3	116.3	120.1	124.8	128.3
100	109.1	111.7	114.7	118.5	124.3	129.6	131.1	135.8	140.2	144.3	149.4	153.2

TEST YOUR UNDERSTANDING

Which type of error (Type I or Type II) do researchers get to explicitly determine when doing their analysis? Researchers get to explicitly determine their Type I error rate, because it is always equal to alpha. Type II error rates rely on many factors, including ones that researchers cannot control, like standard deviation and sample size.

If the null hypothesis is true, is it possible to make a Type II error? Why or why not? No. Type II error rates are False Negatives, which means that we failed to reject the null when it is in reality false. If the null hypothesis is true, by definition we cannot make a Type II error.

Which test statistic(s) (t, z, χ^2) shape is/are affected by degrees of freedom? The shapes of both t and χ^2 are affected by degrees of freedom. The t distribution has thicker tails when degrees of freedom are small and approximates a normal distribution when degrees of freedom are large. Similarly, the χ^2 distribution is an extremely right-skewed distribution when degrees of freedom are small. As degrees of freedom increase, the χ^2 distribution gets less skewed and approximates a normal distribution.

Describe the difference between a parameter and a statistic. A parameter is a description of a population, such as the population mean or standard deviation. A statistic is an approximation (or guess) of a parameter from a sample: for example the sample mean and standard deviation.

If 0 is inside your 95% confidence t-interval, is it possible for your sample mean to be significantly different from 0 at the $\alpha = 0.05$ level? No. All values inside a $(100 - \alpha)$ confidence interval are values which are not significantly different from your sample statistic. A confidence interval lists the range of values that are within one margin of error (ME) of your sample statistic. A t-test only rejects the null when your sample statistic is more than one ME away from the value you're testing against (here, 0). It's impossible for 0 to be less than one ME away from your sample statistic according to the confidence interval, but more than one ME away from your sample statistic according to a hypothesis test. Therefore, it's impossible to have 0 in your 95% confidence interval but have your sample statistic be significantly different from 0 at the $\alpha = 0.05$ level.

Summary

- **Parameters** refer to the population and are typically denoted using Greek letters. **Statistics** refer to samples and are typically denoted using the standard alphabet.

- There are two hypotheses in hypothesis testing: the **null hypothesis** (H_0) and the **alternative hypothesis** (H_a).

- A **Type I error** is the possibility of rejecting the null hypothesis when it is actually true. This is analogous to sending an innocent person to prison. The Type I error rate is set by the statistician and is typically calculated as one minus the confidence level.

- A **Type II error** is the possibility of failing to reject the null hypothesis when it is in reality false. This is analogous to setting a guilty person free.

- The three major components of a test's power are the sample size, the significance level of the test, and the effect size.

- The **critical value** of a test statistic is related to the **rejection region**, as this value marks the edge of the region of rejection.

- There are four steps for constructing a **confidence interval**:
  1. Identify the parameter of interest.
  2. Identify the appropriate type of confidence interval.
  3. Provide the correct mechanics to solve the problem (do the math).
  4. Use the confidence interval to state the conclusion in the context of the problem.

- There are four steps for testing a hypothesis:
  1. State the null and alternative hypotheses.
  2. Identify the correct statistical test and check the assumptions.
  3. Provide the correct mechanics to solve the problem (do the math).
  4. Use the results of the test to state the conclusion in context of the problem: either reject the null hypothesis or fail to reject the null hypothesis.

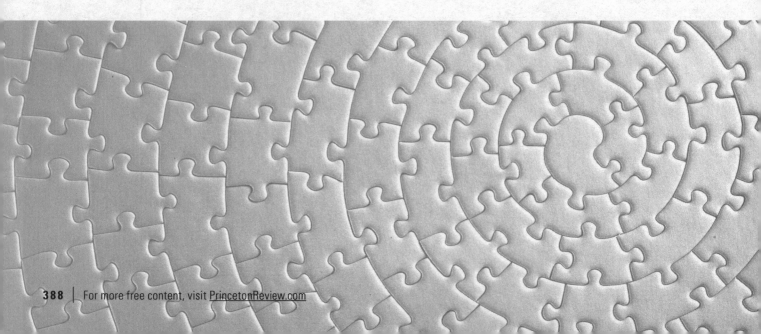

Chapter 7 Review Questions

Multiple-Choice Questions

Answers can be found at the end of this section.

1. A researcher wants to determine whether a new cat food leads to an increased mean weight in cats. Which of the following are the correct null and alternative hypotheses?

   (A) $H_0: \mu_1 < \mu_2; H_a: \mu_1 = \mu_2$
   (B) $H_0: \mu_1 = \mu_2; H_a: \mu_1 < \mu_2$
   (C) $H_0: \mu_1 > \mu_2; H_a: \mu_1 = \mu_2$
   (D) $H_0: \mu_1 = \mu_2; H_a: \mu_1 > \mu_2$
   (E) $H_0: \mu_1 \leq \mu_2; H_a: \mu_1 = \mu_2$

2. Given the null hypothesis that all children sleep 8 hours, which of the following is a Type I error?

   (A) Claiming all children do not sleep 8 hours when, in fact, they do
   (B) Failing to reject the claim that all children sleep 8 hours when that statement is not true
   (C) Claiming all children sleep 8 hours when it is true
   (D) Accepting the claim that all children sleep 8 hours, when that statement is not true
   (E) Accepting the claim that all children sleep 8 hours, when, in fact, they do

3. A grocer would like to determine the proportion of milk cartons that have expired within 0.05 of the true proportion with a 95 percent confidence interval. What is the minimum required sample size?

   (A) 300
   (B) 383
   (C) 384
   (D) 385
   (E) 400

4. Which of the following is FALSE about the power of a test?

   (A) It increases as the sample size increases.
   (B) It increases as the Type I error rate increases.
   (C) It is directly calculated from the error of rejecting the null hypothesis when the hypothesis is true.
   (D) It increases as the effect size increases.
   (E) It increases as β decreases.

5. A 90 percent confidence interval is computed from data to estimate the mean age of summer camp attendees at a local camp. The interval is (4.6 years, 6.3 years). Which of the following is a correct statement based on this interval?

   (A) Ninety percent of the attendees' ages fall between 4.6 and 6.3 years.
   (B) There is a 5 percent probability that no attendee was less than 4.6 years old.
   (C) There is a 90 percent chance that another sample of attendees will get an interval of 4.6 to 6.3 years.
   (D) Ninety percent of the population was sampled and their ages fell between 4.6 and 6.3 years.
   (E) There is a 10 percent probability that the mean age of attendees is not between 4.6 and 6.3 years.

6. Which test is appropriate for analyzing categorical data?

   (A) z-test
   (B) 2 sample t-test
   (C) Chi-square test
   (D) 1-sample t-test
   (E) A nonparametric test

7. When using the rejection region approach, when is it appropriate to reject the null hypothesis?

 (A) The p-value of the test statistic is less than α.
 (B) The test statistic falls within the rejection region, as determined by α.
 (C) The test statistic falls outside of the rejection region, as determined by α.
 (D) The p-value of the test statistic is greater than α.
 (E) The test statistic is less than α.

8. Which of the following is NOT a similarity between the t-distribution and the standard normal distribution?

 (A) Both depend on degrees of freedom.
 (B) Both distribution means are zero.
 (C) Both are continuous distributions.
 (D) Both are bell-shaped.
 (E) Both are symmetric about the mean.

9. A student is surveying her high school population to see whether grade level is related to soda preference. The student takes a large random stratified sample across all four grade levels and asks students to pick a single preferred soda from among six choices. The student then uses this data to construct a two-way contingency table in order to run a χ^2 test of independence. How many degrees of freedom will this test have?

 (A) 1
 (B) 2
 (C) 10
 (D) 15
 (E) 24

Free-Response Questions

10. A researcher wants to see whether there is a connection between a mother's career field type and a daughter's career field type. A random sample of 500 mother–daughter pairs were selected from a large metropolis, and the results are shown in the table below.

		Mother's Career Field		
		Fine Arts	STEM	Social Sciences
Daughter's Career Field	Fine Arts	72	15	24
	STEM	20	99	64
	Social Sciences	44	73	89

Does this data provide significant evidence of an association between the mother's career field type and her daughter's career field type?

11. A fruit distributor ships cases of oranges to grocery stores nationally. The distributor takes a random sample of 10 cases shipped over the course of a month. The weights are as follows: 26.3 lbs; 27.5 lbs; 25.6 lbs; 26.8 lbs; 24.9 lbs; 24.2 lbs; 25.7 lbs; 25.3 lbs; 23.8 lbs; 25.5 lbs.

   (a) Estimate the mean weight of the latest shipment of orange cases using a 95 percent confidence interval and interpret it.
   (b) The mean weight should be 25 lbs/case. Should the shipment be accepted or rejected?

CHAPTER 7 ANSWERS AND EXPLANATIONS

Quick Quiz

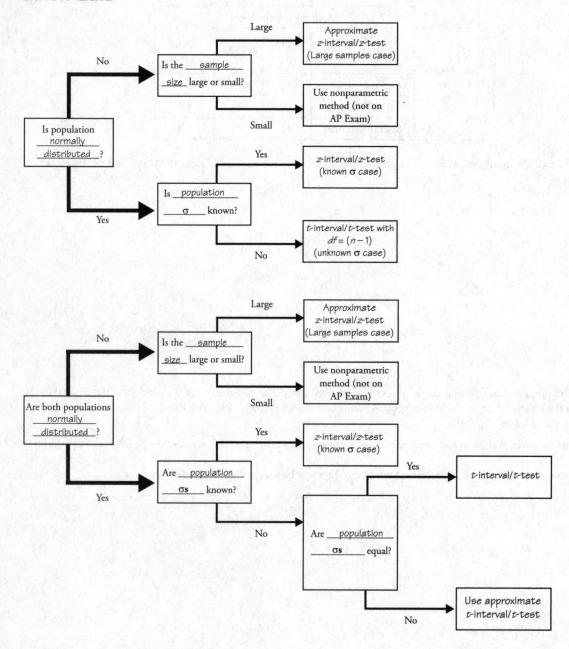

Review Questions

1. **B** The null hypothesis typically is in the form of "no change." In this case, the null hypothesis would state that the mean weight of cats before eating the food, μ_1, is the same as the mean weight of cats after eating the food, μ_2. The alternative hypothesis will be what the researcher wants to test, in this case, that the new food increases the mean weight of cats or the original mean weight of the cats is less than those cats' mean weight after they eat the food. These two hypotheses would be written as: $H_0: \mu_1 = \mu_2$; $H_a: \mu_1 < \mu_2$.

2. **A** A Type I error is the error in which the null hypothesis is rejected when it is true. In this case, the null hypothesis states that children sleep 8 hours, so if someone claims that children do not sleep 8 hours when they really do (as in (A)), that is a Type I error. Note that a Type II error, in contrast, is failing to reject the null hypothesis when the alternative hypothesis is true. In this example, the Type II error is (B).

3. **D** In order to determine the sample size required to estimate a population proportion, use the formula: $n \geq \left(\dfrac{Z_{\alpha/2}}{ME}\right)^2 p(1-p)$. However, if an estimate of p from past experiments is not available, as in this case, use this formula: $n \geq \left(\dfrac{Z_{\alpha/2}}{2ME}\right)^2$. The ME is how far off from the true proportion you are willing to be, in this case, 0.05. $Z_{\alpha/2}$ is equal to the z-score for a certain percentage, $\alpha/2$. In this case, since you want a 95% confidence interval, $\alpha = 0.05$. Because the confidence interval is two-tailed, take $\alpha/2 = 0.025$. The z-score for $\alpha/2 = 1.96$. (See standard normal table or use your calculator.) Finally, plug this information into the inequality for n: $n \geq \left(\dfrac{1.96}{2(0.05)}\right)^2$, $n \geq 384.16$. You need the minimum number of cartons, so you need a whole number. Because the minimum value for n is a decimal, round up to 385.

4. **C** Power of a test $= 1 - P(\text{Type II error})$. Choice (C) is describing a Type I error, which is not directly related to the calculation of the power of a test, although it does influence the power. All other answer choices are correct.

5. **E** A confidence interval describes the mean of the population the sample is drawn from. For a 90% confidence interval, there is a 90% probability that the interval contains the mean of the population. Conversely, there is a 10% probability that the mean of the population is not contained within the interval.

6. **C** A chi-square test is a test for making inferences about categorical data. The other tests are tests for continuous data. Nonparametric tests are not tested on the AP Exam, so you wouldn't be expected to know what they are for (although you may remember that they are an option for continuous data in certain situations).

7. **B** The rejection region approach states that the null hypothesis should be rejected if the test statistic (z, t, etc.) falls within the rejection region, which is determined by α. The p-value approach states that the null hypothesis should be rejected if the p-value of the test statistic is less than α.

8. **A** The t-distribution depends on the degrees of freedom that affect the spread of the data. Thus, as the degrees of freedom increase, the standard deviation of the t-distribution decreases. Another distinction is that the standard deviation of the t-distribution is greater than that of the standard normal distribution, but it approaches 1 as the degrees of freedom increase. The other features are shared by the two distributions.

9. **D** Degrees of freedom for a χ^2 test of independence are calculated as $df = (r - 1)(c - 1)$, where r is the number of rows and c is the number of columns. In this test, there are four rows (for the grades) and six columns (for the sodas). Thus, the formula is $df = (4 - 1)(6 - 1) = (3)(5) = 15$. The answer is (D).

10. The following are the two hypotheses. H_0: There is no association between a mother's career field type and her daughter's career field type. H_a: There is an association between a mother's career field type and her daughter's career field type.

To test these hypotheses, use a chi-square test for independence. Select an α level, for example 0.05.

Compute the row totals, column totals, and expected cell counts using the formula:

$$\text{Expected cell count for a cell} = \frac{(\text{Row total})(\text{Column total})}{\text{Grand total}}$$

		Mother's Career Field			
		Fine Arts	**STEM**	**Social Sciences**	**Total**
Daughter's Career Field	**Fine Arts**	72 (30.2)	15 (41.5)	24 (39.3)	111
	STEM	20 (49.8)	99 (68.4)	64 (64.8)	183
	Social Sciences	44 (56.0)	73 (77.0)	89 (72.9)	206
	Total	136	187	177	500

Check the conditions: (1) The data are counts. (2) The sample is random. (3) The sample is large enough because every cell's expected count is greater than 5.

Calculate the degrees of freedom using: $df = (r - 1)(c - 1) = (3 - 1)(3 - 1) = 4$. Between this and the α-level above, the rejection rule is "reject the null if $p < 0.05$" or, for the rejection region approach, "reject the null if $TS > \chi^2_{0.05}(4) = 9.49$."

Compute the test statistic and p-value: $TS = \sum_3^{i=1} \sum_3^{j=1} \frac{(O_{ij} - E_{ij})^2}{E_{ij}} = \frac{(72 - 30.2)^2}{30.2} + \frac{(20 - 49.8)^2}{49.8} +$

$\frac{(44 - 56.0)^2}{56.0} + \frac{(15 - 41.5)^2}{41.5} + \frac{(99 - 68.4)^2}{68.4} + \frac{(73 - 77.0)^2}{77.0} + \frac{(24 - 39.3)^2}{39.3} + \frac{(64 - 64.8)^2}{64.8} +$

$\frac{(89 - 72.9)^2}{72.9} = 118.6$, and p-value $= P(\chi^2(4) > 118.6) \approx 0$.

Because the p-value is less than 0.05, or, by the rejection region approach, $TS = 118.6 > 9.49$, the null hypothesis should be rejected and the alternative hypothesis can be accepted. In other words, there is significant evidence to conclude that there is an association between a mother's career field type and a daughter's career field type.

11. **(a)** The statistic of interest is an estimate of $\mu =$ the true mean weight of the cases of oranges shipped. A random sample of 10 cases was examined. Check the conditions: (1) The sample is given to be random, and we can assume they are independent because the cases were shipped over the course of a month. (2) A boxplot of the data (not shown) does not show any outliers and appears to be quite symmetric, so it is safe to assume that the weights of the cases are normally distributed.

Because the population standard deviation is unknown—though we can assume a normal distribution—a t-interval for the mean is required.

Compute the sample mean and standard deviation: $x = 25.56$ lbs and $s \approx 1.1217$ lbs.

Compute the degrees of freedom: $df = n - 1 = 10 - 1 = 9$. Because you are constructing a 95% confidence interval, $\alpha = 0.05$. From here, use the t-table for 9 degrees of freedom to find the critical t-value: $t^* = t_{\frac{\alpha}{2}}(9) = t_{\frac{0.05}{2}}(9) = t_{0.025}(9) = 2.262$. Then, the 95%

$ME = t_{0.025}(9) \left(\frac{s}{\sqrt{n}} \right) = 2.262 \left(\frac{1.1217}{\sqrt{10}} \right) \approx 0.8024$ lbs. Thus, the confidence interval is found:

$x \pm ME = 25.56 \pm 0.8024 \rightarrow (24.758, 26.362)$.

In other words, you can be 95% confident that the true mean weight of a case of oranges shipped is between 24.748 lbs and 26.362 lbs.

(b) Now, make an inference in order to test a hypothesis: H_0: $\mu = 25$ lbs (accept the shipment) and H_a: $\mu \neq 25$ lbs (reject the shipment).

The conditions met from part (a) are still valid. As are the degrees of freedom, t^*, and the α value.

The rejection rules are either to reject the null if p-value < 0.05 or reject the null if $t > 2.262$ or if $t < -2.262$.

Next, compute the test statistic: $t = \dfrac{(\bar{x} - \mu_0)}{s / \sqrt{2}} = \dfrac{25.56 - 25.00}{1.1217 / \sqrt{10}} \approx 1.579$ and the p-value: p-value $= P(t < 1.579) = 0.1488$.

Because $p > 0.05$ or because $-2.262 < t < 2.262$, you fail to reject the null hypothesis. Therefore, the distributor should not reject the shipment.

Part VI
Practice Test 2

The Princeton Review®

Completely darken bubbles with a No. 2 pencil. If you make a mistake, be sure to erase mark completely. Erase all stray marks.

1.

YOUR NAME: _____
(Print)　　　　　Last　　　　　　　First　　　　　　　M.I.

SIGNATURE: _____　　　DATE: ___/___/___

HOME ADDRESS: _____
(Print)　　　　　Number and Street

_____
City　　　　　　State　　　　　　Zip Code

PHONE NO.: _____

IMPORTANT: Please fill in these boxes exactly as shown on the back cover of your test book.

2. TEST FORM

_____

3. TEST CODE

⓪	Ⓐ Ⓙ
①	Ⓑ Ⓚ
②	Ⓒ Ⓛ
③	Ⓓ Ⓜ
④	Ⓔ Ⓝ
⑤	Ⓕ Ⓞ
⑥	Ⓖ Ⓟ
⑦	Ⓗ Ⓠ
⑧	Ⓘ Ⓡ
⑨	

4. REGISTRATION NUMBER

| ⓪ ⓪ ⓪ ⓪ ⓪ ⓪ ⓪ ⓪ |
| ① ① ① ① ① ① ① ① |
| ② ② ② ② ② ② ② ② |
| ③ ③ ③ ③ ③ ③ ③ ③ |
| ④ ④ ④ ④ ④ ④ ④ ④ |
| ⑤ ⑤ ⑤ ⑤ ⑤ ⑤ ⑤ ⑤ |
| ⑥ ⑥ ⑥ ⑥ ⑥ ⑥ ⑥ ⑥ |
| ⑦ ⑦ ⑦ ⑦ ⑦ ⑦ ⑦ ⑦ |
| ⑧ ⑧ ⑧ ⑧ ⑧ ⑧ ⑧ ⑧ |
| ⑨ ⑨ ⑨ ⑨ ⑨ ⑨ ⑨ ⑨ |

6. DATE OF BIRTH

Month	Day	Year
○ JAN		
○ FEB	⓪ ⓪	⓪ ⓪
○ MAR	① ①	① ①
○ APR	② ②	② ②
○ MAY	③ ③	③ ③
○ JUN	④	④ ④
○ JUL	⑤	⑤ ⑤
○ AUG	⑥	⑥ ⑥
○ SEP	⑦	⑦ ⑦
○ OCT	⑧	⑧ ⑧
○ NOV	⑨	⑨ ⑨
○ DEC		

7. GENDER
○ MALE
○ FEMALE

The Princeton Review®

5. YOUR NAME

First 4 letters of last name				FIRST INIT	MID INIT
Ⓐ Ⓐ Ⓐ Ⓐ				Ⓐ	Ⓐ
Ⓑ Ⓑ Ⓑ Ⓑ				Ⓑ	Ⓑ
Ⓒ Ⓒ Ⓒ Ⓒ				Ⓒ	Ⓒ
Ⓓ Ⓓ Ⓓ Ⓓ				Ⓓ	Ⓓ
Ⓔ Ⓔ Ⓔ Ⓔ				Ⓔ	Ⓔ
Ⓕ Ⓕ Ⓕ Ⓕ				Ⓕ	Ⓕ
Ⓖ Ⓖ Ⓖ Ⓖ				Ⓖ	Ⓖ
Ⓗ Ⓗ Ⓗ Ⓗ				Ⓗ	Ⓗ
Ⓘ Ⓘ Ⓘ Ⓘ				Ⓘ	Ⓘ
Ⓙ Ⓙ Ⓙ Ⓙ				Ⓙ	Ⓙ
Ⓚ Ⓚ Ⓚ Ⓚ				Ⓚ	Ⓚ
Ⓛ Ⓛ Ⓛ Ⓛ				Ⓛ	Ⓛ
Ⓜ Ⓜ Ⓜ Ⓜ				Ⓜ	Ⓜ
Ⓝ Ⓝ Ⓝ Ⓝ				Ⓝ	Ⓝ
Ⓞ Ⓞ Ⓞ Ⓞ				Ⓞ	Ⓞ
Ⓟ Ⓟ Ⓟ Ⓟ				Ⓟ	Ⓟ
Ⓠ Ⓠ Ⓠ Ⓠ				Ⓠ	Ⓠ
Ⓡ Ⓡ Ⓡ Ⓡ				Ⓡ	Ⓡ
Ⓢ Ⓢ Ⓢ Ⓢ				Ⓢ	Ⓢ
Ⓣ Ⓣ Ⓣ Ⓣ				Ⓣ	Ⓣ
Ⓤ Ⓤ Ⓤ Ⓤ				Ⓤ	Ⓤ
Ⓥ Ⓥ Ⓥ Ⓥ				Ⓥ	Ⓥ
Ⓦ Ⓦ Ⓦ Ⓦ				Ⓦ	Ⓦ
Ⓧ Ⓧ Ⓧ Ⓧ				Ⓧ	Ⓧ
Ⓨ Ⓨ Ⓨ Ⓨ				Ⓨ	Ⓨ
Ⓩ Ⓩ Ⓩ Ⓩ				Ⓩ	Ⓩ

1. Ⓐ Ⓑ Ⓒ Ⓓ
2. Ⓐ Ⓑ Ⓒ Ⓓ
3. Ⓐ Ⓑ Ⓒ Ⓓ
4. Ⓐ Ⓑ Ⓒ Ⓓ
5. Ⓐ Ⓑ Ⓒ Ⓓ
6. Ⓐ Ⓑ Ⓒ Ⓓ
7. Ⓐ Ⓑ Ⓒ Ⓓ
8. Ⓐ Ⓑ Ⓒ Ⓓ
9. Ⓐ Ⓑ Ⓒ Ⓓ
10. Ⓐ Ⓑ Ⓒ Ⓓ
11. Ⓐ Ⓑ Ⓒ Ⓓ
12. Ⓐ Ⓑ Ⓒ Ⓓ
13. Ⓐ Ⓑ Ⓒ Ⓓ
14. Ⓐ Ⓑ Ⓒ Ⓓ
15. Ⓐ Ⓑ Ⓒ Ⓓ
16. Ⓐ Ⓑ Ⓒ Ⓓ
17. Ⓐ Ⓑ Ⓒ Ⓓ
18. Ⓐ Ⓑ Ⓒ Ⓓ
19. Ⓐ Ⓑ Ⓒ Ⓓ
20. Ⓐ Ⓑ Ⓒ Ⓓ

21. Ⓐ Ⓑ Ⓒ Ⓓ
22. Ⓐ Ⓑ Ⓒ Ⓓ
23. Ⓐ Ⓑ Ⓒ Ⓓ
24. Ⓐ Ⓑ Ⓒ Ⓓ
25. Ⓐ Ⓑ Ⓒ Ⓓ
26. Ⓐ Ⓑ Ⓒ Ⓓ
27. Ⓐ Ⓑ Ⓒ Ⓓ
28. Ⓐ Ⓑ Ⓒ Ⓓ
29. Ⓐ Ⓑ Ⓒ Ⓓ
30. Ⓐ Ⓑ Ⓒ Ⓓ
31. Ⓐ Ⓑ Ⓒ Ⓓ
32. Ⓐ Ⓑ Ⓒ Ⓓ
33. Ⓐ Ⓑ Ⓒ Ⓓ
34. Ⓐ Ⓑ Ⓒ Ⓓ
35. Ⓐ Ⓑ Ⓒ Ⓓ
36. Ⓐ Ⓑ Ⓒ Ⓓ
37. Ⓐ Ⓑ Ⓒ Ⓓ
38. Ⓐ Ⓑ Ⓒ Ⓓ
39. Ⓐ Ⓑ Ⓒ Ⓓ
40. Ⓐ Ⓑ Ⓒ Ⓓ

Practice Test 2

AP® Statistics Exam

SECTION I: Multiple-Choice Questions

DO NOT OPEN THIS BOOKLET UNTIL YOU ARE TOLD TO DO SO.

At a Glance

Total Time
1 hour and 30 minutes
Number of Questions
40
Percent of Total Grade
50%
Writing Instrument
Pencil required

Instructions

Section I of this exam contains 40 multiple-choice questions. Fill in only the ovals for numbers 1 through 40 on your answer sheet.

Indicate all of your answers to the multiple-choice questions on the answer sheet. No credit will be given for anything written in this exam booklet, but you may use the booklet for notes or scratch work. After you have decided which of the suggested answers is best, completely fill in the corresponding oval on the answer sheet. Give only one answer to each question. If you change an answer, be sure that the previous mark is erased completely. Here is a sample question and answer.

Sample Question   Sample Answer

Omaha is a

(A) state
(B) city
(C) country
(D) continent
(E) village

Use your time effectively, working as quickly as you can without losing accuracy. Do not spend too much time on any one question. Go on to other questions and come back to the ones you have not answered if you have time. It is not expected that everyone will know the answers to all of the multiple-choice questions.

About Guessing

Many candidates wonder whether or not to guess the answers to questions about which they are not certain. Multiple-choice scores are based on the number of questions answered correctly. Points are not deducted for incorrect answers, and no points are awarded for unanswered questions. Because points are not deducted for incorrect answers, you are encouraged to answer all multiple-choice questions. On any questions you do not know the answer to, you should eliminate as many choices as you can, and then select the best answer among the remaining choices.

GO ON TO THE NEXT PAGE.

STATISTICS
SECTION I
Time—1 hour and 30 minutes
Number of questions—40
Percent of total grade—50

Directions: Solve each of the following problems, using the available space for scratchwork. Decide which is the best of the choices given and fill in the corresponding oval on the answer sheet. No credit will be given for anything written in the test book. Do not spend too much time on any one problem.

1. To check the effect of cold temperature on the viscosity of organic and regular honey, one bottle of organic honey and one bottle of regular honey are tested. Fifty milliliters of organic honey are placed in a refrigerator for five hours and fifty milliliters of regular honey are set at room temperature. The amount of viscosity of both types of honey are measured using a viscometer and graduated cylinder, and the mean viscosity of the refrigerated honey is compared to that of the room temperature honey. Is this a good experimental design?

    (A) No, because the means are not proper statistics for comparison.

    (B) No, because more than two types of honey should be used.

    (C) No, because more temperatures should be used.

    (D) No, because temperature is confounded with type of honey.

    (E) Yes.

2. A biochemist is trying to analyze data derived from a large sample of bacterial cultures. She realized that the measurements that were taken were off by a factor of 8. If she multiplied each value in the data set by the constant 8, which of the following summary statistics would change?

    I.   The mean
    II. The median
    III. The interquartile range

    (A) I only

    (B) I and II only

    (C) I and III only

    (D) I, II, and III

    (E) None of the above

GO ON TO THE NEXT PAGE.

3. The probability that there will be a tornado in Tulsa, Oklahoma, each day of the summer depends on the humidity of the day in question. If the air is dry on a given day, there is a 0.5 percent chance of a tornado in Tulsa; if the air is humid on that day, there is a 5 percent chance of a tornado. On July 1, 2019, local news reported that there was 40 percent chance of the air being humid. What is the probability that there was a tornado in Tulsa on July 1, 2019?

(A) 0.003

(B) 0.020

(C) 0.023

(D) 0.040

(E) 0.060

4. The relationship between the amount of time spent working, q (in hours), and expected score on a group presentation (0–100) in a random sample of groups among AP Statistics students in groups of three was found to be

$$\text{Grade} = 42.01 + 9.68(q)$$

How will a group's expected grade be affected if they work on the presentation for three more hours?

(A) Their expected grade will go up by 32.33 points.

(B) Their expected grade will go up by 29.04 points.

(C) Their expected grade will remain unchanged.

(D) Their expected grade will go down by 29.04 points.

(E) It cannot be determined from the information given.

GO ON TO THE NEXT PAGE.

5. The student government association at a university is interested in the student body's opinions on a docket of topics. The leaders go about this by taking a survey and would like to take a simple random sample of 300 students. Which of the following survey methods will produce a simple random sample?

    (A) Survey the first 300 students that park their cars in the parking garage that day.

    (B) Survey every tenth student that walks into the student center until 300 students are surveyed.

    (C) Choose the first 75 members from an alphabetical roster of each of the freshman, sophomore, junior, and senior classes.

    (D) Put candy under the seats of a lecture hall and interview the first 300 students to discover there's candy under their seats.

    (E) Number the students in the official university enrollment records. Use a table of random numbers to choose 300 students from the records for the survey.

6. An ambitious farmer has set out to maximize the size of the eggs laid by his chickens. After careful thought, he has decided to experiment with a new type of feed. Based on data acquired from the feed manufacturer, he learned that the standard deviation of the eggs laid by the geese that consumed the new feed is 7.5 g. Of the following, which is the fewest number of eggs that should be sampled to obtain an estimate within 0.5 g of the true mean of egg weights, and at the farmer's insistence, at a confidence of 95 percent?

    (A) 29.4

    (B) 100

    (C) 609

    (D) 864

    (E) 865

7. Houston, Texas decided to annex part of its surrounding counties. Statistics graduate students at the UT School of Public Health decided to conduct a survey of registered voters to assess the public's opinion. The found that 77 percent of respondents were against the annexation. During the actual vote, though not every eligible voter voted, only 73 percent of respondents voted against the annexation. Which of the following reasons best describes the difference in percentages obtained from the students' poll and the actual vote?

    (A) It is the systematic difference between a statistic and a parameter caused by the nonrandom selection of surveyed people.

    (B) It is the difference between the same statistics computed from two different samples.

    (C) It is the difference between the statistic and the truth due to the use of a random sample.

    (D) It was caused by the large number of respondents that answered the students' survey.

    (E) It is an example of nonresponse bias, the systematic tendency of individuals with particular characteristics to refuse to answer a survey question.

GO ON TO THE NEXT PAGE.

8. A newly elected mayor sought to improve financial literacy and management in her constituency and assigned a task force to brainstorm an effective initiative. After observing the residents, the task force found that a large majority of these people attend and reportedly benefit from taking courses at the local library. The task force decided to hire financial experts to teach a budgeting series and also employed the experts to rate the effectiveness of the attendees' budgeting practices on a scaled score of 50–100 one month before and one month after taking the course. The following scatterplot shows effectiveness scores after completing the course against the scores from before completing the course.

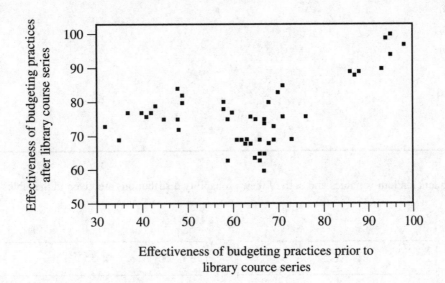

Effectiveness of budgeting practices prior to
library cource series

Which of the following statements correctly interprets the scatterplot?

(A) All the attendees have shown significant improvement in their budgeting effectiveness scores as a result of the library course series.

(B) The library course series failed, as each attendee's budgeting effectiveness score from after the course series did not change from that of before the course series.

(C) The library course series was counterproductive, as each attendee's budgeting effectiveness score decreased after going through the course series.

(D) Attendees who scored below 55 before going through the course series showed appreciable improvement after the course series. Attendees that scored between 55 and 80 before the course series showed slight improvement after the course series. Attendees that scored above an 80 before the course series showed almost no improvement after the course series.

(E) Attendees that scored below 55 before going through the course series showed slight improvement after the course series. Attendees that scored between 55 and 80 before the course series showed moderate improvement after the course series. Attendees that scored above an 80 before the course series showed an appreciable improvement after the course series.

GO ON TO THE NEXT PAGE.

9. A study was recently published showing that Americans frequent libraries more than concerts, amusement parks, or other recreational activity centers. Surprised by this, a UC Berkeley professor decided to look closer at the results. The data showed that the number of patrons served daily by the headquarters branch of the Berkeley library system was normally distributed, with a mean of 1,430 customers and a standard deviation of 172. What is the range of customers served in the middle 50 percent of days?

(A) (1,314, 1,546)

(B) (1,372, 1,546)

(C) (1,372, 1,488)

(D) (1,198, 1,662)

(E) (1,198, 1,546)

10. X and Y are independent random variables and both of their probability distributions are given in the tables below. If $Z = X - Y$, what is $P(Z \geq 4)$?

X			Y	
x	$P(X = x)$		y	$P(Y = y)$
1	0.05		0	0.40
2	0.10		1	0.30
3	0.15		2	0.15
4	0.30		3	0.10
5	0.40		4	0.05

(A) 0.15

(B) 0.30

(C) 0.40

(D) 0.56

(E) 0.88

GO ON TO THE NEXT PAGE.

11. A dentist's office surveyed all 100 of its employees to determine the proportion of them that truly floss their teeth. Which of the following statements is false?

(A) The dentist's office can use the data from the survey because this is an observational study.

(B) The dentist's office can't use the results of this survey to prove that working for a dentist's office causes employees to floss.

(C) The dentist's office surveyed all of its employees, so the survey will provide the dentist's office with useful insights.

(D) The dentist's office doesn't have to use the survey data to construct a confidence interval to estimate the proportion of employees that truly floss their teeth.

(E) The dentist's office needs to use an inference procedure to determine the proportion of employees who truly floss because the survey was a census of all employees.

12. A student that just returned from a trip to the Galapagos Islands is inspired to do some of his own research regarding the ecosystems there. Some of these islands are inhabited by just wildlife (such as in the case of Marchena), while some share their home with humans (e.g. Isabela) and others have volcanic activity (Fernandina). He is looking to see if the differences in these living conditions have supported the livelihoods of finches and turtles. These results are shown in the table below.

Island	Finches	Turtles	Total
Marchena	437	364	801
Isabela	84	32	116
Fernandina	73	89	162
Total	594	485	1079

A chi-square test of independence was conducted, resulting in $\chi^2 = 8.93$. Which of the following statements is best supported by these results?

(A) χ^2 is significant, $p < 0.01$; the counts in the table suggest that the conditions on a particular island of the Galapagos archipelago may affect survival of finches and turtles within a single region.

(B) χ^2 is significant, $p < 0.01$; the counts in the table suggest that the conditions on a particular island of the Galapagos archipelago is independent of survival of finches and turtles within a single region.

(C) χ^2 is significant, $0.01 < p < 0.05$; the counts in the table suggest that the conditions on a particular island of the Galapagos archipelago may affect survival of finches and turtles within a single region.

(D) χ^2 is significant, $0.01 < p < 0.05$; the counts in the table suggest that the conditions on a particular island of the Galapagos archipelago is independent of finches and turtles within a single region.

(E) χ^2 is not significant at the 0.05 level.

GO ON TO THE NEXT PAGE.

13. In an effort to research new trends in the marketing of bottled water, Ice Mountain decided to determine which of two different bottle wrappers would result in more sales. One of the wrappers would be their traditional design and the other would mention buzzwords, such as "minerals", "Fiji", "naturally sourced", "purified", etc. Ice Mountain picked 3000 supermarkets across the US to sell these water bottles. 1500 of these were randomly assigned to sell the water bottles with their traditional design, and the remainder were assigned to sell the water bottles with the "new and improved" wrapper. After collecting sales data on the water bottles at these supermarkets across the nation, Ice Mountain determined that there in fact was a statistically significant difference between the average number of water bottles sold for the two bottle wrappers. Which of the following statements provides both the most accurate conclusion and explanation for the conclusion, based on the results?

(A) It is <u>not</u> reasonable to conclude that the difference in sales was caused by the different wrapper designs because this was not an experiment.

(B) It is <u>not</u> reasonable to conclude that the difference in sales was caused by the different wrapper designs because there was no control group to compare to.

(C) It is <u>not</u> reasonable to conclude that the difference in sales was caused by the different wrapper designs because the 3000 weren't randomly chosen.

(D) It is reasonable to conclude that the difference in sales was caused by the different wrapper designs because the sample size was large.

(E) It is reasonable to conclude that the difference in sales was caused by the different wrapper designs because the stores were randomly assigned to the wrapper design of the bottles they sold.

---

14. Which of the following represents a uniform distribution?

(A)

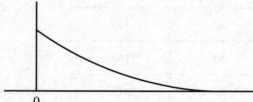

(B)

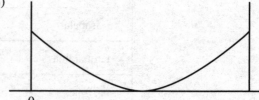

(C)

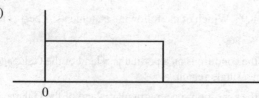

(D)

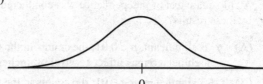

(E)

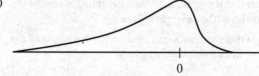

GO ON TO THE NEXT PAGE.

15. A bicycle company has decided to expand its business by offering a combination deal to its customers at a discounted price. This deal would include a bicycle, a helmet, a lock, and an attachable stand. The company's warehouse managers are concerned about the weights of this combined deal and have asked the following question: if the means and standard deviations of the weights of each of the individual components in the combo are as per the table below, what is the standard deviation of the weight of the entire bundle?

Item	Mean Weight (lbs)	Standard Deviation (lbs)
Bicycle	21	1.25
Helmet	2	0.14
Lock	6	0.58
Stand	7	0.69

(A) 6.00 lbs
(B) 2.66 lbs
(C) 2.39 lbs
(D) 1.55 lbs
(E) 1.42 lbs

16. A businessman named Willy decided to start a chocolate factory. He buys fancy machines to fill the bags with chocolates and is interested in how equally the machines will fill the bags. He programs the machine to put an average of thirty grams of chocolate in each bag, with a standard deviation of 4.5 grams. He then randomly selects one hundred of the bags this machine filled. What is the probability that the mean amount per bag of chocolate in his sample is less than twenty-nine grams?

(A) 0.0052
(B) 0.0132
(C) 0.0184
(D) 0.0264
(E) 0.0495

GO ON TO THE NEXT PAGE.

17. For a new study, the American Community Survey is looking to survey a representative sample of children who can't drive. Knowing the importance of study design in the reliability and validity of results, the ACS has filtered its available phone numbers for simply home phone numbers and will follow the following procedure every time a number is dialed:

- If there is no response or if an answering machine is reached, this number is skipped.

- If someone answers, a surveyor verifies that the person is younger than 16 years of age, and if so, the person is surveyed, provided that the parents give consent.

- If the person is older than 16 years of age, a "not valid" response is recorded and this number is skipped.

After reviewing this study design, statisticians are criticizing the methodology as it does not capture all possible children that cannot drive. Which of the following is <u>not</u> a legitimate concern about the procedure used?

(A) Children that are too young to answer the phone or that have been instructed by their parents to not answer the phone may be underrepresented in the sample.

(B) Children in households that have more than one child may be underrepresented in the sample.

(C) Children in households that don't have a home phone may be underrepresented in the sample.

(D) Children with cell phones may be underrepresented in the sample.

(E) All of the following are legitimate concerns about the procedure.

---

18. Assume that the following alternate hypothesis for a hypothesis test on a single population mean is true: H_A: $\mu < 49$. For a fixed sample size n and significance level α, the power of the test will be the smallest if the actual mean is which of the following?

(A) 50

(B) 48

(C) 47

(D) 46

(E) 45

GO ON TO THE NEXT PAGE.

19. To ensure their surgeons were getting enough restorative sleep every night, the Johns Hopkins University medical center decided to survey a random sample of 100 of its surgeons. This resulted in a 99 percent confidence interval for the mean number of hours of REM sleep per night of (1.01, 3.25). Which of the following statements best summarizes the meaning of this confidence interval?

(A) About 99 percent of all random samples of 100 surgeons from this population would result in a 99 percent confidence interval that covered the population mean number of hours spent in REM sleep per night.

(B) A surgeon selected at random from this population gets between 1.01 and 3.25 hours of REM sleep per night 99 percent of the time.

(C) About 99 percent of all random samples of 100 surgeons from this population would result in a 99 percent confidence interval of (1.01, 3.25).

(D) Ninety-nine percent of the surgeons that were part of the survey reported getting between 1.01 and 3.25 hours of REM sleep every night.

(E) Ninety-nine percent of the surgeons at the JHU medical center get between 1.01 and 3.25 hours of REM sleep every night.

20. After a middle school received a high volume of complaints from students who said that the mechanical pencils it buys from the school store broke quickly after purchase, it decided to contact its supplier. The supplier of these pencils was quick to retort that the school's students were simply hard-handed, as its reliability was 95 percent. If reliability is defined as the number of non-defective items divided by the total number of items produced over a given period of time and the supplier's claim is correct, how many mechanical pencils purchased from this supplier would the middle school expect to be non-defective in a random sample of 500 pencils?

(A) 425

(B) 450

(C) 475

(D) 495

(E) 500

GO ON TO THE NEXT PAGE.

21. Apple cider vinegar (ACV) and aloe vera are each highly regarded as a wonderful substance with a number of uses in natural and home remedies, particularly in hair growth. A student decided to perform an experiment to test whether the use of ACV and aloe vera yields any differences in hair growth. She got 50 people to agree to add ACV to their hair care routine for six months and another 52 to do the same with aloe vera. The distributions of data didn't show any evident skewness and there were no outliers in either data set. The results of the experiment are shown below. Which of the following statements best describes the conclusion that can be drawn from this experiment?

	ACV	Aloe Vera
Average number of inches of hair growth per person	3.02	2.79
Standard deviation	0.07	0.02
Sample size	50	52

(A) There is no statistically significant evidence to suggest a difference in the number of inches of hair growth between ACV and aloe vera ($p > 0.20$).

(B) There is no statistically significant evidence to suggest a difference in the number of inches of hair growth between ACV and aloe vera ($p < 0.20$).

(C) There is sufficient statistically significant evidence to suggest a difference in the number of inches of hair growth between ACV and aloe vera ($0.05 < p < 0.10$).

(D) There is sufficient statistically significant evidence to suggest a difference in the number of inches of hair growth between ACV and aloe vera ($0.01 < p < 0.05$).

(E) There is sufficient statistically significant evidence to suggest a difference in the number of inches of hair growth between ACV and aloe vera ($p < 0.01$).

22. Which of the following statements is not an inaccurate criterion to choose a t-test rather than a z-test when making an inference about a population mean?

(A) The mean of the population is unknown.

(B) The standard deviation of the population is unknown.

(C) The sample size is less than 500.

(D) The population is not normally distributed.

(E) The sample selected was not a simple and random one.

GO ON TO THE NEXT PAGE.

23. Which of the following residual plots shows the least amount of bias and the greatest amount of homoscedasticity?

(A)

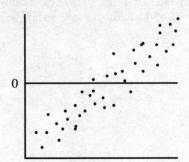

(B)

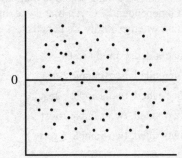

(C)

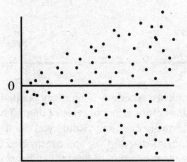

(D)

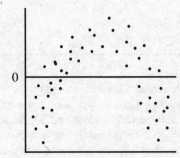

(E)

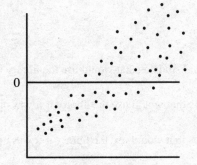

GO ON TO THE NEXT PAGE.

24. Two pencil manufacturers, Entity 1 and Entity 2, are in a dispute over which company makes better pencils. Entity 1 asserts that its #2 pencils are number one in durability—they remain sharper for longer and to test this, sixty of each entity's pencils are tested independently. Given that the assumptions for inference are met, which of the following tests should be performed to determine whether Entity 1's pencils last longer?

   (A) A one-sided, paired t-test

   (B) A one-sided, two-sample t-test

   (C) A one-sided, two-sample z-test

   (D) A two-sided, two-sample t-test

   (E) A two-sided, two-sample z-test

25. A graduate school's library is closed on the weekends, to the disdain of many students. After receiving many pointed suggestions in the school's suggestion box, the administration decided to quantify these results before acting in favor of them. They decided to survey 250 master's students and 300 doctoral students and asked them the following question: "would you use the library if it was open on the weekends?" The administration counted the number of respondents that said yes and constructed a 99 percent confidence interval for the difference in response based on degree by subtracting the proportion of master's students in favor of using the library on the weekends from that of doctoral students. The following confidence interval was the result: (0.23, 0.64). Which of the following statements is a correct interpretation of the interval?

   (A) The interval doesn't contain a negative value, so it can't be interpreted.

   (B) The interval doesn't contain zero, so it can't be interpreted.

   (C) The administration is 99 percent confident that the proportion of doctoral students that would use the library if it was open on the weekends is equal to that of master's students.

   (D) The administration is 99 percent that the proportion of doctoral students that would use the library if it was open on the weekends exceeds that of master's students.

   (E) The administration is 99 percent that the proportion of master's students that would use the library if it was open on the weekends exceeds that of doctoral students.

GO ON TO THE NEXT PAGE.

26. Which of the following is not a discrete random variable?

    (A) The number of days in a leap year

    (B) The number of cakes in a baker's dozen

    (C) The number of buttons on your calculator

    (D) The number of Crayola crayons in a pack

    (E) The amount of galactic dust in the solar system

---

27. A survey had a 7 percent margin of error. Which of the following conclusions can safely be drawn?

    (A) The difference between the sample percentage and the population percentage is likely to be less than 7 percent.

    (B) The difference between the sample percentage and the population percentage is insignificant.

    (C) The difference between the sample percentage and the population percentage is significant.

    (D) About 7 percent of the sample population didn't answer the survey.

    (E) About 7 percent of the sample population couldn't be relied upon to give a straight answer.

GO ON TO THE NEXT PAGE.

28. Ernie and Bert decide to visit Half Price Books. The probability distributions of the number of books they will purchase were calculated based on their previous visits to HPB and are given below. If Ernie and Bert's purchase decisions are independent of each other, what is the probability that they will both buy two books on this visit to HPB?

Number of books Ernie will purchase	0	1	2
Probability	0.06	0.24	0.70

Number of books Bert will purchase	0	1	2
Probability	0.82	0.08	0.10

(A) 0.070
(B) 0.500
(C) 0.800
(D) 0.930
(E) 0.951

29. A company's logo is graphically "constructed" by combining five hues of blue from the expansive set of shades of each color. In this set of hues, 95 percent of the shades would satisfy the public's perception of the logo. If X is to denote the number of acceptable shades of a sample of five hues from the large expansive set, what is the least probable value of X?

(A) 5
(B) 4
(C) 3
(D) 2
(E) 0

GO ON TO THE NEXT PAGE.

30. Which of the following assumptions is required to conduct a valid t-test?

(A) The population standard deviation is known.

(B) The population standard deviation is unknown.

(C) The population mean is large.

(D) The underlying population is normally distributed.

(E) The distribution of the underlying population is unknown.

31. The distribution of the weights of containers of yogurt from a certain farm follows approximately a normal distribution. Based on a very large sample, it was found that 10 percent of the containers weighed less than 14.21 ounces and 20 percent of the containers weighed more than 17.68 ounces. What are the mean and standard deviation of the distribution of weights of the containers of yogurt?

(A) $\mu = 16.30$, $\sigma = 1.00$

(B) $\mu = 16.30$, $\sigma = 1.63$

(C) $\mu = 16.90$, $\sigma = 1.74$

(D) $\mu = 17.32$, $\sigma = 1.74$

(E) $\mu = 17.32$, $\sigma = 3.47$

GO ON TO THE NEXT PAGE.

32. As a head ping pong ball specialist, Randy has been enlisted by his supervisors to determine the proportion of times the balls broke mid-rally last year. Randy's company's manufacturer developed a new formula for making the ball that they hope will reduce the proportion of breaks to below last year's proportion of 0.10. Randy's hypotheses were: $H_0: p = 0.10$ and $H_a: p < 0.10$, where $p =$ the proportion of ping pong ball breaks mid-rally. Suppose Randy decided to hit 5,000 of these balls and 240 of them resulted in breaks, which of the following would be the test statistic for this test?

(A) $z = \sqrt{\dfrac{0.048 - 0.10}{\dfrac{0.048(1-0.048)}{5000}}}$

(B) $z = \dfrac{0.048 - 0.10}{\sqrt{(0.10)(1-0.10)5000}}$

(C) $z = \dfrac{0.048 - 0.10}{\sqrt{(0.048)(1-0.048)5000}}$

(D) $z = \dfrac{0.048 - 0.10}{\sqrt{\dfrac{0.048(1-0.10)}{5000}}}$

(E) $z = \dfrac{0.048 - 0.10}{\sqrt{\dfrac{0.10(1-0.10)}{5000}}}$

GO ON TO THE NEXT PAGE.

33. As an independent project for his statistics class, Carson decided to survey a random sample of 100 gardening students at his university to study the potential correlation between the number of gallons a plant is watered per month and the number of inches it grows in that month. A regression analysis on the data produced the following partial computer output. Carson wants to compute a 95 percent confidence interval for the slope of the least-squares regression line for the population of all the students in his university. Assuming that the conditions for inference are satisfied, which of the following represents the margin of error of the confidence interval?

Predictor	Coef	SE Coef	T	P
Constant	0.349	0.072	11.42	0.000
Number of Gallons	5.238	0.001	2.56	0.001
S = 10.202		R – Sq = 67.1%		

(A) $(1.984)(0.001)$

(B) $(1.984)\left(\dfrac{0.001}{100}\right)$

(C) $(1.984)(10.212)$

(D) $(1.984)\left(\dfrac{10.212}{100}\right)$

(E) $(4.972)(5.238)$

34. Which of the following statements represents for what sample size the sample mean X is approximately distributed, as per the Central Limit Theorem?

(A) The sample size doesn't matter.

(B) A small sample, if the random variable X is slightly skewed.

(C) A small sample, no matter the distribution of the random variable X.

(D) A large sample, if the random variable X is slightly skewed.

(E) A large sample, no matter the distribution of the random variable X.

GO ON TO THE NEXT PAGE.

35. The quality-control people at a pencil case manufacturer want to estimate the proportion of pencil cases whose zippers fail. Unfortunately, the company is facing budget cuts and the team has to to downsize its study. If they decide to decrease the sample size from 450 pencil cases to 45, how will the distribution of the sample proportion change?

    (A) The distribution of the sample proportion will be less spread out.

    (B) The distribution of the sample proportion will be more spread out.

    (C) The distribution of the sample proportion will not change.

    (D) The distribution of the sample proportion will appear to be a normal distribution.

    (E) The distribution of the sample proportion will appear to be a chi-square distribution.

---

36. In response to the common sentiment that has traveled to the far reaches of social media that no one ever finishes an entire tube of lip balm before buying a new one, ChapStick decided to test this hypothesis by surveying a group of 10,000 people on social media. The two-way table below shows the numbers of people by lip balm completion status and if they are a student (K-12 or college) or not. Which of the following statements best represents the relationship between lip balm completion and student status?

	Finishes lip balm completely	Doesn't completely finish lip balm	Total
Students	42	3,458	3,500
Not students	710	5,790	6,500
Total	752	9,248	10,000

    (A) A measure of association cannot be determined from this data.

    (B) There appears to be an association since there are more people that aren't students than those that are students in the sample.

    (C) There appears to be an association since there is a much higher proportion of people that aren't students that finish their lip balm completely than that of those that are students.

    (D) There appears to be no association since there are large numbers of both students and not students.

    (E) There appears to be no association since there is no statistically significant evidence that says so.

GO ON TO THE NEXT PAGE.

37. After much deliberation, a doctor at Harvard decided to finally answer the age-old question: "is cracking your knuckles bad for you?" After obtaining their parents' consent, he enrolled about 100,000 newborns in the Massachusetts area into the study. The parents of half of these children were instructed to encourage their children to crack their knuckles growing up, and the remaining were instructed to prevent their children from cracking their knuckles growing up. The doctor and this team tracked the health of these children until they turned age 70, to see if any association could be drawn. After seventy years, it was concluded that there was no significant difference in health, particularly bone-related illnesses, between the two groups. Which of the following statements is an accurate reflection of the study?

   I.   Because the study included people from Massachusetts, it can be generalized to people across the United States and the rest of the world.

   II.   Because the study was based on the fact that cracking your knuckles can only have an effect in the form of bone-related illnesses, it is fundamentally valid.

   III.   Because the study involved following people across the course of a large period of time, it is a longitudinal study.

   (A) I only

   (B) II only

   (C) III only

   (D) I and II only

   (E) I, II, and III only

38. Based on a survey of a random sample of 1000 adults in the United States, a journalist reports that 80 percent of adults in the United States are in favor of increasing the number of dog parks in the United States. If the reported percentage has a margin of error of 2.07 percentage points, which of the following is closest to the level of confidence?

   (A) 99.0%

   (B) 97.5%

   (C) 95.0%

   (D) 93.0%

   (E) 90.0%

GO ON TO THE NEXT PAGE.

39. A 2019 survey found that 30 percent of the users of a particular social media platform are under the age of 16. The company predicts that the percentage of the social media platform users under the age of 16 is higher now than in 2015 (the midpoint between the year of launch and the year of the study) and that this percentage will only continue to rise. To curate its marketing towards the majority of its users, the company decides to construct a 98 percent confidence interval to estimate the current percentage, with a margin of error no more than 1.5 percentage points. If we assume at least 30 percent of the users of the platform are people that are younger than age 16, which of the following should be used to find the sample size needed?

(A) $1.645\sqrt{\dfrac{(0.5)(0.5)}{n}} \leq 0.015$

(B) $1.96\sqrt{\dfrac{(0.5)(0.5)}{n}} \leq 0.025$

(C) $1.96\sqrt{\dfrac{(0.3)(0.7)}{n}} \leq 0.03$

(D) $2.33\sqrt{\dfrac{(0.3)(0.7)}{n}} \leq 0.015$

(E) $2.33\sqrt{\dfrac{(0.5)(0.5)}{n}} \leq 0.015$

40. A coffee chain has been receiving lots of new recommendations for its seasonal flavors. Instead of simply incorporating some of these suggestions in its not-so-secret menu, the company decided to see if the flavor of the drink (smoked butterscotch, peppermint mocha, caramel waffle, eggnog) is related to the type of drink (latte or cappuccino). They select a random sample of 300,000 people in the US and ask everyone which of the drinks above they get most often. Which of the following procedures would be most appropriate to use for investigating whether there is a correlation between flavor of the drink and type of drink?

(A) A chi-square test of independence

(B) A chi-square goodness-of-fit test

(C) A matched pairs t-test

(D) A two-sample t-test

(E) A two-sample z-test

END OF SECTION I

STATISTICS
SECTION II
Time—1 hour and 30 minutes
Number of questions—6
Percent of total grade—50

Part A
Questions 1–5
Spend about 65 minutes on this part of the exam.
Percent of Section II grade—75

Directions: Show all your work. Indicate clearly the methods you use, because you will be scored on the correctness of your methods as well as on the accuracy and completeness of your results and explanations.

1. A retired CEO decided to embark on an interesting journey in his free time: because sleep is so vital to leading a healthy life, she decided to measure the expandability of fitted sheets. She purchases the sheets from two manufacturers, NapWell and SleepWell, buying cotton fitted sheets from NapWell and silk fitted sheets from SleepWell. The distribution of the expandability of NapWell's cotton fitted sheets is approximately normal with a mean of 5 inches and a standard deviation of 0.5 inches. The probability that a fitted sheet selected at random from SleepWell will have a expandability greater than 5.2 inches is 0.7315. For all the fitted sheets in the bedding section of a mattress store, 60 percent of the fitted sheets are supplied by NapWell, while the remainder are supplied by SleepWell.

   (a) For a fitted sheet selected at random from NapWell, what is the probability that the sheet will have a expandability greater than 5.2 inches?

GO ON TO THE NEXT PAGE.

(b) For a fitted sheet selected at random from that mattress store, what is the probability that the sheet will have a expandability greater than 5.2 inches?

(c) Given that a fitted sheet selected at random from that mattress store has a expandability greater than 5.2 inches, what is the probability that it is a NapWell sheet?

2. The emphasis on wellness and peace of mind is becoming increasingly important and recognized in today's society, and as a result, an osteopathic physician is planning to do research on whether having and maintaining succulents reduces depressive symptoms. The study design is as follows: 2,500 adults who have reported having depressive symptoms were randomly assigned to two groups—1,250 were assigned to the experimental group that took care of a succulent every day for six months and the remainder were assigned to a control group. At the end of the study, 55 people in the experimental group and 79 people in the control group still reported that they experienced depressive symptoms. At the significance level $\alpha = 0.05$, do the data provide sufficient statistically significant evidence that maintaining a succulent every day will reduce the chance of experiencing depressive symptoms among all those that are similar to the volunteers in the study?

GO ON TO THE NEXT PAGE.

3. A university decided to conduct a survey of adults that had just graduated college in an effort to see how nutritiously they ate and how much this would cost. After browsing the internet, the university quickly realized that the best way to eat healthy was to cook meals in an Instant Pot, as it's the up and coming combined epitome of convenience and nutrition. The university asked about 50,000 recent alumni, who reported that they had Instant Pots, how much they spent on not only the Instant Pot but the necessary groceries for it over the last year. After gathering all responses, the university calculated the mean amount spent (amongst the 50,000 alumni surveyed) to be $5,630. Consider the following questions.

(a) What would be a statistical advantage of using the median of the amount spent as opposed to the mean as an estimate of the typical amount spent on an Instant Pot and groceries over a year?

(b) The university believes that its sample might not be representative of the population of recent alumni. It has decided to conduct a more in-depth survey of the recent class of college alumni, to better answer not only this question but also gain more insight into the class. After brainstorming, the university came up with two methods by which to conduct the survey. Which one should the university proceed with to estimate the average amount of money spent on an Instant Pot and the necessary groceries in a year amongst the 4.5 million people that recently graduated college? Explain your reasoning by comparing the two methods and the effect of each method on the estimate.

Method 1: Email all 4.5 million members of the recent alumni class asking them to complete an online survey. We estimate about 630,000 people will complete the survey.

Method 2: Select a simple random sample of members of the recent alumni class and call these members directly. If they have an Instant Pot, follow up with them to ensure all responses are gathered. Because this method will take much longer than method 1, we estimate only about 180,000 people will complete the survey.

GO ON TO THE NEXT PAGE.

4. The director of sales at a gift shop wanted to study the relationship between the number of items purchased and the amount of time (in minutes) spent browsing at the gift shop. She randomly selected a sample of eleven customers whose browsing time and purchases were noted. The results are shown in the following scatterplot and least-squares regression line and computer output.

(a) Identify and interpret in context the estimate of the intercept for the least-squares regression line

(b) Identify and interpret in context the coefficient of determination, r^2.

GO ON TO THE NEXT PAGE.

(c) After analysis, one of the data points was classified as an outlier. Circle the point on the scatterplot and explain why it is an outlier.

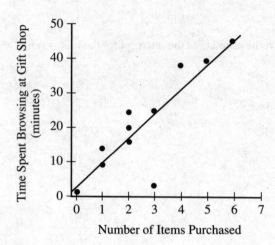

Predictor	Coef	SE Coef	T	P
Constant	1.27	5.38	0.98	0.631
Number of Items Purchased	10.86	2.51	7.36	0.004
S = 20.45		R – Sq = 93.11%		R – Sq (adj) = 81.591%

GO ON TO THE NEXT PAGE.

5. In an attempt to revive "the good ol' days", some retired actors decided to remake Tom and Jerry. To change it up, these actors decided to give all the characters voices and announced a casting call. Eight people were shortlisted for the character of Jerry, four of whom had years behind them as voice actors and four of whom were complete amateurs that auditioned because they loved Tom and Jerry. The actors told the casting directors to choose three finalists at random, of which the actors would make the final call. The casting directors ended up picking three of the amateurs and the actors were then approached by the agents of the experienced voice actors, as none of them were selected.

    (a) Calculate the probability that randomly selecting three finalists from a group of four experienced artists and four amateurs will result in the selection of three amateurs.

    (b) Based on your answer to part (a), is there reason to doubt the casting directors in the fact that they truly chose the three finalists at random? Explain your answer.

GO ON TO THE NEXT PAGE.

(c) The retired actors decide to double check the casting directors in part (b) by creating a simulation to estimate this probability. Their process is described below. Does this process correctly simulate the random selection of three finalists from a group of eight people consisting of four experienced artists and four amateurs? Explain why or why not.

> Each trial in the simulation consists of rolling three fair, eight-sided dice, one die for each of the finalists. For each die, rolling a 1, 2, 3, or 4 represents selecting one of the four experienced artists, while rolling a 5, 6, 7, or 8 represents selecting one of the four amateurs. After 1,000 trials, the number of times the dice indicate selecting three amateurs is recorded.

END OF PART A

STATISTICS
SECTION II
Part B
Question 6
Spend about 25 minutes on this part of the exam.
Percent of Section II grade—25

Directions: Show all your work. Indicate clearly the methods you use, because you will be scored on the correctness of your methods as well as on the accuracy and completeness of your results and explanations.

6. A sports analyst specializing in tennis players and their relative successes reported that the longer that a player had been playing, the more Grand Slams he would win. The report was based on a study that used a random sample of 24 males who had been ranked in the top 24 last year. Information was collected on the number of years each player had been playing for and how many Grand Slam titles he had won. The data are shown in the scatterplot below.

(a) Does the scatterplot support the analyst's statement? Justify your answer.

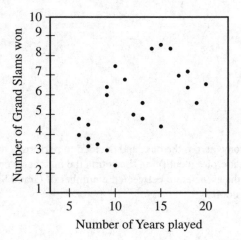

GO ON TO THE NEXT PAGE.

(b) The table below shows computer output from a linear regression analysis on the data. Identify the slope of the least-squares regression line and interpret the slope in context.

Predictor	Coef	SE Coef	T	P
Constant	2.25	0.451	8.72	0.000
Number of Years Played	1.89	0.192	4.91	0.005

S = 8.2103	R – Sq = 34.1%	R – Sq (adj) = 31.4%

(c) A different analyst in the field came across the data and decided to perform a new analysis by separating the data by type of court played on. A revised scatterplot identifying the courts the matches were played on is shown below. Based on the players in the sample, describe the association between the number of Grand Slams won and the number of years played for those slams played on grass courts.

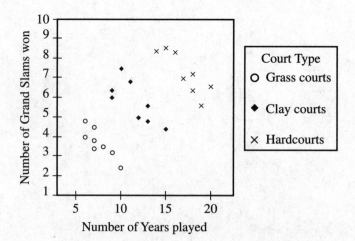

(d) Based on the players in the sample, compare the median number of Grand Slams won on the three types of courts.

(e) Based on the analysis conducted by this new analyst, how could the original analyst's statement be modified to better describe the relationship between the number of years a player plays tennis and the number of Grand Slams he wins, for the players in the sample?

STOP

END OF EXAM

Practice Test 2:
Answers and
Explanations

PRACTICE TEST 2 ANSWER KEY

1.	D		21.	E
2.	D		22.	B
3.	C		23.	B
4.	B		24.	B
5.	E		25.	D
6.	E		26.	E
7.	B		27.	A
8.	D		28.	A
9.	A		29.	E
10.	C		30.	D
11.	E		31.	B
12.	C		32.	E
13.	E		33.	A
14.	C		34.	E
15.	D		35.	B
16.	B		36.	C
17.	E		37.	C
18.	A		38.	E
19.	A		39.	D
20.	C		40.	A

PRACTICE TEST 2 EXPLANATIONS

Section I—Multiple-Choice

1. **D** This experimental design involves changing more than one variable at a time, without adding the necessary number of additional control groups. The answer is (D).

2. **D** When the values in a data set are changed by a constant multiplier, every summary statistic is affected. Since each value in the data set gets larger, the mean and median both increase by the same factor. Increasing each value also increases the spread of the data, as it increases the distance between each of the numbers in the data, so the interquartile range (IQR) is affected as well. Choice (B) would be correct if a constant value were added or subtracted to each value in the data set instead of multiplied, but that is not the case here. The answer is (D).

3. **C** A tree diagram creates a straightforward visual of the problem:

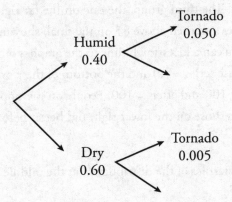

The chance of a tornado depends on whether or not the air is humid, so this is the first branch on the tree. The probability of a tornado, reflected on the next branch, are conditional upon the first branch. The tree ends with the possibility of a tornado, and that probability is: P(humid ∩ tornado) + P(dry ∩ tornado) = (0.40 × 0.050) + (0.60 × 0.005) = 0.020 + 0.003 = 0.023. The answer is (C).

4. **B** The slope of the regression line gives the average increase in expected grade for the group presentation for every additional hour spent working on it. If three extra hours are spent working on the presentation, the expected grade will increase by 9.68(3) = 29.04 points, according to the regression line. It's important to note that this increase isn't based on how much time the group had originally spent preparing for the presentation, it is just concerned with quantifying the expected grade improvement given that the group prepares for three more hours. The answer is (B).

5. **E** A good survey minimizes bias as much as possible. Picking Choices (A), (B), (C), or (D) would subject the survey to convenience bias. Choice (E) would provide an unbiased simple random sample of the entire university.

6. **E** The margin of error is calculated using the formula $ME = Z_\alpha \times \dfrac{\sigma}{\sqrt{n}}$. The farmer is looking for an ME of 0.5 g, and the standard deviation is 7.5 g. $Z_{0.05} = 1.96$. Substituting into the formula gets us:

$0.5 = 1.96\left(\dfrac{7.5}{\sqrt{n}}\right)$, so $n \geq \left(\dfrac{1.96 \times 7.5}{0.5}\right)^2$, so $n \geq 864.36$. Choice (D) rounds down, but because the sample size has to be greater than or equal to the expected value, this is not correct. The answer is (E).

7. **B** If samples are taken from different populations, such as the case here amongst the registered voters and those that actually voted, the resulting estimates will vary. The differences in percentages could be completely a result of sampling variation. The answer is (B).

8. **D** The scatterplot shows three different groups. The group of students on the far left of the scatterplot had the lowest budgeting effectiveness scores (between 30–50), but then scored between 65–85 after going through the course series, showing an appreciable improvement. The middle group scored between 55–80 before the course series and then between 60–85 after the course series, showing a very slight improvement. The third group, the one on the far right of the scatterplot, scored above 85 before the course series and then above 85 on the final, showing almost no improvement. To assist you in seeing this, you can add a straight line to the graph, going from a point on the x-axis at 50 (the score before the course series = 50) and the bottom of the y-axis (the score after the course series = 50) to a point before = 100 and after = 100. People on the upper left of that line did better after the course series, whereas those on the lower right did better before the course series. The answer is (D).

9. **A** Find the first and third quartiles of the distribution, as the middle 50% of the data falls between the first and the third quartile.

$$P(X < Q_1) = 0.25 \Rightarrow Q_1 = \mu - Z_{0.25}\sigma = 1{,}430 - 0.675(172) = 1{,}314$$

$$P(X < Q_3) = 0.75 \Rightarrow Q_3 = \mu + Z_{0.25}\sigma = 1{,}430 + 0.675(172) = 1{,}546$$

The answer is (A).

10. **C** There are three mutually exclusive ways to get a difference greater than or equal to 4: $x = 4$ and $y = 0$, $x = 5$ and $y = 0$, and $x = 5$ and $y = 1$. Because the random variables are independent, you can multiply each pair's probabilities to get the probability of the pair. That is:

$$P(x = 4 \text{ and } y = 0) = P(x = 4) \times P(y = 0) = 0.3 \times 0.4 = 0.12$$

$$P(x = 5 \text{ and } y = 0) = P(x = 5) \times P(y = 0) = 0.4 \times 0.4 = 0.16$$

$$P(x = 5 \text{ and } y = 1) = P(x = 5) \times P(y = 1) = 0.4 \times 0.3 = 0.12$$

Because each of these different possibilities is mutually exclusive, you can sum these probabilities to get the probability of any of them occurring. Thus, $P(Z \geq 4) = 0.12 + 0.16 + 0.12 = 0.40$. The answer is (C).

11. **E** Because the survey was a census of all the employees at the dentist's office, the true proportion of those employees that truly floss is known, so no inference procedure is necessary. The answer is (E).

12. **C** This is a chi-square test, where the test statistic is provided in the question and the levels of significance are provided in the answer choices, so determine the degrees of freedom. The degrees of freedom for this problem would be $(r - 1)(c - 1) = (3 - 1)(2 - 1) = 2$. Upon looking up the critical values for $p = 0.05$ and 0.01 in the table, we find that they are 5.99 and 9.21 respectively. The given test statistic of 8.93 is greater than 5.99, but less than 9.21, hence we can conclude that χ^2 is significant at the 0.05 level but not the 0.01 level. The answer is (C).

13. **E** This was an experiment: it had a control group and an experimental group; the study was conducted over a large number of supermarkets, ensuring the difference in sales was due to the wrapper design and not chance variation; and the random assignment balances out any other uncontrolled factors. Hence, Choice (E) is correct, as it best describes the results that can be drawn from the situation.

14. **C** A uniform distribution is one where every outcome is equally likely over a given interval, and Choice (C) is the visual representation of that.

15. **D** The weight of the bundle of items is calculated as follows: $weight_{bicycle} + weight_{helmet} + weight_{lock} + weight_{stand}$. Each component of the bundle is an independent variable and because the standard deviations of independent variables are not additive, we must calculate the total variance first:

$$\sigma_{combined\ bundle} = \sqrt{\left(\sigma_{bicycle}\right)^2 + \left(\sigma_{helmet}\right)^2 + \left(\sigma_{lock}\right)^2 + \left(\sigma_{stand}\right)^2} = \sqrt{1.25^2 + 0.14^2 + 0.58^2 + 0.69^2} = 1.55 \text{lbs}.$$

The answer is (D).

16. **B** Willy sampled 100 bags of chocolate, which is a large enough prerequisite for the Central Limit Theorem and a resulting approximately normal distribution. We are given that $\mu_x = 30$ grams and we can calculate that $\sigma_x = \dfrac{\sigma}{\sqrt{n}} = \dfrac{4.5}{\sqrt{100}} = 0.45$. Then $P(X < 29) = P\left(Z < \dfrac{29 - 30}{0.45}\right) = P(Z < -2.22)$. From here, use either Table A or the normalcdf function on the DISTR tab of a TI-84: $P(Z < -2.22) = 0.0132$. The answer is Choice (B).

17. **E** Choices (A), (B), (C), and (D) are all valid concerns regarding the methodology of the study. The answer is Choice (E).

18.   **A**   The power of the test is the probability that H_0 is correctly rejected. There are three ways to decrease the power of a test: lower the significance level, lower the sample size, and reduce the distance of the actual mean to the H_A in the opposite direction of H_A. Because the sample size and significance level are fixed, the only remaining option is to look for the answer that is closest to the H_A in the opposite direction. Choices (A) and (B) are both the closest to H_A, and Choice (A) is in the opposite direction, as it is greater than 49, so the answer is (A).

19.   **A**   Choice (A) correctly reflects the meaning of a confidence interval, which is the long-run probability of capturing the true parameter. The answer is (A).

20.   **C**   The expected number of non-defective mechanical pencils would be the total number of pencils in the sample multiplied by the reliability: $500 \times 0.95 = 475$ pencils would be expected to be non-defective. The answer is (C).

21.   **E**   The most efficient way to solve this problem is to run a 2-sample t-test (because the sample sizes aren't the same) on your graphing calculator. The t-statistic ends up being 22.37 and the p-value < 0.01, so the answer is (E).

22.   **B**   An unknown population standard deviation is one of the biggest reasons to choose a t-test over a z-test. The answer is (B).

23.   **B**   Homoscedasticity is the term that is used when the variance around the regression line is the same for all values of the predictor variable. If a plot is to have homoscedasticity and be unbiased, it must have a residual plot with no pattern, so the answer is (B).

24.   **B**   Choice (A) is incorrect because the study involves two sets of random samples of pencils that are studied independently and hence, they wouldn't be paired. Choices (D) and (E) are incorrect as the alternate hypothesis being tested here is ($\mu_1 > \mu_2$), indicating a one-sided test. (C) is incorrect because we are not given the true standard deviations of the durability of Entity 1 and 2's pencils. The answer is (B).

25.   **D**   Because the proportion of master's students that would use the library on the weekends if it was open was subtracted from that of doctoral students, and the entire confidence interval lies above zero, it can be concluded that the proportion of doctoral students that would use the library on the weekends is likely greater than that of master's students. The answer is (D).

26.   **E**   A discrete random variable can only take a countable number of values. Of the options, only (E) fits that bill, so the answer is (E).

27.   **A**   The margin of error is defined as the maximum expected difference between the true population parameter and a sample's estimate of that parameter. The answer is (A).

28.   **A**   Because the question states that these observations are independent, multiply the probability of Ernie buying two books by the probability of Bert buying two books: $0.70 \times 0.10 = 0.070$. The answer is (A).

29. **E** Because 95% of the hues are acceptable, the probability that a hue isn't acceptable is 0.05, and the probability that none of the five hues are acceptable is $(0.05)^5 = 3.125 \times 10^{-7}$, the least probable outcome of those given. The answer is (E).

30. **D** Choice (D) is correct, because a valid t-test is dependent on a population that is normally distributed.

31. **B** We were given that $P(Z > z) = 20\%$. Therefore, $1 - P(Z \le z) = 1 - 0.2 = 0.8$. Look to the z-table to find that this probability corresponds to a z-score of 0.845. Similarly, the other statement was given to be $P(Z \le z) = 0.1$, which corresponds to a z score of -1.28. Then set up a system of equations with what we know about z scores and how they relate to μ and σ: $\dfrac{7.68 - \mu}{\sigma} = 0.84$ and $\dfrac{14.21 - \mu}{\sigma} = -1.28$. Cross-multiplying gets us:

$$17.68 - \mu = 0.845\sigma$$
$$14.21 - \mu = -1.28\sigma$$

Subtracting the second equation from the first results in $3.47 = 2.125\sigma$, so $\sigma = 1.63$. Plugging this back into either equation results in $\mu = 16.30$. The answer is (B).

32. **E** We are given that p_0 is equal to 0.10. $\hat{p} = \dfrac{240}{5000} = 0.048$. The test statistic to be used should be $z = \dfrac{\hat{p} - p_0}{\sqrt{\dfrac{p_0(1 - p_0)}{n}}} = \dfrac{0.048 - 0.10}{\sqrt{\dfrac{0.10(1 - 0.10)}{5000}}}$. The answer is (E).

33. **A** The confidence interval is given as follows: $b \pm t^* SE_b$, of which $t^* SE_b$ represents the margin of error. All five answers have the same t^* (1.984 is the corresponding value on the t chart at a significance level of 0.05 and a sample size of 100), so choose an answer based on which one uses the correct SE_b, which is 0.001 (found under 'SE Coef' in the 'Number of Gallons' row). Thus, the answer is (A).

34. **E** This is one of the tenets of the CLT - the sample mean X will only be approximately normally distributed for a large sample regardless of the distribution of the random variable X, because the large sample size includes enough variation for the sample to be approximately normal. The answer is (E).

35. **B** $\sqrt{\dfrac{p(1 - p)}{n}}$ represents the standard deviation of the sample proportion, which shows that the standard deviation increases as the sample size decreases and therefore, the distribution of the sample proportion will become more spread out as the sample size goes from 450 to 45.

36. **C** Choice (C) is correct because it correctly identifies the difference in outcome proportions between the two groups (students and non-students) and that this difference is indicative of an association.

37. **C** Choice (C) is correct because only III is accurate: following people over a period of time and monitoring effects is the definition of a longitudinal study. Choice (A) is incorrect because the people of Massachusetts may not be a representative sample of the entire US or the world. Choice (B) is incorrect because it highlights a crucial flaw of the study design.

38. **E** We are given the margin of error, the sample size, and the sample proportion, so we can solve for the z score and match it to the table to get the confidence level. Setting $0.0207 = \sqrt{\dfrac{0.8(1-0.8)}{1000}} z^*$ gives us a z^* of 1.64, which corresponds to a 90% level of confidence as per the chart. Choice (E) is correct.

39. **D** The 98% confidence interval indicates a z-score of 2.33, as per the table. Matching that with the answer that has the correct p value (0.3) and margin of error (0.015) gives us Choice (D) as the correct answer.

40. **A** Choices (C), (D), and (E) are all tests of quantitative data. Because these variables are categorical, these options would not apply. Choice (A) is correct because this test is studying two variables, not the one that would be studied in Choice (B).

Section II—Free-Response

Our answers in this section are just guides to how you could or should answer similar questions. Your answers do not need to match ours.

1. (a) If X is the expandability of a randomly selected fitted sheet from NapWell and the question gives that X has an approximately normal distribution with a mean of 5 inches and a standard deviation of 0.5 inches, the z-score for a expandability of 5.2 inches is: $z = \dfrac{5.2-5}{0.5} = 0.4$.

   So, $P(X > 5.2) = P(Z > 0.4) = 0.3446$.

   (b) Let's define the following events: let N indicate that the fitted sheet is from NapWell, let S indicate that the fitted sheet is from SleepWell, and let Y indicate that the expandability of the fitted sheet is greater than 5.2 inches.

   Now, $P(Y) = P(Y \mid N) \times P(N) + P(Y \mid S) \times P(S) = (0.3446)(0.6) + (0.7315)(0.4) = 0.4994$.

   (c) Keeping the same event definitions as in part (b), the probability that is asked for in (c) is:

   $$P(N \mid Y) = \frac{P(N \text{ and } Y)}{P(Y)} = \frac{P(Y \mid N)P(N)}{P(Y)} = \frac{(0.3446)(0.6)}{0.4994} = 0.4140.$$

2.   Step 1: State a correct pair of hypotheses

Let p_{suc} represent the population proportion of adults similar to those in the study who would have continued experiencing depressive symptoms within the six months of the study if they had taken care of a succulent every day. Let p_{con} represent the population proportion of adults similar to those in the study who would have continued experiencing depressive symptoms within the six months of the study if they didn't do anything differently.

The pair of hypotheses are:

$H_0: p_{suc} = p_{con}$

$H_A: p_{suc} < p_{con}$

Step 2: Identifies a correct test procedure and checks appropriate conditions

The appropriate procedure is a two-sample z-test for comparing proportions.

Because this is a randomized experiment, there are two conditions we must check for:

- Random assignment

    o The question gives that the adult volunteers were randomly assigned to either the experimental or the control group, so this condition is satisfied.

- Large sample sizes, relative to proportions

    o This condition is satisfied as well because all the sample counts are large:

        ▪ Succulent group: 55 with depressive symptoms and 1195 without

        ▪ Control group: 79 with depressive symptoms and 1171 without

Step 3: Calculate the appropriate test statistic and p value

The sample proportions who continued experiencing depressive symptoms are $\hat{p}_{suc} = \dfrac{55}{1250} = 0.044$ and $\hat{p}_{con} = \dfrac{79}{1250} = 0.0632$.

The combined sample proportion who continued experiencing depressive symptoms is $\hat{p}_{combined} = \dfrac{55 + 79}{1250 + 1250} = 0.0536$.

The test statistic is $z = \dfrac{0.044 - 0.0632}{\sqrt{0.0536(1 - 0.536)\left(\dfrac{1}{1250} + \dfrac{1}{1250}\right)}} = -2.13$.

The p-value is $P(Z \le -2.13) = 0.0166$, where Z has a standard normal distribution,

Step 4: State a correct conclusion in the context of the study, using the result of the statistical test

Because the *p*-value of 0.0166 is less than α = 0.05, we reject the null hypothesis in favor of the alternate hypothesis because the data provide sufficient statistically significant evidence that the proportion of all adults similar to the volunteers in this study who would continue to experience depressive symptoms if they took care of a succulent every day is less than the proportion of all adults similar to the volunteers in the study who would continue to experience depressive symptoms if they didn't take care of a succulent every day.

3. (a) For a variable such as amount spent, a small number of either very high or very low amount of money spent could drastically increase or decrease the mean amount spent. However, the median is less affected by skewness and outliers, and so it would be preferred to the mean in an effort to accurately estimate the amount of money spent.

(b) Method 2 is better than Method 1, for the following reasons:

- Method 1 involves more bias than Method 2, because the response is purely voluntary. Depending on how much one values nutrition or how high one's income is, they might be more inclined to respond to the survey than others, which would cause errors in estimation.

- Method 2 is more likely to result in a representative sample of the entire class, which would reduce bias and provide a more reliable estimate of how much people spend on an Instant Pot and the associated groceries in a year.

4. (a) The estimate of the intercept is 1.27. It is estimated that the average time spent browsing in the gift shop if no items are purchased is 1.27 minutes.

(b) The coefficient of determination is r^2 = 93.11%. This value indicates that 93.11% of the variability in the amount of time a customer spent browsing in a gift shop can be explained by knowing how many items a customer purchased.

(c) The outlier is the point at $x = 3$ and y near 0. This point is an outlier because the value of y (time spent browsing in the gift shop) is much lower than would be expected when one purchases $x = 3$ items in the gift shop, given the remaining data.

5. (a) The probability that all three finalists that are selected are amateurs can be found using the multiplication rule:

P(all finalists are amateurs) = P(first is an amateur) × P(second is an amateur | first is an amateur) ×

P(third is an amateur | first two are amateurs) = $\dfrac{4}{8} \times \dfrac{3}{7} \times \dfrac{2}{6} = 0.071$.

(b) The probability calculated in part (a) does provide reason to doubt the casting directors and their assertion that the selections were random. There was only about a 7.1% chance that random selection would have resulted in three amateurs being selected, and this is small enough that it might cast doubt on the casting directors and their claim of randomness.

(c) The proposed simulation does not correctly simulate the process of random selection, as the random selection of three finalists is one that is done without replacement, while the dice simulation involves three independent rolls of die, suggesting a process that is done with replacement.

6. (a) The scatterplot supports the analyst's statement about number of years played and number of Grand Slams won because it shows a positive association between the two variables.

(b) The slope is 1.89, so for each additional year a player plays tennis, his predicted number of Grand Slam wins increases by 1.89.

(c) For the Grand Slams won on grass courts, there is a strong, negative linear association between number of years played and number of Grand Slams won—players that have been playing for longer tend to have won fewer Grand Slams.

(d) Grand Slams played on grass courts have resulted in a median of about 3.5 Grand Slam wins, those played on clay courts have resulted in a median of about 6 Grand Slam wins, and those played on hardcourts have resulted in a median of about 7.5 Grand Slam wins.

(e) The original analyst's statement should include type of court played on. Overall, the hard courts yield the highest number of Grand Slam wins, followed by the clay and grass courts respectively, but within a court type, players that have been playing for longer tend to win fewer Grand Slams.

HOW TO SCORE PRACTICE TEST 2

Section I: Multiple Choice

_____ × 1.8750 = _____
Number Correct   Weighted
(out of 40)   Section I Score
                               (Do not round)

Section II: Free Response

(See if you can find a teacher or classmate to score your
Free-Response questions.)

Exact scoring can vary
from administration to
administration. Therefore,
this scoring should only
be used as an estimate.

Question 1: _____ × 2.8125 = _____
            (out of 4)   (Do not round)

Question 2: _____ × 2.8125 = _____
            (out of 4)   (Do not round)

Question 3: _____ × 2.8125 = _____
            (out of 4)   (Do not round)

Question 4: _____ × 2.8125 = _____
            (out of 4)   (Do not round)

Question 5: _____ × 2.8125 = _____
            (out of 4)   (Do not round)

Question 6: _____ × 4.6875 = _____
            (out of 4)   (Do not round)

AP Score Conversion Chart Statistics	
Composite Score Range	AP Score
112–150	5
98–111	4
80–97	3
55–79	2
0–54	1

Sum = _____
      Weighted
      Section II Score
      (Do not round)

Composite Score

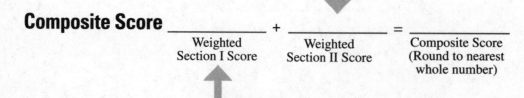

_____ + _____ = _____
Weighted   Weighted   Composite Score
Section I Score   Section II Score   (Round to nearest
                                        whole number)

NOTES

NOTES

NOTES

NOTES